Reference Guides to the World's Cinema

Guide to American Cinema, 1965–1995
Daniel Curran

Guide to African Cinema
Sharon A. Russell

GUIDE TO THE CINEMA OF SPAIN

GUIDE TO THE CINEMA OF SPAIN

MARVIN D'LUGO

Reference Guides to the World's Cinema
Pierre L. Horn, Series Adviser

GREENWOOD PRESS
Westport, Connecticut • London

Library of Congress Cataloging-in-Publication Data

D'Lugo, Marvin.
    Guide to the cinema of Spain / Marvin D'Lugo.
        p.   cm.—(Reference guides to the world's cinema, ISSN
    1090–8234)
    Includes bibliographical references and index.
    ISBN 0–313–29474–7 (alk. paper)
    1. Motion pictures—Spain—History.   I. Title.   II. Series.
PN1993.5.S7D68   1997
791.43'0946—DC20   96–36529

British Library Cataloguing in Publication Data is available.

Library of Congress Catalog Card Number: 96–36529
ISBN: 0–313–29474–7
ISSN: 1090–8234

First published in 1997

Greenwood Press, 88 Post Road West, Westport, CT 06881
An imprint of Greenwood Publishing Group, Inc.

Printed in the United States of America

The paper used in this book complies with the
Permanent Paper Standard issued by the National
Information Standards Organization (Z39.48–1984).

10 9 8 7 6 5 4 3 2 1

For Nena and for José Luis

Contents

Series Foreword

For the first time, on December 28, 1895, at the Grand Café in Paris, France, the inventors of the *Cinématographe*, Auguste and Louis Lumière, showed a series of eleven two-minute silent shorts to a public of thirty-five people each paying the high entry fee of one gold Franc. From that moment, a new era had begun, for the Lumière brothers were not only successful in their commercial venture, but they also unknowingly created a new visual medium quickly to become, throughout the world, a half popular entertainment, half sophisticated art of the cinema. Eventually, the contribution of each member of the profession, especially that of the director and the performers, took on enormous importance. A century later, the situation remains very much the same.

The purpose of Greenwood's *Reference Guides to the World's Cinema* is to give a representative idea of what each country or region has to offer to the evolution, development, and richness of film. At the same time, because each volume seeks to present a balance between the interests of the general public and those of students and scholars of the medium, the choices are by necessity selective (although as comprehensive as possible) and often reflect the author's own idiosyncracies.

André Malraux, the French novelist and essayist, wrote about the cinema and filmmakers: "The desire to build up a world apart and self-contained, existing in its own right . . . represents humanization in the deepest, certainly the most enigmatic, sense of the word." On the one hand, then, every *Guide* explores this observation by offering discussions, written in a jargon-free style, of the motion-picture art and its practitioners, and on the other provides much-needed information, seldom available in English, including filmographies, awards and honors, and ad hoc bibliographies.

Pierre L. Horn
Wright State University

Preface

Film historians have traditionally neglected the study of Spanish cinema. When they do include it at all, they reduce it to the works of two or three "international" figures, such as Luis Buñuel, Carlos Saura, or, more recently, Pedro Almodóvar. Such treatments are usually based on a combination of factors, the principal one being the assumption that, unlike France, Italy, England, or the United States, Spain was never one of the major industrial centers of film production. This argument is often supported by the assertion that, except for a few isolated figures, Spanish film has not spawned any truly international film movements equivalent to German Expressionism, Italian neorealism, or French poetic realism or the later New Wave. Rather, it is often implied that Spanish cinema has been a relatively inconsequential and imitative cinema, constrained by the weight of its history and politics.

The international commercial success of an increasing number of Spanish films since the 1970s has done much to shake off the image of Spanish cinema as a minor national cinema, as has the recognition given to Spanish films at important international film festivals. Interest in Spanish films has been further increased by their frequent nomination for Oscars by the American Academy of Motion Picture Arts and Sciences, culminating in awards in 1983 and again in 1992 in the Best Foreign Film category.

Critical acclaim has been matched in recent years by the publication of a number of scholarly books on Spanish cinema. Among the works that present important and penetrating discussions of major figures, movements, and films are Peter Besas's *Behind the Spanish Lens* (1985); John Hopewell's *Out of the Past: Spanish Cinema after Franco* (1986); Virginia Higginbotham's *Spanish Film under Franco* (1988), and Marsha Kinder's *Blood Cinema: The Reconstruction of National Identity in Spain* (1993). Broad critical views of Spanish film history have been accompanied by other, more specialized studies of particular filmmakers and themes, such as Robin Fiddian and Peter Evans's *Challenges to Authority: Fiction and Film in Contemporary Spain* (1988), Paul Julian's Smith's *Desire Unlimited: The Cinema of Pedro Almodóvar* (1994), and my own *The Films of Carlos Saura: The Practice of Seeing* (1991). The principal audience of these works, however, has been scholars. Very little attention, indeed, has been directed to a more general readership and film audience whose interest in Spanish cinema is broad, yet who are limited in their background knowledge of the historical, political, and theoretic currents that have shaped cinema in Spain.

Guide to the Cinema of Spain grows out of that critical reappraisal of Spanish films for English-speaking audiences. Although I am indebted to the work of those other scholars in the development of the present volume, as well as to the numerous Spanish film historians who have labored to produce a critical context for the development of an important national cinema, my goal, generally, has been to address the needs and interests of that broad English-language audience, first by encompassing in a single volume and in a user-friendly format an overview of major movements, trends, and the careers of individual artists who have shaped nearly a century of film production in Spain. Secondly, I have tried to avoid a lock-step history of particular developments, using instead the format of individual entries for important films, filmmakers, actors, and others related to the development of the film industry. Entries for films and those connected to productions also include additional bibliography and cross-references to enable readers to see both the proverbial forest and the trees. In short, this volume is designed to afford access to and an understanding of both the individual works as well as the larger movements and trends that constitute the special uniqueness of Spanish film.

The eighty works described in detail in the Films section reflect a sampling of those works that have been important in the commercial as well as artistic development of Spanish cinema. These are, generally, the films most frequently commented on by film historians. Though not always works of great artistic merit, they are, nonetheless, films that have been crucial in the career of major directors, have achieved broad popular success in Spain, or have been acknowledged as exemplary of particular periods and genres.

The determination of which directors, producers, and others to include is, in part, the natural consequence of the selection of the particular films. I have also added profiles of a number of directors not represented by major films, yet whose activities in the film industry reflect significant contributions to the development of Spanish cinema. Directors of popular films who have usually been overlooked in other English-language studies of Spanish film are represented here. I have also included some major producers whose contribution to shaping Spanish film has often been ignored. In an effort to fill in many of the details of Spanish film production, I have included entries on a number of important directors of photography, the cinematographers whose contributions have been immense but, owing to the scholarly and theoretic nature of much of the English-language writing on Spanish cinema, have seldom received appropriate critical attention. The selection of nearly one hundred actors is similarly guided by a sense of the key figures who have been associated with the films of commercial or artistic merit of each major period from the late 1920s up to the present.

Several observations should be made about the technical organization of this volume. An asterisk (*) after a film title or individual indicates that there is a separate entry for that work or individual. Spanish surnames often include variations of the preposition *de*, (Antonio del Amo, Juan de Orduña, Eloy de la Iglesia).   For purposes of alphabetization, the "*de*," "*del*," and *de la* are ignored and Antonio del Amo is listed under Amo; Juan de Orduña under Orduña; Eloy de la Iglesia under Iglesia. Spanish capitalization will seem somewhat eccentric to English-language readers. The rule of capitalization is that only the first word and all proper names are capitalized. My general practice is to follow the first reference to any Spanish film title with its English translation. A number of these films, however, have never circulated commercially in English versions. The translated title is, therefore, at best, merely a useful tag for a reader not familiar with Spanish. In very rare instances, Spanish films have circulated internationally with no translation (i.e., *Jamón, Jamón*; *Matador)*. In those instances, the Spanish title is used without English translation.

Acknowledgments

This book could not have been written without the help of individuals and institutions in Spain and the United States. A grant from the Higgins School of Humanities at Clark University enabled me to spend an extended period of time in Madrid viewing many of the films discussed here. I am indebted to Margarita Lobo, Dolores Devesa, and Alicia Potes of the Filmoteca Española who have been tremendously helpful in providing me access to a variety of films and written materials.

My ongoing conversations with José Luis Borau about the historical development of Spanish cinema have deepened my understanding of Spanish film and given conceptual focus to this project. I thank him for his friendship and the boundless generosity with which he has shared his immense knowledge of Spanish cinema.

At Clark University I am fortunate to have had the support of a number of talented and resourceful individuals. I count among these William Ferguson, chair of Foreign Languages and Literatures; Constance Montross, director of the Language Arts Resources Center; and Christine Weinrobe, coordinator of the Hodgkinson Film Archive. I must express my special appreciation to Florence Resnick for her patience, wisdom, and thoroughness in guiding me through the final preparation of the manuscript.

I want also to thank Susan Martin Márquez of Tulane University, for sharing some of her illuminating research on Spanish women filmmakers, and Alicia Merritt, my editor at Greenwood Press, for her encouragement and understanding throughout the evolution of this project.

Finally, my most sincere gratitude goes to Carol Clark D'Lugo, without whose wit and understanding this project could never have been completed. Her keen critical acumen continues to shape the way I look at and talk about Spanish cinema.

GUIDE TO THE
CINEMA OF SPAIN

Introduction: Certain Tendencies in Spanish Cinema

LOCALISM AND INTERNATIONALISM

Spanish cinema is in many ways a microcosm of the tensions and conflicts that have shaped the evolution of the Spanish nation over the course of this century. Throughout the first three and a half decades leading up to the Civil War of 1936–39, Spain was a country living with the isolating effects of cultural traditionalism. Centuries-old patterns of inefficient governance, combined with the accumulated weight of conservative Catholic hegemony, had long since reduced the once-proud Spanish empire to the status of European backwater. This condition of cultural and political underdevelopment was interrupted only sporadically during the early twentieth century by moves toward modernization and national renewal. These were often embodied in literary and cultural movements or generations, such as the famed Generation of '98, which looked outward toward Europe for intellectual and artistic inspiration. The unresolved conflict between these opposing tendencies of traditionalism and modernization would lead to the Civil War as the crucible of modern Spanish identity.

Film as an industry and as a cultural institution serves as one of the privileged sites within which these conflicts are crystallized. Yet, the formative history of Spanish cinema during the early decades of this century was not substantively different from that of other emerging national cinemas in Europe. On one hand, Spanish film innovators struggled to harness the artistic and commercial potential of the rapidly evolving technology of film as an international mass medium; on the other, artists and commercial promoters of Spanish cinema, as well as early audiences, tended to see in the motion picture the reflection of local or national culture. It is not surprising, therefore, to find that Spanish film as a cultural institution is rarely divorced from the political and social currents that have shaped the larger Spanish culture—torn as it was between tendencies of localism and internationalism. This is as true for the fictions represented through the film medium as it is in the efforts to develop and control the production, distribution, and reception of motion pictures in Spain.

Historians often point to the long tradition of official censorship of Spanish films that dates back to 1913 as a demonstration of the localist struggle for ideological control of the medium (Méndez-Leite von Haffe, I: 98). Indeed, there were efforts to direct the course of the medium during various periods, the most elaborate by far being the censorial policies that determined the kinds of films that were produced during the forty years of the Franco dictatorship, right up to 1975. Yet that external ideological apparatus belies a considerably more complex and nuanced struggle, shaped less by institutional coercions than by the tension between popular and elitist notions of culture and society. Here it may be useful to distinguish, as critics of Spanish cultural studies often do, between *popular culture*, and *mass culture*. As Helen Graham and Jo Labany note, for instance, "the current use of the term 'popular culture' as a synonym of 'mass culture' is less frequent in Spanish, where '*cultura popular*' tends to be reserved for popular traditions (produced and consumed by the people, including both rural and urban lower classes) as distinct from '*cultura de masas*' (the mass media, consumed by the people but not produced by them)" (Graham and Labanyi, 8).

In large measure, what is described as popular tendencies in Spanish film is often synonymous with certain expressions of national culture and frequently juxtaposed against its perceived antithesis: elitist and foreign or European values. At various points in the history of Spanish cinema, the efforts to exploit the medium in order to promote notions of traditional Spain, whether for simple commercial appeal to an audience, as in the persistent focus on the native comic and musical forms, the *sainete* and *zarzuela* (popular farces and traditional operettas), or the folkloric imaging, mostly of Andalusian culture known as the *españoladas*, have been met by counter efforts to exploit the mass attraction to films as a way to "Europeanize" or internationalize traditional cultural values. In the decades following Franco's death, despite the dismantlement of the cen- sorship boards and the transition to democratic institutions, many of these same tendencies have persisted, especially the notions that pit a vaguely defined sense of Spanishness against an equally broad notion of internationalism.

PIONEERS OF SILENT CINEMA

The first motion picture shot in Spain was probably Eduardo Jimeno's *Salida de la misa de doce del Pilar de Zaragoza* [*People Coming out of the Noontime Mass at the Cathedral of the Virgin of Pilar in Zaragoza*] (1896), followed by similar shorts made that same year shot by the Lumière brothers' cameraman, Alexander Promio. These included *Llegada de los toreros* [*The Arrival of the Bullfighters*]; *Maniobras de la artillería en Vicálvaro* [*Artillery Maneuvers in Vicálvaro*]; and *Salida de las alumnas del colegio de San Luis de los Franceses* [*Dismissal of Young Schoolgirls from the San Luis de los Franceses School*]. Augusto M. Torres notes that early French films showed the departure of workers from factories, while their Spanish counterparts showed parishioners leaving churches and the arrival of costumed bull fighters (Torres 1994, 8). In 1897 one of the veritable pioneers of filmmaking in Spain, Fructuos Gelabert,* wrote, produced, directed, and performed in *Riña de café* [*Cafe Brawl*], the first fiction film made in Spain. Along with Gelabert, who worked in Barcelona and Paris, Segundo de Chomón,* a native of the eastern province of Teruel, was busy during the final years of the old century developing a series of impressive special effects films that would culminate in his brilliant fantasy, *El hotel eléctrico* [*The Electric Hotel*](1905). Thanks to these efforts, Barcelona became established as the exclusive center for film production on the Iberian peninsula, a distinction it maintained until 1915. This changed when Benito Perojo* and his brother, José, established a production company in Madrid. This enterprise, which involved Benito as producer, scriptwriter, director, cameraman, and actor, would be the start of one of the most prolific careers in Spanish cinema. Though Madrid would gradually see the establishment of many other film production companies, Barcelona remained a major center of motion picture production in Spain for the next two decades.

Early Spanish film productions tended to reflect a marked preference toward localist material. One of the earliest manifestations of this preference came in the exploitation of bullfighting documentaries, which were known to appeal to large audiences. Ricardo de Baños* made the earliest version of Zorrilla's Romantic drama, *Don Juan Tenorio*, in 1906. The film's success led him to produce a number of other adaptations of nineteenth-century Romantic plays over the next decade. To cater to this national taste in Spanish audiences, a special series of "Andalusian fictions" based upon popular regional folklore was commissioned by the French company, Gaumont (Méndez-Leite von Haffe, I: 104). Perhaps the major work of this localist tendency was the French-Spanish coproduction of *Cristóbal Colón* (1916), an epic re-creation of the life of Christopher Columbus, with an international cast that held special patriotic value for Spanish audiences.

By 1920, it was calculated that there were between 925 and 1,000 theaters for the exhibition of motion pictures in Spain (Méndez-Leite von Haffe, I: 181). Many of those theaters were filled with a steady stream of films based on "national" popular cultural themes. In the period immediately following the end of World War I, for example, Jacinto Benavente, the Nobel prize-winning playwright, started directing films, beginning with an adaptation of his own play, *Los intereses creados* [*The Bonds of Interest*] (1920). It was joined by other even more popular Spanish source adaptations, such as the zarzuelas or popular operettas, some of which were directed by the prolific Cantabrian filmmaker, José Buchs* (for instance, *La verbena de la paloma* [*Paloma Fair*]* [1920]). The success of Buchs's adaptation led the way for other filmed zarzuelas, such as *La revoltosa* [*The Rowdy Girl*] (1924) and *Gigantes y cabezudos* [*Giants and Large-Headed Figures*] (1925), both directed by an aspiring actor-turned-filmmaker, Florián Rey.*

Spanish literarature provided a particularly enticing source for film productions. Adaptations of popular nineteenth-century novels, such as Palacio Valdés's

La hermana San Sulpicio [*Sister San Sulpicio*] (1927), a commercial success directed by Florián Rey, proved especially attractive with audiences. It was quickly followed by Francisco Camacho's adaptation of the Pío Baroja novel, *Zalacaín, el aventurero* [*Zalacaín, the Adventurer*] (1927). Also, the highly successful adaptation of Carlos Arniches's popular *¡Es mi hombre!* [*That's My Man!*] (1927), directed by Carlos Fernández Cuenca, was to shape the nature of subsequent Spanish film. Arniches's theater became an especially rich source of material for filmmakers during the early sound period just prior to the outbreak of the Civil War. One of his later plays, *La Señorita de Trevélez*, underwent a mediocre adaptation by Edgar Neville,* but then inspired one of the finest dramas of the 1950s, Juan Antonio Bardem's* *Calle mayor* [*Main Street*]* (1956). The particular attraction of Arniches for Spanish popular cinema clearly derives from two key elements of the playwright's style: his suggestive evocation of the working-class Madrid milieu; and his inventive simulation of an urban, working-class vernacular that was to be emulated in films unrelated to Arniches's own works during the early sound period (Mata Moncho, 229–40).

More popular cultural sources, such as the historical treatment of the themes of emigration and social honor, inspired Florián Rey's *La aldea maldita* [*The Cursed Village*]* (1930), the last great epic silent film made in Spain. The industry, now producing over sixty films a year, was soon to be eclipsed by the advent of talking films, which would alter the course of Spanish film production irretrievably.

One of the most important contributions to the international awareness of Spanish cinema took place outside of Spain during this period: the Paris screening of a surrealist short film, Luis Buñuel* and Salvador Dalí's *Le Chien Andalou* [*The Andalusian Dog*] (1928). The film launched Buñuel's career as Spain's most internationally renowned filmmaker. It also crystallized the tradition, for future generations of filmmakers, of an irreverent and mordant practice of filmmaking; this characteristic would remain, at least for foreign audiences, one of the hallmarks of Spanish directors.

THE ADVENT OF SOUND AND THE SECOND REPUBLIC

The first sound film produced in Spain was Francisco Elías's* *El misterio de la Puerta del Sol* [*The Mystery of the Puerta del Sol*] (1929), starring Juan de Orduña,* which used the less than adequate Phonofilm technology for synchronized sound, with very disappointing results. Three years later, when Edgar Neville made his debut as director of *Yo quiero que me lleven a Hollywood* [*I Want Them to Take Me to Hollywood*] for Star Films, the technology had not improved greatly. During the intervening years, new improvements in sound technology were revolutionizing motion picture production in the United States and other parts of Europe. Yet Spanish filmmakers continued to make films conceived essentially as silent works, then later synchronized for sound. This was the case, for instance, with Florián Rey's *Fútbol, amor y toros* [*Soccer, Love, and Bullfighting*] (1929) and *The Cursed Village* (1930), as well as José Buchs's historical-epic film, *Prim* (1930).

The first sound cinema for Spanish audiences was not made with Spanish technology but rather through the efforts of Hollywood film companies that wanted to maintain their grip on international markets during the early sound period. A plan was devised for "international productions." Spanish casts and directors were assembled in Hollywood (later, these productions took place at the Paramount Studios at Joinville, outside of Paris) to refilm English-language productions using the same sets, but with a Spanish-language translation of the script. Though the technical quality of such films was vastly superior to anything that Spanish companies could produce during the same period, they usually lacked Spanish cultural specificity in their story lines or settings (Gubern, 1993, 16).

By contrast, the domestically produced silent cinema of this period tended to remain strikingly localist, relying very often on aspects of the *españolada* tradition, that is, celebrations of regional Spanish customs, myths, and folklore. Given the near total lack of an industrial infrastructure for a national film industry during the late silent period, it was inevitable that these years would see a dramatic migration of film professionals from Spain to Hollywood or Paris to participate in productions that would not have been possible in their native country. During this period, for instance, Florián Rey shot *Melodía de arrabal* [*Song of the Shantytown*] (1932) in France with the famed Argentine tango singer, Carlos Gardel, and Imperio Argentina,* while Benito Perojo* was able to direct *Mamá* (1931) and *Primavera en otoño* [*Springtime in Autumn*] (1932), two of the very few Spanish-language films not translated from English-language originals. As Caparrós-Lera points out, by 1931 the extensive production of Spanish-language motion pictures produced abroad had essentially monopolized the peninsular market (Caparrós-Lera 1981, 15–16). Spanish-language films shot in either Hollywood or the Joinville studios probably numbered over fifty by this time. These included Benito Perojo's adaptation of Miguel de Unamuno's novel, *Niebla* [*Fog*], made in France in 1931. Some recent studies, such as Manuel Rotellar's *Cine español de la República*, suggest that by 1935 the number of these international productions may have reached 129 (23–57).

In an effort to remedy this situation, a meeting of interested Spanish and Latin American film professionals was held in Madrid in October of 1931. This first ever Congreso Hispanoamericano de Cinematografía [Hispanic American Film Congress] called for government action to establish protection for national film industries. It advocated efforts to impede Spanish-language productions outside of Hispanic countries, specifically, the United States, and proposed developing a formula to require theater owners to show a specific number of Spanish films yearly. While generally viewed as a landmark in the development of a united effort to defend Spanish-language cinema, the congress, according to various film historians, failed to produce any concrete results beyond the establishment in 1933 of Spain's Consejo Nacional de Cinematografía [National Film Board], which was aimed at developing protectionist supports for Spanish cinema. The board's functions were redefined the following year but produced no tangible results in defense of Spanish films (Gubern 1993, 57–58).

Of the early Republican cinema, by far the most striking film is Luis Buñuel's ethnographic documentary, *Tierra sin pan* [*Land Without Bread*]* (1932), which was commissioned by the government but later repudiated by it. The film's depiction of the poverty, hunger, and social backwardness of the rural Spanish region of Las Hurdes was perceived as offensive to the Spanish nation. Given the shift to the right in the general elections of 1934, there seemed very little chance that the film or its director would receive any support from official Spain.

The establishment of the Orphea Studios in Barcelona, the first sound studios in Spain, also took place in 1932. Orphea was a partnership among Francisco Elías; French producer, Camille Lemoine; and the Spanish technical engineer, José María Guillén García. Their first colaboration, *Pax* (1932), though actually filmed in a French version, marked the beginning of the development of a viable technological infrastructure for sound film production in Spain. The following year, Cinematografía Española Americana (CEA), a Madrid-based sound studio, was established in Ciudad Lineal, and later, Estudios Cinema Español S.A. (ECESA), in Aranjuez, just outside of Madrid. While CEA and ECESA produced films of quality comparable in the quality to those turned out in Hollywood or Joinville they could not compete numerically with the foreign Spanish-language film factories. Following these "majors," some fourteen other studios producing Spanish-language films emerged in Spain over the next two years. Thus, by 1935–36, it was possible to speak of a boom in national cinema in Spain, spurred in part by the extraordinary support of Spanish films by the general populace.

Between 1932 and 1936, 109 sound films were produced in Spain. The vast majority of these were escapist fare, reflecting very little effort by producers or directors to connect with contemporary society. Of the significant production companies formed during this period, however, two broke with this pattern and produced films of distinctive cultural quality as well as popular appeal. The first was Vicente Casanova's Compañía Industrial Film Español S. A. (CIFESA), which began producing films in 1933 and would, within a very brief time, establish itself as the leading film production company of Republican Spain. The company boasted not only some of the most commercially successful films of the day, but the most prominent directors as well. CIFESA's early major hits in the pre-Civil War period include Florián Rey's *El novio de Mamá* [*Mama's Suitor*] (1934), Benito Perojo's *Rumbo a Cairo* [*On the Road to Cairo*] (1934) and *He's My Man!* (1935).

The other company that produced important films, Filmófono, was founded by Ricardo Urgoiti, scion of the liberal newspaper family, who was involved in sound engineering for motion pictures. When the company shifted from importation of foreign films and domestic motion picture distribution to actual production, Urgoiti hired Luis Buñuel as his executive producer. Though Filmófono's productions were few, the significance of its popular productions, as well as Buñuel's participation in all aspects of the company's activities including directing films under the guise of other directors' names, would place Filmófono, along with the expanding CIFESA enterprise, among the most serious efforts at the development of a national cinema in Spain. (Torres 1994, 18).

However promising this period may have been in terms of the emergence of an actual Spanish film industry, Román Gubern reminds us that the general economic and ideological context of that development effectively limited the impact of cinema in Spain. All production was confined to two cities, Barcelona and Madrid, and, as Gubern points out, the cultural models of such a cinema were essentially the same as those of the silent period: folkloric films that fed off conservative cultural models; and works of escapist tendencies, now refined through the medium of sound (Gubern 1983, 33–34). The aesthetic models of such a cinema reflected the essential conservativism of the investors in the motion picture industry, who proved ultimately far less daring than their counterparts in theater and serious literature.

Yet, on the surface, Spanish cinema appeared to have achieved in a brief period of no more than three years a very wide popular audience. The hits of this period include Florián Rey's La hermana San Sulpicio [Sister Saint Sulpicio] (1934); Nobleza baturra [Rustic Gallantry] (1935),* and Morena clara [The Light-Skinned Gypsy]* (1936); Luis Marquina's Don Quintín, el amargao [Bitter Don Quintín] (1935); Benito Perojo's Rumbo a Cairo [On the Road to Cairo] (1935), ¡Es mi hombre! [He's My Man!] (1935), and La verbena de la paloma [Paloma Fair]* (1936). If these popular successes can be taken as an indication, what pleased Spanish audiences most were films in the popular cultural vein, specifically regional, folkloric works; musicals, especially those with zarzuela roots; films with working-class characters; and films that played off the familiar, urban milieu and vernacular speech.

To be sure, some social criticism was evident in Spanish cinema, although in considerably smaller measure than in Spanish literature or theater of the same period. The earliest example of a film with a purely social theme was the 1932 Fermín Galán, directed by Fernando Galán, which was clearly aimed at justifying the advent of the Second Republic (García Fernández, 57). Prior to the actual Civil War period, however, social thematics were consciously directed away from the immediate political issues of the day. Examples are films such as Edgar Neville's adaptation of Arniches's play, La señorita de Trevélez (1935); Alfonso Benavides and Adelquín Miller's Madrid se divorcia [Madrid Gets Divorced](1934); and Sáenz de Heredia and Buñuel's ¿Quién me quiere a mí? [Who Loves Me?] (1936). These films only confronted certain contemporary social themes, such as divorce and gender relations.

In light of the period that followed, this golden age of Spanish cinema, that is, the years of film production immediately preceding the Civil War, were striking for the general appeal that popular cinema held for national audiences. All of this was done, notably, without any governmental subsidies to help shape or protect the emerging film industry. Equally notable was the emergence of popular film stars, such as Miguel Ligero,* Manuel Luna,* Rosita Díaz Gimeno,* and

Antoñita Colombé. But by far the most popular of all screen personalities of the period was Imperio Argentina,* the young star who had appeared in Florián Rey's silent films. In the early 1930s, she developed a vivacious screen persona built around her spunky screen characters and lilting singing voice.

There were also a few highly visible directors, each with his own strong celebrity persona. Of these, the two most significant were Benito Perojo and Florián Rey. Perojo's cosmopolitan film style led him to develop some of the most technically sophisticated films of the thirties, such as *Paloma Fair* (1935), which, though based on a popular zarzuela, was also an urban, working-class musical comedy of manners that both imitated and rivaled the treatment of the urban milieu in certain French films of the period. Less daring and ultimately more ideologically conservative than Perojo, Rey became the master of a regional folkloric cinema in films like *Rustic Gallantry* (1935) and *The Light-Skinned Gypsy* (1936), which captured the very spirit of Spanish traditional cultural values and stereotypes.

THE CIVIL WAR

By mid-1936, on the eve of the Civil War, the Spanish film industry had at last achieved the industrial, commercial, and artistic vitality that foretold solid development of film culture (García Fernández, 82). This progress first would be halted, then nearly collapse entirely, under the weight of the prolonged struggle that gripped the country over the next three years.

A number of films already in production had to be either delayed or abandoned. Production of Benito Perojo's *Nuestra Natacha* [*Our Natacha*] (1937), based on the popular Alejandro Casona play, was delayed some two years before being completed, as was Fernando Delgado's *El genio alegre* [*The Happy Spirit*], based on a play by the Alvarez-Quintero brothers. In order to complete his film, Delgado had to use doubles to replace the lead actors who had been Republican sympathizers. The advent of the war was problematic on all sides. Barcelona and Madrid, the principal centers for commercial production as well as the location of film laboratories, were in Republican hands throughout the war. Producers sympathetic to the Republican cause, while having an obvious technological advantage, were nonetheless hampered by the exigencies of the war effort and the loss of a considerable portion of their audience. Filmmakers and producers who supported the Nationalist uprising were simply cut off from the production centers. They did, however, have the friendship and collaboration of Franco's fascist allies in Germany and Italy. This led to the formation of Hispano-Film-Produktion in Berlin, a company whose facilities enabled Florián Rey and Imperio Argentina to continue making Spanish-language films abroad, such as *Carmen, la de Triana* [*Carmen, the Girl from Triana*]* (1938), and Benito Perojo's *Suspiros de España* [*Spanish Sighs*] (1938). Perojo went on to shoot *Los hijos de la noche* [*Children of the Night*] (1940) in Rome.

Although domestic production was curtailed, first by the war effort, then by the destruction of production centers, films already completed by the summer of

1936 continued to be shown with great commercial success. This was strikingly the case of Rey's *The Light-Skinned Gypsy*, which remained immensely popular and commercially successful with both Republican and Nationalist audiences right up to the end of the war.

The real core of film production during the war, however, was not commercial, escapist fare, regardless of how appealing individual films might have been; it was documentary and newsreel, a type of film that required very little of the technological infrastructure or support staff of the elaborate, studio-produced commercial narrative films. Both sides made an enormous number of documentary and newsreel shorts laden, understandably, with the ideological content of their respective cause. To these must be added the endless series of sympathetic documentaries shot by British, French, Soviet, and Mexican filmmakers whose work chronicled not only the battles but also the human struggle of the war. Though historically interesting for the sheer quantity of documentaries produced on both sides, film production of this period would achieve note only later, as these materials were reworked in artistic documentaries.

THE POST–CIVIL WAR DECADE

The Nationalist victory in 1939 meant that a wedge effectively had been driven into the development of Spanish cinema. Members of the film industry who had sided with the Republicans were in exile or had been killed and a considerable portion of the infrastructure that made production possible had been destroyed. There were also a series of ideological forces that contributed to the end of the flowering of a popular Spanish film tradition. These included the establishment of a rigid censorial apparatus, the banishment of languages other than Spanish from Spanish movie screens, and the coercive strategies of governmental subsidies and classifications aimed at intimidating the renascent film industry into producing the type of films that would coincide with or even enhance the cultural and ideological pretensions of the state.

On November 2, 1938, while the war was still raging, the Ministry of Interior of the Nationalist government in Burgos issued a decree establishing film censorship boards throughout the reconquered territories. At the war's end, this censorial apparatus was expanded to include censorship review prior to actual production of scripts for all films. Interestingly, the orders establishing these censorial controls were clear about the composition of censorship boards, but said nothing about the criteria to be used to judge the appropriateness of various films. This arrangement had the effect of transferring the censorial activity from the government to the production teams—scriptwriters, directors, and producers—who were understandably chastened by the possibility of a total prohibition of their works.

A second government order in April of 1941, this time from the Ministry of Industry and Commerce, established Spanish as the only language to be spoken in films shown on Spanish territory. As Augusto M. Torres points out, the edict is consistent with the spirit of the immediate postwar period as a general effort to hispanize all aspects of culture and commerce took hold (Torres 1994, 21).

Such a xenophobic move, however, had the unforeseen economic consequence of placing foreign films on an equal linguistic footing with domestic products since all films shown in Spain, regardless of their origin, had to be spoken in Spanish. Thus, in a short time these better-made and more sophisticated foreign films gained a strong foothold in the Spanish market. But the measure had at least one major point of attractiveness to the new regime: The dubbing of foreign films, even the altering of dialogues, served the objectives of the censorship boards. Spanish audiences would eventually become so adjusted to viewing dubbed films that the practice would remain for the low-cost production of Spanish films long after the actual edict had been abandoned.

Third and perhaps most debilitating of the bureaucratic interventions into the film industry of the postwar period was the effort to induce producers to make the kind of films the government wanted through a system of official subsidies for production, based on film classifications begun in 1943. Tied for a time to the granting of lucrative import licenses, the subsidy strategy would endure in various forms right up to the present and enfeeble Spanish film production by making it continually dependent upon government subsidies.

Post–Civil War cinema is characterized, in part, by the continuation of some of the film genres and of the notable filmmakers of the 1930s. Three, in particular, continued to produce significant films: Benito Perojo, Florián Rey, and the youngest of the three, José Luis Sáenz de Heredia,* who, as he later revealed, had been under the tutelage of Luis Buñuel at Filmófono shortly before the war. Rey's 1942 remake of his silent masterpiece, *The Cursed Village*; Perojo's adaptation of the *zarzuela*, *Goyescas* (1942); and Sáenz de Heredia's inventive comedy, *El destino se disculpa* [*Destiny Apologizes*] (1944), are examples of post–Civil War productions that clearly follow the model of prewar popular genres. As Fernando Vizcaíno Casas notes, "for Spanish cinema, it was as if the Civil War had not existed. It continued with the eternal themes: the *zarzuela*, the gypsies, and *folletín* melodramas"(70).

Despite efforts to provide audiences escape from the squalor and depravation that resulted from nearly three years of continuous fighting, the Spanish film industry was forced to make some acknowledgment of the radical social and ideological changes that the Nationalist victory had brought. Relatively few films, though, addressed the theme of the war in the immediate postwar period. Román Gubern, who has studied the period extensively (Gubern 1986, 82–103), points to only a few films of the genre he calls the crusade, the term euphemistically applied by those associated with the military uprising against the constitutionally elected Republic in 1936. Of these, Enrique del Campo's *El crucero Baleares* [*The Cruiser Baleares*] (1940) was never released, and Carlos Arévalo's *Rojo y negro* [*Red and Black*] (1942) was removed from circulation shortly after its initial release. The principal remaining films included Edgar Neville's *Frente de Madrid* [*Madrid Front*] 1939), Augusto Genino's *Sin novedad en el Alcázar* [*No News From the Alcázar*] (1940), Antonio Román's *Escuadrilla* [*Squadron*] (1941), and Carlos Arévalo's *¡Harka!* (1941).

There was an understandable tendency toward the aggrandizement of the heroic, militant values of The New Era even in films unrelated to the theme of the war. Indeed, as Gubern notes, a related subgenre emerged during the early postwar years that did not deal explicitly with the war but connected with it by exalting the army and militarism generally. Notable works of this group include Juan de Orduña's* ¡A mí la legión! [The Legion's For Me!]* (1942) and Antonio Román's Los últimos de Filipinas [Martyrs of the Philippines]* (1945), each of which in its own way fetishized fighting and dying.

By far the most important film of the heroic-militaristic-war genre was Raza [Race]* (1941), directed by Sáenz de Heredia and scripted by Franco himself under a pseudonym. Race seemed less the embodiment of a coherent set of values than what John Hopewell has called "an unconscious but consuming and structuring neurosis" (34). Largely sketched from distortions of details of Franco's own biography, the film emphasized Franco's obsession with heroic death, his vision of the ideal Spanish family as the ideological apparatus that produced "good" Spaniards, and finally, the weight of Spain's bellicose history as it defined Spanish cultural identity. Despite its dramatic and thematic limitations, Race succeeded where nearly all previous efforts had failed, by situating some semblance of the Nationalist cultural thematics within a highly melodramatic plot that foregrounded the chaste love between the two romantic leads, Alfredo Mayo* and Ana Mariscal.* The popularity of the film enabled both actors to sustain their careers throughout the rest of the 1940s in roles not unlike the ones they played here.

Akin to the excesses of the heroic genre was the emergence of a chain of films loosely based on historical themes, events, or merely icons, rooted in the regime's obsessive penchant for the past. Opulent costume dramas became a staple, with films such as Manuel Augusto García Viñola's Inés de Castro (1944), José López Rubio's Eugenia de Montijo (1944), and two key films of the decade's end, Juan de Orduña's Locura de amor [The Madness of Love]* (1948) and Agustina de Aragón (1950), both produced by CIFESA. Spun off from the same ideological predilection was a series of religious dramas that purported to reaffirm Catholic faith: Rafael Gil's 1946 Reina Santa [Saintly Queen], Juan de Orduña's Misión blanca [White Mission] (1947), Sáenz de Heredia's La mies es mucha [Bountiful Harvest] (1948), and José Diáz Morales's El capitán de Loyola [The Captain from Loyola] (1948). Because of their sources in the lives of saints and martyrs, many of these were also historical costume films.

A more perverse expression of the historical costume drama were adaptations of nineteenth-century Spanish novels triggered by the resounding commercial success of two adaptations of Pedro Antonio de Alarcón novels, José Luis Sáenz de Heredia's El escándalo [The Scandal] (1943) and Rafael Gil's El clavo [The Nail] (1944). Superficially, these films and their imitators followed the fairly popular tradition of adapted novels, such as Benito Perojo's version of Galdós's Marianela (1940), but their melodramatic eroticism tapped into Spanish audiences' desire for a prurient kind of escapism. These enormously popular films, were, in fact, closer in temperament to the contemporary *novela rosa* than to the realist classics of the previous century. The genre held its audience throughout the 1940s with a combination of adaptations of literary works and costumed biographies, with films such as Antonio Román's biopic, *Lola Montes* (1944), Rafael Gil's *La pródiga* [*The Prodigal Daughter*] (1946), Antonio del Amo's *El huésped de las tinieblas* [*The Guest from the Shadows*] (1948), and Edgar Neville's biographical film, *El marqués de Salamanca* [*The Marquis of Salamanca*] (1948).

Two areas in which strong vestiges of pre–Civil War film tradition remained were in the folkloric musical comedies and in popular comedic vehicles that, like some of the most popular comedies of the mid-1930s, showed their clear indebtedness to Spanish theatrical forms: Perojo's *Goyescas* (1942), and Juan de Orduña's *La Lola se va a los puertos* [*Lola Goes Down to the Ports*] (1947).

Clearly imitating the patterns of the Hollywood film industry, Spanish cinema generated its own star system as a pattern of inducement for audiences to return to the theater (García Fernández, 136–44). Prominent actors of this period included Rafael Durán* as the quintessential romantic male lead, Alfredo Mayo in both heroic and romantic films, and Luis Peña.* Among the important actresses of this period were Amparito Rivelles* in melodramatic roles, along with Ana Mariscal and Luchy Soto.* By the end of the decade, however, Aurora Bautista,* who had begun her acting career in the theater in Barcelona, and had been discovered by Juan de Orduña, achieved almost mythic stardom as the heroine of a number of costume melodramas beginning with Orduña's epic *The Madness of Love* (1948), followed in rapid succession by *Pequeñeces* [*Trifles*] (1950) and *Agustina de Aragón* (1950).

These Orduña films were products of CIFESA, a studio that during the post–Civil War period gained a reputation as the quasi-official film studio of the regime. This reputation was based not only on the favoritism the company had gained from the state (Font, 107) but on its development of films that reflected the narrative and thematic preferences of the Franco government. CIFESA was, for instance, the studio that produced *¡Harka!*, *The Legion's for Me!*, *The Nail*, *The Madness of Love*, and *Agustina de Aragón*. CIFESA's studio style showed a marked preference for opulently produced historical-biographical films in the grand style of its American counterpart, MGM. Throughout its history, however, until the company's demise in the 1950s, the thematic focus of the films it produced was intimately connected with and at times indistinguishable from state propaganda (Font, 109).

FILM CULTURE OF THE FIFTIES

The early 1950s saw the continuation of much of the drab postwar culture of the 1940s, intensified by a new period of international ostracism of Spain after the defeat of Franco's axis allies at the end of World War II. The essential contradiction for film culture of this period is described by Diego Galán as an effort by the government to harmonize the maintenance of its old ideological schemes and biases with the demands of a modernized and democratized Europe within which Spain needed to find a place (Galán 1983, 146). For the first time since the war, government controls led to dissension among filmmakers, some of whom were in prominent positions and supported changes in cultural direction.

Film, of course, was only one avenue through which that resistance developed. In truth, the implacable nature of repression maintained by the regime during the second decade of its triumphant new era led to the emergence of a *cultura de disidencia*, a culture of dissidence (Heredero, 36), which found its expression in literary magazines such as *Insula, Indice, El Ciervo,* and *Revista.* There was also an effort to "Europeanize" Spanish literary culture by embracing French and American novelistic tendencies. This produced a broad realist generation in fiction that found its cinematic cognates in the Madrid film journal, *Objetivo,* and its Salamanca counterpart, *Cinema Universitario,* both of which advocated stronger engagement with everyday social reality for Spanish films.

Official historians of Spanish cinema might look at the 1950s, from one perspective, as a continuation and embellishment of movie traditions from the previous decade, especially in the area of popular, folkloric cinema. Yet, more recent film historians have emphasized the series of problems that arose within the development of Spanish film during the 1950s, many of which derived from the government's own misguided policies, which served to spawn conflicts.

In 1951, a government reorganization of ministries placed the general responsibility for film under the Ministry of Information and Tourism, with José María García Escudero named to head the new film office. García Escudero had hoped to modernize Spanish cinema by bringing into focus a more socially contemporary and liberal view of Spain and Spaniards, but he almost immediately fell out with various groups. In attempting to provide state protection by way of subsidies for José Antonio Nieves Conde's *Surcos [Furrows]** (1951), a Neorealist portrait of urban ambience and moral decay, García Escudero ran into the opposition of ecclesiastical authorities who had condemned *Furrows.* At the same time, others who supported CIFESA's production of Juan de Orduña's historical epic about Columbus and the discovery of America, *Alba de América [Dawn in America]* (1951), were piqued by the designation of *Furrows* for subsidy purposes as a film of National Interest. García Escudero was no match for the forces of traditionalist power, and his departure from office only foreshadowed the conflicts that would mark much of the decade.

Paralleling those in official positions who supported Orduña's historical genre films, popular Spanish audiences were largely wed to the formula films they had become accustomed to in the previous decade. Of these, the most conspicuous were a newly emerging genre of religious and pseudo-religious cinema, obviously inspired by the lingering ideological fetish of Catholic Spain. Films featuring priests in leading roles such as Nieves Conde's *Balarrasa* (1950), Rafael Gil's *La señora de Fátima [The Lady of Fatima]* (1951), and *La guerra* de Dios *[God's War]* (1953), Ignacio Iquino's *El Judas [Judas]* (1952), and *El beso de*

Judas [*The Kiss of Judas*] (1953), and Pedro Lazaga's *El frente infinito* [*The Infinite Front*] (1956), only begin to suggest the volume and persistence of such a genre, built at times on the flimsiest and most melodramatic of religious premises. One of the biggest commercial successes of the decade in this genre was Ladislav Vajda's *Marcelino, pan y vino* [*Marcelino, Bread and Wine*]* (1953), a tale of a newborn baby abandoned at the door of a monastery and taken in by the friars. The film owes its popularity as much to its narration of religiosity and faith as to the presence of the child actor, Pablito Calvo, in the title role. Calvo not only managed to forge a career from his performance, but also seems to have founded another popular genre of the period, the child-star film. Subsequent spin-offs of this model included the figures of Marisol*(Pepa Flores) and Joselito, each of whom would in time become a box-office phenomenon not unlike their American counterpart, Shirley Temple.

The folkloric comedy, a highly refined escapist genre, was also abundantly represented on Spanish screens of the decade. Like the pre–Civil War films to which this genre owes its origins, these were stylized traditional comedies, conveniently punctuated by songs at various points. Luis Lucia's version of *La hermana San Sulpicio* [*Sister Saint Sulpicio*] (1952) is an emblematic expression of this tendency. Based on a nineteenth-century Palacio Valdés novel, it was first adapted for the screen in a silent version by Florián Rey in 1927, then remade by the same director with the same star, Imperio Argentina, as a sound film in 1934. Rey's remake was an important commercial success, as was Lucia's remake of 1952, which was followed by yet another version, again directed by Lucia in 1971. The obvious popularity of such remakes, similar to the Hollywood approach to sequels, was clearly based on their appeal to the audience's familiarity with the characters, story, and most importantly, the popular spirit embodied in these.

In one of the most successful comedies of the decade, José Luis Sáenz de Heredia's *Historias de la radio* [*Radio Stories*]* (1955), many of the values, stereotypes, clichés, and views of drab Spanish life codified into filmic narrative were clearly on display. Sáenz de Heredia, whose film career goes back to before the Civil War, was by now a master at presenting such views in ways that were familiar and yet notably nonjudgmental, a formula that other mainstream filmmakers of the period would attempt to emulate.

Indeed, the attraction of folkloric films was their appeal to the static values of the familiar as portrayed usually in rural settings involving stereotyped figures. This tendency is brilliantly lampooned in Luis García Berlanga's* *Bienvenido, Mister Marshall!* [*Welcome, Mister Marshall!*]* (1953), in which the fantasies of the members of a rural Castilian community about their own world and the world outside of Spain is cleverly portrayed.

Although Berlanga mocked these tendencies, the familiar stereotypes and clichéd plots he derided remained an irresistible formula for commercial success for movie producers as well as an emotional attraction for Spanish audiences. Two of the most telling expressions of that relation may be found in Juan de

Orduña's spectacularly successful musical production of *El último cuplé* [*The Last Song*]* (1957) and Luis César Amadori's *¿Dónde vas, Alfonso XII?* [*Where Are You Going, Alfonso XII?*]* (1958). The former film catapulted Sara Montiel, a popular romantic starlet of the 1940s and early 1950s, into the status of superstar and film legend (Heredero, 127). The appeal of this backstage musical melodrama, the last major CIFESA production before the company's demise, derived from two possible sources, as Diego Galán argues: The first was simply the recuperation of an alternative, popular musical tradition to the Andalusian folkloric trend that had been a staple on Spanish screen since the 1930s; the other was the attraction of the kind of eroticism, embodied both in the person of Sara Montiel and in her fictional story, that Spanish censors had shielded Spanish audiences from for the better part of two decades. (Galán, 20). Amadori's fairy-tale melodrama, based on details of the ill-fated love between the late nineteenth-century Spanish king and his Sevillana bride, starred the popular heartthrob, Vicente Parra, in the title role. Between the popular adulation of the actor and the audience's embrace of the most pedestrian of romantic melodramatic plots, the film became one of the biggest box-office hits of the decade.

Despite fleeting impressions to the contrary, these commercial successes confirm that much of the dominant Spanish cinema of the 1950s remained static as it reflected a view held by Spaniards of their own world. The culmination of that static view came in 1960 when César Fernández Ardavín's adaptation of the Spanish Golden Age narrative, *Lazarillo de Tormes** won the Golden Bear at the Berlin Film Festival. The prestige of the prize suggested to Spaniards that the outside world both ackowledged and praised the traditional culture the regime had so long espoused.

This status quo cinema served, however, to fire a younger generation of filmmakers and critics to formulate a cinema of mild opposition during the 1950s. Ironically, some of that opposition came into focus through a government-sponsored institution, the National Film School (Instituto de Investigaciones y Experiencias Cinematográficas: IIEC), founded in 1947. Though its curriculum was largely negligible during its early years, the school's chief accomplishment was to have brought together a group of precocious young men intrigued by film and politically opposed to the regressive nature of the Franco regime. The principal figures of this group were Berlanga and Juan Antonio Bardem,* whose heated discussions of film themes clearly influenced another generation of young directors and other film professionals.

The ferment of the group was clearly abetted by the fortuitous organization of an Italian Cinema Week in Madrid in 1951, to which the Italian consulate invited students from the film school. This introduction to the classics of Italian Neorealist cinema exposed these young men for the first time to the political and social potential of certain filmmaking strategies that were clearly within their own grasp. This impulse was already apparent in the works of an older generation of directors familiar with American gangster films, and who emphasized working-class milieus in police films such as Julio Salvador's

Apartado de correos 1001 [*Mailbox 1001*] (1950) and Ignacio Iquino's *Brigada criminal* [*Criminal Division*] (1950). Nieves Conde's controversial *Surcos* and Antonio del Amo's *Día tras día* [*Day after Day*] (1951) also pointed the way toward a Spanish equivalent of the early Italian Neorealist spirit.

These latter films, however, were fairly tentative explorations of Neorealism. It was the works of the National Film School's younger filmmakers that would combine Neorealism's strategies of on-location shooting and proletarian characters with a series of pointed social critiques. The first Bardem-Berlanga collaboration, *Esa pareja feliz* [*That Happy Couple*]* (1951), for example, appeared to be merely a light comedy about the Madrid housing shortage. But the film's narrative emphasized urban exterior locations as an implicit critique of life in drab working-class Madrid; the film was a gentle prelude to Bardem's later films where the Neorealist treatment of mise-en-scène was more biting and pointed. *Muerte de un ciclista* [*Death of a Cyclist*]* (1955) exposed the hypocrisy of class divisions in the seemingly stable world of well-to-do Madrid, while *Calle Mayor* [*Main Street*]* (1956), debunked the myth of the idealized Spanish provinces. Even an apparently frivolous comedy, such as Fernando Fernán-Gómez's *La vida por delante* [*Your Life before You*]* (1958), which borrowed the theme of the Madrid housing shortage, aimed its barbs at the pathetic state of working-class Spaniards.

Given the spirit of discontent of the period, it is not surprising that a more focused effort was made for a public airing of the grievances of this younger generation of filmmakers. In the spring of 1955 the film magazine, *Objetivo* in conjunction with the University of Salamanca Cine-club organized a series of "national conversations" about the state of Spanish cinema. Professionals and students of all political persuasions were invited to attend. Although much fiery rhetoric was voiced, including Bardem's scathing denunciation of the state of the film industry, the meeting concluded with only a mild set of demands, the principal one of which was a plea for the government to rationalize its censorship practices. What motivated many of those who participated in the Salamanca "conversations" was not a political agenda, although some of the prominent spokesmen at the meeting, such as Bardem and Ricardo Muñoz Suay, were members of the clandestine Communist party. It was the desire to connect in meaningful ways with a popular Spanish audience. Bardem's complaint about the state of Spanish film, for instance, was that it did not connect in any meaningful way with the reality of Spanish life.

Symptomatic of the spirit of intransigence of the period, the government's response to these efforts was to dismantle the film magazine and to blacklist a number of the more prominent participants of the meeting. In the ensuing years, however, the demand of this younger generation for that vital connection with a popular cultural base would persist. The most notable achievements of this cinema of dissidence were films by Marco Ferreri* and Rafael Azcona* which combined the Neorealist penchant with classically Spanish gallows humor in *El pisito* [*The Little Apartment*]* (1958) and *El cochecito* [*The Little Car*]* (1960), as well as Carlos Saura's* debut film, *Los golfos* [*Hooligans*]* (1959), perhaps the quintessential Neorealist film of protest against the patterns of social marginalization. These were, in fact, the kind of films that showed the everyday struggles and aspirations of ordinary Spaniards characteristically living the contradiction between official cultural views of Spanish life and the reality of poverty, social marginalization, housing shortages, and the like. The apparent Neorealism of Saura's and Ferreri's films at the decade's end contrasts pointedly with the benign images of folkloric and pious Spain that had dominated film screens through most of the 1950s.

On a less politically charged plane, another chain of events was transpiring in terms of the industrial structure of Spanish film production that was to have far-reaching impact on the complexion of Spanish film production during the 1960s. These events were set in motion by the arrival of the U.S. producer, Samuel Bronston, who had come to Spain in 1959 with the intention of setting up a major Hollywood-style studio for a series of American superproductions that could take advantage of the newly stabilized *peseta* and the dramatically lower wage scale of Spanish workers. Bronston was not the first to see the financial benefits of lower production costs in Spain. Since the middle of the 1950s, films like Robert Rossen's *Alexander the Great* (1956) and Bronston's own *John Paul Jones* (1959) had been shot in Spain. In the 1960s he was developing a series of superproductions, beginning with Nicholas Ray's *King of Kings* (1961), and including *El Cid* (1961) and *55 Days at Peking* (1963), and concluding with the massive commercial failure, *The Fall of the Roman Empire* (1964) before the Bronston studios finally closed down. As Peter Besas argues, the importance of this venture was that Bronston's studio gave firsthand training and influenced the professional course of a generation of Spanish film technicians who continued to work on international as well as Spanish productions over the coming years (53–54).

THE FINAL DECADE OF FRANCOISM

The portentous changes that were to shape the 1960s in Spanish culture date back to a radical shake-up of Franco's government that occurred in 1959, when the technocrats seeking to modernize the country and to bring it into closer contact with Europe finally gained definitive control in key government ministries. Among the newly important ministries was that of Information and Tourism, which held the reigns on the official film administration. As one of those forward-looking new ministers, Manuel Fraga Iribarne sought to change the publicity image of Spain by liberalizing press and literary censorship that had kept tight control over mass information in Spain since the end of the Civil War. Fraga believed that Spain could effect an evolution towards modernity in small, incremental steps. One of his first actions was to return García Escudero to the leadership of the film office. Fraga encouraged him to take action to loosen film censorship policies in ways that would be consistent with his own view of liberalized press censorship. This García Escudero did in 1963 by issuing the first published statement of norms for film censorship. This was a simple measure but it allowed filmmakers to carve out a more reasonable series of narrative and thematic elements for a modern Spanish cinema. García Escudero's tenure as the head of the film division lasted some four years and came to an end in 1967 after a series of reversals of Fraga's policies. The Minister of Information was himself removed from his position and his liberal policies were repudiated in 1969.

The 1960s in film and popular media was known as the era of *destape* or opening up, owing principally to Fraga's liberalizing moves. Yet despite the loosening up of censorship norms popular Spanish cinema was generally impervious to substantive changes; it simply continued earlier and easy patterns of no resistance in presenting popular, folkloric comedies and musicals, albeit with more sexually explicit scenes and situations as well as never-before-seen scenes of nudity. Ramón Fernández's abysmal comedy, *No desearás al vecino del quinto* [*Though Shalt Not Covet Thy Neighbor on the Fifth Floor*] (1970), with the popular comic actor, Alfredo Landa,* turned out to be the most commercially successful Spanish film in decades (Torres 1994, 55), in no small measure due to its patently sexual comic style that seemed perfectly designed to show off Landa's particular appeal. Indeed, Landa had achieved such universal popularity throughout the 1960s and 1970s that his comic style and the genre of comedies in which he appeared became known as *Landismo*. Other popular comic films of the decade included Pedro Lazaga's *Nuevo en esta plaza* [*New in This Place*] (1966) and the debut film of the popular teenage heartthrob singer, Raphael, *Cuando tú no estás* [*When You're Not Here*] (1966), directed by Mario Camus.*

While this surface of Spanish popular film was all but static, another scenario was evolving for the small but critically significant artistic cinema of Spain. In 1960, the legendary Luis Buñuel returned from his twenty-five-year exile to make *Viridiana*,* a Mexican-Spanish coproduction from a script passed by Spanish censors with only minor changes. When the resulting film, as the official Spanish entry to the prestigious Cannes Film Festival in 1961, won the Gold Palm, it was summarily condemned by *L'Osservatore Romano*, thereby provoking an international scandal in which Spanish government officials were made to look like dupes to the cunning Surrealist, Buñuel. The Spanish company that had coproduced the film, UNINCI, was dissolved; the film was banned commercially and even mention of Buñuel or *Viridiana* in the Spanish press was prohibited; those involved in government supervision of the film were removed from their positions.

The only way the regime knew to respond to criticism or opposition was to reaffirm its own power in the eyes of would-be dissidents. This was accomplished through harsh censorial cuts in films or, in some instances, by denying licenses to directors to shoot certain projects. Because of Buñuel's cameo appearance in Carlos Saura's second film, *Llanto por un bandido* [*Lament for a Bandit*] (1963), that film suffered important censorial cuts as well as a low distribution classification, thus making it unattractive to domestic distributors.

As Fraga and García Escudero well understood, such repressive moves might make conservative members of the Franco regime feel good, but they also confirmed the outside world's notion of cultural tyranny under the dictatorship. García Escudero's mission as he assessed it was to advance Fraga's goal of promoting a new image of Spain in the international media by addressing what he saw as the two implacable forces that seemed to be provoking conflict: the censorship apparatus, and the clamor by aspiring young directors for a chance to make films (Rodero, 44). His strategy evolved on a variety of fronts that would shape filmmaking in Spain over the next decade. He promoted a new approach to film subsidies called *Nuevo Cine Español* [New Spanish Cinema]. The scheme called for establishing a new subsidy category for films designated as being of "Special Interest," to replace the old "National Interest" subsidy category.

This mechanism, it was hoped, would recognize serious artistic work, as opposed to merely politically correct works. As well, the government established special subsidies for younger filmmakers, particularly the younger generation coming out of the recently reorganized National Film School, renamed *Escuela Oficial de Cine* (EOC).

Also, by establishing a series of published censorship norms, García Escudero was able to cultivate an impressive number of talented young and innovative filmmakers while sponsoring some of the most original and powerful Spanish films of recent decades. This promotion of a distinct kind of Spanish cinema also called for a different pattern of domestic distribution that the government provided through the establishment of a separate category of movie house: small art-house cinemas called *salas de arte y ensayo*.

By 1966, these new strategies for support had shown dramatic results in film production, with an all-time record of 174 films produced that year (Rodero, 68). From 1963 through 1967, roughly the years that encompass the promotion of New Spanish Cinema, Spain saw the emergence of some of the most talented and original works since the pre–Civil War period. These included critically praised and commercially successful films such as Miguel Picazo's* *La tía Tula* [*Aunt Tula*]* (1964); Carlos Saura's third film, but the first in collaboration with the gifted scriptwriter-producer, Elías Querejeta,* *La caza* [*The Hunt*]* (1965); Basilio Martín Patino's innovative *Nueve cartas a Berta* [*Nine Letters to Bertha*]* (1965); Manuel Summers's *Del rosa al amarillo* [*From Pink to Yellow*]* (1963), Angelino Fons's *La busca* [*The Search*] (1966); and Mario Camus's *Los farsantes* [*The Actors*] (1963) and *Con el viento solano* [*With a Wind from the East*] (1966).

After a certain initial euphoria about the enlightened transformation of the film climate, the harsh reality set in that though censorship had somehow been "rationalized," the censorial sword of Damocles remained as a form of implacable intimidation on young filmmakers. Preproduction censorship of scripts persisted, and, in many cases, excessive cuts ordered by the censors for completed films severely marred the finished product. Then, in 1967, as the censors appeared to gain increasing power, García Escudero's office was eliminated, and government supervision over domestic film production was transferred to a new organism, the *Dirección General de Cultura Popular y Espectáculos*. Following this move, the subsidies for films of Special Interest were eliminated, prominent film journals began to disappear, and even the National Film School was transferred to the University of Madrid's Faculty of Information Sciences in an effort to reduce its personality (Rodero, 92).

While some later critics dismiss the New Spanish Cinema as merely the regime's short-lived window-dressing for its own propagandistic aims that seldom connected with the popular Spanish audience, it is clear that the kind of support given younger filmmakers, as well as the modifications made in the censorial system, contributed to the rich and innovative film style of young directors who over the coming decade radically altered the complexion of Spanish cinema. It is perhaps no coincidence that most of these men who developed elaborate, allegorical styles in their films of the 1970s had already learned to cope with the censorship boards during the heyday of New Spanish Cinema. As Peter Besas notes: "The trick was to expand upon the nebulous fringe of the permissible, which might also greatly enhance the commercial returns of the film, provided it got past the censors at all" (80).

This was certainly the case with some of the 1970s films by the men who had benefited from García Escudero's plan. These included Saura, with a trilogy of three political films (*Jardín de las delicias* [*Garden of Delights*] (1970), *Ana y los lobos* [*Ana and the Wolves*] (1972), and *La prima Angélica* [*Cousin Angelica*]* (1973); José Luis Borau* who coscripted *Mi querida señorita* [*My Dearest Señorita*]* (1971) and wrote and directed *Furtivos* [*Poachers*]* (1975); Víctor Erice,* whose *El espíritu de la colmena* [*Spirit of the Beehive*]* (1973) is often cited as one of the most important films of the final decade of the dictatorship; and Basilio Martín Patino* whose *Canciones para después de una guerra* [*Songs for after a War*]* (1971) confronts for the first time in a Spanish film the powerful blockage of popular cultural memory by the repressive regime.

Much of the drama of Spanish cinema's attempt to modernize itself through this politicization of narratives took place in Madrid, which, after the Civil War, was the center of film production as well as national politics. In direct response to the emergence of New Spanish Cinema, a brief but important counter movement, the Barcelona School, took form in Spain's second city. By the mid-1960s, and clearly as a result of the modernization policies that had transformed Spain over the past decade, a group of young filmmakers now took aim at not only Castilian-based culture but also the presumably conventional films being promoted as New Spanish Cinema. A radically different look and visual style, as well as a more European type of narrative, came into focus in Jacinto Esteva and Joaquín Jordá's *Dante no es únicamente severo* [*Dante Is Not Only Severe*] (1967) and Carlos Durán's *Cada vez que . . .* [*Each Time That . . .*] (1967). These films sought to express through images and story an alternative to the often drab and traditional views of a Castilianized Spain. Their directors emphasized a sleek and cosmopolitan culture like the very city of Barcelona with whose cultural style their work implicitly identified. By far the most impressive works to come out of this movement were Gonzalo Suárez's* *Ditirambo** (1967) and Vicente Aranda's* *Fata morgana** (1967), enigmatic tales set in a futuristic space but actually shot in Barcelona. John Hopewell sees the use of genre style in the two films—espionage in Suárez's film and science fiction in Aranda's—as strategies to express covert political themes in seemingly vanguardist experimental films (70). Despite such efforts, the Barcelona School members generally ignored the emerging efforts of a Catalan national movement of the period and instead focused their attention on a cultural struggle against *los de Madrid*, the Madrid gang (Rodríguez Lafuente, 253). By the end of the decade, the group had disbanded and only Suárez and Aranda went on to establish careers as filmmakers.

The last five years of Franco's life, 1970–1975, often characterized by social and political historians as the final stage of the forty-year Franco dictatorship, has been read in more recent years as the beginning of the transition from dictatorship to democracy (Monterde, 7). Many of the filmmakers who sought a frontal attack on Francoism were tempered by expediency to conform to some degree to censorial pressures. This led them to the strategies of double readings, elliptical narration, and cryptic allusions through which they hoped to bypass the literal-minded censors and address sympathetic audiences. In the process of these conceptual rewritings, Saura's political trilogy and Borau's *Hay que matar a B* [*B Must Die*] (1973) and *Poachers* (1975) being excellent examples, audiences were brought to witness more than mere attacks on Francoist actions and policies; they were led to ponder the ideological weight of decades of postwar coercion. In *Garden of Delights* (1970)* just as in Patino's brilliant documentary, *Songs for after a War* (1971), the representation of the blockage of popular cultural memory was brought home to audiences. In the Armiñán-Borau collaboration, *My Dearest Señorita* (1971), as in Víctor Erice's haunting *Spirit of the Beehive* (1973), the vision of repressive provincial life in the immediate post–Civil War period as it shaped social, especially female identity, was vividly portrayed. Buñuel's second feature-length Spanish film, his first since *Viridiana* ten years earlier, was *Tristana** in 1970, which similarly questioned the conceptual relation of women to the patriarchal traditionalism of Spanish culture. Based on a nineteenth-century Galdós novel, the film's success led to an increased interest by other filmmakers in adapting literary classics to the screen.

Augusto M. Torres notes a growing rift between the Church and the regime that made it possible for more popular filmmakers to treat the hitherto untouchable narrative theme of ecclesiastic indiscretions, essentially through the filmed adaptations of certain novelistic masterpieces (Torres 1994, 40). These included Rafael Moreno Alba's adaptation of Juan Valera's *Pepita Jiménez* (1974), Gonzalo Suárez's version of Clarín's *La regenta* [*The Regent's Wife*] (1974), and Pedro Olea's version of Galdós's *Tormento* [*Torment*] (1974). These were followed by more contemporary representations of the critique of ecclesiastic mores.

These tendencies both coincided with and in certain instances were actually part of a strategy loosely termed *tercera vía*, or the "Third Route." Filmmakers and producers made a conscious effort to chart a course for their productions that avoided the extremes of the low, popular cinema epitomized by the films of Pedro Masó* and Pedro Lazaga,* and the intellectual and often hermetic art-house films of the Querejeta-Saura collaborations, which often seemed more geared for cosmopolitan and international audiences than for the general Spanish public (Caparrós-Lera 1978, 49-51). The Third Route cinema was aimed at a middle-brow, socially and politically progressive, usually urban audience born in the immediate post-Civil War period and now coming to maturity and beginning to raise their own families. The principal voice of *tercera vía* was the producer José Luis Dibildos, who promoted early films by Roberto Bodegas* such as *Vida conyugal sana* [*Healthy Married Life*] (1973), *Españolas en París* [*Spanish Girls in Paris*] (1971) and *Los nuevos españoles* [*New Spaniards*] (1974); and films by Antonio Drove* such as *Tocata y fuga de Lola* [*Lola's Toccata and Fugue*] (1974) and *Mi mujer es decente dentro de lo que cabe* [*My Wife Is Decent As Far As That's Possible*] (1975).

What thus emerged was a gradual but persistent critique of the social legacy of the dictatorship that broached the truly profound problems of identity and cultural ideology that would shape the direction of the cinema of transition. When Franco died in 1975, two of the pivotal films of the transition had already been completed: Saura's *Cría cuervos* [*Raise Ravens*] (1975) and José Luis Borau's *Poachers* (1975). Saura's film dramatizes the wake for a military officer as a symbolic image of Franco's death; even more violently, Borau portrays a matricide that is clearly aligned to the killing off of the ideology of the past. Though violence increasingly becomes an element of the cinema of transition—characterized by Marsha Kinder as a "Blood Cinema" (*Blood Cinema: The Reconstruction of National Identity in Spain*)—these films led the way for the type of cinematic interrogation of cultural and political values that provided a uniqueness to Spanish cinema during this difficult period.

DECADES OF TRANSITION

As in earlier decades, a certain core of low-grade, popular domestic cinema remained one of the staples on Spanish screens well beyond Franco's death. The only real alteration in these films was the increase in scenes of nudity and soft-core pornography. But a cluster of serious films continued to be made during these years as well, principally by members of the generation of filmmakers who had been able to sustain their careers after the demise of New Spanish Cinema. These included Saura, Borau, Manuel Gutiérrez Aragón,* Camus, and Armiñán, as well as several younger directors developed under the tutelage of Elías Querejeta's production company, including Ricardo Franco* and Jaime Chávarrí.* Others, just starting out in film, sought to break with what they saw as the ponderous style of these opposition filmmakers; they cultivated, instead, the image and spirit of the rapidly changing cultural milieu of post-Franco Spain.

Notable among this group were Fernando Colomo,* José Luis Garci,* and Fernando Trueba.*

One of the most striking tendencies of the five or six years following Franco's death was what might be called the genre of political and historical revision, including that of the conception and impact of the Civil War (Rodríguez Lafuente, 258; José Enrique Monterde, 8–14). These were films such as Ricardo Franco's adaptation of Camilo José Cela's brutal novel, *Pascual Duarte** (1975), which modified a contemporary Spanish literary masterpiece to coincide with a critique of the political forces shaping social behavior in Spain. Jaime Camino's* *Las largas vacaciones del '36* [*The Long Summer Vacation of '36*] was a simpler form of historical retrospection about the summer of 1936 and the outbreak of the Civil War. Pedro Olea's *Pim, pam, pum . . . ¡fuego!* [*Bang, Bang . . . You're Dead!*]* (1975) evoked the memories of the harsh and depressing life of food rationing and struggle in the Madrid of the immediate post–Civil War. Manuel Gutiérrez Aragón's *Camada negra* [*Black Brood*]* (1978) and *Corazón del bosque* [*The Heart of the Forest*] (1979) focused on aspects of the enduring legacy of Francoist ideology; in the former film, through the rise of right-wing urban violence; in the latter, through the story of sustained resistance to the dictatorship more than a decade after the Republican defeat of 1939. As diverse as was the surface subject matter of such films, the common thread of the persistence of historical memory brought these works together. In *Sonámbulos* [*Sleepwalkers*] (1977), Gutiérrez Aragón presented a stunning dreamlike reenactment of scenes of urban violence clearly related to the recent experience of the dictatorship. Perhaps the most scathing, certainly one of the most highly original of the directorial approaches to this theme was Jaime Chávarri's stunning documentary, *El desencanto* [*Disenchantment*]* (1976), a unique series of interviews with the wife and three sons of the Falangist poet, Leopoldo Panero, more than a decade after his death. In the process of retrospection, Chávarri provides a cathartic view of the burden of the dictatorship and its ideology on the members of a presumably exemplary Spanish family. Chávarri's next film, *A un dios desconocido* [*To an Unknown God*] (1977), posed a fictional equivalent of a similar process of recollection, this time from the point of view of a middle-aged gay magician remembering his childhood contacts with the poet, Federico García Lorca.

Perhaps the most critical moment in the evolution of this historical/political tendency came in 1979 when Pilar Miró* directed a film version of a little-known incident in the notorious history of the dreaded Spanish Civil Guard in which two men were wrongly tortured then forced to confess to the murder of a shepherd in the rural province of Cuenca early in the century. *El crimen de Cuenca* [*The Crime at Cuenca*]* (1979) was confiscated by the Civil Guard and charges were brought against Miró and her producer, Alfredo Matas,* for maligning its reputation. The situation provoked a governmental crisis since the Guard claimed historical jurisdiction that predated the 1978 constitution. If the Civil Guard's decision were allowed to stand, then not only Miró but the entire

Spanish film industry would remain at the mercy of the old forms of political coercion and censorship. The crisis was eventually resolved when the Guard was persuaded to let the charges be shifted to a civil court where they were finally dropped. When *The Crime at Cuenca* eventually did achieve normal distribution, the film became a popular commercial success, in part due to the scandal, in part due to the rumors of sensationalist depictions of the torturing of the two innocent men.

While such films found a receptive audience at home as well as abroad, the vast majority of Spaniards tired quickly of such brooding introspection and historical revisions of the recent, bloody past. Thus, as in every decade since the war's end, many of the most commercially successful films turned out to be lighter fare. Of particular note, however, is the work of more serious filmmakers in comic genres in an effort to address more mainstream commercial audiences. One of the comedies made by well-established filmmakers was Luis García Berlanga's social satire, *Escopeta nacional* [*National Rifle*]* (1977), which boasted an impressive ensemble cast in a film that stylistically harked back to that director's most impressive successes of the 1950s and 1960s, *Welcome, Mister Marshall!* (1953) and *Plácido** (1961). This time the object of Berlanga's scathing criticism was the interplay between nouveau riche businessmen and enterprising politicians on the take, with the action set against a backdrop of the decadent and impoverished Spanish nobility. Also, Saura's *Mamá cumple 100 años* [*Mama Turns 100*] (1979), broke the mold of the Aragonese director's introspective symbolic narratives. Here he created a comic sequel to his earlier *Ana and the Wolves* (1972), in order to chart the course of a new generation's abandonment of Francoist traditions. While both films were enormous commercial successes in Spain, and Saura's film even garnered an Oscar nomination, the field for Spanish comedy had already ceded to a younger generation.

Fernando Colomo's 1977 debut film, *Tigres de papel* [*Paper Tigers*],* starring Carmen Maura,* helped to establish a spirit of critical unrest echoed in a contemporary comedy of manners that quickly established itself as one of the characteristic genres of the years of transition. The *Nueva Comedia Madrileña* or New Madrid Comedy, usually but not always set in the Spanish capital, played off the ironic and often confused attitudes of a younger, progressive generation of Spaniards caught in the foibles of achieving social status and a perspective on their own lives. José Luis Garci's *Asignatura pendiente* [*Pending Examination*]* (1977) and Fernando Trueba's* debut film, *Opera prima* [*First Work* or *Cousin in Opera*]*(1980), seemed to define the terms of a genre that was strikingly akin to Woody Allen's mature comedies of the 1970s, such as *Manhattan*. At the same time, Colomo, Garci, and Trueba appealed to an audience quite distinct from that of other directors. They were addressing Spaniards who, like the Woody Allen heroes, were aware of styles and trends, but were not as politically engaged as the audiences of the late Francoist cinema were presumed to be. Political themes, such as the general elections of 1978, entered these films, but usually only as the backdrop for plot.

Against such moves toward a less pronounced Spanishness in Spanish cinema and a desire to embrace more international contemporary trends, a decided counterforce is noted in the advent of strong regional cinema. This is sometimes referred to as *cine de autonomías* [Cinema of the Autonomous Communities], so called in recognition of the 1978 constitution that organized Spain as a federation of seventeen "autonomous regions." Many of these regions were expedient constructions to suggest an even-handed political plan for post-Franco Spain. Two of them, however, Catalonia and the Basque Country, were, in fact, traditional historical communities that had long claimed autonomy from the Castilian hegemony of the peninsula. In an effort to reassert their regional identity, each community developed local governmental plans to promote regional cinema. Ironically, the strategy in many ways coincided with the old Francoist plan to create a "national" cinema through subsidies and other supports. In the first decade of the post-Franco era, both the Basque and Catalonian regional governments supported production of some of the most important contemporary Spanish films. These included, in Catalonia, Antoni Ribas's *La ciutat cremada* [*Burnt City*]* (1976), Jaime Camino's *La vieja memoria* [*The Old Memory*]* (1977), and Ventura Pons's *Ocaña: retrato intermitente* [*Ocaña: An Intermittent Portrait*] (1978). While filmmakers such as Ribas sought to affirm a totally autonomous Catalonian identity in film as in culture, Camino and Pons seemed to rely on a more balanced tradition that saw Catalonia as distinct in terms of language and customs but still part of a larger Spain. This was an image that coincided with earlier representations of Catalonian identity, such as Llobet-Gracia's unique *Vida en sombras* [*Life in the Shadows*]* (1948) and Josep María Forn's* *La piel quemada* [*Burnt Skin*]* (1964).

Unlike Catalonia, which had a long historical tradition of filmmaking dating back to the start of the century, Basque filmmakers had no equivalent industrial infrastructure on which to rely, nor a regional film tradition from which to draw inspiration. Yet, oddly enough, Basque films achieved a greater circulation than their Catalonian counterparts. Imanol Uribe's trilogy about the Basque terrorist group, ETA, *El proceso de Burgos* [*The Trial at Burgos*] (1981); *La fuga de Segovia* [*Flight from Segovia*] (1982); and his masterpiece, *La muerte de Mikel* [*The Death of Mikel*]* (1983), traced the historical evolution of the separatist bent in Basque thinking. Montxo Armendáriz* made his debut as a commercial filmmaker with the prize-winning *Tasio** (1984), telling the story in an almost ethnographic style of two generations of Basque carbon workers. Two years later, in *27 horas* [*Twenty-Seven Hours*](1986), he turned his attention to the problem of drug culture among youths in San Sebastián. A similar configuration of themes of generation, regional identity, drugs, and the law emerges in Eloy de la Iglesia's* *El pico* [*The Shoot*]* (1982) and its sequel, *El pico II* (1983), both of which used the Basque country as a critical setting within which to situate contemporary social themes.

In 1982, with the Socialist electoral victory, Pilar Miró, the most prominent Spanish woman filmmaker, was named director of the film section of the

Ministry of Culture. As one of the rare examples of a professional trained in the industry who achieved such authority in Spain, Miró set out to support Spanish cinema in a way that, it was believed, would enable Spanish cinema to flourish on its own. The *Ley Miró* or Miró Law, as it was known, called for a series of subsidies to producers against box-office receipts. The plan was an effort by the Socialist government to influence the kinds of films that were to be made. In truth, most of the films that received such support simply could not have been made without the government's backing. Left unchecked for decades, Hollywood cinema had so encroached into the Spanish distribution market that by 1985 it represented over seventy percent of all box-office receipts in Spain.

One of the films that received a Ministry of Culture subsidy was Pedro Almodóvar's* *La ley del deseo* [*Law of Desire*]* (1987), an improbable choice for official subvention since the film's content dealt explicitly with gay and transsexual characters. Such official support, however, was itself part of an agenda to help undo the legacy of the Franco years by supporting those artistic efforts that might contribute both within Spain and abroad to the climate of greater toleration of cultural and social diversity.

Even before *Law of Desire*, his sixth film, Almodóvar was considered by Spaniards as well as international audiences to be the most prominent embodiment of countercultural and antitraditionalist sentiments in Spanish film. Self-taught as a filmmaker, his first two films, *Pepi, Luci, Bom y otras chicas del montón* [*Pepi, Luci, Bom, and Other Girls Like That*]* (1980), and *Laberinto de pasiones* [*Labyrinth of Passion*] (1982), were not only the effervescent expressions of the so-called *Movida* or counterculture movement in Madrid, but a clear rebuke to the polished and controlled cinema that had, since the early 1970s, been the presumed core of serious art film in Spain. Here, however, was a truly popular and populist cinema whose characters and audiences were an exuberant generation who mocked restraint and reveled in illicit drugs, sex, and scatological humor (Smith, 32–34).

Each successive Almodóvar film suggested a gradual evolution in technical mastery of film form. Thus, five years after the technically flawed *Pepi, Luci, Bom*, Almodóvar's *¿Qué he hecho yo para merecer esto?* [*What Have I Done to Deserve This?*] (1985) achieved cross-over success and enthusiastic praise by American critics. With each new film, Almodóvar's reputation and commercial success grew. His 1988 film, *Mujeres al borde de un ataque de nervios* [*Women on the Verge of a Nervous Breakdown*],* proved to be the most commercially successful Spanish film in the U.S. market up to that time and was nominated for an Oscar in the Best Foreign Film category.

Given Almodóvar's status as a filmmaker who developed outside of the semi-official channels of a national film school or the film industry, it is difficult to extrapolate from his meteoric rise any general sense regarding the Spanish film industry in general. Yet, his evocation of a new, young Spain, his treatment of exuberant sexuality, and his efforts to move beyond the traditional images of Spain to address an international audience are all hallmarks of new directions of

Spanish cinema of the post 1985 period.

Some of that movement to an international context is to be noted earlier in the 1980s. Miró's campaign to support the Oscar nomination for José Luis Garci's otherwise forgettable *Volver a empezar* [*To Begin Again*]* (1982) resulted in the first Oscar ever for a Spanish film in the Best Foreign Film category. (Buñuel's 1972 Oscar for *The Discreet Charm of the Bourgeoisie*, it is often argued, was for a French film, shot and spoken in French). The next year, Carlos Saura's flamenco dance film, *Carmen*,* was an international critical and commercial success. It too was nominated for an Oscar.

By all standards, the Oscar remains the highest accolade of international recognition for a motion picture, a filmmaker, and a national cinema. The Spanish cinema, which had for so long languished in industrial and artistic underdevelopment, would wait nearly another decade for recognition, until the 1992 award for Fernando Trueba's *Belle Epoque*.* Trueba's success, as well as the international recognition for Garci and Almodóvar, however, were only the most conspicuous indications of a cinematic tradition that had gradually broken out of its historical cultural isolation. Vicente Aranda's *Amantes* [Lovers]* (1990) and Bigas Luna's* *Jamón Jamón* (1992),* are only two of many examples of the expanding international popularity of a cinema that has managed to reconnect with its national audience over the two decades since the end of the Franco dictatorship. The international celebrity of Spanish film actors, such as Victoria Abril,* Carmen Maura, Antonio Banderas* also suggests that Spanish cinema, while remaining rooted in the specificity of its own popular cultural styles, has finally succeeded in stabilizing its identity within the global community of cinema.

WORKS CITED

Besas, Peter. *Behind the Spanish Lens: Spanish Cinema Under Fascism and Democracy*. Denver: Arden Press, 1985.

Caparrós-Lera, José María. *El cine político visto después del franquismo*. Barcelona: Dopesa, 1978.

———. *Arte y política en el cine de la República (1931–1939)*. Barcelona: Ediciones 7 1/2, 1981.

Font, Domènec. *Del azul al verde: el cine español durante el franquismo*. Barcelona: Editorial Avance, 1976.

Galán, Diego. "Aquel cine de los 50." In *Cine español años 50*: 14–21. Vol. 2 of *Tiempos del Cine Español*. San Sebastián: Ayuntamiento de San Sebastián, N.D.

———. "1950–1961." *Cine español 1896–1983*, edited by Augusto M. Torres, 146–67. Madrid: Filmoteca Española, 1983.

García Fernández, Emilio C. *Historia ilustrada del cine español*. Barcelona: Planeta, 1985.

Graham, Helen, and Jo Labanyi. "Culture and Modernity: The Case of Spain." In *Spanish Cultural Studies: An Introduction* edited by Helen Graham and Jo

Labanyi, 1–19. Oxford: Oxford University Press, 1995.

Gubern, Román. *El cine sonoro de la II República: 1929–1936*. Barcelona: Editorial Lumen, 1977.

———. "1930–1936." In *Cine español 1896–1983*, edited by Augusto M. Torres, 32–45. Madrid: Filmoteca Española, 1983.

———. *1936–1939: La guerra de España en la pantalla*. Madrid: Filmoteca Española, 1986.

———. "La traumática transición del cine español del mudo al sonoro." In *El paso del mudo al sonoro en el cine español*, edited by Román Gubern, 5–24. Madrid: Universidad Complutense, 1993.

Heredero, Carlos F. *Las huellas del tiempo: cine español 1951–1961*. Valencia: Filmoteca de la Generalitat Valenciana, 1993.

Hopewell, John. *Out of the Past: Spanish Cinema after Franco*. London: BFI Books, 1986.

Kinder, Marsha. *Blood Cinema: The Reconstruction of National Identity in Spain*. Berkeley: University of California Press, 1993.

Mata Moncho, Juan de. "Arniches, un autor multiadaptado por las cinematografías de Hispanoamérica." In *Estudios sobre Carlos Arniches,* edited by Juan A. Ríos Caratalá. Alicante: Instituto de Cultura Juan Gilm Albert, 1994.

Méndez-Leite von Haffe, Fernando. *Historia del cine español*. 2 Vols. Madrid: Ediciones Rialp, 1965.

Monterde, José Enrique. "Crónicas de transición: cine político español 1973–1978." *Dirigido Por*, 58 (September, 1978): 7–14.

Rodero, José Angel. *Aquel "nuevo cine español" de los '60*. Valladolid: 26 Semana Internacional del Cine de Valladolid, 1981.

Rodríguez Lafuente, Fernando. "Cine español: 1939–1990." In *Cultura*, edited by Antonio Ramos Gascón, 241–79. Vol. 2 of *España Hoy*. Madrid: Cátedra, 1991.

Rotellar, Manuel. *Cine español de la República*. San Sebastián: 25 Festival Internacional del Cine, 1977.

Smith, Paul Julian. *Desire Unlimited: The Cinema of Pedro Almodóvar*. London: Verso, 1994.

Torres, Augusto M. (ed.) *Cine español 1896–1983*. Madrid: Filmoteca Española, 1983.

———. *Diccionario del cine español*. Madrid: Espasa Calpe, 1994.

Vizcaíno Casas, Fernando. *Historia y anécdota del cine español*. Madrid: Ediciones ADRA, 1976.

Films

¡A mí la legión! [*The Legion's for Me!*] (1942: Juan de Orduña*). Juan de Orduña moved from a career in acting, in such films as *Nobleza baturra* [*Rustic Gallantry*]* (1935), to making shorts during the Civil War period, to this, his first major commercial success and an early indication of his ideological allegiances. As more than one Spanish film historian has pointed out, not far beneath the surface of this, the most popular of Spanish legionnaire films, lurks the spirit of the martial culture of the early post–Civil War period.

The story revolves around two legionnaires of different social and cultural backgrounds. El Grajo (Alfredo Mayo*) is of a low social caste, a onetime petty criminal who joined the legion to forget a woman. Mauro (Luis Peña*) is actually the heir to the throne of a fictitious central European kingdom, but this is kept secret from his comrades. He too has joined to get away from a woman. When Mauro saves Grajo's life on the battlefield, the pivotal knot of the plot is fixed. So strong is the bonding between the two men, hinging on a homoerotic narrative, that when Mauro leaves the legion to return to his kingdom and assume the throne, his buddy, Grajo, is despondent and also eventually leaves. When Grajo shows up in Eslonia, he manages to pay the debt owed to Mauro by saving the king's life. When he is brought to the royal palace, he discovers Mauro's true identity. Mauro names Grajo his personal secretary and it appears as though the film is about to come to a complete narrative standstill when word reaches the operetta-style central European kingdom that civil war has broken out in Spain. The two men depart with joy to join in the fighting to defend Spain and the Legion.

The plot of *The Legion's for Me!* is at best merely a chain of odd adventure sequences strung together by an improbable cast of characters. The two principal characters, however, clearly reflect the dominant view of manly power related to the official ideology of early Francoism. This was an ideology that saw tedium in anything but war and evolved a masochistic aesthetic in bringing characters to want to fight and die in battle rather than lead normal, peaceful lives. The two leads in the film continually underscore their misogyny by speaking negatively of women and insisting on the higher value of male camaraderie. Not coincidentally, the film was produced by CIFESA, the Valencian production company that by the early forties was clearly identified as the ideological film factory of the regime. Also worthy of note is the presence of Alfredo Mayo in the role of Grajo, a character who reaffirms Mayo's emerging screen persona as Francoism's militaristic ideal of the epic hero who never flinches at risking his own life or well-being for the higher ideal of the nation or a comrade.

BIBLIOGRAPHY
Gubern, Román. *1936–1939: La guerra de España en la pantalla*. Madrid: Filmoteca Española, 1986.
Méndez-Leite, Fernando. *Historia del cine español en 100 películas*. Madrid: Jupey, 1975.

La aldea maldita [*The Cursed Village*] (1930: Florián Rey*). The last great epic film of the silent period in Spain, *The Cursed Village* focuses on precisely those themes of Spanish culture—the eternal values of Castile and the honor and dignity of the peasants—that would become the hallmarks of official Francoist cultural ideology within a decade. The script, written by Rey in six days, focuses on the fortunes of a poor Castilian farmer, Juan (Pedro Larrañaga) who lives with his wife, Acacia (Carmen Viance), their small child, and the family patriarch, Juan's blind grandfather. After years of failed harvests, other farmers prefer to abandon the area in search of a more hospitable zone in which to farm. Thus begins a huge exodus presented in the film as though repeating the biblical exodus. Rather than abandon his land, Juan takes out his frustration by striking down the local landlord and usurer, Tío Lucas (Ramón Meca), for which he is sent to jail.

Instead of waiting for Juan, Acacia lets herself be persuaded by her friend, Magdalena (Amelia Muñoz), to find work in the nearby city of Segovia. Once in the city, Acacia is forced to become a prostitute. Juan is eventually released from jail and discovers his wife in a low-class bar. He forgives her and brings her home but she is punished by not being allowed to go near her child.

Both in terms of style and plotting, *The Cursed Village* represents an amalgam of motives related to traditional Castilian values: the peasants' rootedness to the land; the spiritual strength they find in the eternal force of Castile; and their strong sense of personal honor, a theme that harks back to Spanish Golden Age honor plays by Lope de Vega and Calderón de la Barca. Interestingly, the characterization of the evil Lucas is built on the way he thwarts the peasants' communion with their eternal and natural identity. In terms of the honor theme, the melodramatic narrative follows closely the Calderonian notion of the wife's betrayal of her husband's honor, not so much by her sordid activities in the city as by her decision to abandon the family and the land, a violation of the traditional conception of the patriarchal order.

In its emphasis on the cultural motif of the peasants' abandonment of the land

and the moral decadence of the city, *The Cursed Village* develops a variation on the conservative political view of traditional Spain in the face of cultural modernization soon to be embodied in the policies of the Second Spanish Republic. Critics have often commented on the pictorial renditions of those traditional virtues in the film as conveyed in the static but spiritual Castilian landscape.

The success of the 1930 version of *The Cursed Village* led Rey to do a sound remake in 1942. In 1986 the Filmoteca Española restored the original silent version and added a newly composed score to accompany it on its soundtrack.

BIBLIOGRAPHY
Kinder, Marsha. *Blood Cinema: The Reconstruction of National Identity in Spain.* Berkeley: University of California Press, 1993.
Méndez-Leite von Haffe, Fernando. *Historia del cine español.* Vol. 1. Madrid: Ediciones Rialp, 1965.

Amantes [Lovers] **(1991: Vicente Aranda*).** This is Aranda's ninth film with Victoria Abril,* and in no small measure, the film's phenomenal international success is due to the ways in which Aranda's script combines the Abril persona as the femme fatale with a series of highly marketable commonplaces about Spanish culture under the Franco dictatorship. The story is based on the general scheme of a well-known Madrid crime of the late 1940s involving the murder of a woman by her fiancé and his lover. Aranda originally developed the script for a Spanish television series but when production was delayed he revised and enlarged it as a feature-length film project.

The story is set in Madrid during the Christmas season sometime in the early 1950s and involves a former soldier, Paco (Jorge Sanz*), his housemaid fiancée, Trini (Maribel Verdú*), and Paco's improbable landlady, a young widow, Luisa (Victoria Abril). Trini embodies traditional Spanish Catholic sexual modesty, fending off Paco's sexual advances. Rejected by Trini, Paco finds himself seduced by Luisa, who, besides initiating him into sexual activities, also enlists his help in her underworld activities. When Trini senses that Paco has strayed, she is persuaded by her employer's wife to snare Paco into marriage by offering herself to him sexually. A sexual triangle is thus established in which Paco becomes the passive object of desire manipulated by two very different conceptions of Spanish womanhood. This situation is shattered when Paco is pressured by Luisa to murder Trini and to steal the dowry the maid had been saving. In a coda to the film, we learn that the two plotters were eventually captured after the murder.

Two elements in the film's treatment of female figures are particularly noteworthy. The first is the number of explicit scenes of sexual activities between Paco and Luisa designed to underscore the female's domination of the male, even in terms of his sexual identity. The other is the formulation of the cultural scenario of the "two Spains" as embodied in Paco's two female rivals. Identified with the images of rural Spain, Trini is the traditional stoically self-sacrificing embodiment of Catholic Spain. Luisa, conversely, identified with the city and with the iconography of foreign culture (kimonos, Christmas tree ornaments), represents the modernizing version of Spain. Though the narrative eventually casts Luisa as the heartless author of Trini's murder, Aranda treats her with a certain ambivalence, part villainess, part rebel against the oppression of Spanish *machista* culture. In this respect, Victoria Abril's powerful performance adds special richness to the film's thematic focus.

Equally noteworthy is the film's striking cinematography by José Luis Alcaine,* with whom Aranda had previously worked on no fewer than five films. Alcaine is especially adept at evoking the "sooty" look of Madrid winters, which conveys the somber qualities of drab urban life during the early decades of the dictatorship.

BIBLIOGRAPHY

Alvares, Rosa, and Belén Frías. *Vicente Aranda: El cine como pasión*. Valladolid: 36 Semana Internacional de Cine, 1991.
Heredero, Carlos F. *El lenguaje de la luz: entrevistas con directores de fotografía del cine español*. Alcalá de Henares: 24 Festival de Cine de Alcalá de Henares, 1994.

Arrebato [Rapture] **(1979: Iván Zulueta*).** This is only the second film by Iván Zulueta, some ten years after his first, equally unconventional *Un, dos, tres, al escondite inglés* [*Hide and Seek*] (1969). Though *Rapture* failed commercially in its original release, over the years it has become a cult favorite for Spanish audiences. The plot is highly self-conscious both in parallels to the filmmaker's own life and in its interrogation of cinematic representation. The film traces the final days in the life of José Sirgado (Eusebio Poncela*), a hack filmmaker dedicated to grade-B terror films who has just completed a vampire film and has become obsessed with a videocassette he has received detailing various moments of his life. These memories, told through a series of flashbacks from the point of view of Sirgado's alter ego, Pedro P. (Wil More), recount Sirgado's sexual relations with Ana Turner (Cecilia Roth); his failed efforts to free himself from drug-addiction; his former lover and star of his most recent film; his own obsession with the movie camera; and, in the final scene in which José sits blind-folded facing the camera, the possibility of his suicide as recorded by the camera.

In ways that few Spanish films have done, *Rapture* self-consciously interrogates the nature of visual representations of lived experience through a complex flow of narrative fragments. Zulueta uses a variety of techniques, including overexposed stock and slow-motion or sped-up images in order to render the persistent and hallucinatory quality of images as they relate to the protagonist's memories of his experiences. His design for *Rapture* clearly builds on some of the past treatments of the film-within-the-film structures in Spanish cinema, most notably Llobet-Gracia's *La vida en sombras* [*Life in the Shadows*]* (1948) and Víctor Erice's *El espíritu de la colmena* [*Spirit of the Beehive*]* (1973). Most conspicuously, his strikingly self-referential questioning of the meaning of the visual artifact in cinema prefigures Erice's later interrogation of the medium in *El sol de membrillo* [*The Quince-Tree Sun*]* (1992).

BIBLIOGRAPHY
Heredero, Carlos F. *Iván Zulueta: la vanguardia frente al espejo*. Alcalá de Henares: Festival de Cine, 1989.

Asignatura pendiente [*Pending Examination*] (1977: José Luis Garci*). José Luis Garci's first feature-length directorial credit is often described as one of the key films of the political transition to democracy in Spain. Made at a time when the sense of euphoria over the end of the dictatorship was still necessarily mixed with profound uncertainty about Spain's future, the film depicts a limited time frame in the lives of José (José Sacristán*), a successful progressive labor lawyer, and Elena (Fiorella Faltoyano), a woman who was once his adolescent sweetheart. She is now married to an economist and locked into a boring marriage so that when José, also married and with a young son, spots her on the street, the two are ready for an affair. Though Elena initially resists his advances, José's description of the dilemma of their generation, caught, as José says, with "pending examinations," quickly moves her to identify with that generation of Spaniards born in the years immediately following the end of the Civil War who were shaped by repressive social, intellectual, and sexual taboos.

Elena lets herself be seduced by José and the two soon set up a clandestine apartment where they meet at regularly scheduled times. But the relationship quickly falls into a domestic routine and in the end the couple agree to separate. In their parting conversation, Elena explains to José that she knows that this affair has been for him an attempt to recapture his lost youth. However, she is no longer the adolescent girl of his dreams but a woman of thirty-three. Acknowledging the truth of her assessment of him, José says they must learn to live for the future, not the past.

Pending Examination is an important example of the genre of generational films that were spawned during the period of the transition. Its structural strategy is to transform what might otherwise be an innocuous story of middle-class marital infidelity into an exemplary narrative of the political coming of age of a generation of Spaniards who, by the time of Franco's death in 1975, represented the progressive, professional class that presumably would lead the country over the coming decades. This construction, cleverly exploited through much of José's dialogue and underscored by the clever final dedication to the audience's memories of their bittersweet childhood and adolescent illusions, accounts for the film's extraordinary commercial appeal in Spain.

In terms of its formal qualities, *Pending Examination* is consciously constructed in the style of recent Hollywood romantic films, making specific allusions to Sidney Pollack's *The Way We Were* and using expansive establishing shots to give the story the "look" of Hollywood construction. Garci also adds a nostalgic soundtrack with popular Spanish songs and singing groups of the 1960s and 1970s in a montage of sound and image that borrows from Mike Nichols' use of this device in *The Graduate* a decade earlier.

José Sacristán's performance as José is one of the crucial elements that brings life to *Pending Examination*. His portrayal of a socially awkward young man whose verbal skills are honed around self-denigrating humor gives an important self-conscious edge to the film not unlike that of certain Woody Allen comedies. This performance contributed greatly in bringing Sacristán to wide popularity in other films of the late 1970s and 1980s.

BIBLIOGRAPHY
Hopewell, John. *Out of the Past: Spanish Cinema after Franco.* London: BFI Books, 1986.

***Belle Epoque* (1992: Fernando Trueba*).** One of the most resounding commercial and artistic successes of Spanish cinema of the 1990s, this winner of the 1992 Academy Award for Best Foreign Film owes more than a little of its success to a masterful blend of narrative, fine ensemble acting, and a striking visual style. The film grew out of the earlier collaboration of director Fernando Trueba, screenwriter Rafael Azcona,* and leading actor Jorge Sanz,* in *El año de las luces* [*The Year of Light*] (1986). As in *The Year of Light*, the narrative is a light erotic coming-of-age story set in a lush, rural locale at some point in the past. In *The Year of Light*, that past was 1940 and the culture of deprivation that of the immediate post–Civil War period. In *Belle Epoque* the focus is on April 1931, the fall of the Spanish monarchy and the advent of the Second Republic.

Trueba's pairing of the nostalgic view of the "beautiful time" of sexual and social liberation of the Republican years is charmingly presented through the erotic adventures of Fernando (Jorge Sanz), a deserter from the army who has strayed into the household of Manolo (Fernando Fernán-Gómez*), an aging painter and father of four daughters who are soon to arrive from Madrid. Manolo's wife, a traveling opera singer (Mari Carmen Ramírez) is off on the road with her manager/lover (Michel Galabru). Fernando lingers and meets up with the four daughters who each take a liking to the young deserter. Clara (Miriam Díaz-Aroca), the oldest, still mourns the untimely death of her husband. Rocío (Maribel Verdú*) is being pursued by a wealthy local boy, Juanito (Gabino Diego*), with a religion-obsessed mother (Chus Lampreave*). Violeta (Ariadna Gil) prefers cross-dressing and appears sexually ambivalent. It is ultimately the youngest and most innocent of Manolo's daughters, Luz (Penelope Cruz*), with whom Fernando is smitten.

The interplay between the obvious historical portent of the story's time and place and the peculiarly light comedy of mixed identities and confused relationships makes *Belle Epoque* appear to be more frivolous than it really is. The film cleverly sets the cynical wit and wisdom of the aging Manolo against the sexual energies of the younger generation to suggest an unusually reflective view of the passage of time. To this is added a clever visual counterpoint to the action in the lush, edenic setting of southern Spain (actually Portugal), which evokes comparisons with Jean Renoir's 1935 *Une partie de Campagne* [*A Day in the Country*]. These visual and thematic points underscore the contemporary 1990s historical position that looks back to that pre–Civil War past with a bittersweet nostalgia for a simpler time when social, sexual, and political freedom were much less troublesome than they are for contemporary Spaniards. As well as receiving international acclaim with an Oscar, the film won a number of Goyas, including Best Film of the Year, and a Goya for José Luis Alcaine* for Best Cinematography.

BIBLIOGRAPHY
Alegre, Luis. "Entrevista: Fernando Trueba." *Dirigido Por*, no. 208 (December 1992): 38–41.
Fernández Valenti, Tomás, "*Belle Epoque*: La España soñada." *Dirigido Por*, no. 208 (December 1992): 34–37.

***Bienvenido, Mister Marshall!* [*Welcome, Mister Marshall!*] (1953: Luis García Berlanga,*).** This is Berlanga's first solo-directed film, based in part on a script by his earlier codirector, Juan Antonio Bardem,* and the noted Spanish comic playwright, Miguel Mihura. The film was originally conceived as a way of capitalizing on the popular fifties Andalusian musical genre that had recently brought so much fame and profit to flamenco stars such as Lola Flores* and Carmen Sevilla.* *Welcome, Mister Marshall!* was intended as a vehicle for the film debut of Lolita Sevilla but Berlanga provided a script that went well beyond that mere commercial goal.

More than any other Spanish film since the Civil War, *Mister Marshall* underscored contemporary topical politics: the discredited efforts of the government to improve the plight of the Spanish people, which left the populace, as the film demonstrates, to their childlike daydreams of improving their economic plight by simple "fixes," manna from heaven in the form of a U.S.-sponsored Santa Claus. The plot of *Mister Marshall* expands on the back story of *Esa pareja feliz* [*That Happy Couple*]* (1951) in which radio contests and correspondence-school courses were seen as the quick solution to economic hardships. Another dimension of the film's critique is the mocking characterization of the local authorities, who are considered foolish and corrupt.

The plot of *Welcome, Mister Marshall!* is a simple one. The mayor of Villar del Río is informed by the regional authorities that American officials are passing through the town and the local population should provide some sort of welcome for them. After rejecting a series of modest projects, a visiting theatrical manager, Manolo (Manolo Morán*), who is in Villar del Río to promote his latest singing discovery, María Vargas (Lolita Sevilla), the songbird of Andalusia, suggests that the entire town disguise itself as carefree Andalusians. As the Americans know little about Spanish culture and geography, he feels they would be more enchanted with Andalusia than their own arid Castilian culture and landscape. The town is easily mobilized by Manolo, and the mayor (José

Isbert*) clothes the populace as Andalusians and refurbishes building fronts, bringing the town government into debt. Each citizen is promised a "wish" from the wealthy Americans. When the day of the arrival of the foreign visitors comes, the Americans' schedule is altered and they race through town without even stopping, leaving the dejected townspeople to ponder their plight.

Through its parodic structure, *Welcome, Mister Marshall!* lampoons the gullible Spaniards as they, in turn, mock their American visitors. But the film is replete with a series of other parodies, especially of film styles. In one of the most famous sequences, Berlanga shows the dream of each of five different local citizens regarding their anticipation of the Americans. Each dream parodies a different film genre. The mayor dreams he is a western sheriff; the priest, don Cosme, evokes the image of Spaniards meeting Americans through a film noir scene in which he is first interrogated by hard-boiled detectives and then condemned by the House Un-American Activities committee. Perhaps the two most biting parodies are of Spanish cinema itself. The first is simply the way the townspeople are shown converting their little hamlet into what appears to be the movie set of a Spanish folkloric film in the style of Florián Rey's* *Morena clara* [*The Light-Skinned Gypsy*]* (1936). The second scene, the most often shown clip from the film, is the rehearsal of the arrival of the Americans, which is a parody but also an homage to those folkloric Andalusian musicals, with a large cast of characters donning their typical Andalusian garb.

Welcome, Mister Marshall! was selected to represent Spain at the 1953 Cannes Film Festival where it won an award for Best Comedy. Along with *Plácido*★ (1961), and *El verdugo* [*The Executioner*]* (1962), *Welcome, Mister Marshall!* is generally considered one of Berlanga's three film masterpieces.

BIBLIOGRAPHY
Gómez Rufo, Antonio. *Berlanga, contra el poder y la gloria*. Madrid: Temas de Hoy, 1990.
Hernández-Les, Juan and Manuel Hidalgo. *El último austro-húngaro: conversaciones con Berlanga*. Barcelona: Editorial Anagrama, 1981.

Bilbao **(1978: José Juan Bigas Luna*).** This is the second feature-length film by the Catalan designer-artist turned filmmaker, and his first effort to discard his previous popular commercial cinema in favor of a more artistically motivated narrative and visual style. The plot, based on a soft-porn short story written by Bigas, follows the experiences of an antisocial and maladjusted young man, Leo (Angel Jove), living in Barcelona with María (María Martín), the lover of Leo's uncle (Jordi Torras). María is not only a substitute for Leo's deceased mother, but variously a nanny and a sexual partner.

Leo prowls Barcelona by night and eventually discovers a young prostitute whom he names Bilbao (Isabel Pisano), a name suggested as much by the Basque city as by the Kurt Weil song of the same name. He trails Bilbao, eventually engaging her in sex. In an effort to possess her fully, Leo kidnaps the prostitute and brings her to an abandoned warehouse, where, in order to maintain her in an unconscious state, he covers her mouth with a cloth doused in chemicals. The dose is too strong and Bilbao dies. Undeterred, Leo sets up a series of ropes in the middle of the warehouse in order to suspend Bilbao's naked body there in simulation of the Ribera painting, *The Martyrdom of St. Bartholomew*, a copy of which hangs on the garage wall. Eventually, Leo must confront Bilbao's death, and he tells María, who informs Leo's uncle. The prostitute's body is disposed of at the sausage factory and Leo returns to his habitual prowling of Barcelona's underworld at night.

On the surface, *Bilbao* might appear to be only one more of the chain of pornographic films released in Spain during the early post-Franco years, which saw the dismantlement of the old Francoist censorship apparatus. A closer inspection, however, reveals a precise and highly controlled visual and narrational structure charged with a series of other, "oppositional" messages. At the very least, the depiction of Leo's sexual obsessions forces the audience to question the illusion of post-Franco social freedom. Even in the reputedly liberated atmosphere of Barcelona, the force of old bourgeois family repressions still orders the individual's perception of his social reality. This particular message is strikingly underscored by the film's use of Leo's persistent voice-over monologue as the dominant verbal text of the film.

Similarly, his obsessive interest in consumerist objects—toothpaste tubes, yogurt containers, fish, sausage—all underscore the culture of commodification that orders this world. Indeed, the dynamic of Leo's pathological behavior appears to be the need to possess objects; he ultimately transforms the female into an object. Special visual force is given to that thematics of commodity fetishism through Bigas's elaborate development of metaphoric images. Just as María is understood to be a substitute for Leo's mother, Bilbao is a substitute for María, and a fish with a sausage in its mouth is a substitute for Bilbao performing oral sex.

At the time of its release, *Bilbao* was chosen as the official Spanish entry to the 1978 Cannes Film Festival. Unlike the vast majority of Spanish films of that year, it received wide commercial distribution in France and Italy and helped establish Bigas Luna as one of the most promising young filmmakers of the period of Spain's transition to democracy.

BIBLIOGRAPHY
Espelt, Ramón. *Mirada al Món de Bigas Luna*. Barcelona: Editorial Laertes, 1989.
Kinder, Marsha. *Blood Cinema: The Reconstruction of National Identity in Spain*. Berkeley: University of California Press, 1993.

Calle Mayor [Main Street] **(1956: Juan Antonio Bardem*).** Made immediately after the politically controversial *Muerte de un ciclista [Death of a Cyclist]** (1955), *Main Street* is not so much a political attack as a critique of the spiritually confining and repressive life in the provincial cities so venerated in Francoist discourse. The action is centered on the oppressive life in a Spanish provincial city in which boredom leads young men to become practical jokers. The main focus of one of their pranks is a spinster, Isabel Castro (Betsy Blair), who at thirty-five feels she will never marry. The men pressure Juan (José Suárez) to confess love to Isabel and then propose marriage, hoping to humiliate her when the marriage is publicly announced. Though feeling that the joke has gone too far, Juan is too much of a coward to tell Isabel the truth and simply chooses to disappear. It is up to his friend, Federico, to tell Isabel and also to encourage her to leave the oppression of the provincial city.

Main Street combines the fine acting of Betsy Blair with an acerbic political indictment of the oppression and mediocrity of life in Franco's idealized provincial cities. Particularly impressive are the several scenes on the Calle Mayor, the city's main street, where on Sundays the inhabitants regularly promenade. Here the audience gets a feel for the oppressive nature of provincial life where everybody knows everybody else's business. To avoid the impression of singling out one particular provincial city, Bardem did location shooting in a number of Spanish cities, including Palencia and Valladolid.

The film's credits acknowledge as their source the play, *La Señorita de Trevélez*, by Carlos Arniches, but there are clear modifications of the original 1916 play (first adapted for the screen in 1936 by Edgar Neville*) that underscore Bardem's contemporary social critique. Another source for the script is Federico Fellini's 1953 film, *I Vitelloni*, which also focuses on the social maladjustment of a group of young men in a provincial city who prefer to live the reverie of their youth rather than assume serious roles in local society.

BIBLIOGRAPHY
Heredero, Carlos F. *Las huellas del tiempo: cine español 1951–1961*. Valencia: Filmoteca de la Generalitat Valenciana, 1993.
Méndez-Leite, Fernando. *Historia del cine español en 100 películas*. Madrid: Jupey, 1975.

***Camada negra** [Black Brood]* **(1977: Manuel Gutiérrez Aragón*).** Gutiérrez Aragón's second film credit as a director and his second scriptwriting collaboration with producer/director José Luis Borau* is one of the key political films of the early years of transition to democracy. Marked by scenes of graphic violence, the film in many ways mirrors the tensions of the political and social environment of Spain in the years immediately following Franco's death.

The story traces the life of fifteen-year-old Tatín (José Luis Alonso), the youngest of the three sons of Blanca (María Luisa Ponte), a shrewish mother who encourages her two older sons, José (Joaquín Hinojosa*) and Ramiro (Manuel Fadón), in their activities as Falangist terrorists. While Tatín follows his brothers in their more socially proper activity as members of a church choir, Blanca feels that Tatín is still too young to be involved in the group's terrorist activites. Tatín, nonetheless, seeks to imitate his brothers in all ways. To be a member of the group, however, he must fulfill the three fascist requirements: to keep their path secret; to seek revenge against their enemies; finally, to be prepared to sacrifice his closest friend or relative for the cause. Rejected by his mother, Tatín sets out to fulfill these three commandments on his own. The means through which he will be able to do so comes about through his encounter with Rosa (Angela Molina*), an unwed mother of a four-year old son, who becomes involved with Tatín. After participating in a terrorist attack on a book store and committing other acts that fulfill the fascist credo, Tatín is inexorably led to kill Rosa in order to prove his fidelity to the cause.

Despite its strikingly realistic evocation of the mentality of violence of the period of transition, *Black Brood* is constructed around the notion of a perverse fairy tale, with the figure of Tatín torn between the two maternal figures, Rosa and Blanca, each embodying part of the Manichaean structure of good and evil that is as much a part of fairy-tale structure as it is of the political polarization of Francoist and early post–Francoist Spain.

The film's formulation of its narrative around the centrality of the family holds particular political importance on several levels. First, it harks back to the early post–Civil War film plotting of *Raza* [*Race*]* in which Spain's political divisions were likened to a fratricidal struggle within one symbolic family. The metaphor of the nation as a corrupt and violent family thus serves to undo Francoist mythology. At the same time, the narrative underscores in literal terms the way the family under Francoism was exploited as the ideological core of the nationalist philospohy, which molded the minds and outlooks of generations of Spaniards.

Of particular dramatic note in this context are the two female leads. María Luisa Ponte gives a terrifying portrayal of the savagely fascistic mother whose powerful will has shaped her sons' spirit and action. Rejecting the sexual desires of her second husband, she prefers to glorify the memory of her first husband with a portrait of him in Falangist uniform in her bedroom. Not coincidentally, the conception of Blanca bears a strong resemblance to the violent and devouring mother, Martina, played by Lola Gaos* in Borau's *Furtivos* [*Poachers*],* coscripted with Gutiérrez Aragón. Angela Molina, in one of her earliest important roles, plays a sexually provocative Rosa who is nonetheless able to shift quickly from her seductress role to a maternal identity. The film won the Silver Bear at the 1978 Berlin Film Festival.

BIBLIOGRAPHY
Heredero, Carlos F. *José Luis Borau: teoría y práctica de un cineasta*. Madrid: Filmoteca Española, 1990.
Torres, Augusto M., ed. *conversaciones con Manuel Gutiérrez Aragón*. Madrid: Editorial Fundamentos, 1985.

Canciones para después de una guerra [*Songs for after a War*] (1971, 1976: **Basilio Martín Patino***). This is a documentary compilation film that, as its very title suggests, covers popular Spanish songs from the Civil War period to the early 1960s. The vividly nostalgic sound track is synchronized with newsreel footage that coincides historically with the period covered, if not always the subject matter or the context of particular songs. The evocation of period songs, on the surface, merely triggers a nostalgia among Spaniards for an earlier time of simple pleasures such as Christmas lotteries and pole climbing. It also evokes, however, some of the harshest memories of food lines and shortages of material goods during the decade following the end of the Civil War.

There is almost no voice-over commentary to explain or identify the footage. Rather, the film appears to work on the premise of an evocation of popular cultural memory of the postwar period and of the transformation of Spain from its traditional to its modern image.

Despite this appearance of pictorial innocence, a quality that Patino developed in order to get his film through the rigid censorial process, *Songs for after a War* is one of the most powerful and sophisticated political films of the 1970s; it confronts the ideological impact of what by then were three full decades of the Francoist domestic propaganda machine. By directly addressing its audience's "popular," presumably unmediated, memories of the past, and employing a radical juxtaposition of both sound and visual tracks, the film gradually engages its ideal audience in a reflection of the ways in which Francoism has effectively infantilized the Spanish people.

Released in 1971 but later suppressed by the government, *Songs for after a War* did not have normal public distribution until 1976, although other filmmakers were well aware of the work. It may be for that reason that a number of other films of the earlier 1970s, such as Carlos Saura's* *Jardín de las delicias* [*Garden of Delights*] (1971), and *La prima Angélica* [*Cousin Angelica*]* (1973), and Víctor Erice's* *El espíritu de la colmena* [*Spirit of the Beehive*]* (1973) also focus on the problematic nature of a distorted and controlled popular cultural memory.

BIBLIOGRAPHY
Company, Juan M, and Pau Esteve. "Habla Patino." *Dirigido Por*, no. 38 (November 1976): 27–29.
Lara, Fernando. "*Canciones para después de una guerra*," *Revista de Occidente* (October 1985): 92–101.

Carmen (1983: Carlos Saura*). *Carmen* is the second installment of a trilogy of flamenco dance films made as a collaboration between Saura, producer Emiliano Piedra,* and the Antonio Gades flamenco dance company. Unlike their first collaboration, *Bodas de sangre* [*Blood Wedding*] (1980), which was planned initially as a filming of the rehearsal of a ballet that Gades had already prepared, *Carmen* was created especially for the screen. In this variation of the Carmen story, Antonio (Antonio Gades*) is a choreographer planning a ballet version of the Prosper Mérimée story of the sultry gypsy. In an effort to find the right female lead for the ballet, Antonio searches various flamenco dance studios until at last he sees Carmen (Laura del Sol*), whom he recruits. Though Carmen is clearly less talented than his lead dancer, Cristina (Cristina Hoyos), Antonio falls hopelessly in love with her, therein beginning a real-life mirroring of the Bizet version of the Carmen myth.

Antonio frequently confuses real-life situations with those of the Bizet plot, and the film is edited in such a way that the audience is never really certain if the particular dance numbers the group rehearses are part of the ballet they are preparing, his real experiences with Carmen, or simply his reverie. This confusion of planes of reality and theater is not fully explained in the film, which adds an intellectual enigma to the powerful dance sequences.

The artist's inability to separate his own life and consciousness from that of the Bizet opera is key to one of the film's central themes: the susceptibility of Spaniards to the imposture of their own culture. At the outset, Antonio rejects the Bizet opera as a falsification of the true spirit of Andalusian culture, preferring the original Mérimée story which appears to him to be more authentic. By the midpoint in the action, he conjures up the clichéd image of Bizet's Carmen wearing a mantilla with a rose clenched in her lips, signifying his seduction by these false foreign constructions of Spanish cultural identity.

One of the most striking dimensions of the film, and what sets it apart from most other dance films is the stunning collaboration between Saura's filming strategies and the powerful dance performance by Gades and Cristina Hoyos. The film was extraordinarily successful commercially and was nominated for an Oscar in the Best Foreign Film category.

BIBLIOGRAPHY
D'Lugo, Marvin. *The Films of Carlos Saura: The Practice of Seeing*. Princeton, NJ: Princeton University Press, 1991.
Sánchez Vidal, Agustín. *El cine de Carlos Saura*. Zaragoza: Caja de Ahorros de la Inmaculada, 1988.

Carmen, la de Triana [*Carmen, the Girl from Triana*] (1938: Florián Rey*). This first Spanish sound version of the famous Mérimée story (there were at least two silent versions made in Spain) was actually shot in Nazi Germany, where Rey and his wife, Imperio Argentina,* had been personally invited by the German government to make films. Hitler, it was said, had been impressed by Rey's earlier *Nobleza baturra* [*Rustic Gallantry*]* (1935), which he considered an excellent example of a film about racial purity. *Carmen* was the first production to be sponsored by the recently established Hispano-Film-Produktion, formed by the Spaniard, Norberto Soliño, a representative of the CIFESA Studios, and Johann Ther, his German partner, who provided the capital and the technological infrastructure for what was hoped would be a series of a popular Spanish films. Two versions of the film were in fact produced: one was in German, *Andalusische Nachte* with Argentina in the cast and the other in Spanish. Both versions were immensely popular upon their release.

Carmen, the Girl from Triana is especially noteworthy for its elaborate depiction of Andalusian folkloric culture so prominent in Rey's earlier *Morena clara* [*The Light-Skinned Gypsy*]* (1936). Given the moral restrictions of Spanish Nationalist culture, the fictional Carmen's depiction as the eroticized gypsy had to be substituted with Imperio Argentina's tamer screen persona, that of a spunky and outspoken young woman. But authenticity to the source material was clearly less important than the exploitation of Rey's succesful formula for Spanish folkloric cinema.

Set in nineteenth-century Seville, the plot follows much of Prosper Mérimée's original short novel, with some noticeable plot changes. Carmen (Imperio Argentina) seduces the erstwhile soldier, José Navarro, who abandons his superior's order to follow her, thereby becoming an outlaw. Rather than having Carmen completely smitten with José, however, Rey has her torn between the soldier and her former lover, the popular bullfighter, Antonio Vargas Heredia (Manuel Luna*). This plot twist repeats a situation in which Manuel Luna vied for Imperio Argentina in *Rustic Gallantry*. Between a series of impressive musical numbers involving a large cast masterfully photographed from dolly cranes, Carmen strings the two lovers along, unable or unwilling to choose between them. When Antonio is gored by a bull and dies, Carmen grieves for him, but she also grieves for José when he is accidentally killed while setting a bomb under a bridge with his smuggler friends. Thus the film alters the more traditional Bizet ending, by having Carmen die in melodramatic grief for her two stricken lovers.

Despite such changes, *Carmen, the Girl from Triana* proved to be commercially successful in Germany as well as in Spain, although it fared less well in France, perhaps owing to the French familiarity with the Bizet version. Rey and Argentina next worked on the poorly received *La canción de Aixa* [*The Song of Aixa*] (1939). *Carmen, the Girl from Triana* proved to be the couple's last commercial success.

BIBLIOGRAPHY
Galán, Diego. "El largo viaje de Carmen en el cine," In *Carmen: el sueño del amor absoluto*, edited by Carlos Saura and Antonio Gades, 34–45. Madrid: Círculo de lectores, 1984.
Gubern, Román. *1936–1939: La guerra de España en la pantalla*. Madrid: Filmoteca Española, 1986.

Las cartas de Alou [*Letters from Alou*](1990: Montxo Armendáriz*). This is only Armendáriz's third feature length film, all three of which were produced by Elías Querejeta.* Like the two earlier films, *Tasio* (1984)* and *27 horas* [*Twenty-Seven Hours*] (1986), there is an effort to capture and sustain a documentary realism with a minimum of professional actors and a story that is compelling in its own topical quality. In *Tasio* Armendáriz told the story of carbon workers in the region of Navarre; in *Twenty-Seven Hours*, he explored the youth drug culture of San Sebastián. In *Letters from Alou* he examines the problems of black African immigration to Spain and the racism and hypocrisy that surrounds it.

The story is a simple, linear tale, built out of actual events. A group of Africans land secretly on the southern coast of Spain. Among them is a twenty-eight-year-old Senegalese, Alou (Mulie Jarju). His friend, Mulai (Akonio Dolo), who has been living in Catalonia for some time, has encouraged Alou to emigrate, promising to find him work when he arrives. Upon arriving in Almería, Alou works picking fruit. He then moves north. His possessions are stolen at one point and he is forced to find more work in Madrid. While he continues his search for Mulai, from time to time Alou writes letters to his family in Senegal telling them of his experiences.

At one town he meets Carmen (Eulalia Ramón) with whom he develops a relationship, but not without others in the community questioning the presence of a black man who is interested in a white woman. Eventually Alou meets up with Mulai in Barcelona but is disappointed by the help he finds from his old friend. Mulai exploits his fellow emigrés by placing them as illegal workers in a garment factory. Alou tries to maintain his relationship with Carmen despite her father's objections but is eventually arrested and deported. By the film's end we see him on the African coast starting out anew for his journey to Spain.

Based upon a series of preparatory documentaries shot in video to obtain an immediately contemporary and accurate picture of the plight of Africans in Spain, *Letters from Alou* was gradually built up from that documentary source. Its central theme, however, the vision of an inhospitable, xenophobic, and ultimately racist Spain, was there from the film's original conception. The film won a Concha de Oro at the 1990 San Sebastián Film Festival for Best Film. Mulie Jarju won an award in the best actor category.

BIBLIOGRAPHY
Pérez Manrique, José María. *Montxo Armendáriz: imagen y narración de libertad.* Burgos: Encuentro Internacional de Cine de Burgos, 1993.

La caza [*The Hunt*] **(1965: Carlos Saura*).** Saura's third feature-length film and the first made under the stewardship of producer Elías Querejeta* is an effort to capitalize on the Franco government's liberalized policies toward the films of young directors. The film is a complex critique of cultural censorship and the corrupt atmosphere of Spanish society after a quarter century of the stifling dictatorship.

The plot focuses on a day-long excursion by four comrades who go off to hunt rabbits on a game preserve in the province of Toledo during a hot summer day. Three of the men, Paco (Alfredo Mayo*), Luis (José María Prada), and José (Ismael Merlo), were buddies together during the Civil War. The fourth man, Enrique (Emilio Gutiérrez Caba*), much younger than the other three, is the brother-in-law of the well-to-do Paco. Almost from the start of the outing, old rivalries and animosities surface. Paco has fared the best of the older men economically, while José's business is on the verge of collapse. The latter has instigated this reunion by inviting Paco to go hunting with the intention of soliciting a much needed loan from his old friend. The haughty and vain Paco sees through the ploy and refuses to lend José money.

As the afternoon hunt progresses, Paco shoots one of the ferrets belonging to José's gamekeeper. He claims it was an accident, but José believes it was merely an effort to reassert his own superiority over the others. Crazed as much by the heat as by the pressures upon him, José aims his rifle at José and shoots him down. This, in turn, leads Luis to lose control and gun José down. Before dying, José takes aim at Luis. As Enrique, sole surviving witness of the carnage, runs for help, the three old war buddies lie dead.

Beneath this tale of violence lies a precise political message as Saura takes aim at the aging process of the victors of the Civil War. Though the censors refused to allow any direct mention of the conflict, references to the fratricidal struggle abound in the film. The hunting preserve, for instance, was in fact the site of a pitched battle during the war. Alfredo Mayo, the actor playing the triumphalist Paco, had an early career as a stalwart Nationalist in a number of Civil War films of the early 1940s, including Sáenz de Heredia's *Raza* [*Race*] (1941)* and Antonio Román's* *¡Harka!* (1941). Enrique, who knows nothing of the war to which the other men allude, comes to represent a generation of Spaniards shaped by a near total ignorance of the war, who are thus forced to bear witness to the long-simmering effects of the repression of national history.

Among the most striking features of the film is the splendid black-and-white photography by Luis Cuadrado,* which serves to underscore the narrative thematics of men reduced to the level of animals. *The Hunt* received the Silver Bear at the 1966 Berlin Film Festival with special note made of Saura's courage in depicting the social environment of his country.

BIBLIOGRAPHY

D'Lugo, Marvin. *The Films of Carlos Saura: The Practice of Seeing*. Princeton, NJ: Princeton University Press, 1991.

Sánchez Vidal, Agustín. *El cine de Carlos Saura*. Zaragoza: Caja de Ahorros de la Inmaculada, 1988.

La ciutat cremada [*Burnt City*] **(1976: Antoni Ribas*).** Though Catalan cinema had flourished before the Civil War and gradually began to normalize its existence under the dictatorship beginning in the late 1960s with films such as the works of Josep Maria Forn* and Jaime Camino,* it was not until 1975 with this highly ambitious historical/political epic (two hours, forty-five minutes) that a truly Catalanist, "national" cinema came into being. The story, meticulously researched by a team of historians, covers a ten year period in Spanish and Catalan history beginning with the return of the defeated Spanish armies from Cuba, Puerto Rico, and the Philippines in 1899. The narrative details the general strike of 1901 culminating in the Tragic Week in 1909 when anarchosindicalists and workers formed a general strike in opposition to the central government's order to conscript troops to be sent to fight in Spain's Morrocan colony. The ensuing struggle between local and government troops, symbolically depicted as a staging of the later Catalan autonomy move, left the city in flames, as underscored by the title *Burnt City*.

In order to dramatize these historical events, Ribas and his co-scriptwriter, Miquel Sanz, developed an elaborate script involving an upper middle-class family, Dr. Palau, his wife, and their daughters, Remei and Roser. Remei has married Josep (Xabier Elorriaga*) a veteran of the disastrous Cuban war, and now a worker who, rejecting the lifestyle of his wife's family, affiliates himself with the workers' movement. While the thread of the narrative continually returns to the Palau family, much of the film focuses on the actions of important politicians and intellectuals of the period, such as Alejandro Lerroux (Alfred Luccheti), Francesc Cambó (Adolfo Marsillach*), and Enric Prat de la Riba (José Luis López Vázquez*). In this manner, the film evokes a panoramic view of social and political conflicts that characterized the Barcelona of the first decade of the new century. The central dramatic figures of the entire film are played by Xabier Elorriaga,* Jeannine Mestre, Angela Molina,* Adolfo Marsillach,* José Vivó,* and José Luis López Vázquez.*

Perhaps owing to a a general liberal sympathy of Spaniards toward the martyrdom experienced by Catalonia under the Franco dictatorship, *Burnt City* had a highly successful run in its Spanish-language version in other parts of Spain. The film went on to win first prize at the Iberoamerican and Latin American film festival at Biarritz in 1976.

BIBLIOGRAPHY
Balló, Jordi, Ramón Espelt, and Joan Lorente (eds.). *Cinema català 1975–1986.* Barcelona: Columna, 1990.
Rigol, Antoni. "La historia de Cataluña en la pantalla: *La ciutat cremada* (1976) de Antoni Ribas." In *El cine en Cataluña: una aproximación histórica.* Edited by Sergi Alegre et al. Barcelona: Centro de Investigaciones Film-Historia, 1993: 83–100.

El cochecito [The Little Car] (1960: Marco Ferreri*). Marco Ferreri's third film, coscripted by Rafael Azcona,* is a black comedy produced by Films 59, the liberal production company that had recently produced Carlos Saura's* first feature-length film, *Los golfos [Hooligans]** (1959), and was soon to be instrumental in the production of Luis Buñuel's controversial *Viridiana** (1961). Like those two films, *The Little Car* is a bitingly critical view of Spain of that period, told through a symbolic narrative. Though the film received a low government classification rating, which limited its domestic distribution, it was selected as the official Spanish entry to the 1960 Venice Film Festival where it won the prestigious Critics' Award.

Superbly acted by a brilliant cast of comic actors headed by José Isbert* and supported by Pedro Porcel, José Luis López Vázquez,* María Luisa Ponte, Lepe, and Chus Lampreave,* *The Little Car* tells the story of Don Anselmo (José Isbert), a retired man who lives with the family of his son, Carlos (Pedro Porcel), and a variety of relatives who generally treat the old man as a dotty fool. When Anselmo's only friend in the world, Lucas (Lepe), an invalid who similarly lives under the neglect of his grown children, obtains a small motorized car, Anselmo immediately becomes consumed by the desire to have his own motorized vehicle.

The little car comes to symbolize freedom of movement for Anselmo, indepen-
dence from his family and from his own aging body, and finally, perhaps most
importantly, friendship and companionship with the bizarre variety of new
friends he meets through Lucas.

Anselmo tries various ruses to coax his son into buying him the little car, but
to no avail. Having already made arrangements with the owner of an orthopedic
supply store to buy the desired vehicle, Anselmo is desperate to obtain the
money for the car from his son. He pawns family jewels, but Carlos find out and
thwarts the scheme. Driven to desperation, Anselmo poisons his son's entire
family and then takes the money from his desk, obtains the little vehicle and
drives off, presumably to live happily on his own. Soon, however, he is
apprehended by the Civil Guard.

Though the censors forced Ferreri and Azcona to change the ending in the
domestically-circulated version of the film, in order to show Anselmo's remorse,
much of the biting critique of Spanish ethical and social values remains intact.
In fact, scathing social criticism pervades the film on numerous levels. Perhaps
the most central of these is the depiction of the ways the changing economic
fortunes of Spain in the late 1950s, under the impetus of the government's plan
for economic revitalization, had left Spanish acquisitive desires largely
unrealized. Anselmo's dream of his own "little car" is quite explicitly a parodic
version of the Spanish populace's love affair with the tiny Seat 600, a car that
similarly embodied the desire for movement and the dream of a freedom from
the dreary life that had been Spanish reality for much of the period following the
end of the Civil War.

The generational conflict among Spaniards, the new petty acquisitive desires
of Carlos's generation, and more particularly, the disdain between father and son,
are all underscored by the way Azcona's cynical script leads to the poetic justice
of Anselmo's plan to obtain the money and rid himself of his family. The family,
after all, was the bulwark of Francoist cultural ideology, the spiritual source of
Spain's presumed greatness. Anselmo's family constitutes a clear rebuke of this
thesis. Finally, and quite central to the visual force of the film, is Juan Julio
Baena's* photography, which uses exterior shots of Madrid streets and thorough-
fares to underscore the oppresive mise-en-scène of a decrepit and antiquated
culture and the parallel lure of social modernization.

BIBLIOGRAPHY

Méndez-Leite, Fernando. *Historia del cine español en 100 películas.* Madrid: Jupey, 1975.
Riambau, Esteve (ed.). *Antes del apocalipsis: el cine de Marco Ferreri.* Madrid: Cáte-
    dra, 1990.

***Cómicos* [*Comedians*] (1953: Juan Antonio Bardem*).** This is Juan Antonio
Bardem's first independent film, made immediately after his collaboration with
Luis García Berlanga* in *Esa pareja feliz* [*That Happy Couple*]* (1951). It tells
the story of actors struggling in a second or third-rate touring company in Spain

in the late 1940s or early 1950s. Inspired by Joseph Mankiewicz's 1950 film, *All About Eve*, it has a heavy dose of talk about theater, but it also provides a vivid picture of the life of actors as they struggle with ambition and hope in the midst of mediocrity. The script is also inspired by Bardem's own knowledge of the world of actors gleaned first-hand from his parents' life as traveling actors.

The plot of *Comedians* focuses on the struggle of Ana Ruiz (Christian Galvé), a bit player who struggles to make it in the theater. She confronts a ruthless producer and must decide between ambition and personal morality. At the film's end, she chooses the latter.

From a visual point of view, *Comedians* plays with the relation of stage illusion and reality. In a number of scenes, Bardem cleverly juxtaposes the two as actors mix their personal life with the plays they are in while waiting either in the wings, or on stage, to speak their lines.

Even though the film appears entirely devoid of political themes, there is an implicit political message in the depiction of individuals struggling between hope for personal success and the mediocre reality that surrounds them in the provincial Spain of the period. This is, in fact, a theme to which Bardem will return with more explicit criticism of Francoist culture in *Calle Mayor* [*Main Street*]* (1956). Of special note is the strong supporting cast of the film, which included Fernando Rey* appearing as the second-string romantic character actor, Miguel Solís, who prefers to give up the elusive hope of theatrical reality to confront the outside world.

BIBLIOGRAPHY
Egido, Luis G. *J. A. Bardem*. Huelva: Festival de Cine Iberoamericana, 1983.
Heredero, Carlos F. *Las huellas del tiempo: cine español 1951–1961*. Valencia: Filmoteca de la Generalitat Valenciana, 1993.

El crimen de Cuenca [*The Crime at Cuenca*] (1979: Pilar Miró*). This controversial film is based on a notorious travesty of justice that occurred in the second decade of this century, the "crime at Cuenca," as it was popularly known. The film recounts the disappearance of an illiterate Castilian shepherd, José María Grimaldos, and the charges brought against two local farmers, León Sánchez (José Manuel Cervino) and Gregorio Barredo (Daniel Dicenta) for the shepherd's murder, despite the fact that no body was ever found. Initially released, the two farmers were later recharged for the crime, and the Civil Guard allegedly tortured the two men into confessing. Though innocent of the crime, the two men finally signed confessions but were understandably unable to lead authorities to the shepherd's body. Their death sentence was eventually commuted to life imprisonment, but they were released after serving sixteen years. After their release, Grimaldos, who had merely moved to a nearby village, reappeared.

The taut narrative is constructed as a series of flashbacks as told by a town crier recounting various of the more lurid details of the arrest, torture, and trial of Sánchez and Barredos. This framing device foregrounds the gullible crowd that not only follows the fragments of the story, but comes to demand blood and justice, even though there is no concrete evidence of the crime. In this way, Miró's film, based on a Lola Salvador screenplay, serves as a cautionary tale for a contemporary Spanish audience about the dangers of a passive and malleable public, easily manipulated by demagogic leaders. Like other historical films made during the early post-Franco period, the film encourages its audience to interrogate the negative traditions of Spain's past in an effort to repudiate those excesses.

Owing to the volatile political message of *The Crime at Cuenca*, especially the explicit depiction of the Civil Guard's procedures of torturing confessions from the two accused men, efforts were made to suppress the film by having charges brought against Miró and her producer, Alfredo Matas.* The film's release was thus delayed nearly a year and a half while protests were lodged against the military actions taken against Miró and Matas. Such publicity assured the film an extraordinary box-office appeal and it became the most commercially successful of all of Miró's films.

Notwithstanding such controversy, *The Crime at Cuenca* poses a thoughtful reconstruction of the events of the Grimaldos case. Hans Burmann's* lush photography of tranquil Castilian landscape serves as a striking counterpoint to the violent story enacted in that setting.

BIBLIOGRAPHY

Pérez Millán, Juan Antonio. *Pilar Miró: directora de cine*. Valladolid: Semana Interna-
    cional de Cine, 1992.
Kinder, Marsha. *Blood Cinema: The Reconstruction of National Identity in Spain*.
    Berkeley: University of California Press, 1993.

Del rosa al amarillo [From Rose to Yellow] (1963: Manuel Summers*). This first Manuel Summers film is structured around two tales of the difficulties of love, one about early adolescence, entitled *From Rose*, the other, *To Yellow*, about an aging couple in a home for the elderly run by nuns. The two stories are shot on location with nonprofessional actors, giving the film a documentary feel of authenticity that connects with other early works of New Spanish Cinema, especially first films by Carlos Saura* and Basilio Martín Patino.*

The first and more elaborate of the two stories focuses on the struggles of twelve-year-old Guillermo (Pedro Díez de Corral), who lives in a comfortable middle-class Madrid neighborhood and attends a religious school. He has fallen in love with Margarita (Cristina Galbo), a year older than he, who eventually responds to his advances. Despite efforts by Margarita's mother to thwart the romance, and a series of school problems for Pedro occasioned by his day-dreaming about his sweetheart, the young couple appears to maintain an innocent courtship. The relationship dissolves after the two separate for summer vacation.

To Yellow recounts the improbable courtship of Valentín (José Manuel Cerrudo), an octagenarian, with Josefa (Lina Onesti), a woman in her seventies who, though living in the same hospice for old people, is physically removed from Valentín by the nuns' rule of a strict separation of the sexes. After a progression of love letters sent clandestinely between the two, Valentín proposes that they flee the convent and live together. The fearful Josefa refuses and Valentín eventually abandons the plan.

From Rose to Yellow is striking more for its depiction of aspects of Spanish social life in the 1960s than for the particular qualities of the two stories it develops, both of which, finally, depend upon certain predictable clichés about frustrated courtship, adolescence, and old age. More arresting are the off-hand characterizations of the world of middle-class Spanish Catholic youth whose natural instincts are continually frustrated by the networks of surveillance at school and at home. A similar visual-thematic motif runs throughout the second story in which the physical separation between the two chaste lovers is sustained not only by the barriers put in their way but by the nuns who appear to function as prison guards enforcing daily routines that serve to isolate characters from one another.

The film was extremely well received at the the San Sebastián Film Festival; it won five awards including the Concha de Plata for direction.

BIBLIOGRAPHY
Castro, Antonio. *El cine español en el banquillo.* Valencia: Fernando Torres, 1974.
Hopewell, John. *Out of the Past: Spanish Cinema after Franco.* London: BFI Books, 1986.

El desencanto [*Disenchantment*] (1976: Jaime Chávarri*). This brilliant documentary was shot in 1974 and originally planned as a short on the members of the family of Leopoldo Panero, the putative "official" poet of the Franco regime, who died in 1962. Under the guidance of his producer, Elías Querejeta,* Chávarri expanded the project into a feature-length film. The title, *Disenchantment*, was to become the catchword for a generation of Spaniards who, in the years of the transition to democracy, identified their own position—vis-à-vis the culture of the dictatorship—with the painful disenchantment of the dead poet's family.

On the surface, the film is a very simple, straightforward attempt to have Panero's widow, Felicidad Blanc, and his three sons, Michi, Leopoldo María, and Juan Luis, recall their experiences in the family of the great poet. On this level, the film works simply as a family album of memories, a theme that is, itself, emblematic of the approach of a number of younger filmmakers of the period, most characteristically, Carlos Saura* and Víctor Erice,* who narrated the symbolic trauma of the nation during the dictatorship by recourse to the experiences of particular families.

In the process of interviewing the four surviving family members, however, the film evolved into a profound exploration of the conceits of Francoist culture and society. Although Felicidad attempts at various points to maintain the facade of a happy family, a certain amount of bitterness and enmity emerges in her long interviews with Chávarri. As the sons recall their childhood experience with their parents, they begin to turn on their mother and eventually on each other, shattering the public image of their father while exposing the fraudulent nature of the Francoist ideal of the harmonious Spanish family.

The effect of these ruptures in the facade of decorum functions as literary invention: the death of the patriarch occasions the children's symbolic emolation of their father's memory, and then they set upon their mother. Juxtaposing family pictures, newsreels, and newspaper photos of the dead poet and his supposedly happy family, Chávarri invites the audience to penetrate the constructed facade of the Francoist ideal of the family and to perceive within that constructed ideal of Nationalist ideology a basic correlation between the individual experience of Spaniards and that of the larger national community.

Of the three sons, perhaps the most striking figure is that of Leopoldo María, a poet in his own right. Drunk and on drugs during much of the interviewing process, he converts the film into an event in which the sordid details of his father's life, as well as his mother's struggle to maintain proper appearances, become the targets.

In 1990 Felicidad Blanc died, and her three sons went their own bitter ways. In 1994 Panero's youngest son, Michi, proposed a continuation of the film to Chávarri, who turned down the project. Ricardo Franco,* a close friend of Panero's, eventually made the film under the title *Después de tantos años* [*After So Many Years*]. In this sequel, Michi now stands as the central narrational figure, guiding the film through a reflection of the effect of the earlier *Disenchantment* on the lives of the three brothers, and also reflecting upon the destinies of that generation that came of age in the final years of the dictatorship.

BIBLIOGRAPHY

Caparrós-Lera, José María. *El cine español de la democracia: de la muerte de Franco al "cambio" socialista (1975–1989)*. Barcelona: Anthropos, 1992.

Kinder, Marsha. *Blood Cinema: The Construction of National Identity in Spain*. Berkeley: University of Califronia Press, 1993.

¿Dónde vas, Alfonso XII? [*Where Are You Going, Alfonso XII?*] (1958: Luis César Amadori). One of the most popular commercial hits of the 1950s, this historical drama owes much to the commercial success of the so-called *Sissi* films, a series of three German-language fictionalized tales involving members of the Austro-Hungarian royal family during the late nineteenth century. Those films, starring Romy Schneider, were enormously popular throughout Europe. This Spanish variation on the genre boasts among its many charms two romantic leads, Vicente Parra* as the future king, Alfonso XII, and Paquita Rico as his bride, María de las Mercedes. The film script was, in fact, based on a highly successful stage play of the same title by Juan Ignacio Luca de Tena, who also collaborated on the film script.

The story is inspired by a series of events in nineteenth-century Spanish political history involving the abdication by Queen Isabella II (Mercedes Vecino) in 1870 in favor of her son, Alfonso (Vicente Parra) who was then a cadet at an English military school. He had made frequent visits to Paris to visit his exiled mother and during one of these visits had met his cousin, María de las Mercedes (Paquita Rico).

It is this narrative of the doomed love of Alfonso and his queen, the *Romeo and Juliet* of the Spanish monarchy, rather than the historical details, that gives the film its coherence and indeed explains much of its commercial success. When Alfonso is named king, he insists on marrying Mercedes, despite his mother's objections. Having won both his throne and his bride, all is well for the young king. But when Mercedes takes ill, that happiness ends. She dies, and her death is mourned by not only the king but also the people, who had taken to their new queen with great affection.

The highly melodramatic quality of the story of doomed love, combined with the monarchical backdrop, made the film an extraordinary commercial success in the late 1950s. Though critics mocked it when it was rereleased in the 1970s and later shown on Spanish television in the early 1980s, there are serious critics of Spanish film who see *Where Are You Going, Alfonso XII?* as a revealing expression of the cultural outlook of the period of its original production. As with the *Sissi* stories, the film's appeal lies in its evasionistic embrace of a simpler time for Spaniards, when political allegiances could be more readily explained by individual emotions than by ideological or political differences. As in other popular film successes of the period, most notably *El último cuplé* [*The Last Song*] (1957)*, the focus on a colorful, historical evocation by means of melodrama seems to have been the ideal formula for addressing the tastes of a Spanish audience who saw little else of color in their culture.

BIBLIOGRAPHY
Heredero, Carlos F. *Las huellas del tiempo: cine español 1951–1961*. Valencia: Filmoteca de la Generalitat Valenciana, 1993.
Méndez-Leite, Fernando. *Historia del cine español en 100 películas*. Madrid: Jupey, 1975.

Elisa vida mía [***Elisa, My Life***] **(1977: Carlos Saura*).** Saura's first film entirely made after the death of Franco is an effort to move beyond the political themes that had shaped much of his work during the preceding decade. Saura describes *Elisa* as a personal film dealing with the emotional life of a young woman, Elisa (Geraldine Chaplin*), in the throes of the painful breakup of her marriage, and her reencounter with her father, Luis (Fernando Rey*), with whom she has agreed to spend several days in his isolated country house in the Segovian countryside.

The story line itself is minimal, consisting of conversations and reminiscences between the two, punctuated by scenes of Luis's declining health and Elisa's replacement of her father as director of a small theatrical production at the nearby girls' Catholic school. What sets the story apart, and indeed the entire film, is the intricate narrative structure this simple story involves: multiple narrations, calling for Geraldine Chaplin to play at least three separate roles— Elisa, Elisa's mother, and the anonymous widow described in the story told by her father.

That narrational complexity is structurally rooted in the autobiographical material Luis is seen writing during Elisa's visit. Instead of using a conventional first-person perspective, he tells the story of his own life from the perspective of Elisa. The film actually begins with lines spoken by Luis but subsequently understood as being related to Elisa's failed marriage and emotional crisis. At the film's end, after Luis's death, Elisa reads these same lines as though finally occupying the position constructed for her by her father's narrative. This eccentric point of view and the fact that Elisa comes to occupy that position are the keys to the film's themes of liberation from social constraints and individual creativity.

Having left his wife and family some twenty years earlier, Luis has rebelled against the imposed values, perspectives, and representations of conventional society. In writing his memoirs, he attempts to impart some of that message to his daughter in ways that mirror his relation to the young girls whom he tutors at a religious school. He has them rehearse scenes from one of the most rigorous works in Spanish Catholic orthodoxy: Calderón de la Barca's *Gran teatro del mundo*, (Great Theater of the World). His aim is to position the young girls within the confining structures that conservative society has constructed for them so that they might see for themselves the nature of the ideological repression that awaits them.

Splendidly photographed by Teo Escamilla,* *Elisa, My Life* is performed with exceptional force both by Chaplin, who had appeared in five earlier Saura films, and by Fernando Rey, who won the award for Best Actor at the 1977 Cannes Film Festival for this performance.

BIBLIOGRAPHY
D'Lugo, Marvin. *The Films of Carlos Saura: The Practice of Seeing*. Princeton, NJ: Princeton University Press, 1991.
Sánchez Vidal, Agustín. *El cine de Carlos Saura*. Zaragoza: Caja de Ahorros de la Inmaculada, 1988.

Esa pareja feliz [*That Happy Couple*] (1951: Juan A. Bardem* and Luis G. Berlanga*). This first film by two of the principal filmmakers of the 1950s is a disarmingly light comedy that deals with nothing more profound than the problems of a young couple confronting the everyday crises of housing shortages and job insecurities in the big city. It is, in fact, this engagingly comic approach to everyday life in the second decade of the Franco dictatorship, combined with an equally disarming visual approach to cinematic realism, that clearly sets the film apart even from other films of the period that challenged status quo social representation.

The plot is a simple one: Juan (Fernando Fernán-Gómez*) and Carmen (Elvira

Quintillá) are the struggling couple, forced by the severe housing shortage to rent one room in an apartment. Their continual absence of privacy leads the couple to a series of desperate moves in an attempt to fulfill their dreams of well-being. The couple's economic woes, symptomatic of the workplace instabilities of a younger generation of Spaniards in the late 1940s, are rooted in Juan's job insecurity. After being laid off as a stagehand at a movie studio, he works as a movie extra while struggling through a correspondence course in radio electronics. Carmen clips soapbox coupons in the hope of winning a big prize. In the midst of a domestic squabble over Juan's loss of his job, the representative of the soap company shows up to tell them that they have won the "Happy Couple" contest and will be treated to twenty-four hours on the town.

What ensues is a series of comic confusions and misunderstandings stemming from the discrepancies between the couple's real needs and this fantasy solution. After Juan provokes a brawl in a fancy nightclub, the couple winds up at a police station with the officer in charge telling them to forget about contests and get to work. As they leave the station, they see a group of hobos and give them the last remaining prizes from the contest. The film ends with Juan and Carmen finally embracing as a truly happy couple.

The underlying theme of *That Happy Couple* is clearly the critique of the sad illusions of struggling Spaniards in the face of a world that only provides the surface appearance of well-being. The bittersweet unmasking of false illusions is masterfully presented on multiple levels. For instance, the film opens on the movie set of a Spanish historical epic, clearly a parody of Juan de Orduña's *Locura de amor* [*The Madness of Love*]* (1948), in which the set collapses as an actress makes a wrong move to exit. In this way, Bardem and Berlanga announce their theme of exposing the false images that films have presented to Spaniards. Later scenes at a music hall expose the paltry efforts of theatrical groups to present a series of tableaux of historical moments of pomp and grandeur. One of those scenes, showing a short actor pretending to be an admiral attempting to disembark from his boat, was taken to be a parody of Franco himself.

This type of imaginative visual parody of the dominant style of Francoist culture contrasts cleverly with the illusions of the couple whose problems seem to derive not only from the pathetic style of everyday culture of the period, but more pointedly, from the illusions they have been fed to keep them going. Juan expresses those illusions when, in a flashback of his first date with Carmen, the ferris wheel they are on breaks down and the tiny cabin they are in becomes immobile. Juan looks out at the city and pines: "*Me gusta ver Madrid desde arriba. Es como si fuera amo de todo.*" ["I like seeing Madrid from on high. It's as if I were the boss of everything."] But the amusement park illusion proves to be exactly that. The truly happy couple, as the film's ending suggests, is the couple that has given up these false illusions.

BIBLIOGRAPHY
Heredero, Carlos F. *Las huellas del tiempo: cine español 1951–1961.* Valencia: Filmoteca de la Generalitat Valenciana, 1993.
Méndez-Leite, Fernando. *Historia del cine español en 100 películas.* Madrid: Jupey, 1975.

El escándalo [The Scandal] (1943: José Luis Sáenz de Heredia*). Based on the novel of the same name by the popular nineteenth-century writer, Pedro Antonio de Alarcón, this historical melodrama was, in its day, a resounding commercial success. Critics attributed its success to the film's opulent period sets, which showed once and for all that Spain could produce films on a par with other countries. But its success was more likely due to the film's melodramatic intensity, its presumably risqué theme—adultery and social ignominy—which was the kind of escapist formula that audiences in postwar Spain needed to help them forget their troubles.

Following the original story, the plot tells of the rake, Fabián Conde (Armando Calvo*), who has sustained an adulterous affair with Matilde (Mercedes Vecino) while her husband (Manuel Luna*) is off in the Canary Islands. To divert suspicion of their relationship, Matilde suggests that her innocent young niece, Gabriela (Trini Montero), come and live with her so that it will appear that Fabián is really visiting the younger woman. When Gabriela discovers the plan, she runs off to a convent. Eventually, Fabián repents of his wicked ways and begs forgiveness of Gabriela and implores her to marry him. This plan is thwarted when a new scandal erupts over Fabián's old reputation.

The importance of *The Scandal* resides in the way its popularity appeared to draw upon a desire by the Spanish public for a different type of film, one that would be escapist, and also emotionally jolting, and thus cathartic. Sáenz de Heredia's success in tapping into that formula led other filmmakers, such as Rafael Gil,* to look to Spanish novels of the nineteeth century for their cinematic inspiration. But whereas the historical adaptation was nothing new in Spanish films, the particular inspiration in Alarcón and in other lesser authors of the nineteenth century, such as Father Coloma, inadvertently spawned a subgenre of pseudohistorical dramas that relished sordid melodramatic plotting. This was certainly the case with Gil's 1944 film, *El clavo* [*The Nail*], also based on an Alarcón novel.

BIBLIOGRAPHY
Sanz de Soto, Emilio. "1940-1950." In *Cine español 1896–1983*, 102–41, edited by Augusto M. Torres. Madrid: Filmoteca Española, 1983.
Vizcaíno Casas, Fernando. *De la checa a la meca: una vida del cine.* Barcelona: Planeta, 1988.

Escopeta nacional [*National Rifle*] (1978: Luis García Berlanga*). This is the first part of a phenomenally successful trilogy of comic looks at Spanish social types during the period of the political transition from dictatorship to democracy. In contrast to his earlier comic successes, such as *Plácido* (1961),* and *El* *verdugo* [*The Executioner*]* (1962), in which Berlanga's sense of comedy revealed an essential tenderness for the working class and for otherwise marginalized Spaniards, in *National Rifle* he focused almost entirely on the powerful, would-be titans of government and industry, presenting a nastier kind of parody. This shift, according to some film historians, was due to the black humor and well-known misogyny of Rafael Azcona,* Berlanga's scriptwriter on the trilogy, who also collaborated with him on the earlier scripts of *Plácido* and *The Executioner*.

The plotline is a simple one, though convoluted with a series of comic subplots. Jaime Ganivel (José "Saza" Sazatornil), a Catalan manufacturer of electric-door security devices, decides to participate in a weekend hunting party for important members of Madrid high society, thinking that this will be an excellent way of making valuable business connections and help him expand his business to a national level. Ganivel attends the weekend hunt with his mistress (Mónica Randal), where he meets an assortment of venal, petty, and self-absorbed types. He becomes involved in a series of slapstick mishaps, then sadly concludes that the advice his father had given him long ago was correct: The best way to sell your product is as a traveling salesman.

National Rifle boasts an all-star comic cast with Antonio Ferrandis* as Alvaro, the venal government minister with more interest in sex and business than in his position in the government. Agustín González* plays Padre Calvo, a reactionary priest comfortably situated to maximize his influence among the rich and powerful. José Luis López Vázquez* is Luis José, the oversexed young marquis, estranged from his hysterical wife, played by Amparo Soler Leal,* and interested only in spending time with his young mistress.

National Rifle follows in the style of Berlanga's earlier ensemble comedies, *Bienvenido, Mister Marshall* [*Welcome, Mister Marshall!*]* (1953), *Los jueves, milagro* [*Every Thursday a Miracle*]* (1957), and *Plácido* * (1961), with a large and varied cast. In a style slightly different from those earlier works, however, Azcona and Berlanga's script combines two seemingly opposing currents in the director's work. On the one hand, the film involves a cast of well-known Spanish character actors in a series of situations involving the kind of slapstick antics deeply ingrained in popular Spanish film humor; on the other, it poses a clever allegory of all the petty social mentalities of the old regime—political corruption, social pretension, religious hypocrisy—that have survived the dictatorship and seem to continue to shape the new order. Deftly balancing the two, Berlanga secures one of the few truly popular comic masterpieces of the period of transition.

BIBLIOGRAPHY

Gómez Rufo, Antonio. *Berlanga, contra el poder y la gloria*. Madrid: Temas de Hoy, 1990.
Harguinday, Angel S. "La saga picaresca de la aristocracia española," *El País Semanal*, no. 180, 21 September 1980: 14–16.

El espíritu de la colmena [Spirit of the Beehive] (1973: Víctor Erice*). Erice's first feature-length film, produced by Elías Querejeta,* won the grand prize at the 1973 San Sebastián Festival and was warmly received internationally as one of the most moving and original expressions of opposition to the Franco dictatorship. The story focuses on a few basic events in the life of a little girl, Ana (Ana Torrent*), as she lives with her family in a Castilian village in the dreary winter of 1940, just after the final Fascist victory. Though the war is never explictly depicted, and barely even alluded to, it is the remembrance of the war and its aftermath that serves as the critical intertext of the film.

Ana and her sister, Isabel (Isabel Tellería), have gone to see the weekly film that has been brought to the village: James Whale's 1931 film, *Frankenstein.* Ana becomes obsessed with the film's monster, whose eyes she peers at as if they were the double of her own jet-black eyes. She sees the monster as having been tormented for being different. Ana recedes into fantasy because she is unable to communicate her feelings or fears with either of her parents, both of whom are absorbed in their own problems. Her mother (Teresa Gimpera*) writes letters to a friend who is obviously in exile in France. Her reclusive father (Fernando Fernán-Gómez*) keeps bees and each night divides his time between listening clandestinely to a shortwave radio and composing a treatise on the "spirit of the beehive."

When a stranger takes refuge in an abandoned house in the outskirts of the town, Ana believes him to be the monster. She brings him some of her father's clothing, shoes, and a pocket watch. Eventually, the local authorities discover the man's hideout and shoot him down when he attempts to escape. His body is brought to the town hall, and laid out for identification. This is the very same room in which Ana had previously seen the movie *Frankenstein.* Ana's father is brought to identify the corpse since his pocket watch was found on the body. He later confronts his daughter. Ana flees in pursuit of the monster whom she finds has disappeared. She wanders in search of the monster but is eventually found in a state of shock by her parents who bring her home to recuperate.

The simplicity of the plot of *Spirit of the Beehive* belies its complex themes and style. Much of the story is told without dialogue; instead, Erice employs a series of powerful images. The insistent chiaroscuro, beautifully photographed by Luis Cuadrado,* similarly reflects the somber inward-looking world of post-Civil War Spain. All of these elements contribute to a somber evocation of life in the early years of the Franco dictatorship.

Part of the film's complexity derives from the distinctive way each of the principal characters defines his or her relation to the outside world. Ana, for instance, makes a critical conflation between the world of movies and her own experiences, thus opening the entire film to a powerful self-referential reading. Her father, Fernando, in an effort to survive as a former Republican supporter in a society ruled by the Francoist victors of the Civil War, occupies himself by composing a treatise on the behavior of bees. This is clearly his effort to embrace the spirit of conformism of the postwar world. Finally, Teresa pines for the outside world by writing letters to an unnamed male friend in France. The plotline of *Spirit of the Beehive* is frequently punctuated by one or another of these personal discourses, expressed visually or as voice-over, thus adding a high measure of complexity to the otherwise linear narrative.

Ana Torrent's portrayal of the little girl has often been noted as one of the stellar performances of modern Spanish cinema. In particular her piercing black eyes suggest a maturity and cynicism beyond her tender years.

BIBLIOGRAPHY

Arocena, Carmen. *Víctor Erice*. Madrid: Cátedra, 1996.

Kinder, Marsha. "The Children of Franco in the New Spanish Cinema." *Quarterly Review of Film Studies* 8, no. 2 (Spring 1983): 57–76.

El extraño viaje [*The Strange Journey*] (1963: Fernando Fernán-Gómez*). Generally acknowledged to be Fernando Fernán-Gómez's best directorial work, *The Strange Journey* is a minor masterpiece of black humor. The film was inspired by an idea of Luis García Berlanga's* who, responding to a notorious unsolved double murder popularly known as *el crimen de Mazarrón* [the crime at Mazarrón], proposed a narrational solution. The resultant film, scripted by Pedro Beltrán, borrows freely from the details of the murder, but focuses on one of the dominant themes of opposition cinema of the 1950s and 1960s—the oppressive life in Spanish provincial towns. In this respect, Fernán-Gómez's film holds a thematic kinship to Juan Antonio Bardem's* earlier *Calle Mayor* [*Main Street*]* (1956) and Miguel Picazo's* later *La tía Tula* [*Aunt Tula*]* (1964).

Like many films of the period, *The Strange Journey* builds upon the tension created in traditional Spain by the advent of foreign modernity, in this instance, the presence of contemporary popular music (the Twist) brought to the small Castilian town each week by the regularly scheduled performance of a dance band. The band energizes the young people while the old women appear shocked by the immorality of the gyrations of the young. The old men of the town use the occasion to gape voyeuristically at the young girls.

This tension provides the thematic and social backdrop for the story as it focuses on the three grown children of the wealthy family in this anonymous Castilian town. Ignacia (Tota Alba), the domineering spinster, tyrannizes her brother Venancio (Jesús Franco*) and her sister Paquita (Rafaela Aparicio*). Ignacia has seduced one of the musicians, Fernando (Carlos Larrañaga), with promises of money. She has a series of secret trysts with him in her bedroom and now plans to leave the town and run off with him to Paris. In the middle of a family squabble, Venancio accidently kills Ignacia and he and Paquita get Fernando to help dispose of the body in a wine vat and plan their escape from the town. The surviving brother and sister are found dead on a beach in southern Spain and the clues eventually lead back to the not-so-innocent Fernando.

The film is replete with social criticism of provincial life, including persistent characterizations of the distorting effects of sexual repression in Francoist Spain.

Visually, it is marked with touches of parody of Hitchcock's *Psycho* and narrated with a series of visual enigmas to engage the audience on various levels. Fernán-Gómez's highly original visual and sound gags combine with a firm grasp of gallows humor, perhaps only matched by Ferreri's *El cochecito* [*The Little Car*]* (1960) and Berlanga's *El verdugo* [*The Executioner*]* (1962). After a poor opening in Madrid, the film was rediscovered by the critics six years after it was made. Fernán-Gómez and the film won a number of awards from the Círculos de Escritores Cinematográficos.

BIBLIOGRAPHY
Angulo, Jesús, and Francisco Llinàs. *Fernando Fernán-Gómez: El hombre que quiso ser Jackie Cooper*. San Sebastián: Ayuntamiento de San Sebastián, 1993.
Contracampo, no. 35 (Spring 1984): 6–82. Special issue devoted to Fernando Fernán-Gómez.

Fata Morgana (1965: Vicente Aranda*). Though usually considered Vicente Aranda's second film, after the 1964 *Brillante porvenir* [*Bright Future*], codirected with Román Gubern,* this is really the first film in which Aranda achieved complete directorial control. Originally coscripted with the novelist and later filmmaker, Gonzalo Suárez,* a series of disagreements between the two led to Aranda's assuming most of the control over the content of the script.

The story is inspired by the convergence of a number of influences: the advent of intense consumer culture in Spain throughout the decade of the 1960s; the implacable force of Spanish film censorship that had thwarted the freedom of expression of aspiring young filmmakers in Catalonia; finally, a general rejection of the style and substance of films produced by the young generation of directors being supported by the government's program of New Spanish Cinema.

Because Aranda worked within the group of dissident filmmakers and critics that took the name of the "Barcelona School" in order to promote their own aesthetic and political cause, *Fata Morgana* was initially seen as an emblematic expression of the loosely conceived group. In their rejection of dominant modes of Spanish representation of culture and their insistence on modernity and innovation, the group and the film were seen as an aesthetic attack on Francoist culture.

The story itself is posed as an enigma. Set in a futuristic city that could, in fact, be any modern European city, the plot involves Gim (Teresa Gimpera*), a highly successful publicity model who is widely recognized and avidly pursued by groups of youths who want to possess her in the same way they desire other consumerist objects. One day Gim discovers that the population has fled the city, possibly in fear of a nuclear blast. Gim refuses to leave but soon learns from a blind man that she will be the victim of an assassin's bullet. The assassin is a professor (Antonio Ferrandis*) who lectures on the psychology of assassination victims. He stalks Gim through the city. Meanwhile, J.J. (Marcos Martí) has accepted the mission of saving Gim by killing her assassin. Gim seeks out

Alvaro, her lover (Alberto Dalbes), for help but receives none. As she roams the streets she eventually encounters the professor whose efforts to kill her are thwarted by one of the roving gangs of youths that become enamored of Gim's publicity posters.

More than merely a fascinating cinematic enigma, *Fata Morgana* presents one of the most strikingly original visual texts of Spanish cinema of the period. Eschewing any traditional cultural representations of a recognizable touristic Spain, instead it proposes a totally modern, international space of action. This, in turn, is supported by the insistence on sleek publicity images as embodied in the figure of Teresa Gimpera, the real-life publicity model who inspired the film in which she makes her acting debut. Aranda attempted to structure the narrative through editing according to popular comic strip patterns, highly simplified, yet action-based. The modernity of the ambience is further accentuated by lighting and photography that clearly marks an advance over the traditionally somber imagery of Spanish films of the period.

Aranda went so far as to argue that the film had an influence on the way other, more mainstream filmmakers began to visualize their work. The most conspicuous example, he claimed, was the work of Carlos Saura,* who appeared to have reconceptualized his images of Spanish narrative space after *Fata Morgana*.

BIBLIOGRAPHY
Alvares, Rosa, and Belén Frías. *Vicente Aranda: el cine como pasión.* Valladolid: 36 Semana Internacional de Cine, 1991.
Guarner, José Luis, and Peter Besas. *El inquietante cine de Vicente Aranda.* Madrid: Imagfic, 1985.
Vera, Pascual. *Vicente Aranda.* Madrid: Ediciones JC, 1989.

Función de noche [*Evening Performance*] (1981: Josefina Molina*). *Evening Performance*, Josefina Molina's second commercially released film, is based on her own theatrical staging of an adaptation of the Miguel Delibes novel, *Cinco horas con Mario* [*Five Hours with Mario*]. Developed as a cinema verité project with the original female protagonist, Lola Herrera, of the one-character play, *Evening Performance* is mostly set in Herrera's dressing room where she has a long soul-searching conversation with her estranged husband, the film actor, Daniel Dicenta. Their dialogue, largely improvised, is drawn from the real-life experiences of the couple, their failed marriage, the raising of their two children, Lola's experiences of cosmetic surgery, and finally, a series of painful recognitions about the failed nature of their sexual life.

The film is noteworthy as the expression of a growing body of female-enunciated films made by women. It probes the consciousness of a couple whose experience of marriage, family, and sexuality were largely shaped by Francoist cultural ideology in the repressive atmosphere of the Spanish provinces. In this respect, it is a fitting companion piece to films like Juan Antonio Bardem's* *Calle Mayor* [*Main Street*]* (1956) and Miguel Picazo's* *La tía Tula* [*Aunt*

*Tula]** (1964), both of which dramatize similar scenarios of the female deformed by Spanish provincial culture.

At the same time, and within an even more ambitious framework, the film's foregrounding of the real-life experiences of the actress in the role of Carmen presents a highly original twist on this theme. The dramatic encounter between Herrera and Dicenta is triggered when the actress begins to sense a certain identification-revulsion with her dramatic character as drawn by the male writer, Delibes. In this way, Herrera's intense exploration of her own background begins to challenge Delibes's conception of the dutiful, traditional wife as the embodiment of repressive provincial culture. The Herrera figure as captured by Molina reveals the actress to have been just the opposite, a naive victim of the dominant cultural values of her time, still struggling years later to fully understand the price she had paid for such conformity.

Herrera reveals certain curious parallels with Delibes's protagonist in that she comes to see herself as the victim/product of a repressive cultural education. At a telling moment in the film both Dicenta and Herrera echo the same line: "*Nos han estafao.*" ["They (the social network) have conned us, our generation]". By formulating her subject matter in this fashion, with a probing multiple set of cameras within the tightly constructed space of the actress's dressing room, Molina connects her film with a series of other important docudramas of the transition period, such as Jaime Chávarri's* *El desencanto* [*Disenchantment*]* (1976) and Jaime Camino's* *La vieja memoria* [*The Old Memory*]* (1977), which similarly exposed the burden of decades of dictatorship on the lives of its survivors.

BIBLIOGRAPHY
García Domínguez, Ramón. *Miguel Delibes: La imagen escrita.* Valladolid: 38 Semana Internacional de Cine, 1993.

Furtivos [Poachers] (1975: José Luis Borau*). This is Borau's fourth feature-length film and one of the most widely acclaimed and commercially successful of modern Spanish films. Coscripted with Manuel Gutiérrez Aragón,* the film is set in an unnamed Spanish province and details the web of relations between Martina (Lola Gaos*), her son Angel (Ovidi Montllor*), and the provincial governor, Santiago (José Luis Borau*), who is Angel's *hermano de leche*, (as babies, they were both suckled by Martina). Martina and Angel are caretakers for one of the provincial restricted game preserves. Mother and son are clearly involved in an incestuous relationship that is mirrored in their clandestine activities as the principal poachers of the governor's preserve.

To add to the complex set of relations, the governor and his entourage come for a day of autumn hunting just as Angel has returned home from the city with Milagros (Alicia Sánchez), a young girl who has picked him up in the city. Milagros is also the lover of *El Cuqui* (Felipe Solano), an escaped convict who eventually traces Milagros to the game preserve. Thus the film sets up a series of tense rivalries: Martina and Milagros as the two women in Angel's life; Angel and *El Cuqui* as the two rivals for Milagros's affection; finally, the two fraternal rivals, Angel and Santiago.

El Cuqui arrives at the house pursued by the governor's men, but he is allowed to escape by Angel. Embarrassed by the discovery that Angel is an illegal poacher, Santiago makes his "breast brother" an official gamekeeper. When Angel discovers that Martina has murdered Milagros, he takes revenge by killing her while dressed in his official uniform.

The complexity of the various social and psychological relations among the characters reflects the equally complex social thematics of the film. On one level, this is a not-too-veiled allegory of the corrupt social and moral order of the Franco dictatorship, with Santiago, the provincial governor, clearly evoking the figure of Franco. In this same allegorical key, the idea of poaching obtains a variety of social, political, even moral connotations: The petulant infantile behavior of the governor in relation to his own wet nurse suggests the senility of the old dictator. As well, his legalization of Angel's social status becomes a reflection of the quasi-public acknowledgment of social corruption that became part of the dictatorship in its final years. Beneath these social themes lies the motif of incest and the image of the cruel and vicious Martina, who represents the kind of unwielding and violent matriarchal structure that belies traditional Spanish machismo.

Particularly noteworthy in *Poachers* is the extraordinary performance of Lola Gaos in the role of Martina. Borau claims to have been inspired in the writing of the film by Gaos's performance as Saturna, the cynical maid in Luis Buñuel's* 1970 *Tristana*.* Picking up on the allusion in the Buñuel text to the Goya painting of *Saturn Devouring His Children*, he thus fashioned a film with the central thematic and visual motif of a female Saturn devouring her son.

BIBLIOGRAPHY
Heredero, Carlos F. *José Luis Borau: teoría y práctica de un cineasta.* Madrid: Filmoteca Española, 1990.
Kinder, Marsha. *Blood Cinema: The Reconstruction of National Identity in Spain.* Berkeley: University of California Press, 1993.

Los golfos [Hooligans] **(1959: Carlos Saura*).** Saura's first feature-length film is generally considered the culmination of the Neorealist trend in Spanish film, the visual and thematic style that had shaped some of the most important cinematic expressions of political dissidence during the decade of the 1950s, including José Antonio Nieves Conde's* *Surcos [Furrows]** (1950) and Juan Antonio Bardem's* *Muerte de un ciclista [Death of a Cyclist]** (1955). Inspired by a series of newspapers articles by Daniel Sueiro about a Madrid street gang, Saura's script, developed in collaboration with his former student, Mario Camus,* traces the efforts of the members of a Madrid gang to help their friend, Juan (Oscar Cruz) enter a *novillada*, a special bullfight for aspiring novices. In order to have his name entered in the program, however, Juan must first pay certain fees. The rest of the film details the efforts of Juan's comrades to raise the money through a series of petty robberies. Eventually, one of the victims of the gang's efforts, a cabdriver, recognizes one of the members and the police set to tracking the gang. The police finally catch up with the gang at the bull ring just as Juan's long-dreamed of debut turns to failure.

Most striking in the film are Saura's astounding visual skills both in capturing a view of working-class Madrid districts and also in editing the narrative to emphasize the rapidly paced actions of the group. This latter element, filled with striking narrative ellipses between scenes, which adds to the quick-paced plot, appears to coincide with if not to precede techniques soon to be identified with the French *Nouvelle Vague*. Also, the film's photography by Juan Julio Baena* provides a powerful visual expression of the drab and confining social spaces that provoke the youths' struggle to break out. Because of the film's dreary vision of life in working-class Madrid, the classification board charged with establishing all-important film production subsidies gave *Hooligans* its lowest possible rating, effectively blocking it from any state subsidy, a move that delayed the film's commercial release some three years.

BIBLIOGRAPHY
D'Lugo, Marvin. *The Films of Carlos Saura: The Practice of Seeing*. Princeton, NJ: Princeton University Press, 1991.
Sánchez Vidal, Agustín. *El cine de Carlos Saura*. Zaragoza: Caja de Ahorros de la Inmaculada, 1988.

Historias de la radio [*Radio Stories*] **(1955: José Luis Sáenz de Heredia*).** Although Sáenz de Heredia had forged his reputation as the stolid quasi-official filmmaker of the Franco regime with *Raza* [*Race*]* (1941) and *Franco, ese hombre* [*Franco, that Man*] (1964), his career was also marked by a number of exceptionally successful lighter films, such as the comic *El destino se disculpa* [*Destiny Apologizes*] (1944), the musical comedy remake of *La verbena de la paloma* [*Paloma Fair*] (1964) and, in the mid-1950s, this light comedy, the most commercially sucessful film of his long career. Indeed, during the three years following its release, *Radio Stories* sustained the record of having achieved the largest domestic film audience of any Spanish film.

The plot is light and whimsical, making no pretensions to anything but entertainment. Picking up on a theme that was originally developed as the centerpiece of the first Bardem-Berlanga collaboration, *Esa pareja feliz* [*That Happy Couple*]* (1951), *Radio Stories* sets its plot in motion around a zany radio contest in which various individuals need to come to the radio station to claim their prizes. Although focusing on the radio contest, the film really poses three interrelated stories. The first one deals with two old inventors who need the prize money for a patent for their invention of a piston. The second recounts an odd pact between a house robber and the owner of the house who plan to share the prize since the radio station's phone call came in the middle of the robbery. The third story deals with money desperately needed for a young child to go to Sweden for an operation to save his life. All of the stories reinforce the film's central theme of the importance of radio to boost the spirits of Spaniards who have very little else to cheer them. Francisco Rabal* and Margarita Andrey are the station announcers. José Isbert* plays an inventor who rushes to be the first to arrive at the radio station dressed as an eskimo.

Perhaps the most interesting aspect of the narrative structure of *Radio Stories* is the intricate series of social narratives that are interwoven around the three principal episodes. The film is framed at the beginning by the comic activities of two pudgy middle-aged bachelors in a boardinghouse who do their morning calisthenics by following the exercises on the radio health program; they, in turn, introduce the love story between the Rabal and Andrey characters, which then leads to the series of interviews Rabal conducts on air with bullfighters and soccer players. What eventually emerges from this chain of comic and romantic situations is a suprisingly rich and unstereotyped panorama of Spanish social types during the second decade of post–Civil War peace, and a revealing view of the popular culture of evasion as embodied in radio that sustained everyday life in Francoist Spain during this period.

BIBLIOGRAPHY

Heredero, Carlos F. *Las huellas del tiempo: cine español 1951–1961.* Valencia: Filmoteca de la Generalitat Valenciana, 1993.
Méndez-Leite, Fernando. *Historia del cine español en 100 películas.* Madrid: Jupey, 1975.

***Historias del Kronen** [Stories from the Kronen Bar]* (1995: Montxo Armendáriz*). Montxo Armendáriz's fourth film, produced by Elías Querejeta,* is similar to his earlier works in that it constructs its narrative as an almost ethnographic look at a distinct Spanish subculture. Adapted from the novel of the same name by José Angel Mañas, who also collaborated with Armendáriz on the script, the story focuses on a group of contemporary alienated youths in Madrid whose pattern of life revolves around drugs, sex, and acts of defiance against parental and other social authority.

The central figure of the film is Carlos (Juan Diego Botto) who, at the age of twenty-one, leads an aimless existence during what appears to be his summer vacation. He hangs out with his friends Roberto (Jordi Mollà) and Pedro (Aitor Merino), at the local tavern, the Kronen Bar; it is clear that he is the leader of the group. In defiance of his bourgeois family, who literally bail him out of his many financial and legal problems, Carlos sleeps by day and cruises the city for adventure by night.

The apparent randomness of the film's plot belies two sets of interconnected relations: one with his comrade, Pedro, whom Carlos takes a sadistic pleasure in enticing with homosexual overtures, which are rejected; the other with his family, whom he sees as the institution against which he must rebel. These two focuses are joined in the film's final portion when Carlos's grandfather, who had served as something of a mentor to him, dies, and his comrade, Pedro, dies at his own birthday party as the result of having been forced by Carlos to drink a bottle of scotch.

As a powerful chronicle of a certain sector of contemporary Spanish youth that has grown disaffected precisely with the achievement of economic and social freedom, *Stories from the Kronen Bar* is clearly derivative of earlier works such as Armendáriz's own *27 horas* [*Twenty-Seven Hours*] (1986) Carlos Saura's* *¡Deprisa, deprisa!* [*Hurry, Hurry!*] (1980) and Eloy de la Iglesia's* *Colegas* [*Pals*] (1982). As in those earlier films, the generational struggle is linked to themes of the dissolution of the Spanish family and the economic transformation of Spain. Here, for the first time, Armendáriz locates his story in an affluent Madrid, a cityscape that has become all but indistinguishable from that of any European or American city. The film was the official Spanish entry to the 1995 Cannes Film Festival.

BIBLIOGRAPHY
Pérez Manrique, José María. *Montxo Armendáriz: imagen y narración de libertad.* Burgos: Encuentro Internacional de Cine de Burgos, 1993.

Jamón, Jamón (1992: José Juan Bigas Luna*). Bigas Lunas's eighth film is his most critically acclaimed and commercially successful work to date. The rich visual and narrative style of *Jamón, Jamón* focuses on the transformation of traditional Spain by a new commercial and consumerist logic in which people as well as objects are part of the intricate social economy. The story, set in contemporary rural southern Spain, opens with the passionate young lovers, Silvia (Penelope Cruz) and José Luis (Jordi Mollà), confronting the reality of the young woman's pregnancy. José Luis is the son of the owners of·a highly successful intimate garment company—Sansón—run by José Luis's domineering mother, Concha (Stephanie Sandrelli), who has eclipsed his father, Manuel (Juan Diego*). Silvia is an employee at the factory, the daughter of a prostitute mother, Carmen (Ana Galeana), who works in a roadside brothel.

Fearing his mother, José Luis cannot bring himself to tell her of his planned marriage or of Silvia's pregnancy. When she finds out, Concha sets out to break up the affair, recruiting a young man, Raúl (Javier Bardem*), to seduce Silvia away from her son. Problems arise when Concha herself becomes smitten with Raúl and jealous of his developing relationship with Silvia.

As planned, Silvia falls out of love with José Luis and is smitten with Raúl. José Luis becomes despondent at the loss of Silvia and vows to kill Raúl, tracking him to the ham factory where the two men have a sparring match with ham legs in which Raúl kills José Luis. The film ends with a complex rearrangement of couples: Raúl with the grieving Concha; Silvia with Manuel; Carmen with the dead would-be son-in-law.

Jamón, Jamón marks the refinement of a filmic style and conception that Bigas Luna as auteur has been developing since his first major success, *Bilbao* (1978), within which political themes are insistently aligned with sexual narratives. In *Jamón, Jamón*, Bigas's theme is now economics, and he depicts a Spain moving away from its macho-obsessed patriarchal past into a period of modernization and economic prosperity in which the ineffectual male figure is displaced by the more aggressive female. Here, the dominant roles of women in the workplace are expressed through their predatory sexual moves, which contrast with the debilitating social and economic characterizations of males, especially father figures.

To underscore this notion, Bigas uses the visual power of certain icons of Spanish culture—the predominance of hams, bulls' testicles, and close-ups of crotches and breasts. This is immediately made clear in the credits and opening shots of the film, stunningly photographed by José Luis Alcaine,* which show a highway in southern Spain as seen from between the legs of a billboard representation of a black bull in silhouette, the logo of a local brandy company. Although the film's narrative is initially framed by the commercial and sexual image embodying male dominance, the plot ultimately reveals that it is women who control and manipulate these commercial symbols.

Jamón, Jamón was a resounding box-office success throughout Spain as well as an extraordinarily marketable film abroad. It became the first part of a trilogy of "Iberian Portraits," followed by *Huevos de oro* [*Golden Balls*] (1993), and *La teta i la lluna* [*The Tit and the Moon*] (1994), both of which explored other aspects of the themes of Spains's economic transformation.

BIBLIOGRAPHY
D'Lugo, Marvin. "Bigas Luna's *Jamón, Jamón*: Remaking the National in Spanish Cinema. In *Spain Today: Essays on Literature, Culture, Society*, edited by José Colmeiro, et al., 67–81. Hanover, NH: Dartmouth College Department of Spanish and Portuguese, 1995.
Weinrichter, Antonio. *La línea del vientre: el cine de Bigas Luna*. Gijón: Festival de Cine de Gijón, 1992.

Los jueves, milagro [*Every Thursday, a Miracle*] (1957: **Luis García Berlanga***). This is the Berlanga film most mutilated by the censors. The problems apparently arose from the film's focus on religious practices and belief in Spain. Set in the fictional community of Fontecilla, whose spa was once prosperous, the film features five prominent local citizens, a doctor, a schoolteacher, the owner of the spa, the mayor, and the barber, who decide to imitate the miracles of Lourdes and Fatima by creating their own local miracle in order to drum up business for their community. The mayor (José Isbert*) is recruited to dress up in the garb of Saint Dimas, a local saint. The plan is for the saint to appear to a local hobo, Mauro, and to have him spread the word that Saint Dimas will appear each Thursday. The plan works moderately well with local gentry easily conned.

Problems arise when Martín, a modern-day Saint Dimas (Richard Basehart) arrives in town and begins to work a series of quasi-miracles. These, in turn, so upset the five local leaders, who by now have been touched by the power of faith, that they publicly denounce themselves. The truth, however, proves less powerful than faith, for Saint Dimas disappears as crowds continue to worship the saint in hopes of miraculous cures.

The first half of the film is cut from the same cloth as Berlanga's earlier *Bienvenido, Mister Marshall!* [*Welcome, Mister Marshall!*]* (1953), with its incisive views of the demagoguery of the local powers in Spain and the gullibility of the masses towards these deceptions. With the appearance of Martín, however, the humor of the film begins to slacken as the theme of creating miracles of belief becomes quite heavy. That appearance, in fact, had been dictated by the priest hired by the film's producers to tone down the apparent anti-Catholicism of Berlanga's original script.

The underlying theme of *Every Thursday, a Miracle* is, as in so many of Berlanga's works, the easy self-deception of Spaniards rooted in their own childlike illusions. This is a theme never far from the political implications of Spain under Franco.

BIBLIOGRAPHY
Gómez Rufo, Antonio. *Berlanga, contra el poder y la gloria.* Madrid: Temas de Hoy, 1990.
Hernández-Les, Juan, and Manuel Hidalgo. *El último austro-húngaro: conversaciones con Berlanga.* Barcelona: Editorial Anagrama, 1981.

Lazarillo de Tormes (1959: César F. Ardavín). At the time of its release, this adaptation of the sixteenth-century picaresque novel was considered by most Spanish critics to faithfully capture much of the satiric and often mordant spirit of the original Spanish classic. The film dramatizes four key episodes from the original novel: Lazarillo's origins and experiences with the brutal blind man, with the cleric, with the impoverished squire, and finally with the imposter friar who sells indulgences to gullible townsfolk. As well as praising the script, critics note the apparent authenticity of the settings and ambience of the film. Shot in various historical sites in Castile, these settings, interiors as well exteriors, lent a tremendous sense of realism to the film. An Italian child actor, Marco Paoletti, played the title role of Lazarillo. Carlos Casaravilla* rendered a vivid performance as the blind man and Margarita Lozano* played Antonia, Lazarillo's mother.

The importance of this adaptation of *Lazarillo de Tormes* lies in several areas connected to the historical moment of the film's production and release. First, Ardavín transcended the limits of the usual deadly literary adaptation that had been a staple of Spanish cinema during the two decades following the Civil War; at the same time, he remained relatively faithful to his literary sources. While affirming a particular national literary heritage consistent with the cultural politics of the Franco regime, the film also, ironically, fed into certain negative conceptions of Spanish culture popular among foreign audiences—poverty, cruelty, blind honor, and religious hypocrisy. It was thus able to make an impact at least in critical circles and festivals that was especially rare for Spanish films during this period. In its own way, the foreign success of the film suggested a potential road for other filmmakers to follow.

Worthy of special note is the presence of Carlos Casaravilla as the blind man, a tour de force performance that underscored the theme of cruelty to which the picaresque hero is subjected. The impressive photography by Manuel Berenguer splendidly conveys the glaring poverty amidst the wealth of Spain during its Golden Age. Less successful is Marco Paoletti's performance in the title role. Giving the character of Lazarillo a wholesome and warm demeanor, his performance undercuts the theme of the young hero's continuing education into the corrupt and hypocritical values that belie the religious and opulent facade of Spanish culture. The film won the Gold Bear, the highest award, at the 1960 Berlin Film Festival.

BIBLIOGRAPHY
Heredero, Carlos F. *Las huellas del tiempo: cine español 1951–1961*. Valencia: Filmoteca de la Generalitat Valenciana, 1993.
Méndez-Leite, Fernando. *Historia del cine español en 100 películas.* Madrid: Jupey, 1975.

La ley del deseo [*Law of Desire*] (1987: Pedro Almodóvar*). Though Almodóvar's sixth feature-length film and his first major international sucess was originally promoted abroad as a gay comedy, the film is actually more in the thematic line of his first film, *Pepi, Luci, Bom, y otras chicas del montón* [*Pepi, Luci, Bom, and Other Girls like That*]* (1980), which similarly celebrated the liberated sexual and social atmosphere of Madrid of the 1980s. Unlike that first film, however, *Law of Desire* boasts an intricate yet totally coherent plot. After the premiere of one of his films, Pablo, a popular gay filmmaker, is abandoned by his lover, Juan (Miguel Molina), who goes off to the Andalusian coast. During the sultry Madrid summer, Pablo prepares the script of a semiautobiographical film involving the participation of his transsexual brother, now sister, Tina (Carmen Maura*), who is also in the midst of an emotional crisis, recovering from the breakup with her lesbian lover (Bibi Andersen). To add to his agitated life, Pablo finds himself pursued and seduced by Antonio (Antonio Banderas*), a closet gay from Andalusia. When Antonio returns to the south, he asks Pablo to write love letters to him, but to cover up the nature of their relations by signing the letters with the name "Laura P." Jealous of Pablo's continuing desire for his former lover, Antonio murders Juan, leaving a piece of his shirt, identical to one Pablo owns, at the site of the crime.

All of these circumstances eventually lead the police to suspect that Pablo has murdered Juan. When Pablo crashes his car, he suffers amnesia and is hospitalized. Meanwhile, Antonio, fearing betrayal, courts Tina. Eventually, Pablo recovers his memory and is led to Tina's house where Antonio has held her captive. In exchange for releasing his sister, Pablo spends one final night of love with Antonio who kills himself rather than give himself up to the police.

Though marketed as a gay film, *Law of Desire* shows all the signs of

Almodóvar's clever, almost allegorical rewriting of Francoist cultural history: the conflation of sexual identities, the mock pietà scene at the site of Antonio's death, finally the enlightened view of the police and Civil Guard in their treatment of the new sexual morality. Among the striking ensemble performances, clearly the most noteworthy is that of Carmen Maura, who is called upon to play the part of a gay man who has undergone a sex change operation.

As he did in each of his preceding films, Almodóvar gives special emphasis to the allure of Madrid in *Law of Desire*. José Luis Alcaine's splendid photography captures the intimate and even sensual qualities of a city seldom depicted in any positive light in Spanish cinema.

BIBLIOGRAPHY
Smith, Paul Julian. *Desire Unlimited: The Cinema of Pedro Almodóvar*. London: Verso, 1994.
Kinder, Marsha. "Pleasure and the New Spanish Mentality: A Conversation with Pedro Almodóvar." *Film Quarterly* (Fall 1987): 33–44.
Vernon, Kathleen and Barbara Morris (eds.). *Post-Franco, Postmodern: The Films of Pedro Almodóvar*. Westport, Ct: Greenwood Press, 1995.

Locura de amor [*The Madness of Love*] (1948: Juan de Orduña*). Juan de Orduña's prominence as a director throughout the 1940s and up to the mid-1950s was closely aligned to the fortunes of the Valencian production company, CIFESA, under whose patronage he directed a series of important historical epics, of which *The Madness of Love* is often considered the most representative. This extravagant epic adaptation of the nineteenth-century historical melodrama by Manuel Tamayo y Baus reflects the Francoist notion of epic historical traditions of modern Spain, combining details of historical events and personages with more than a touch of xenophobic bombast and a good deal of melodramatic excess. The result is at once an absurd and dated film, but also a highly engrossing historical melodrama.

The film tells the story of the frustrated love of Juana de Castilla (Aurora Bautista*), daughter of the Catholic Kings, Isabel and Fernando, and her unreciprocated love for her rakish husband, Felipe, dubbed "*el hermoso*," or "the pretty one" (Fernando Rey*). In a famous incident following Felipe's death, grieving Juana dragged her deceased husband's decomposing body across Castile so that the people could mourn his death and their loss. The life of the historical Juana was filled with significant and transcendent events but in Orduña's clever script he reduces her life to two main plotlines: the frustrated love of the queen for her husband, and the plotting on the part of his ministers to have her declared mad so as to shift the center of power away from the Castilian crown to the hands of "foreigners."

To fill in the gaps in the story, a secondary love interest is developed around the characters of don Alvar de Estúñiga (Jorge Mistral*), the queen's aide, who secretly loves her, and Aldara (Sara Montiel*), Felipe's mistress, who was taken into the palace as a handmaiden to the queen. Through conformity to the requirements of genre rather than historical accuracy, *The Madness of Love* achieved a popular acceptance that reflected clever commercial interest as well as the underlying ideological spirit of Francoist culture of the period.

The story unfolds as a flashback told by Alvar to Juana's son, the emperor Carlos, who has come to visit his mother during her confinement. The acknowledgment of Juana's madness at the outset thus gives the ensuing narrative a sense of predestination and closure, heightened by Alvar's off-screen narration. The focus of his account of the queen's passion and madness covers a period from 1504 to 1506, running from the death of Queen Isabel and Juana's ascent to the throne to the death of Felipe and Juana's legendary necrophiliac embrace of his body.

The immense commercial success of *The Madness of Love* is often imputed to the opulent CIFESA production scale of the period, which was determined to compete with Hollywood by means of lavish historical reconstructions of major national themes. But it also owes some of its appeal to Orduña's cultivation of a popular melodramatic style that emphasized the highly theatrical nature of particularly charged emotional moments. The extravagant histrionic style of Aurora Bautista in the role of the mad queen did much to accentuate the melodramatic qualities of the film while driving home quite graphically to the audience the image of the queen's madness.

BIBLIOGRAPHY
Méndez-Leite, Fernando. *Historia del cine español en 100 películas.* Madrid: Jupey, 1975.
Vizcaíno Casas, Fernando. *Historia y anécdota del cine español.* Madrid: Ediciones ADRA, 1976.

Marcelino pan y vino [*Marcelino, Bread and Wine*] (1954: Ladislao Vajda*). One of the major commercial hits of Spanish cinema in the 1950s—popular with both domestic and foreign audiences—*Marcelino* is by far the most commercially and critically successful of the more than two dozen films made by the Hungarian emigré director, Ladislao Vajda. The story is told through a framing device in which a local monk, played in a cameo role by Fernando Rey,* comes to minister to a family whose young daughter is suffering from a grave illness. To comfort the child and also to prepare her parents for the possibility of her death, the monk tells the story of Marcelino, the child whose saint's day is being celebrated that very day.

Marcelino's story is set in the aftermath of the Napoleonic wars at the beginning of the nineteenth century. In a small town, a group of Franciscan friars establish a monastery that eventually grows and flourishes. One day, a small male child is left at the monastery door and taken in by the monks. Unable to place him with a proper family, they refuse to give Marcelino up for adoption to the local blacksmith who will eventually become the mayor of the town (José Marcos Davo), thus making him the arch enemy of both Marcelino and the friars. Instead, the friars raise Marcelino themselves. The main portion of the film is devoted to the presentation of the idyllic days of Marcelino's childhood when he is about five years old, as portrayed by the child actor, Pablito Calvo.

All goes well in this fairy-tale world until one day when Marcelino discovers that he has no mother. When asked where she is, the friars tell him she is in heaven. A second crucial event comes to alter Marcelino's life. When told he cannot enter the upstairs attic area because there is a thin, hungry man who is there, Marcelino's curiosity is naturally piqued. He disobeys the friars and goes into the room where he discovers a nearly life-size crucifix and carving of Christ with whom the little boy begins a dialogue and to whom each day he brings food. Marcelino tells Christ he would like to go to heaven to see his mother. When the friars later enter the room they find that Marcelino has died "and gone to heaven."

Suffused with a fairy-tale quality that makes the first part of the story seem almost like a religious version of Snow White and the Seven Dwarfs, the second part of *Marcelino* shifts tone radically and becomes a quasi-religious parable. Unabashedly purporting to be a tale to soften the blow of a child's death, the film mixes a variety of comic stereotypes of good and evil, humor and seriousness, into a popular message that is rooted in Spanish Catholic culture. The tenderness and sentimentality of the treatment of the little hero and his death, in fact, become something of a hallmark for a wide range of popular Spanish films.

When completed, *Marcelino, Bread and Wine* became the official Spanish entry to the 1955 Cannes Film Festival. Its positive commercial and critical reception led Vajda to attempt a continuation of this formula with two subsequent "child films" with Pablito Calvo, *Mi tío Jacinto* [*My Uncle Jacinto*] (1956), and *Un ángel pasó por Brooklyn* [*An Angel Passed through Brooklyn*] (1958).

BIBLIOGRAPHY
Heredero, Carlos F. *Las huellas del tiempo: cine español 1951–1961*. Valencia: Filmoteca de la Generalitat Valenciana, 1993.
Kinder, Marsha. *Blood Cinema: The Reconstruction of National Identity in Spain*. Berkeley: University of California Press, 1993.

Mi querida señorita [*My Dearest Señorita*] (1971: Jaime de Armiñán*). This collaboraton between Armiñán* and producer-director-scriptwriter José Luis Borau,* on Armiñán's third feature-length film was a resounding critical and commercial success in Spain. It was nominated for an Oscar the year following its debut.

The film tells the story of Adela (José Luis López Vázquez*), a fortyish spinster in a small Galician town, who suffers a series of emotional crises. First, she is confused by her feelings of sexual attraction toward her young maid, Isabelita (Julieta Serrano*). Then, she suffers a fall when refereeing a local soccer match. After an examination by her local physician (Borau himself in a cameo), Adela discovers that she is really a man. Since her childhood, he, Juan, had been sheltered by his parents, dressed in female clothing as was a Spanish tradition, then progressively shielded from anything having to do with sex. The film's improbable premise that Juan–under the protected identity of Adela–could, in fact, grow to adulthood never seeing another person naked nor recognizing his own biological gender poses a biting criticism of the repressive environment nurtured by the conservatism of the Franco dictatorship. The discovery that he is, indeed, a man, helps explain Juan's otherwise aberrant attraction for his maid, Isabelita.

Fleeing the town in which he has spent his entire life, Juan comes to Madrid to try to begin his life anew. He takes up residence in a boardinghouse, but soon discovers that the provincial education of women in Francoist Spain has not prepared him for modern urban life. He reencounters Isabelita, who discerns something familiar about him but appears not to recognize him. Juan eventually assumes a full masculine identity when he makes love with Isabelita, but the film ends on an ironic note when he tells her that there is a secret about himself he will someday tell her. She replies, "*¿Qué me va a contar, señorita?*" ["What are you going to tell me, miss?"] thereby indicating that she knows Juan's secret.

The plot of *My Dearest Señorita* functions as a grotesque parody of Francoist cultural ideology: the lampooning of the idyllic world of the country and the narrow, anachronistic education of women, all of which leads to the unnecessary deformation of the individual. Juan's escape to the city reveals that modernity and tolerance are, in fact, the only antidotes for this fossilized culture that the dictatorship has imposed upon Spaniards.

Worthy of special note in the film is the stunning performance by José Luis López Vázquez as Adela/Juan. Although López Vázquez was trained as a comic actor and was one of the most popular film actors of the 1960s, this role makes extraordinary demands on his talents, since in order to make the story plausible, he must play the drag role of Adela with total seriousness. Significantly, the script of *My Dearest Señorita* emphasizes the grotesque cultural distortions of sexual identity, yet avoids the obvious sensationalism built into the situation. Instead, it focuses on the cultural and ideological implications of sexual marginalization in Francoist Spain, thereby prefiguring a trend that will gain increasing prominence in serious Spanish film over the next two decades, in films such as Bigas Luna's* *Bilbao**(1978), Vicente Aranda's* *La muchacha de las bragas de oro* [*The Girl in the Golden Panties*] (1979), Antonio Giménez Rico's* *Vestida de azul* [*Dressed in Blue*] (1983), and in Pedro Almodóvar's films of the second half of the 1980s.

BIBLIOGRAPHY
Crespo, Pedro. *Jaime de Armiñán: los amores marginales*. Huelva: Festival de Cine Iberoamericano, 1987.
Kinder, Marsha. *Blood Cinema: The Reconstruction of National Identity in Spain*. Berkeley: University of California Press, 1993.

La mitad del cielo [*Half of Heaven*] (1986: Manuel Gutiérrez Aragón*). Gutiérrez Aragón's ninth film is possibly his most fully realized blend of folkloric storytelling traditions and modern political allegory. The film is a companion piece to his earlier *Demonios en el jardín* [*Demons in the Garden*] (1982), which narrated the political and emotional dynamics of the Spanish generation of the immediate post–Civil War years by focusing on the conflicts within a single family.

The time frame of *Half of Heaven* runs from the late 1950s up to the period of the political transition from dictatorship to democracy, following the fortunes of Rosa (Angela Molina*) from her adolescence in the Cantabrian mountains to her struggles and eventual success as a restauranteur in Madrid. The tension within a rural family is told through the conflicts among four generations of women. Rosa is guided by her grandmother (Margarita Lozano*), who is endowed with a magic power of prophecy and who predicts the death of Juan, Rosa's husband. Left to fend for herself and her newborn baby daughter, Olvido, Rosa is sent off to Madrid to serve as a wet nurse for a child of the local commissioner of public markets, Pedro (Fernando Fernán-Gómez*).

The story eventually focuses on Rosa's efforts to achieve economic well-being while raising her daughter. The principal problems that ensue for her in Madrid include continual sexual pursuit by Pedro, political differences with his assistant, Delgado (Nacho Martínez), and the arrival of Rosa's two malevolent sisters who nearly wreck her chances for commercial success. Through a deft, almost fairy-tale style of narration, the plot of *Half of Heaven* spans two decades in modern Spanish history. More than being mere background, that history makes crucial intersections with Rosa's fortunes, first as she battles the corrupt bureaucracy involved in the the public markets where she works, later in her influential contacts made through the restaurant she owns that caters to government ministers. In this way, Gutiérrez Aragón chronicles the evolution of traditional Spanish culture, especially as it is reflected in the pivotal roles assumed by women, while also recounting the parallel evolution of national politics.

Angela Molina gives a rich and nuanced performance in the lead role of Rosa, playing a character who is at once rooted in the material struggle of surviving in a harsh economic reality but who also is surrounded by characters drawn from a fairy-tale and popular folkloric tradition. Of equal note, Margarita Lozano as Rosa's grandmother affects a striking iconic force as the nearly silent and all-knowing matriarch. Her movements and knowing glances frame the story of Rosa's struggle but effectively avoid the snare of reducing her character to a cartoon or fairy-tale figure.

BIBLIOGRAPHY
Hopewell, John. *Out of the Past: Spanish Cinema after Franco*. London: BFI Books, 1986.
Kovacs, Katherine S. "Half of Heaven." *Film Quarterly* 41, no. 3 (Spring 1988): 33-37.

Morena clara [*The Light-skinned Gypsy*] **(1936: Florián Rey*).** Along with Florián Rey's earlier *Nobleza baturra* [*Rustic Gallantry*]* (1935) and Benito

Perojo's *La verbena de la paloma* [*Paloma Fair*]* (1935), this is generally considered among the most artistically accomplished films of the pre–Civil War sound period in Spain. The film is based on a theatrical success of the time, but most critics conclude that the stage version's often static, vaudevillesque features were greatly improved upon in Rey's handling of the material.

The story is set in a splendid studio reconstruction of Seville in the 1930s as two gypsies, Trini (Imperio Argentina*) and her brother, Regalado (Miguel Ligero*), are arrested and brought to trial for having robbed hams from a local Sevillano innkeeper. The district attorney, Enrique (Manuel Luna*), is annoyed with the pair's mocking attitudes and in his closing summation makes a strong attack upon the antisocial, often criminal behavior of gypsies. He demands that the two be sentenced to six months in prison. The defense lawyer challenges Enrique's condemnation of the gypsies and suggests that if he took them in to work in his own house he might see that they are not as bad as he claims. The judge takes the defense lawyer's side, suspending the sentence and sending Trini to work in Enrique's house.

When Trini arrives at the house, Enrique's mother immediately takes her under her wing and makes her a maid. In the ensuing days, Trini becomes involved in a series of family problems involving Enrique, his brother, and his philandering father. Gradually, Trini discovers that she is in love with Enrique. When she resolves the family's difficulties, showing herself to be an honorable person, Enrique softens his view of her and eventually expresses reciprocated sentiments of love. The film ends with the suggestion that the couple will marry.

The Light-Skinned Gypsy is a perfect example of the elegant CIFESA studio style of the 1930s. Essentially a musical comedy, complete with a Busby Berkeley-style chorus number to celebrate the Cruz de Mayo festival, the film offers a picture-postcard version of Andalusian folkloric styles: the bravado of the gypsies, the elegant style of the regional architecture and decor, and the frivolity of the Sevillano men as embodied in Enrique's spendthrift brother, Rafael (Manuel Dicenta).

This popular folkloric evocation is further enhanced by the development of the two central gypsy characters, Regalado and Trini. Their dress, their often comic simplicity, but most of all, their speech, a stylized, staged form of Andalusian gypsy speech, reinforce the popular stereotypes of the gypsy as an astute but likeable character living just beyond the law. In fact, the plot's twists and turns do much to suggest that Trini's sense of justice is much more potent and valuable than Enrique's formal and intransigent notion of the law.

One of the most fascinating aspects of the film is its candid and unapologetic portrayal of the prejudices against gypsies. Enrique's impassioned racist outpouring against gypsies is not even repudiated by the defense attorney, whose only argument is that gypsies can be redeemed if they are helped.

Owing to Imperio Argentina's immense popularity, *The Light-Skinned Gypsy* was shown regularly in Republican and Nationalist zones during the Civil War, despite the fact that the star and the director had publicly stated their allegiance to the Nationalist cause. In 1954, Luis Lucia* remade *The Light-Skinned Gypsy* in a color version with the famed gypsy singer, Lola Flores,* in the role of Trini and Fernando Fernán-Gómez* in the role of Enrique.

BIBLIOGRAPHY
Caparrós-Lera, José María. *Arte y política en el cine de la República (1931–1939)*. Barcelona: Ediciones 7 1/2, 1981.

Muerte de un ciclista [*Death of a Cyclist*] (1955: Juan Antonio Bardem*). This is Bardem's best-known and most biting denunciation of the hypocrisy and moral corruption of Spanish society under the Franco dictatorship. The film boasts a scathing script that indicts not only the "victors" of the Civil War, but also the conservative Catholic bourgeoisie—the social foundation of the regime. Borrowing heavily from Michelangelo Antonioni's *Cronaca di un amore* [*Chronicle of a Love Affair*] (1950), the plot details a crisis in the adulterous affair between Juan (Alberto Closas*) and María José (Lucía Bosé*). After one of their clandestine trysts, their car runs down a bicyclist on a deserted highway. At first María José stops the car and Juan approaches the fallen body, but fearing that to become involved in the accident will expose their immoral relationship, she coaxes him back to the car and they drive off. The guilt and fear that grip the couple during the following days shape the rest of the film.

María José's husband, Miguel (Othelo Tosso), a self-made man, who has not suspected anything about his wife's relationship with Juan, begins to note her tenseness. Juan, a university professor of mathematics who has gotten his position through family connections, is racked with guilt. When Rafa (Carlos Casaravilla*), an intellectual friend, begins to note María José's nervousness and surmises that she and Juan are involved in an adulterous affair, he perceives the opportunity to blackmail them. Juan's emotional distraction leads him to mistreat a female student in one of his classes which, in turn, leads to a student strike at the university during which students demand Juan's resignation.

All the diverse strands of the plot come together when Miguel discovers his wife's adultery and demands that she come with him on a business trip to separate her from Juan. She is put in a quandary as Juan, now finding an inner moral strength, demands that she accompany him to the police to confess their guilt in the crime. Fearing that her life will be ruined, María José runs down Juan with her car, thus repeating the death with which the film opened. However, as she rushes down a rain-swept road to meet her husband, she sideswipes another cyclist and goes off the road and is killed. The final image of the film is that of the cyclist, now torn between running away or calling for help. Unlike the egotistical heroine, he runs for help.

Death of a Cyclist is perhaps most noteworthy for its daring denunciation of the morally corrupt environment of the Spanish upper classes. Bardem's script even points to the Civil War, only referred to as "the war," as the source of contemporary immorality and corruption. Particularly striking is the film's formulation of a schism between the uncaring upper classes and the rest of Spanish society. The exaggerated use of crosscutting emphasizes the violent contrast between the wealth and frivolity of María José's circle of friends and the dreary poverty of the urban workers.

For obvious reasons, the film was heavily censored before its release. The Spanish censorship boards insisted that the film's ending be rewritten to show that María José's crimes would not go unpunished. Similarly, there was great concern about the representation of the corrupt university system in which favoritism rather than ability determined positions. The censors were especially uncomfortable with the depiction of a violent university student strike, and the scene was deleted from the Spanish version of the film. The Italian coproducers of *Death of a Cyclist* retained the original scene in the version distributed outside of Spain. When shown at the Cannes film festival in 1955, the film won a special award for its director.

BIBLIOGRAPHY
Egido, Luis G. *J. A. Bardem*. Huelva: Festival de Cine Iberoamericano, 1983.
Kinder, Marsha. *Blood Cinema: The Reconstruction of National Identity in Spain*. Berkeley: University of California Press, 1993.

La muerte de Mikel [*The Death of Mikel*] (1983: Imanol Uribe*). This is the third part of Uribe's trilogy of "Basque" films that focus in a variety of ways on the Basque terrorist group *Euskadi Ta Askatasuna* (ETA) and their relation to contemporary Spanish politics. In *El proceso de Burgos* [*The Trial at Burgos*] (1978) and *La fuga de Segovia* [*Flight from Segovia*] (1981), Uribe tried to humanize the hitherto demonized figures of the Basque separatist group. In *The Death of Mikel*, his attitude toward the clandestine political and military group changes radically.

In this beautifully filmed fictional narrative, the focus is on a young man, Mikel (Imanol Arias*), who is involved in the Basque autonomy movement and who is also, apparently, a collaborator with the terrorist group. Though ETA takes a decidedly secondary position within the narrative, the Basque autonomy party is thematically characterized as an intransigent group that not only stifles self-expression, but is not above hypocritically exploiting events and people to aid its political ends.

The story is framed by the funeral mass for Mikel. At first the circumstances surrounding Mikel's death are unclear. Through a series of flashbacks that punctuate the process of the funeral, however, the audience is able to piece together the details of Mikel's life and death.

In a small Basque town not far from Bilbao, Mikel and his wife, Begoña (Amaia Lasa), are in the throes of an unspecified marital crisis. When Mikel's friend, Martín (Martín Adjemian), suggests that he see a psychiatrist in Bilbao, it becomes clear that Mikel's problem is his sexual orientation. In Bilbao, Mikel meets a female impersonator, Fama (Fernando Tellechea), in a nightclub. They spend the night together but the next morning Mikel repents his actions and quickly leaves Fama's apartment. When Fama shows up in the small town, Mikel's life reaches a crisis point. Motivated by Fama's words, Mikel decides not to hide his sexual orientation, and even kisses Fama in public.

His acknowledged homosexuality causes the Basque autonomy party to remove his name as a candidate from the election lists; his mother (Montserrat Salvador) is similarly appalled by her son's actions and orders him to keep things discreet. In a seemingly unrelated action, Mikel is sequestered and tortured by the police under the antiterrorist laws. It becomes clear to him that his friend, Martín, has informed upon him. Mikel finally returns home with the determination to leave the town and go to live in Bilbao. The next morning his brother (Xabier Elorriaga*) finds Mikel's dead body. At the funeral, the Basque political group, having once rejected Mikel for his sexual orientation, now organizes a protest against the police arguing that he was killed by the authorities and that "his death belongs to the people." The final image of the film, that of Mikel's mother staring stoically out her window, suggests that it was she, and not the police, who killed Mikel.

The power of *The Death of Mikel* lies in two spheres: First, this is the emotionally charged story of a young man attempting to sort out his sexual identity amid conflicting commitments both to family and to political party; second, it poses a devastating indictment of the repressive nature of those social and political institutions. In the immediate post-Franco period, the depiction of the repressive family was the focus of a number of films. Especially striking in Uribe's film is the alignment of that characterization with the depiction of presumably more liberal political groups on the left, whose repressive and hypocritical actions reveal the persistence of a mind-set that many Spaniards had long equated exclusively with the dictatorship.

Equally worthy of note is Uribe's critical position in relation to Basque culture. Unlike his earlier works, which embrace regional cultural identity unquestioningly, *The Death of Mikel* derives a special force by interrogating the nature of cultural communities as its central narrative theme. As such, it offers a much more complex vision of social affiliation and community than may be found in most Spanish films of the period.

BIBLIOGRAPHY
Angulo, Jesús, Carlos F. Hererdero, and José Luis Rebordinos (eds.). *El cine de Imanol Uribe: entre el documental y la ficción*. San Sebastián: Filmoteca Vasca, 1994.
Gutiérrez, Begoña, and José Manuel Porquet. *Imanol Uribe*. Huesca: Festival de Cine de Huesca, 1994.

Mujeres al borde de un ataque de nervios [*Women on the Verge of a Nervous Breakdown*] **(1988: Pedro Almodóvar*).** Nominated for an Oscar as Best Foreign Film, this is one of the most commercially successful Spanish films of all time. Apparently conceived to appeal to a foreign mainstream audience, *Women on the Verge* is notable for the conspicuous absence of the major plot elements usually associated with Almodóvar's earlier films, namely drugs and sex. It does, however, contain other distinctive signature elements of the director's style: a complicated plot involving a fairly large ensemble of Almodóvar regulars, the interpolation of scenes from Hollywood movies, and a series of parodies of Spanish television programs.

The plot involves the crisis brought on when Iván (Fernando Guillén*), a successful movie dubber, abandons his lover, Pepa (Carmen Maura*), about the time she discovers that she is pregnant with his child. The rest of the film details Pepa's efforts to locate Iván, who has disappeared and who, as it turns out, is attempting to run off to Stockholm with his new lover, Paulina Morales (Kitty Manver), a callous feminist lawyer. In the process of Pepa's investigations, she encounters Iván's estranged wife, Lucía (Julieta Serrano*), recently released from an asylum, who is now pursuing him with the intention of murdering him; Iván's son, Carlos (Antonio Banderas*); and Carlos's fiancée, Marisa (Rossy de Palma). After numerous plot twists, Pepa and Lucía meet up with Iván at the airport. Pepa saves Iván's life and realizes that she is no longer emotionally bound to him. She is determined to have the baby on her own.

The often zany plot of *Women on the Verge*, although similar to some of Almodóvar's earlier work, appeared more controlled. Little other than the skyline view of Pepa's penthouse apartment and a number of exterior shots mark the film as specifically Spanish or *madrileño*. However, the thematic focus of *Women on the Verge* grows out of an evolving narrative emphasis in Almodóvar's films on the gradual self-liberation of female characters. In this regard, Carmen Maura's portrayal of Pepa seems to have developed out of her earlier roles in Almodóvar comedies, especially her performance as the repressed Gloria in *¿Qué he hecho yo para merecer esto?* [*What Have I Done to Deserve This?*] (1985). In that film, it was the catalyst of the modern city that provided the heroine the impetus to shed her feeling of inferiority to male characters. A similar scenario seems to guide the narrative logic of *Women on the Verge*.

The film boasts a striking visual style, marked by José Luis Alcaine's* stunning photography, which uses strong basic colors, particularly reds and yellows, to convey the vividness of the liberated cultural milieu of Madrid. That spirit of liberation imbues not only the Maura character but the other two major female characters, Julieta Serrano and Rossy de Palma. *Women on the Verge* was the final colllaboration between Almodóvar and Carmen Maura, who had appeared in six of his previous films.

BIBLIOGRAPHY
Smith, Paul Julian. *Desire Unlimited: The Cinema of Pedro Almodóvar*. London: Verso, 1994.
Vidal, Nuria. *El cine de Pedro Almodóvar*. Barcelona: Ediciones Destino, 1988.

El nido [*The Nest*] (1980: Jaime de Armiñán*). Armiñán's ninth film is his second work, the first being *Mi querida señorita* [*My Dearest Señorita*]* (1971), to be nominated for an Oscar in the Best Foreign Film category. The story follows in the style Armiñán had stabilized over the preceding decade: the construction of a narrative fixed on a character's sexual obsession and power, which is loosely connected to a political context that enables audiences to read the film allegorically.

In this instance, the story focuses on the relation between Alejandro (Héctor Alterio*), a widower in his sixties, who is pursued by and gradually becomes obsessed with Goyita (Ana Torrent*), a thirteen-year-old girl living in a small town in the province of Salamanca. Alejandro finds a series of cryptic, rhymed messages that Goyita has left for him, which eventually leads him to meet her as she is rehearsing for a school version of Shakespeare's Macbeth in which she plays Lady Macbeth. A sexual fascination ensues in which Goyita quickly shows her dominance and control over Alejandro. A good deal of attention is paid to her family situation. Members include a henpecked father (Ovidi Montllor*), a member of the Civil Guard, his superior (Agustín González*), who frequently chides Goyita for her actions; and a mother who also continually criticizes her and forces her husband, at one point, to take a strap to Goyita.

To avenge this treatment, Goyita pressures Alejandro to challenge the sergeant to a duel. Reluctantly, the older man obeys, but in an apparent act of self-sacrifice for his love, Alejandro uses blanks, thus tricking the Civil Guard into killing him and allowing Alejandro to become a martyr to his love.

Beneath this tale of perverse sexual and power relations, one notes the striking social thematics of the film. Women are the forceful and dominant characters, and Goyita clearly mirrors the aggressive force of her mother just as Alejandro reflects the weakness of her father. Goyita's alignment with the figure of Lady Macbeth not only underscores her personal yearning for power but also identifies the plot of the film as a variation on the Macbeth narrative. Also, Alejandro is a Republican refugee from the Civil War and Goyita's family is affiliated with the Civil Guard. The film thereby resonates as an allegorical reenactment of the ideological clash between the left and the right in the Civil War.

Beyond these embellishments of cultural thematics lies a more intimate tension in the troubled relation between Alejandro and Goyita. Alejandro is at once a father figure and the embodiment of a storybook lover. We see him from the very beginning on a white horse as a chivalric knight riding to the rescue of his imprisoned maiden in distress.

The film is beautifully photographed by Teo Escamilla.* It is also splendidly acted by Alterio as the weak but obsessed Alejandro and Ana Torrent as Goyita, playing what is a difficult transitional role as both an adolescent who must convey the childlike qualities of innocence and an embittered and power-obsessed female seeking revenge from her family.

BIBLIOGRAPHY
Crespo, Pedro. *Jaime de Armiñán: los amores marginales*. Huelva: Festival de Cine Iberoamericano, 1987.

Kinder, Marsha. "*El nido.*" *Film Quarterly* 35, no. 1 (Fall 1981): 34–41.

Nobleza baturra [*Rustic Gallantry*] (1935: Florián Rey*). Filmed largely on location in the rural regions of Aragon, the film is one of the most poetic expressions of popular Spanish folklore. The director, Florián Rey, was a native of Aragon, and the film reveals a deep appreciation for details of traditional folkloric customs without falling into maudlin sentimentality. Some of the early scenes of the harvest, though shot with professional actors, have the quality of an ethnographic documentary.

The story is inspired by the lyrics of a popular *jota*: "*A eso de la media-noche/dicen que han visto saltar/ un hombre por la ventana/ de María del Pilar*" ["At about midnight they say that they saw a man jump from the window of María del Pilar"]. The song became the basis for the plot of a 1925 silent film from which Rey's film was developed as a remake. In this new version, Pilar (Imperio Argentina*) is the daughter of the wealthy farmer, Don Eusebio (José Calle), who is reminded by his neighbor, Marco (Manuel Luna*), that as small children Pilar and Marco were promised to each other in marriage by their fathers. Unfortunately, Pilar prefers Sebastián (Juan de Orduña*), the poor farm-hand. Marco tries a variety of ploys to gain Pilar's affections, including a fight with Sebastián. Roundly rejected, he plots revenge by sneaking up to Pilar's room at night and arranging for men of the town to see him leave, in order to suggest the young woman's dishonor. Marco circulates the verses and Pilar is publicly humiliated. Marco repents of his revenge and resolves the problem by leaving town, writing a confession to the wronged Sebastián, and leaving the latter his lands so that Don Eusebio cannot oppose his marriage with Pilar because he is poor.

The film is notable for its traditional conservative representation of family honor and female chastity. Few Spanish films have so forcefully depicted the power of honor on the actions of men and women. In this respect, the story harks back to a variety of Spanish Golden Age sources, including Lope de Vega's *Peribáñez*, in which tales of infidelity are circulated through song, and a number of Calderonian honor plays in which male and female characters prefer death to public dishonor. Rey's earlier *Aldea maldita* [*The Cursed Village*]* (1930), also depicts a rigid code of male honor that destroys the female.

Equally noteworthy is the extraordinary evocation of Aragonese folkloric culture and tradition. The opening sequence, which shows workers gathering the harvest and singing a traditional *jota*, is very close to poetic documentary. The later party sequence in which Pilar sings a *jota* and dances with a group of youths is one of the most evocative of traditional Aragonese cultural images to appear in a fictional film. This sense of local folkloric color is, in turn, enhanced by the use of a simulated Aragonese dialect among the actors, even Imperio Argentina and Miguel Ligero,* who were both more conventionally characterized in others films by their Andalusian speech patterns.

BIBLIOGRAPHY

Caparrós-Lera, José María. *Arte y política en el cine de la República (1931-1939)*. Barcelona: Ediciones 7 1/2, 1981.

Gubern, Román. *El cine sonoro de la II República: 1929–1936*. Barcelona: Editorial
Lumen, 1977.

Nueve cartas a Berta [*Nine Letters to Berta*] (1965: Basilio Martín Patino*).
Patino's first feature-length film prefigures the underlying duality of his later
work: There is a tension between narrative and documentary cinema that
produces a unique, intriguing, and ultimately enriching film. Here, for instance,
he chooses as his subject matter a simple narrative situation that illustrates one
of the persistent social criticisms of the Francoist status quo: the confining nature
of provincial life. Lorenzo Carvajal (Emilio Gutiérrez Caba*), a law student at
the University of Salamanca, has recently returned from his first trip abroad,
where he met the Berta of the title, the daughter of an exiled Republican writer
living in London. The impact of the contact, presumably amorous, becomes the
catalyst for Carvajal's reflections on the state of life in provincial Spain. His
strong feeling of discontent, immediately focused on his family and girlfriend,
is a critique of the reality of provincial Spain under Franco.

Beyond this grounding situation, there is little real plot to the film. The action
opens sometime after Lorenzo's return, as he recounts in his early letters to Berta
his reactions to the people and situations he has encountered since his homecom-
ing. Among those Lorenzo views in a newly critical light are his parents, who
have taken note of their son's changed attitudes. His father is a former military
officer and now a bank official, and his mother a conservative religious woman
who recognizes her own unhappy marriage. Lorenzo reassesses his relationships,
first with his girlfriend, Trini, then with a French friend, Jacques, whom he looks
up during a trip to Madrid.

A family crisis erupts when Lorenzo fails a course and is about to lose his
scholarship. In an effort to help him regain his former equilibrium, his family
urges him to visit his uncle, an aging cleric. After spending several days with the
old man in a nearby village, Lorenzo is apparently "cured," which pleases his
family and girlfriend.

The film is broken up into nine sections, each preceded by an intertitle. The
entire film is preceded by the precredit: "*Esta es la historia de un español que
quiere vivir, y a vivir empieza . . .* ["This is the story of a Spaniard who wants
to live and so begins to live . . ."]. Shots of street scenes and people in the old
university town of Salamanca are presented as freeze-frames. At one point,
Lorenzo, in voice-over, explains that his family had given him a camera and thus
the freeze-frames give the appearance of photographs. The visual style is quite
clearly derived from French New Wave films, especially the early films of Jean-
Luc Godard, whom Patino acknowledges as an influence. At certain points, the
voice-over narration disappears and what remains is a series of quasi-documenta-
ry shots and freeze-frames of the city.

Contextual footage of Salamanca, such as images of sterile family life and shots of a typical conservative provincial city, poses a social critique of life in the Francoist provinces that is common to other works of New Spanish Cinema. The film also shares one of the key thematic/stylistic features of New Spanish Cinema: the contrast between old Spain and the new air of modernity evident in contemporary music, dance, and the customs of young people. *Nine Letters to Berta* was winner of the Concha de Plata at the San Sebastián Film Festival, but distributors saw little commercial potential for it, which delayed its release for nearly three years.

BIBLIOGRAPHY

Hopewell, John. *Out of the Past: Spanish Cinema after Franco.* London: BFI Books, 1986.

Rodero, José Angel. *Aquel "Nuevo cine español" de los '60.* Valladolid: 26 Semana Internacional del Cine de Valladolid, 1981.

Nunca pasa nada [*Nothing Ever Happens*](1963: Juan Antonio Bardem*). After a series of failures in the mid-to-late 1950s, Juan Antonio Bardem returned to prominence with this film that appears to combine elements of his own theatrical past, reminiscent of his 1953 *Cómicos* [*Comedians*],* with the anti-Francoist theme of a critical view of Spanish provincial life as reflected in the film's title. Despite this latter dimension, *Nothing Ever Happens* was chosen as the official Spanish entry to the 1963 Venice Film Festival. Though Bardem considered it one of his best works, European critics generally treated it harshly, judging it a reworking of his earlier success, *Calle Mayor* [*Main Street*]* (1956).

The plot of the film is a relatively simple one involving a traveling theater company that is forced to make an unexpected stop in a Castilian town because one of its young starlets, a French girl, Jacqueline (Corinne Marchand), has had an attack of appendicitis. Don Enrique (Antonio Casas), the town doctor, performs the operation and has Jacqueline remain in the village to recuperate. He quickly falls passionately in love with the exotic French actress and is prepared to compromise his reputation and leave his wife (Julia Gutiérrez Caba) to run off with her. The close-knit townspeople, even the schoolboys, comment on the doctor's affair. Finally, Enrique comes to his senses as he realizes that in this town, as in all of Spain, nothing ever happens.

The thematic focus of the film joins two of the insistent themes of opposition cinema of the fifties and sixties: the comparison between Spain and the outside world, and the critique of provincial life. The appearance of foreigners, especially those involved in theatrical enterprises, as the narrative suggests, only points up the anachronistic and puritanical culture of Spain. By setting the action in the Castilian heartland, as he had in his last critical success, *Main Street*, Bardem takes aim at the Francoist insistence that the true Spanish values lie in the provincial heartlands and not in the cities.

BIBLIOGRAPHY
Egido, Luis G. *J. A. Bardem*. Huelva: Festival de Cine Iberoamerico, 1983.

***Opera prima* [*First Work* or *Cousin in Opera*] (1980: Fernando Trueba*).**
Fernando Trueba's first feature-length film is one of the key works of the New
Madrid Comedy of the late 1970s and early 1980s. Like Fernando Colomo's*
Tigres de papel [*Paper Tigers*]* (1978) and José Luis Garci's* *Asignatura
pendiente* [*Pending Examination*]* (1978), Trueba's film depends for its impact
on its self-conscious embrace of a new generational spirit in Spanish culture
during the early post-Franco period. In a modest, almost self-deprecating way,
the director discards the look and feel of recent serious Spanish cinema by
openly borrowing from the light visual and narrative style of Hollywood
romantic comedies of the 1940s and their updated reincarnation in the early New
York comedies of Woody Allen.

His effort to emulate the cosmopolitan style associated with Woody Allen is
especially noticeable in the characterization of his principal male character,
Matías, a lanky and striking figure with prominent eyes, played by Oscar
Ladoire,* a part-time entertainment journalist and would-be novelist. Like
Woody Allen's and earlier Spanish incarnation in Colomo's and Garci's films,
José Sacristán,* Matías is more verbal than sexy and spouts dialogue that runs
from cinematic self-references to literary allusions of the type common in the
Allen comedies. When by chance he meets his younger cousin, Violeta (Paula
Molina), at the Madrid Opera Plaza, he finds himself completely drawn to her.
The film details their rocky relationship. After an initial phase of seduction,
Matías becomes jealous when he discovers that Violeta's hippie violin teacher,
Niki (Luis González-Regueral), has convinced her to run off with him to Peru.
The film culminates in a classic Hollywood comedy ending as Matías pursues
Violeta to the airport. She changes her mind and returns to their apartment, and
the couple is romantically reunited on the plaza at night as a pop jazz band plays
on the street.

Despite the obvious derivative nature of the film, or perhaps because of it,
First Work comes to embody for a large Spanish audience the generational break
in Spanish cinema as characters, and their creator, forcefully stake out a new
cultural identity that totally rejects the usual marks of Spanishness. Through the
subplots related to Matías's work with his photographer partner, Leon (Antonio
Resines*), and his several reencounters with his former wife, Ana (Kitty
Manver), Matías's world comes into focus as one that is closer to the cinematic
concoctions of certain American and French light comic fare than to the
ponderous historical and political thematics of some Spanish films of the 1970s.
For his offbeat performance as Matías, Ladoire received the best acting award
at the 1980 Venice Film Festival.

BIBLIOGRAPHY
Caparrós-Lera, José María. *El cine español de la democracia: de la muerte de Franco al
    "cambio" socialista (1975–1989)*. Barcelona: Anthropos, 1992.

Hopewell, John. *Out of the Past: Spanish Cinema after Franco*. London: BFI, 1986.

El pájaro de la felicidad [*The Bird of Happiness*] **(1993: Pilar Miró*).** This seventh film by Spain's foremost woman director has been critically acclaimed as her most fully realized work to date. In many ways the film parallels the narrative structure of Miró's earlier *Gary Cooper que estás en los cielos* [*Gary Cooper Who Art in Heaven*] (1980), in which Mercedes Sampietro,* Miró's cinematic alter ego, also appeared in a role that suggested a number of autobiographical details. In this instance, and working from a script authored by Mario Camus,* Miró traces the emotional crisis suffered by Carmen when she is robbed and nearly raped in Madrid. A successful restorer of important paintings, she is nonetheless unfulfilled as a woman. The attack becomes the occasion for her to take account of her life. She begins by visiting her aging parents in Catalonia, then proceeds to the barren coast of Almería where she rents a house. Her goal, it appears, is to recede not only from the violence around her but apparently from all social contacts.

This effort is thwarted, however, first by the arrival of the owner of the rented house (José Sacristán*), who becomes amorously involved with Carmen, then by the appearance of the woman (Aitana Sánchez Gijón*) with whom her son had borne a child but whom he now has abandoned. Carmen is initially frustrated by these encounters, but gradually regains her equilibrium. She develops a lesbian attraction to her son's lover, but the woman soon runs off with a new lover, leaving Carmen to care for her grandson. Through her new solitude and communion with the child, Carmen appears at last to have achieved a measure of the happiness she has sought.

The thematic complexity of *The Bird of Happiness* derives as much from the portrayal of social spaces in contemporary Spain as from the rich visual counterpoint between the details of Carmen's life and the Murillo painting, *The Virgin Mary and Santa Isabel*, that she is restoring. She describes Murillo's work as an effort to portray the positive side of life. Shortly afterward, she and Aitana Sánchez-Gijón will, in fact, re-create a contemporary version of the painting's figuration of two females.

Carmen's self-conscious effort to achieve happiness is situated within a clearly defined contemporary social geography. After the attempted rape, she extricates herself from her egotistical lover, then departs from the city, making a stop at a nearby farm to bid farewell to her former husband, then her parents, and finally arrives at the southern coastal village. Her trajectory makes clear a process of disengagement from the fetters of society and family and is marked by a progressively deeper identification with open, natural locales, beautifully captured by the luminous photography of José Luis Alcaine.* Carmen's process of physical disengagement and personal renewal is continually paralleled by the words of Pío Baroja, the Generation of '98 writer, whose works she is shown reading at various points. By the film's end, alone with her grandson and a newly acquired dog, she appears to have at last achieved that equilibrium.

BIBLIOGRAPHY

Martí-Olivella, Jaume. "Toward a New Transcultural Dialogue in Spanish Film." *Spain Today: Essays on Literature, Culture, Society*, edited by José Colmeiro et al., 47–66. Hanover, NH: Dartmouth College Department of Spanish and Portuguese, 1995.

Pérez Millán, Juan Antonio. *Pilar Miró: directora de cine*. Valladolid: Semana Internacional de Cine, 1992.

Pascual Duarte (1975: Ricardo Franco*). This brilliant adaptation of the famous novel by Camilo José Cela portrays, through flashbacks of the final days of his life, the tragic peasant figure, Pascual Duarte (José Luis Gómez*). Little by little, the spectator is able to reconstruct a fragmented biography of Pascual from the age of seven through the subsequent stages of the development of his violent personality. The film presents flashbacks triggered by words, objects, or events in the present, as though these could somehow explain the circumstances that have shaped and motivated the hero's life. In fact, the distinctive feature of Franco's film is that its enigmatic pseudo-psychological structure leads the audience gradually to perceive not the emotional origins of the protagonist's actions, but rather the social underpinnings of his violent life and death.

Raised in a brutalizing family environment, Pascual witnesses the violence of his father (Héctor Alterio*) who, in bouts of drunkenness, batters his mother (Paca Ojea). Upon his father's death from rabies and the departure of his sister, Rosario (Diana Pérez de Guzmán), to the city to work as a prostitute, Pascual is left alone with his mother. He falls in love with a woman named Lola (Maribel Ferrero) but she soon dies. As if to avenge her death, Pascual kills the mule that was the cause of Lola's death. The latter half of the film details a crescendo of violence in Pascual's life from his shooting of his sister's boyfriend, El Estirao (Joaquín Hinojosa*), his mother, and finally, the local landowner, Don Jesús (Eduardo Calvo). The motivation for these murders is not explained but simply chronicled as a crescendo of brooding anger that gradually swells up in Pascual as he is confronted by the loss of the two females who had apparently meant most to him: his sister, Rosario, and Lola.

The final scene of the film is the point at which the past and present join: Pascual appears to have been tried and brought to be executed by garrote for the murders of his mother and Don Jesús. In contrast to most of the film, in which Pascual remains taciturn in the face of violence, these last moments are marked by his prolonged howling and shrieking as he faces state-inflicted violence. The final image of the film is a medium close-up of Pascual's screaming face transformed into a freeze-frame that lingers on the screen for nearly a minute.

The brilliant script of *Pascual Duarte* transposes the often ambiguous time frame of the original Cela novel into a precise chronology that runs through the 1920s and 1930s and situates key actions within the period of the Second Spanish Republic and the outbreak of the Civil War (Pascual is executed in 1937). This historical contextualization thus serves as a means through which the cinematic narrative provides a symptomatic social/political context for the aberrant actions of the title character. It is ultimately the tension between the unspoken, often silent narrative of individual characters and the historical backdrop of Spain moving inexorably to fratricidal violence that constructs the thematic core of what is possibly the most explicitly violent film of the post-Franco era.

Pascual Duarte bears the clear marks of Elías Querejeta's* productions of the 1970s: a characteristically elliptical plot with a marked political theme that makes clear connections between a fictional narrative and the Franco regime; splendid photography by Luis Cuadrado* that continually underscores the oppressive milieu of impoverished rural Spain; finally, a talented cast headed by José Luis Gómez, the noted Spanish stage actor who makes his screen debut in this film. Gómez won the Best Actor award at the Cannes Film Festival for this performance.

BIBLIOGRAPHY
Hernández-Les, Juan. *El cine de Elías Querejeta: un productor singular.* Bilbao: Ediciones Mensajero, 1986.
Vernon, Kathleen M. "La politique des Auteurs: Narrative Point of View in *Pascual Duarte*, Novel and Film." *Hispania* 72, no. 1 (March 1989): 87–96.

Pepi, Luci, Bom, y otras chicas del montón [*Pepi, Luci Bom, and Other Girls like That*] **(1980: Pedro Almodóvar*).** Almodóvar's first feature-length film was made on a minimal budget in 16mm and later blown up to 35mm for commercial viewing. The film captures the spirit of *La Movida*, the effervescence of Madrid counterculture of the late 1970s. Though often criticized for its poor technical quality, the film captures much of the improvisational style of the movement and its irreverent attitudes toward nearly all the conventions of middle-class propriety. At the time of its release, most critics dismissed *Pepi, Luci, Bom* as unprofessional and incoherent. Only a few were able to argue that the series of assaults on the staid modes of conventional cinematic narrative and the presentation of a series of bizarre characters engaged in sexual hijinks were indications of a serious revaluation of Spanish cinema.

The action centers around the figure of Pepi (Carmen Maura*), who, attempting to take revenge for her rape by a police detective (Félix Rotaeta), has her friends, members of a punk rock band, assault the detective. The discovery that they have accidently beaten up the detective's twin brother only infuriates Pepi more. She thus seeks a greater revenge: having the detective's meek wife, Luci (Eva Silva), seduced by Pepi's girlfriend, Bom (Alaska). When it turns out that Luci is not only a lesbian but has masochistic tastes, a friendship among the three women quickly develops and leads to a series of misadventures. Eventually, the detective is able to win back his wife by so brutalizing her that she has to be hospitalized. After visiting Luci in the hospital, Pepi and Bom realize that Luci will remain with her husband, so they plan a new life together and discuss plans for Bom's career as a bolero singer.

Though marked by conspicuous technical flaws and narrative inconsistences, *Pepi, Luci, Bom* nonetheless reveals some highly creative marks, such as the effort to shape the film's narration around the techniques associated with underground comics. Each of the film's major sections, in fact, is preceded by a comic strip that announces the general action of the sequence to come. These touches, along with the many narrative flaws of the film, contributed to making *Pepi, Luci, Bom* a cult favorite for a number of years, shown at special weekend midnight screenings in Madrid. The film was released abroad after Almodóvar achieved international success in the the the late 1980s, and foreign audiences were able to view the sources of many of the sexual and social themes that had become the hallmark of his later films.

BIBLIOGRAPHY

Smith, Paul Julian. *Desire Unlimited: The Cinema of Pedro Almodóvar*. London: Verso, 1994.
Vidal, Nuria. *El cine de Pedro Almodóvar*. Barcelona: Ediciones Destino, 1988.

***El pico* [*The Shoot*] (1983: Eloy de la Iglesia*).** De la Iglesia's most resounding commercial hit follows the large commercial successes of three earlier films, *El diputado* [*The Deputy*] (1978), *Navajeros* [*Knife Fighters*] (1980) and *Colegas* [*Pals*] (1982), and shares with those films a common cluster of themes of Spanish youth for whom drugs and homosexuality offer the comforts otherwise denied them by faltering families and oppressive economic marginalization. With *The Shoot*, however, a new and telling element is introduced: the theme of Basque nationalism. Because de la Iglesia and his producer and coscriptwriter, Gonzalo Goicochea, are native Basques, the theme may appear merely autobiographical. In fact, however, it coincides with efforts in political and cultural circles to give prominence to Basque cultural identity, and this film, despite many of the strongly negative reviews it received at the time of its release, provides exactly that type of prominence within the larger polemical context of an emerging multicultural identity for Spain.

The story involves paired father-and-son relations: a Civil Guard commander, Evaristo Torrecuadrada (José Manuel Cervino), discovers that his seventeen-year-old son, Paco, (José Luis Manzano), is a drug addict, as is his best friend, Urko, (Javier García) the son of a politician (Luis Iriondo) affiliated with one of the groups pushing for Basque autonomy. Paco flees his family, stealing two of his father's pistols. He takes refuge with the only person who has shown him any warmth, a gay sculptor (Quique San Francisco). Torrecuadrada's search for his son eventually leads him to Urko's father, with whom political differences are overshadowed by their common need to find and help their sons. In the meantime, the two youths have gotten mixed up in a complicated drug ring involving the police, which only creates more dramatic crises for the boys and their families and connects the larger political and social themes with issues of family unity.

The powerful attraction of *The Shoot* to huge audiences in Spain at a time when much of the Spanish public was ignoring domestic films lies in its dramatic treatment of contemporary issues of alientated youth as well as its daring linking of gay thematics with the issue of Basque nationalism. Here, as throughout de la Iglesia's films, a highly popular, unproblematic narration that emphasizes plot and drama over refined visual technique makes for a kind of immediacy that appeals to Spanish popular audiences much more than the work of other filmmakers ostensibly dealing with the same thematic and political agendas.

BIBLIOGRAPHY
Smith, Paul Julian. *Laws of Desire: Questions of Homosexuality in Spanish Writing and Film 1960–1990*. Oxford: Clarendon Press, 1992.

La piel quemada [Burnt Skin] **(1968: Josep Maria Forn).** Made during the period of liberalization in film censorship in the late 1960s, this film is one of the first to address explicitly issues of Catalan cultural identity during the Francoist period. In *Burnt Skin* Forn views Catalan culture as distinct and yet still part of a larger Spanish national culture. Though his conception is much less radical than the views of some of his contemporaries among Catalan filmmakers, particularly Antoni Ribas,* this film helped set the cultural and historical contexts within which subsequent Catalan cinema was to emerge in the next decade.

Burnt Skin tells the story of an Andalusian worker, José (Antonio Iranzo), who has come as a *charnego* (a non-Catalan) to find better economic opportunities as a laborer on the Costa Brava. The film details a brief period, the journey made by José's wife and two children from the Andalusian village to the Catalan coast, while José celebrates the end of his enforced bachelorhood with friends. The narrative enables Forn to pose a series of fascinating themes and issues, among them the contrast between internal migrations caused by the faltering Spanish economy and the promotion of foreign tourism, embodied by the French female tourist who, in the context of the period, appeared to represent all the sexual and social freedom that Spaniards yearned for.

To this must be added the peculiar regional thematics surrounding the *charnegos*. Forn is directly attacking the closed mentality of his fellow Catalans who are hostile to internal Spanish migrations to their region. Though over time this attitude largely dissipates, it nonetheless remains, from a historical perspective, a portent of the issues of regional autonomy that were to surface in the post-Franco period.

Especially noteworthy in *Burnt Skin* is the stunning black-and-white photography by Ricardo Albiñán as well as the impressive editing that juxtaposes scenes of José's life as a worker with his family's struggle to join him. There is also a particularly impressive sequence without dialogue that details the pattern of departure and forced migration that is at the heart of the narrative. Though Forn's view of Catalan culture as being situated within the larger sphere of Spanish culture was eventually eclipsed by more strident filmmakers who posed themes of regional autonomy, Forn's vision was shared by a number of important Catalan filmmakers of the 1970s, most notably Jaime Camino.*

BIBLIOGRAPHY
Batlle, Joan, and Ramón Sala. "Entrevista con Josep Maria Forn." *Contracampo*, no. 7, Año 1 (December 1979), 13–19.
D'Lugo, Marvin. "Catalan Cinema: Historical Experience and Cinematic Practice." *Quarterly Review of Film and Video* 13, nos. 1–3. (1991): 131–147.

Pim, pam, pum . . . ¡fuego! [Bang, Bang . . . You're Dead!] **(1975: Pedro Olea*).** During the early 1970s, Olea established himself as a promising young filmmaker through a series of powerful dramas beginning with *El bosque del lobo* [*The Wolf's Forest*] (1970). His reputation was to be solidified by a trilogy of films of the mid-1970s set in and dealing with life in Madrid at various moments in its modern history. The trilogy consisted of *Tormento* [Torment] (1974), an adaptation of a nineteenth-century novel by Benito Pérez Galdós, followed by *Bang, Bang, You're Dead!* (1975), and ended with the least appreciated of the three films, *La Corea* (1976). *Bang, Bang, You're Dead!* was, for its time, certainly the most controversial of the three films, owing to its strong use of popular vulgar language and several scenes of sexual acts never before shown in Spanish films. But the real importance of the film lies in its evocation of life in the Madrid of the early postwar period.

From a script written in collaboration with Rafael Azcona,* Olea presents the underside of life in the years immediately following the Nationalist triumph; this was, of course, one of the themes Azcona would return to time and again over the next twenty years. In the immediate context of the 1970s, however, this evocation of post–Civil War Madrid clearly coincided with the theme of blocked popular memory that had already been the basis of Carlos Saura's* *Jardín de las delicias* [*Garden of Delights*] (1970) and Basilio Martín Patino's* *Canciones para después de una guerra* [*Songs for after a War*]* (1971, 1976).

The protagonist is Paca (Concha Velasco),* a struggling chorus girl who is the sole support for her disabled father, who was wounded during the recent war. She comes under the protection of a shady underworld figure, Julio (Fernando Fernán-Gómez*), while maintaining a relationship with Luis (José María Flotats), a *maquis*, an underground resistance fighter against the regime.

The dramatic focus of the story involves Julio's discovery of Paca's relationship with Luis and his revenge against the two. In its portrayal of the venal behavior necessary simply for survival, as exemplified by Paca and Julio, Olea's film contributes to the first critical revision in the consciousness of the historical processes that connect the contemporary aura of prosperity in 1970s Spain with its political and historical roots in the Civil War.

Though melodramatic in plotting and tone, *Bang, Bang, You're Dead!* derives emotional force from the powerful performance by Concha Velasco, who, up to this point in her career, had been largely relegated to light comedy and musicals.

Her performance as a streetwise kept woman clearly saves the film from the excesses of melodrama. Also worthy of note is Olea's treatment of the poverty and the tawdry milieu created in the war's aftermath. The film stunningly captures the feel of post–Civil War Madrid as much by its vivid mise-en-scène as by the presentation of an array of secondary characters whose speech and actions evoke the drab and oppressive ambience of the period.

BIBLIOGRAPHY
Angulo, Jesús, Carlos F. Heredero, and José Luis Rebordinos, (eds.). *Un cineasta llamado Pedro Olea*. San Sebastián: Filmoteca Vasca, 1993.

El pisito [The Little Flat] **(1958: Marco Ferreri*).** This first Spanish film by Italian director Ferreri is based on a novel by Rafael Azcona,* who also collaborated on the script. Throughout the 1950s, Spanish filmmakers attempted to use plots involving the extreme housing shortage as the basis for veiled critiques of the regime. *Esa pareja feliz [That Happy Couple]** (1951), the first film by Juan Antonio Bardem* and Luis García Berlanga*, and Fernando Fernán-Gómez's* *La vida por delante [Your Life before You]** (1958) are the most striking examples of this treatment. Both of these films exploit comic elements as a way of softening the critique of social situations. Also, both resort to the formula of the happy ending in order to secure at least the impression of comic innocence. The Ferreri-Azcona script breaks with that tradition by proposing a black comedy with no happy ending.

The story involves the seemingly endless courtship of Rodolfo (José Luis López Vázquez*) and Petrita (Mary Carrillo*) as the two attempt to find an apartment. Rodolfo lives in an apartment converted into a boardinghouse in a prime location near one of Madrid's main avenues, the Gran Vía, owned by the aging Doña Martina (Concha López Silva). The old lady shows real affection for Rodolfo and even promises him that when she dies he will inherit the apartment with all of her beloved possessions. When he informs her that legally she cannot bestow the apartment on anyone but a family member, the plot is hatched to have Rodolfo marry Doña Martina and upon her death inherit the apartment as her legal heir, thus enabling him to then marry Petrita.

Plot complications ensue after Martina and Rodolfo marry and the old lady begins to take an active hand in controlling her new husband's behavior, demanding that he hand over his whole monthly salary to her. Petrita becomes vexed and goads Rodolfo to assume a more assertive role in his "marriage." It is, in fact, Petrita's own aggressiveness that annoys both Martina and the other tenants. When Martina finally does fall ill, Petrita begins to assess the apartment and her new possessions. At Martina's funeral, as Rodolfo mourns his recently departed friend, Petrita, in a shrewish move, parades the new clothes she has bought for the celebratory funeral. The film ends as the couple ride off to the cemetery.

This first collaboration between Azcona and Ferreri worked so well that it led to their even blacker comedy, *El cochecito* [*The Little Car*]* (1960). Their collaborative activities were so successful that over the next twenty-seven years they worked together on twelve additional films, all made in Italy, including the international hit, *La grande abbuffata* [*La Grande Bouffe* or *The Big Blow-Out*] (1974).

BIBLIOGRAPHY
Frugone, Juan Carlos. *Rafael Azcona: atrapados por la vida.* Valladolid: 32 Semana de Cine de Valladolid, 1987.
Riambau, Esteve (ed.). *Antes del apocalipsis: El cine de Marco Ferreri.* Madrid: Cátedra, 1990.

Plácido (1961: Luis García Berlanga*). The first of Berlanga's many script collaborations with Rafael Azcona,* *Plácido* is a scathing indictment of social and political life in provincial Spain. It is also an exposure of the moral corruption of a bourgeois Catholic society in which the doctrines of Christian charity are ostentatiously observed but in which true charitable behavior is often absent. As with many of Berlanga's projects, the film went through a series of radical modifications before it found a producer willing to finance it. Denied access to the Venice or Cannes festivals by the intentionally slow censorship boards, *Plácido* was eventually nominated for an Oscar in 1962 in the Best Foreign Film category.

Formally, *Plácido* is a perfect embodiment of what would later come to be known as the Berlanga ensemble film, a narrative that involves a vast array of characters all thrown into an extreme situation that calls for a series of collective interactions. In this instance, the centerpiece is a campaign organized for Christmas in a provincial city in which various citizens of note are encouraged to "seat a poor person at the Christmas Eve table." The plan involves not only the recruitment of suitable beggars and old people and the pairing of these with appropriate citizens, but also the participation of what is presumed to be a group of noted Spanish film and stage stars and starlets brought in from Madrid.

The plot sets these characters and situations in the background as the film's title character ("Cassen"), the struggling owner of a vehicle for hire, tries to amass the appropriate amount of money before dark on Christmas Eve to pay the first installment of his bank loan on the van. Plácido is continually thwarted in his efforts by the chaotic activities related to the arrival of the trainload of actors, which makes it difficult for him to claim his salary in time to make his payment. He is further frustrated by the activities of Gabino Quintanilla (José Luis López Vázquez*), the local organizer of the campaign, who forces Plácido to accompany him on a series of trips related to the evening's activities. Part of the film's cynical view of organized charity comes precisely from the community's indifference to the real needs of one of their own, Plácido. At long last, Plácido is able to make the needed loan payment and to get his family home barely before midnight for a makeshift Christmas Eve celebration.

One of the most distinctive stylistic features of Berlanga's films, the complex long-take with a large ensemble of characters, is much in evidence in *Plácido*. The most elaborate of these scenes occurs in the home of the couple whose Christmas Eve guest, an ailing beggar, takes ill. Gabino is quickly summoned, and he, in turn, is followed by Plácido and his entire family who are attempting to get home for their own celebration. The sequence runs some five minutes with the camera in continuous movement without cuts. Through the camera's versatility suggested by the length of the take, the episode thematically underscores the interrelatedness of characters from a variety of social classes who are, in fact, oblivious to their own social interconnectedness.

Much of the contagious humor of *Plácido* is the result of impressive timing and the interaction of a number of well-known Spanish actors (Elvira Quintillá, Manuel Alexandre, Luis Ciges, and Amparo Soler-Leal* among others), as well as the extraordinary character acting of both "Cassen" and López Vázquez, who become comic foils for each other. While Cassen as Plácido, with his blank everyman expression, tries to contend with the local forces of establishment power, López Vázquez portrays Gabino as the insensitive architect of planned charity who is oblivious to the real needs of people around him. Together, the two character actors sum up the underlying tensions of the callous world evoked by Berlanga and Azcona.

BIBLIOGRAPHY
Hernández-Les, Juan, and Manuel Hidalgo. *El último austro-húngaro: conversaciones con Berlanga*. Barcelona: Editorial Anagrama, 1981.
Méndez-Leite, Fernando. *Historia del cine español en 100 películas*. Madrid: Jupey, 1975.

La prima Angélica [*Cousin Angelica*](1973: Carlos Saura*). Of the nine feature-length films made by Saura during the Franco dictatorship, this is, by far, the most politically controversial, provoking bomb scares by right-wing groups in theaters in Madrid and Barcelona and leading to prohibition of public showings of the film in a number of provinces for fear of repeated violence. The powerful reactions against *Cousin Angelica* came from the fact that the film presented a sympathetic portrayal of the Republicans during the Civil War while apparently mocking the Nationalists. Beyond these external elements, the film is a moving portrayal of a man's enduring memory of the traumas of the Civil War. Although he has reached middle age, he continues to be haunted by the memories of his experiences.

Luis (José Luis López Vázquez*) is a middle-aged bachelor who feels compelled to fulfill his mother's deathbed wish and return her remains, which are in a tomb in Barcelona, to the family crypt in Segovia. Luis has not been to the Castilian city since his childhood when, left at his grandmother's house in the fateful summer of 1936 for part of his summer vacation, he found himself stranded for three years in Francoist territory when the Civil War broke out. Because he had been raised in a Republican family, Luis was tormented by his pro-Nationalist relatives.

When he returns to Segovia, many of his long-festering childhood memories resurface in odd and disconcerting ways. Luis's memories of the past are triggered by sounds, images, words, and places, but when he involuntarily relives them, he confuses his friends and relatives of contemporary Segovia with those from the past. Thus, his childhood sweetheart, his cousin Angelica (played as an adult by Lina Canalejas), seems to be Luis's aunt, while the adult Angelica's daughter, little Angelica (María Clara Fernández de Loaysa) becomes Luis's beloved cousin of 1936. However, throughout these reveries, Luis images himself as the balding middle-aged man of 1973, and he is able to suggest the innocence of little Luis through gestures and facial expressions.

The significance of this curious representational mode is intimately connected to Saura's notion of the historical trauma of the Civil War visited upon the individual psyche. The adult Luis thinks of himself as the little boy of 1936 trapped in the body of a man. This same conflation of past memories with present-day realities plagues his recollection of others, so when he meets the adult Angelica's husband, Anselmo (Fernando Delgado), and begins to recall Angelica's tyrannical father, Luis imagines the old fascist as looking just like Anselmo.

As well as being a clever approximation of the tricks of the human mind, Saura's development of Luis's waking-dream mode also underscores a political theme: the continuity between the fascist roots of contemporary Spain and the positions and attitudes of a number of contemporary Spaniards. The theme of blocked and deformed memory, which is the thematic centerpiece of Cousin Angelica, becomes one of the signature elements of Saura's style in a number of films of the post-Franco period, especially Cría cuervos [Raise Ravens] (1976) and Elisa vida mía [Elisa, My Life]* (1977). It is also part of a fabric of opposition films of the last five years of the Franco dictatorship that includes Basilio Martín Patino's* Canciones para después de una guerra [Songs for after a War]* (1971, 1976), Víctor Erice's* El espíritu de la colmena [Spirit of the Beehive]* (1973), and Ricardo Franco's* Pascual Duarte (1975)*.

BIBLIOGRAPHY
D'Lugo, Marvin. The Films of Carlos Saura: The Practice of Seeing. Princeton, NJ: Princeton University Press, 1991.
Galán, Diego. Venturas y desventuras de La prima Angélica. Valencia: Fernando Torres, 1974.

Raza [Race] (1941: José Luis Sáenz de Heredia*). Based on a script by Francisco Franco himself (under the pseudonym, Jaime de Andrade), Race is generally considered the emblematic expression of the bellicose Francoist cultural ideology during the decade following the Nationalist victory in the Civil War. Its themes are the importance of family, religion, subordination of individuals to the greater national cause, and, finally, the belief in the historical continuity from

Spain's imperial past to the recent Civil War.

Race was an officially commissioned film with Sáenz de Heredia, a first cousin of José Antonio Primo de Rivera (the founder of the Falangist Party), chosen as the director from a group who had submitted treatments of a text authored by Franco. As a quasi-official project, *Race* enjoyed a lavish production budget rare in the devastating immediate postwar period. The production included more than five hundred costumes and fifty different sets.

The plot of the film parallels striking aspects of Franco's life. The central characters, members of the Churruca family, bear a resemblance, albeit greatly romanticized, to Franco's own family. The obvious Manichaean structure of the film attempts to rewrite centuries of Spanish history as a family melodrama in which the good brother is pitted against the bad brother in a struggle to define the true nature of the national community. The three central figures of the plot are the good Churruca brother, José (Alfredo Mayo*); Pedro (José Nieto*), the bad brother; and Jaime (Luis Arroyo), the younger, religious brother who becomes a priest and is killed by Republicans during the Civil War.

The action of *Race* covers a period of roughly forty years, running from the eve of Spain's defeat by the United States in the Spanish American War to the triumph of the Nationalists in the Civil War (1936–1939). This action is divided into three clearly defined sections and an epilogue. The first section establishes the ideological basis of the film's reading of history by presenting naval captain Churruca who, on the eve of Spain's loss of its last imperial possessions in 1898, gives his three children a lesson in the moral roots of family history and patriotism. Churruca goes off to die courageously in Cuba, leaving his wife to care for their three children.

A montage sequence covers the next three decades with the fall of the monarchy and the formation of the Republican government. The children have grown and the animosity between Pedro and José is now sharply delineated as a struggle between patriotic and self-sacrificing values (José) and cynical capitalist deceits that would sell Spain out to its foreign enemies, presumably Russian communists (Pedro). Another montage introduces the contemporary action of the film: the Civil War itself and the parallel tales of the rise to prominence of each brother. We see José risk his life to get an important message across enemy lines. Caught, he is prepared to die heroically before a firing squad. Miraculously saved and brought to the Nationalist zone, he continues the fight. We see the gentle brother, Jaime, executed by ruffian soldiers of the Republic who have no compassion for either defenseless priests or the orphans being cared for by them. Finally, Pedro recognizes the error of his ways and actively betrays the Republican cause—a sign of his Churruca blood and his underlying patriotic feelings.

The film ends with an epilogue in which the victorious Nationalist troops enter Madrid and the film's underlying theme that there is a special race of heroic and patriotic Spaniards is emphasized. *Race* was rereleased in a slightly more cosmetic version in 1950 under the title *El espíritu de una raza* [*The Spirit of a Race*]. Much of the racist, xenophobic dialogue was toned down through dubbing and the focus of the film shifted from the earlier fascistic style to adjust to Cold War geopolitics in which the enemy was perceived not as Republicans but as Communists.

BIBLIOGRAPHY

Gubern, Román. *Raza: un ensueño del General Franco*. Madrid: Ediciones 99, 1977.
Méndez-Leite, Fernando. *Historia del cine español en 100 películas*. Madrid: Jupey, 1975.

***El rey pasmado* [*The Flustered King*] (1991: Imanol Uribe*).** This film marked a change of pace for the Basque filmmaker. It is an adaptation of a contemporary retelling of an apocryphal story of the inexperienced seventeenth-century adolescent monarch, Philip IV (Gabino Diego*), involving a series of comic adventures based on the novel by Torrente Ballester, *Crónica del rey pasmado* [*Chronicle of the Flustered King*]. On the morning of a fateful day, the young king is brought to the house of Marfisa (Laura del Sol*), a courtesan. When he sees her nude he becomes dumbfounded. The beauty and nudity of the young woman leads him to demand that he also see nude his otherwise chaste wife, the queen (Anne Roussel). The rest of the film is a series of complications and plot twists in which the king's advisers struggle to provide him with the desired view of the unwilling queen.

This is an ensemble film with a huge cast that includes, besides Gabino Diego in the title role, Eusebio Poncela* as the King's friend, Peña Andrada; Fernando Fernán-Gómez* as his grand inquisitor; Juan Diego* as the bishop, Padre Villaescusa; and Javier Gurruchaga as the king's valet.

Of the most impressive elements of the film, two are especially worth noting. The lighthearted script, coauthored by Torrente Ballester, mixes historical pageantry with a well-calculated sense of humor hitherto absent from Uribe's political and genre films. As well, the striking re-creation of court life in the Spanish Golden Age is done with an eye for historical accuracy that, unlike recent attempts at historical drama, most notably Carlos Saura's *El Dorado* (1988), does not weigh down the film. A popular commercial success in Spain, *The Flustered King* won a prize for its director at the 1991 Biarritz Film Festival.

BIBLIOGRAPHY

Angulo, Jesús, Carlos F. Heredero, and José Luis Rebordinos (eds.). *El cine de Imanol Uribe: entre el documental y la ficción*. San Sebastián: Filmoteca Vasca, 1994.
Gutiérrez, Begoña, and José Manuel Porquet. *Imanol Uribe*. Huesca: Festival de Cine de Huesca, 1994.

***Los santos inocentes* [*Holy Innocents*] (1984: Mario Camus*).** Following his practice of more than a decade of adapting most of his films from established modern literary classics, Mario Camus, along with coscriptwriters Antonio Larreta and Manuel Matji, built a powerful filmic narrative from the novel by Miguel Delibes, one of Spain's most prestigious contemporary writers. Though much revered in Spain, Delibes is little known outside of his native land, largely owing to his very demanding style that emphasizes the spoken language of his native Castile and the presentation of hermetic and socially marginalized characters.

The story is a linear one developed through Camus's script around a series of fragmented flashbacks. Set in a seemingly timeless 1960s on a country estate in the isolated area of Extremadura in southwestern Spain, the monotonous life of the workers is broken by the arrival of the Marquise (Mary Carrillo*) and her son, "El señorito Iván" (Juan Diego*), a cruel and pompous figure accustomed to getting his way. For the family of one gamekeeper, Paco el Bajo (Shorty Paco), (Alfredo Landa*), the visit only seems to add to his drudgery and to the difficulties of his family, for Iván, a hunting enthusiast, depends upon Paco to guide him in the hunt.

This is, indeed, the story of Paco's family of marginalized Spanish rural workers as told through a series of pointed juxtapositions with the Marquise's family, who represent decadent rural aristocracy. The central moment of the narrative comes when Iván insists that Paco assist him in the hunt even though the worker has broken his ankle. By going with Iván, Paco does irreparable damage to his foot, making it impossible for him to continue with the hunt the following day. Azarías (Francisco Rabal*), Paco's retarded brother-in-law, replaces him in the hunt. But when Iván purposely kills Azarías's pet bird, the retarded old man takes simple vengeance by hanging Iván.

The tragic story of the arrogant abuse of power by the Marquise's family and the shattering effect of Iván's actions on Paco's family forms a poignant tale of class struggle and the traditional backwardness of Spanish society under the old regime. The splendid acting by Alfredo Landa as Paco and Francisco Rabal as Azarías earned them an unprecedented shared award for acting at the 1984 Cannes Film Festival.

BIBLIOGRAPHY
Frugone, Juan Carlos. *Oficio de gente humilde . . . Mario Camus*. Valladolid: Semana de Cine de Valladolid, 1984.

El sol de membrillo [*The Quince-Tree Sun* or *Dream of Light*] (1992: Víctor Erice*). Halfway between a documentary and a fiction film, *The Quince-Tree Sun*, only Víctor Erice's third feature-length film in twenty years, tells the story of the creative struggle of the renowned Spanish painter, Antonio López, to capture on canvas the play of light on the surface of quinces hanging on a tree in the garden of his Madrid home. Originally planned as a single half-hour episode for a Spanish television series, over time the collaboration between Erice and López took on a life of its own. The resulting film presents a complex exploration of the creative struggle of the traditional painter to capture the fleeting natural light of autumn on a living tree.

Erice situates López's story within his own vision of a post-Franco Spain in which the contemplative art of oil painting is violently juxtaposed against a series of contemporary forms of representation: radio, television, photography, even mass-produced reproductions of the works of great masters. While documenting López's struggle, Erice's camera gradually brings in cinema itself as part of the indictment of the displacement of classical modes of representation by the technologies of mechanical reproduction. During the final moments of the film, as López has given up the effort to paint the tree, he narrates a dream of his struggle and the screen shows an image of a movie camera, undaunted by the rain and wind that hampered the artist, now filming the growth and deterioration of the quince fruit.

Filmed ostensibly as a documentary, with intertitles documenting the exact dates of filming, the story line gradually becomes blurred by two alternate emerging fictions. One involves López's wife, the painter María Moreno, who has her husband pose as a reclining figure on a bed. The other details the work of Polish artisans who have come to remodel some rooms in López's house and whose actions are frequently crosscut with López's work on his painting.

The more prominent of these two narrative threads shows María Morena as she paints her husband's motionless body, ambiguously posed as if sleeping or perhaps dead. The spectator is brought to appreciate the circular patterns of life and death that inform the passage of time. The dream sequence ends with the film's final images, those of a juxtaposition between the rotten remains of last year's fruit and the springtime image of a young quince tree awaiting the arrival of the painter.

Though scarcely distributed commercially in Spain, *The Quince-Tree Sun* won a special jury prize at the Cannes Film Festival and the top fiction film award at the subsequent Chicago Film Festival.

BIBLIOGRAPHY
Arocena, Carmen. *Víctor Erice*. Madrid: Cátedra, 1996.
Erlich, Linda. "Interior Gardens: Víctor Erice's *Dream of Light* and the Bodegón Tradition." *Cinema Journal* 34, no. 2 (winter 1995): 22–36.

El sur [*The South*] (1983: Víctor Erice*). Erice's second feature-length film, *The South*, loosely based on a short story by Adelaida García Morales, bears unmistakable visual and narrative similarities to his first film, *El espíritu de la colmena* [*Spirit of the Beehive*] (1973), which was made a full decade earlier. Both are set in rural areas of Castile during distinct moments of the long period of Francoism. Each presents a portrait of a reclusive father who has been emotionally scarred by the Civil War and its cruel aftermath and his problematic relation with his young daughter. Similarly, a major part of each narrative deals with the impact of a particular motion picture in the life of the young girl.

The South is told as a flashback from the apparent point of view of Estrella (Sonsoles Aranguren), a teenage girl, in the autumn of 1957. The narrative begins as Estrella is awakened by a distant gunshot, that of her father's act of suicide. A series of flashbacks ensues covering approximately a decade and detailing the affectionate relation between Estrella, beginning when she was seven or eight, with her father, Agustín (Omero Antonutti), a doctor who has relocated with his family from some place in the "south" and now lives in a quiet country house, "La gaviota" ("The Seagull"). Estrella's recollections focus on two specific periods in the father-daughter relation: her first communion, when her paternal grandmother (Germaine Montero) and the family servant, Milagros (Rafaela Aparicio*), arrived from the south to attend the religious ceremony, and an event approximately seven or eight years later, when Estrella discovered, amidst apparent discord between her parents, that her father had had some intimate relation with a woman in the south named Laura. Laura, Estrella learns, has gone on to a career in movie melodramas.

The discovery of this relation is brought to the surface when one of Laura's films is shown in the town and Estrella finds a paper on which her father had repeatedly written Laura's stage name, Irene Ríos. Father and daughter seem separated by an immense emotional gulf and are thus unable even to talk about the other woman. After Agustín's suicide, Estrella is invited by her grandmother to visit the south. At this point the film ends.

Thematically, *The South* updates certain of the central themes of the earlier *Spirit of the Beehive*, especially the idea of a generation of Spaniards formed in the isolated atmosphere created by the Republican defeat. Erice's film beautifully states that theme in its construction of the solitary Castilian settings. Even in urban scenes, as when Estrella spies her father's motorcycle outside the movie theater, the sense of emptiness of the street, and of the pervasive silence and darkness through which Estrella's world is defined, underscores the weight of Francoist culture on the remembrance of Spaniards. Especially noteworthy in comparing *The South* with Erice's earlier film is the contrast between the powerful, dark evocation of *Spirit of the Beehive* as shot by Luis Cuadrado* and the photography of José Luis Alcaine* in *The South*. While playing with the patterns of shadow and light of the earlier film, Alcaine adds more vivid colors to express the light that guides Estrella's pursuit and evocation of the past.

BIBLIOGRAPHY

Arocena, Carmen. *Víctor Erice*. Madrid: Cátedra, 1996.

Marías, Miguel, and Felipe Vega. "Una conversación con Víctor Erice." *Casablanca*, nos. 31–32 (July–August 1983): 59–70.

Surcos [*Furrows*] (1951: José Antonio Nieves Conde*). This is one of the landmark works in the gradual return of Spanish cinema to some form of social realism in the post–Civil War period. Unlike the vast majority of films that preceded it, *Furrows* attempts to pose a critique of the social as well as economic circumstances of contemporary Spain. The film was obviously inspired by the Italian Neorealist movement and it is replete with location scenes of lower-class street life in Madrid. Yet it was defended by its director and by Spanish critics as being not a Spanish variant of the Neorealist school, but rather a film rooted in a Spanish tradition of Critical Realism found in the fictions of Quevedo in the seventeenth century and Pío Baroja earlier in the twentieth century. Such arguments aside, *Furrows* includes a number of self-conscious citations to Italian Neorealist films, and, like the Italian movement, clearly seeks to pose a scathing critique of the official representations of working-class culture.

The story traces the fortunes of a family of farmers who arrive in Madrid in search of work. The family patriarch (José Prada) fails first in a factory job, then as a street vendor, and is humiliated by his wife (María Francés). Their daughter, Tonia (Marisa de Leza), similarly fails as a theatrical singer and becomes the companion of the corrupt Don Roque, "El Chamberlain" (Félix Dafauce), a sinister underworld figure. A similar fate awaits each of the sons, which completes the image of the dissolution of the family by the forces of industrial modernization.

One of the regressive images that emerge from this narrative is that of the city as a place where the traditional male is destroyed and where females come to assume a greater social prominence. In order to stem this collapse of the family, the father rises up against his wife and orders the family to return to the provinces, where at least they will be able to partake of the natural order of things. In a version of the film cut by the censors, Tonia rejects this plan and jumps off the train before it returns to the provinces.

Furrows is clearly marked by conceptual ambiguity as a film. Visually and stylistically, it signals the opening up of a critical discourse on contemporary society in Spanish film. The scenes of Madrid streets as well as the tenement in which the family lives are striking models of a visual representation that would have an impact on the way younger filmmakers would depict urban life over the next decade. At the same time, the film's conservative narrative and theme, with its polarized connotations related to urban and rural lifestyles, the roles of men and women, and the devastating power of the city on the family all partake of the regressive ideology of the Francoist regime.

When it was released, *Furrows* received a designation as a film of "national interest," qualifying it for government subsidies. The designation angered those who objected to the film's portrayal of the underside of Spanish life and eventually led to the removal José María García Escudero from the Ministry of Information's film section, as he had defended the film's special status.

BIBLIOGRAPHY
Kinder, Marsha. *Blood Cinema: The Reconstruction of National Identity in Spain.* Berkeley: University of California Press, 1993.
Méndez-Leite, Fernando. *Historia del cine español en 100 películas.* Madrid: Jupey, 1975.

Tasio **(1983: Montxo Armendáriz*).** Along with the early works of Imanol Uribe*, Montxo Armendáriz's first feature-length film is one of the most striking examples of Basque regional cinema. Based on the life of a charcoal-pit worker from a rural area of Navarre, whom Armendáriz met while shooting a documentary short, the film appears to be a cross between ethnographic documentary and fictional cinema, creating a lyrical visual and narrative style that incorporates the landscape of the Basque country as graphic embodiment of the spirit of Basqueness.

The story covers approximately fifty years in the life of Tasio, a prototypical Basque: his world as a child of about eight; his youth and marriage to Paulina (Amaia Lasa); the birth of their child; his wife's death; finally, his old age as he continues to tend his charcoal mound even as his daughter, now a young woman of about eighteen, tells him she is going off to work in the city of Vitoria.

A number of narrational elements are quite distinctive in the film. There is very little dialogue; much of the narrative is conveyed through the stunning images of the different stages of Tasio's life from childhood to old age as shot by José Luis Alcaine.* The presence of different actors representing three different ages of Tasio's life—Garikoitz Medigutxia as a small child, Isidro Solano as an adolescent, and Patxi Bisquert as the adult Tasio—help intensify the sense of passing time.

This sensation of growth and change is counterbalanced by the aura of an eternal, edenic world in the the rural Basque areas. Although a few small cues, such as the presence of an automobile, signal a movement of the characters through time, the community's sense of conservative tradition counteracts this historical progression. At the end of the film, when the daughter announces her departure, Tasio says, "*No me muevo,*" ("I will not move"), suggesting the constancy of the position. Yet, as an ironic twist, the very next moment he offers a drink to his old enemy, the guard (Paco Sagarzazu), who for years has pursued Tasio as a poacher. This ambivalent dynamic of movement and status ultimately provides a thematic focus to the film in that the two opposing currents defining rural life in the Basque country underscore the tension between tradition and modernity within modern Basque culture as well. *Tasio* was the first of four Armendáriz feature-length films produced by Elías Querejeta.* It won the grand prize at the Biarritz Film Festival in 1984.

BIBLIOGRAPHY
Pérez Manrique, José María. *Montxo Armendáriz: imagen y narración de libertad.* Burgos: Encuentro Internacional de Cine de Burgos, 1993.

La tía Tula [Aunt Tula] (1964: **Miguel Picazo***). *Aunt Tula* is the debut film of Miguel Picazo. During the 1960s, the film was considered one of the clearest indications of the advent of a New Spanish Cinema as well as the arrival on the scene of a fresh, new talent. Unlike many of the other films promoted by special governmental subsidies as part of the New Spanish Cinema, *Aunt Tula* was to be well received by the general Spanish audience and critics alike, winning the prestigous award for best direction at the 1964 San Sebastián Film Festival.

The film is a loose adaptation and update of the novel of the same title by the renowned writer, Miguel de Unamuno. In the original work, the story of the provincial spinster who takes charge of the upbringing of her dead sister's children was the basis for a philosophical inquiry into the nature of maternity and immortality through procreation. In the Picazo version, the emphases change in order to focus on the repressive environment of the much revered provincial life under the Franco dictatorship, and the parallel sexual repression that was also synonymous with the regime's social agenda. Ironically, although supported by the government's film office and defended by its director, José María García Escudero, the film was subject to censorial cuts precisely in the sections that dealt with the theme of repressed sexuality. This led Picazo to claim his work had been mutilated by government censors.

Tula (Aurora Bautista*), the spinster of the tale, assumes responsibility for the care of her deceased sister Rosa's children. Tula's brother-in-law, Ramiro (Carlos Estrada), appears sexually drawn to his sister-in-law, but is frustrated by Tula's inflexible rectitude. She has turned down one marriage offer in the village in order to care for her new "family" and eventually turns down Ramiro's offer of marriage as well, defying the advice of her local priest. On a family outing, Ramiro seduces the maid, Juanita, who becomes pregnant with his child. He is forced to marry the girl and take his children to live with the them, thus depriving Tula of her family. This plot twist reinforces Picazo's theme of the self-mutilating nature of sexual repression in Spanish culture, as Tula's own moral dictates precipitate her separation from the children she loves and thus deny her even a chaste form of maternity.

Especially noteworthy is the extraordinary photography by Juan Julio Baena* and the striking editing that suggests a stylistic coincidence with French New Wave films. Aurora Bautista, who plays an emotionally taut Tula, was an actress who had become a major star in a series of patriotic epics under the direction of Juan de Orduña* in the late 1940s. Though she continued to appear in films throughout the 1950s and early 1960s, her performance in *Aunt Tula* brough her new critical attention, including a best actress award from the Sindicato Nacional de Espectáculos.

BIBLIOGRAPHY

Castro, Antonio. *El cine español en el banquillo*. Valencia: Fernando Torres, 1974.
Higginbotham, Virginia. *Spanish Film under Franco*. Austin: University of Texas Press, 1988.

***Tierra sin pan** [**Land without Bread**]* **(1932: Luis Buñuel*).** The first film made by Luis Buñuel in Spain is also his only documentary. Shot after Buñuel disengaged himself from the Surrealist circle in Paris and returned to Madrid, *Land without Bread* is generally viewed by film historians as a complete break from Buñuel's two earlier surrealist works made in collaboration with Salvador Dalí, *Le Chien Andalou* [*The Andalusian Dog*] (1928) and *L'Age d'Or* [*The Age of Gold*] (1930).

While apparing devoid of the visual tricks that characterized his two earlier works, a closer examination of the visual/narrational structure of the film reveals a number of basic links between *Land without Bread* and its surrealist antecedents. The most conspicuous of these is the radical juxtaposition between sound and image. Although shot without a sound track, with a musical background score and voice-over commentary only added later, the juxtaposition between Brahms' Fourth Symphony and some of the horrific scenes of social backwardness hark back to the iconoclastic style of the two earlier films.

Inspired by a scientific treatise by Maurice Legendre on the cultural geography of the region of Las Hurdes in the northwest Spanish province of Salamanca, the modest film was financed by Buñuel's anarchist friend, Ramón Acín. In the spring of 1932, accompanied by a small technical crew, Buñuel made the harsh trip through nearly all of the fifty-two villages of the Hurdano region and filmed scenes that reflected the social backwardness and economic marginalization of a population that dated back to the original expulsion of Jews from fifteenth-century Spain. In particular, Buñuel contrasts scenes of economic exploitation and social abandonment with the prosperity of the town of La Alberca, only some sixty miles from the university town of Salamanca.

One of the most striking structural features of *Land without Bread* is Buñuel's formulation of his material as a parody of film travelogues, shifting from what appears at times to be an example of serious ethnographic film to that of fluffy touristic cinema. His objective is obviously to mock his audience's assumed dispassionate objectivity to the world they are brought to see.

The reaction of the Spanish Republican government to the public screening of the film was so negative that it was officially banned, and it was the first of many of Buñuel's films to suffer that fate in his native country.

BIBLIOGRAPHY
Aranda, J. Francisco. *Luis Buñuel: biografía crítica.* Barcelona: Editorial Lumen, 1969.
Sánchez Vidal, Agustín. *Luis Buñuel: obra cinematográfica.* Madrid: Ediciones JC, 1984.

Tigres de papel [Paper Tigers] (1977: Fernando Colomo*). Colomo's first feature-length film is one of the key cinematic works of the late 1970s. Set in the Madrid of the period just before the general elections of 1978, the film focuses on three characters who reflect the progressive political and cultural values of Spain during the transition to democracy. Carmen (Carmen Maura*), a young woman separated from her liberal husband, Juan (Joaquín Hinojosa*), has met Alberto (Miguel Arribas) while touring Italy. Back in Madrid they enter into an easy relationship as Carmen introduces Alberto to Juan. The loose plot traces the interaction among the three as they attend a political rally, discuss philosophical issues including love and liberty, and expose their respective emotional and sexual needs.

Although giving the appearance of a somewhat open and rambling narrative, the film gradually establishes its own dynamic as a focus on the interplay of appearances and illusions among the three exemplary characters. Juan, who likes to mouth his liberal political beliefs, is shown to be a hypocrite when he hides as Carmen and Alberto are beaten by right-wing thugs when they post political billboards. Carmen, who appears to be a sexually free spirit, resists making love with Alberto, and Alberto shows himself to be merely an opportunist, more interested in keeping a mistress than in developing a relationship with Carmen.

Colomo's bittersweet comedy is formally and conceptually inspired by the cerebral style of Eric Rohmer's films, especially *Ma Nuit chez Maud* [*My Night at Maud's*] (1969), with its insistence on sequence shots and intricate intellectual dialogues. Shot with direct sound, a rarity for Spanish films of this period, the open style and focus on the small crises of young urban progressives helped establish the *Comedia Madrileña*, "New Madrid Comedy" genre, of the late 1970s and 1980s, of which Colomo was one of the chief proponents.

BIBLIOGRAPHY

Caparrós-Lera, José María. *El cine español de la democracia: de la muerte de Franco al "cambio" socialista (1975–1989)*. Barcelona: Anthropos, 1992.

Hopewell, John. *Out of the Past: Spanish Cinema after Franco*. London: BFI Books, 1986.

Monterde, José Enrique. *Veinte años de cine español (1973–1992): un cine bajo la paradoja*. Barcelona: Paidós, 1993.

***Tristana* (1970: Luis Buñuel*).** Buñuel's third film shot in Spain, *Tristana* is also his second film made during the Franco dictatorship. The story is based on a minor novel of the same title by the famed nineteenth-century Spanish novelist, Benito Pérez Galdós. Buñuel had previously directed an adaptation of another Galdós novel, *Nazarín*, in Mexico in 1958. With the help of coscriptwriter Julio Alejandro, he transferred the action from Galdós's original late nineteenth-century Madrid to the Toledo of the 1920s, a location that not only captures the antiquated spirit of Galdós's vision of Spanish society, but also enables Buñuel to underscore one of his implicit political themes: the very conservative nature of Spanish life.

The aging "Don Juan," Don Lope (Fernando Rey*), becomes the guardian for his young orphaned niece, Tristana (Catherine Deneuve), only to fall passionately in love with her and to seduce her. In his ambivalent relation with Tristana, Lope displays two sides of his personality: One side is responsible for filling Tristana's mind with dreams of self-improvement for women through education and a disdain for the Catholic church and marriage; the other side surfaces as a jealous and tyrannical lover. Tristana remains submissive to Lope's will until, on an innocent stroll with her maid, Saturna (Lola Gaos*), she meets the young painter, Horacio (Franco Nero), with whom she falls in love at first sight.

She abandons Lope and runs off with Horacio only to have the painter return her to Lope's house several years later when she has been stricken by a malignancy on her leg. Embittered by Horacio's willingness to abandon her, Tristana submits to the amputation of her leg and remains in Lope's house.

Having now rejected her younger lover, she sets about tyrannizing the aging Lope. She eventually agrees to marry Lope, but during his protracted illness, she lets him die, feigning that she has called the doctor.

Tristana, often viewed by critics as Buñuel's most complex and profound work, is constructed around the interweaving of a number of thematic and formal threads. It is not only a denunciation of the social backwardness of Spanish society, but also an attack on the hypocrisy of liberal thinkers who adjust their beliefs to suit their own desires. Also, Buñuel's characterization of the struggle of the female for emancipation and equality is barbed, revealing how Tristana's dream of freedom has become a snare in which she ends up entrapped by her own bitterness and mutilated in physical, sexual, and, ultimately, moral terms. Two particularly striking performances in the film are those of Fernando Rey, one of Buñuel's preferred Spanish actors, who plays a lead in all three of Buñuel's Spanish fictional films; and Lola Gaos as Saturna, the maid.

BIBLIOGRAPHY

Colina, José de la, and Tomás Pérez Turrent. *Luis Buñuel: prohibido asomarse al interior*. Mexico: Joaquín Mortiz, 1986.

Kinder, Marsha. *Blood Cinema: The Reconstruction of National Identity in Spain*. Berkeley: University of California Press, 1993.

El último cuplé [The Last Song] **(1956: Juan de Orduña*).** This last major production by the CIFESA studios is the most commercially successful of the thirty-eight films directed by Juan de Orduña. It is also the pivotal work that changed the career of the film's star, Sara Montiel*, converting her into one of the very few true movie legends in Spanish cinema. Though both Orduña and Montiel had worked together earlier in *Locura de amor [The Madness of Love]** (1948), it was not until this particular combination of melodramatic narrative and nostalgia for the popular Spanish ballad, the *cuplé*, that the talents of director and star came together with one of the most resounding successes of Spanish film history. The film, which opened in May of 1957, remained in its initial Madrid run for over a year, playing to packed houses. A number of the more than one dozen songs sung by Montiel became popular hits in their own right, adding to the general appeal of the film with Spanish audiences.

Spanish critics and film historians have tried to understand the curious success of the film, especially since it lacks strikingly innovative techniques or materials and its principals, including its director, were already well-known to Spanish audiences. It may well be that the film's treatment of the life of a fictitious musical hall singer had just enough suggestive appeal in a period of rigid censorship to add a special charge. Also, Sara Montiel's sensual delivery of a number of the songs, replete with moist and open lips and other provocative gestures, added a specific sexual subtext to the film that was all but unknown in Spanish cinema of the previous decade and a half. To these suppositions must be added Orduña's very unique talent as an experienced architect of immensely popular melodramas as evidenced by his earlier CIFESA works, *The Madness of*

Love (1948), *Agustina de Aragón* (1950), and *Pequeñeces* [*Trifles*] (1950).

The story is a very simple one but told through Orduña's characteristic penchant for flashback. It begins sometime in the 1950s when María Luján (Sara Montiel) is performing in a lower-class musical hall in Barcelona. She is visited by a group of friends, including Juan Contreras (Armando Calvo*), María's former manager and ex-lover. He recalls her past greatness and offers to arrange her professional comeback. From there the story shifts to the retelling of María's life: Juan's discovery of María in a music hall during the early decades of the century, his effort to seduce her, the prompting by her aunt and guardian, Tía Paca (Matilde Muñoz Sampedro), and María's unwilling separation from her true love, Cándido, a humble watchmaker (José Moreno) who gives up María for the sake of her career.

The story follows Maria's rise to national and international fame and success under Juan's tutelage until their breakup some time in the 1920s when she meets Pepe (Enrique Vera), an aspiring bullfighter. Juan is persuaded to support Pepe's career even though he knows he has lost María. When Pepe is killed in the bullring, María becomes distraught and falls ill. She is so weakened that she can no longer perform on stage. She abandons Spain, taking to drink and gambling, until she reaches the bottom of her career. It is at this point that Juan discovers her in Barcelona and organizes her comeback. On the night of her performance, she is warmly received but falls ill again and quickly dies of an apparent heart attack. Juan must appear on stage to the exultant audience to tell them that they have just heard María's "*último cuplé,*" her last song.

The narrative is punctuated with well over a dozen ballads, some of which are, in fact, authentic songs of the periods in which they are sung in the film. Throughout many of these musical interludes, María's song corresponds to details of her life or her emotional state, thus reinforcing the highly melodramatic nature of the film's construction and intensifying audience appeal. One of the most striking of these is "El relicario ["The Shrine"], the song María sings during her performance shortly after Pepe's death. She cannot finish the song and must be taken off stage. It is this kind of dramatic overstatement in both story and staging that lends particular emotional appeal both to Montiel's performance and to the film as a whole.

BIBLIOGRAPHY

Galán, Diego. "Aquel cine de los 50." In *Cine español años 50:* 14–21. Vol. 2 of *Tiempos de Cine Español*. San Sebastián: Ayuntamiento de San Sebastián, N.D.

Méndez-Leite, Fernando. *Historia del cine español en 100 películas*. Madrid: Jupey, 1975.

***Los últimos de Filipinas** [**Martyrs of the Philippines**] (1945: Antonio Román*).*
One of the most commercially successful of the war genre films of the 1940s, this dramatization of bizarre events that occurred during the final days of the Philippine campaign of the War of 1898 clearly held a patriotic message of persistence against all odds for Spanish audiences of the post–Civil War period.

Made at the time of the final Axis defeat and the increased political and economic isolation of Spain, the film concerns a group of Spanish soldiers during the insurrections of 1898 who took refuge in the Baler fortress in the Philippines and were able to hold out against continual bombardment for 337 days, a full five months after the Spanish capitulation to the rebels. The obvious parallels between the narrative of valiant defiance by Spanish soldiers against superior forces and Spain's isolation after the axis defeat in 1945 was clearly one of the principal selling points of the film among Spanish audiences.

Román's script traces the final days of the garrison commander, Captain Las Morenas (José Nieto*), whose strategy of resistance to the local Tagalog uprising is to have his men take refuge in the tiny fort. When Las Morenas succumbs to fever, he is replaced by the equally stalwart Lieutenant Martín Cerezo (Armando Calvo*), who so embodies the Spanish bellicose virtue of resistance until death that he even refuses to accept the various proofs given him that the Spanish government has capitulated. Instead, he and his men hold on for five months after the war's end. These two figures, played with the kind of exaggerated, almost plastic acting that the Román's histrionic script demands, are set off against a number of humanizing elements in the film. The most noteworthy of these include the appearance of Manolo Morán*, the famed comic actor, as Pedro Vila, the source of humorous diversion among the other soldiers; as well, there is a romantic subplot involving a young recruit played by Fernando Rey* who is smitten with Tala, a Tagalog woman (Nani Fernández), the only female character in the entire cast.

One of the more enduring aspects of the film, in fact, is the song, "Yo te diré" ("I Will Tell You") sung by Fernández to entertain the soldiers, which later became a popular hit and was used prominently by Basilio Martín Patino* in his compilation documentary, *Canciones para después de una guerra* [*Songs for after a War*]* (1971, 1976).

BIBLIOGRAPHY
García Fernández, Emilio C. *Historia ilustrada del cine español*. Barcelona: Planeta, 1985.
Méndez-Leite, Fernando. *Historia del cine español en 100 películas*. Madrid: Jupey, 1975.

Vacas [*Cows*] (1992: Julio Medem*). Julio Medem's first feature-length film was much praised for the startlingly poetic historical vision it presented of Basque culture. Also, the extraordinary complexity of its narrational structure daringly treated a somewhat traditional historical subject matter in an especially striking and original way. Through the structuring device of four separate stories within which there is a recurrence of characters from two rural Basque families, *Cows* recounts both family and regional history from the time of the second Carlist war in the late nineteenth century up to the start of the Civil War in 1936. While focusing on this fairly predictable historical ordering, Medem has given a unique twist to his film by also recounting three generations of cows—the film's title. Such an eccentric perspective serves, on the one hand, to underscore a certain note of rural tranquility in terms of individual and community experiences, and on the other, to juxtapose these values surrealistically with the scenes of violence that grip the families, communities and region over nearly half a century.

Indeed, the film is embued with a strong poetic quality that is emphasized through the frequent linking of animals with humans in a number of sequences and the use of eccentric camera angles to frame various actions. The talented cast includes Carmelo Gómez,* Emma Suárez,* Ana Torrent* and Manuel Blasco. *Cows* was shown to a very warm reception at the 1992 Berlin Film Festival, and won the Gold First Prize at the Tokyo Film Festival. It also won an award from the British Film Institute in the category of first films.

BIBLIOGRAPHY
César, Samuel R. "*Vacas* de Julio Medem." *Dirigido Por*, no. 201 (April 1992): 81-82.

La verbena de la Paloma [Paloma Fair] (1935: Benito Perojo*). Considered by film historians to be one of the major artistic achievements of the early sound period in Spanish cinema, *Paloma Fair* was opulently produced by CIFESA, the undisputed Spanish prestige film studio of the 1930s. The film is an adaptation of the popular Spanish *zarzuela* of the same name, which had been produced as a silent film in 1921 by José Buchs*.

The story follows fairly faithfully the details of the well-known musical. Set in Madrid on a single day, August 15, 1893, the celebration of the day of the *Virgen de la Paloma*, "Virgin of the Dove," the action focuses on the travails of a young couple who are obviously in love: Julián (Roberto Rey), a printer's assistant, and Susana (Raquel Rodrigo), a seamstress. Julián is extremely jealous of the overtures any other man makes to his beloved. For her part, Susana wants to goad Julián, so, following the advice of her aunt, Señá Antonia (Dolores Cortés), she agrees to attend the *verbena* with the wealthy old pharmacist, Don Hilarión (Miguel Ligero*), accompanied by her sister, Casta (Charito Leonis). The pharmacist is delighted but can't decide which of the two girls he prefers, the brunette Susana or her blonde sister Casta. When Julián spies Susana in a horse-drawn carriage with a man whose face he cannot see, he becomes infuriated. He goes to the *verbena* with his godmother, Señá Rita, who tries to get Julián to stop thinking about Susana. Predictably, problems arise at the street fair and Julián is arrested. Everything works out when the young man is released and reunited with Susana.

Paloma Fair is notable for its lavish sets, which reconstruct end-of-the-century Madrid street scenes in spectacular detail. Also, smooth camera work effectively masks the fact that all but the opening sequence was filmed within a studio. Particularly noteworthy in this regard is the opening musical number that cuts between exteriors and the interior of a horse-drawn tram as it passes through the streets. The excellent editing of the scene highlights the technical polish that pre–Civil War productions had achieved. A similarly elaborate musical number showing how the various characters spend the hours just prior to the festivities reveals similar resourcefulness in both filming and editing. Though rooted in very local folkloric tradition, *Paloma Fair* reveals Perojo's technical virtuosity as a director. Having worked earlier in the decade in film studios in Paris, Berlin, and Hollywood, his conception of the staging of this film suggests a sophistication rivaling international productions of the period.

Especially noteworthy in the cast are the female characters—Raquel Rodrigo, Charito Leonis, and Dolores Cortés—each of whom does a masterful job in underscoring the comic features that define their respective characters. Similarly, Miguel Ligero in the role of Don Hilarión is often singled out by critics as one of the most richly achieved characters in the film. In 1962, Benito Perojo produced a highly successful remake of *Paloma Fair* directed by José Luis Sáenz de Heredia* that starred the same actor, Miguel Ligero, in the role of the decrepit pharmacist, Don Hilarión.

BIBLIOGRAPHY
Caparrós-Lera, José María. *Arte y política en el cine de la República (1931–1939)*. Barcelona: Ediciones 7 1/2, 1981.
Gubern, Román. *Benito Perojo: pionerismo y supervivencia*. Madrid: Filmoteca Española, 1994.

La verdad sobre el caso Savolta [*The Truth about the Savolta Case*] (1980: Antonio Drove*). This daring political film of the early post-Franco years is loosely based on the popular historical novel of the same title by Eduardo Mendoza. Unlike other films of the period that sought to engage their audiences in reflections on the nature of contemporary political tensions, Drove's film chooses a complex historical dramatization as his vehicle. The film details a corruption scandal and cover-up in Barcelona in 1917 involving workers' grievances and their political implications.

Savolta (Omero Antonutti) is a factory owner whose partner, Claudeu (Ettore Manni), is not against using violence to thwart workers' strikes. When an anarchist worker is murdered, Savolta and partner claim innocence, but a journalist, Domingo "Pajarito" de Soto (José Luis López Vázquez*), publishes an underground pamphlet denouncing the Savolta connection with the murder. In his investigations, Domingo discovers that the Savolta company is involved in illegal and clandestine trade in international arms. He convinces the workers to hold off their general strike in the hopes of pressuring Savolta with exposure if he does not meet the workers' demands. Savolta ignores the pressure and then is found murdered. The anarchists are blamed for his death as an act of retaliation. The film thus ends with the thwarting of the workers movement in Barcelona.

A taut historical drama, the film seeks to enter a larger arena of political discourse and historical revision by proposing a correspondence between the docudrama about workers' grievances and managerial duplicity and the subsequent rise of Spanish fascism. As such, the message seems to have had a particular poignancy for a contemporary Spanish audience in 1980 as they viewed the forces of repression at work during the early and uncertain stages of the Spanish transition toward democracy.

The intense quality of the acting, most notably López Vázquez's performance, as well as the finely crafted script contributed to making this a major critical success of the early transition period. Before making *Savolta*, Antonio Drove's work as a director of feature-length films was restricted to the so-called *tercera vía* or "Third Route" cinema, films that attempted to pose topical social themes for a wide audience. Unlike those earlier, uneven films, *Savolta* appears to be both the consummate work of a film author and a film of popular appeal.

BIBLIOGRAPHY
Hopewell, John. *Out of the Past: Spanish Cinema after Franco*. London: BFI Books, 1986.

El verdugo [*The Executioner*] (1963: Luis García Berlanga*). Following the splendid *Plácido* (1961)*, the creative team of Berlanga and scriptwriter Rafael Azcona* made this equally black comedy of Spanish life and customs under the dictatorship. Though the film is generally seen within the narrow confines of a biting attack on capital punishment, it is also an insightful but bitter look at the discrepancy between the static values of the past in Spanish culture and the intensifying changes of contemporary European culture provides much of the film's scathing black humor.

The story involves the struggles of José Luis (Nino Manfredi), a grave digger and funeral parlor employee, who makes the acquaintance of a state executioner, Amadeo, comically portrayed by José Isbert.* José Luis is obsessed with the idea of going to Germany as a guest worker and learning a productive trade as a mechanic. His plan is thwarted when he meets Amadeo's daughter, Carmen (Emma Penella*), who, like José Luis, is slightly past her prime. She is unable to find a suitable marriage partner because of her father's profession. José Luis laments to her that girls are also turned off by his profession. When the two are discovered by Amadeo to have been having sexual relations, the father is duly outraged. When Carmen learns she is pregnant, José Luis promises to marry her, but the problem arises as to where the couple will live, once married.

Through Amadeo's position as a state employee, he can obtain a modern apartment, the kind of cheap high-rise flat that the Franco regime ordered constructed in the early 1960s to relieve the decade's long housing shortage in major cities. In order to qualify for the apartment, however, Amadeo must first resign his position and maneuver the situation so that his son-in-law replaces him. Despite José Luis's resistance to the distasteful job of executioner, he is cajoled into accepting the plan.

The scene then shifts to several years later when the child has arrived and the family, including father-in-law, is living in the new apartment. José Luis receives his first official certified letter calling him to perform an execution in the resort city of Palma de Mallorca. The final portion of the film chronicles José Luis's comic acceptance of his new job.

Berlanga's biting denunciation of the inhumanity of Spanish capital punishment is, of course, the centerpiece of the film, a tour de force of almost literal gallows humor. Also noteworthy is the way in which the brilliant Azcona script situates that blistering attack in the equally grim landscape of working-class Spain, where the material questions of housing and economic improvement influence the social ethics of the members of the executioner's family. At the beginning of the film, Amadeo laments the changing times and the lack of respect his profession now receives. He thus initiates a critical discourse around the contradictory nature of Spanish culture in the 1960s, which is torn between the repressive institutions of the past, such as garrote, and the contemporary energy of new generations thwarted in their efforts to realize a different vision of Spain. Manfredi's José Luis is a brilliant expression of that defeated optimism.

The excellent camera work by Tonino Delli Colli also deserves mention as it captures the continuously changing but persistently confining landscapes of a real Spain that reminds José Luis of both his aspirations and his confinement. That particular quality is perhaps best crystallized in the scene in which José Luis, Carmen, and Amadeo come to survey their dream apartment in a structure that is no more than a skeleton of a building and end up fighting with another family over this imagined space. The film won the Critics' Award at the 1963 Venice Film Festival.

BIBLIOGRAPHY
Frugone, Juan Carlos. *Rafael Azcona: atrapados por la vida.* Valladolid: 32 Semana de Cine de Valladolid, 1987.
Hernández-Les, Juan, and Manuel Hidalgo. *El último austro-húngaro: conversaciones con Berlanga.* Barcelona: Editorial Anagrama, 1981.

Vida en sombras [*Life in the Shadows*] **(1948: Lorenzo Llobet-Gracia*).** The only film by this Catalan film aficionado turned director was completed in 1948, but its commercial release was delayed nearly five years. Ignored by the critics and audiences of the period, the film disappeared, only to be discovered some three decades later when it underwent a meticulous reconstruction by the Filmoteca Española. *Life in the Shadows* has since come to be recognized as one of the most aesthetically sophisticated Spanish films of the pre-1950 period.

The reasons for the film's initial commercial failure and its long disappearance are easy to understand in light of the period in which it was made. An eccentrically self-conscious film about filmmaking, made by an unknown director, set in the Barcelona of the Spanish Republic and early post–Civil War period, was bound to be less than pleasing to the Spanish censors. A low distribution classification further delayed the film's release until 1953. Even then, it was shown only in a second-run house during the slow summer months. When finally rediscovered by a Catalan cine-club years later, neither the film nor its director were known except by a minority of aficionados.

The story line of *Life in the Shadows* traces the life of Carlos Durán (Fernando Fernán-Gómez*) from his birth during a carnival presentation of Lumière Brothers shorts in turn-of-the-century Barcelona through his adolescent fascination and even passion for the cinema. As a young man, Carlos becomes a documentary newsreel cameraman and marries his childhood sweetheart, Ana (María Dolores Pradera). All seems ideal for the couple as they await the birth of their first child. But on the very day that the military insurrection against the Republic breaks out, Carlos is called to shoot footage of fighting in the streets of Barcelona. When he returns to the couple's apartment, he discovers that Ana has been killed by a stray bullet. Blaming his own dedication to filmmaking for his wife's death, he vows never to have anything to do with cinema again.

The film then cuts to some seven years later, after the Nationalist victory over the Republic. Carlos is now living in a boardinghouse in Barcelona, the window of his room looking across to the illuminated marquee of a movie theater where Hitchcock's *Rebecca* is playing. Urged by the boardinghouse owner's daughter, Clara (Isabel de Pomés), to accompany her to the movie, he at first refuses but eventually relents. Once in the darkness of the theater, Carlos succumbs to his old passion for cinema. He returns to his room and looks at old movies of Ana and himself, and he becomes determined to return to cinema. The film ends with the opening shots of the film Carlos has made, *Life in the Shadows*, the story of his own life, in effect, the film we are viewing.

The narrative of *Life in The Shadows* is explicitly constructed to repeat the plot of *Rebecca* in which the second Mrs. de Winters (Joan Fontaine), attempts to get her husband, Max (Laurence Olivier), to stop blaming himself for his wife's death. In Llobet's film, Clara assumes the Fontaine role, pushing Carlos to move beyond his past sense of guilt. This particular aspect of the film is especially signficant in that it transforms the art-versus-life motif of the Hitchcock plot into a social message for a Spanish audience, emphasizing the need to move beyond the self-recriminations of recent national history. In a broader context, however, *Life in the Shadows* is significant as being perhaps the first Spanish film of the post–Civil War period to actively seek to relate Spanish cultural experience—here embodied by the artistic potential of cinema—to the world outside of Spain.

BIBLIOGRAPHY

Kinder, Marsha. *Blood Cinema: The Reconstruction of National Identity in Spain.* Berkeley: University of California Press, 1993.

Méndez-Leite, Fernando. *Historia del cine español en 100 películas.* Madrid: Jupey, 1975.

La vida por delante [*Your Life before You*] (1958: Fernando Fernán-Gómez*). This is Fernán-Gómez's third attempt at an independent film, and commercially as well as cinematically it is his most successful effort up to this point in his career. It is inspired in obvious ways by the earlier Juan Antonio Bardem*–Luis

García Berlanga* film, *Esa pareja feliz* [*That Happy Couple*]* (1951), in which Fernán-Gómez played the male lead. Like that earlier film, this one presents the problems of a young couple starting out married life in the Madrid of the 1950s. *Your Life before You* picks up on the absurdity of the housing shortage by developing a mise-en-scène in which the couple's tiny apartment becomes a continual source of humor. Whenever Antonio (Fernán-Gómez) opens the curtains to his living-room window, he encounters his neighbors from the building across the way seated at their dining room table, ready to comment on any of the problems of Antonio or his wife, Josefina (Analía Gadé).

Your Life before You works as a beguiling series of episodic anecdotes that capture the bittersweet life of a professional couple in the first year of marriage. Antonio is an unemployed lawyer who takes on a variety of incongruous jobs (vacuum cleaner salesman, movie extra, night club master of ceremonies), until he is at last able to begin his own modest law practice. Josefina is a psychologist, with a particular knack for hypnotizing her patients. She proves to be more successful and astute than her husband. Indeed, among the interesting aspects of Spanish life documented by the film is the emerging professional role of women in Spain in the 1950s and the ways in which female superiority is portrayed.

Especially noteworthy is the film's pattern of narration. From the very start, Antonio addresses the camera directly and speaks to the audience. This device, more common in theater than film (a notable exception in Spain was Sáenz de Heredia's *El destino se disculpa* [*Destiny Apologizes*] [1945]), adds a dimension of humor and camaraderie between audience and character. This is particularly striking in the sequence in which Josefina is involved in a car accident, and a group of characters must retell their version of the accident. Each telling combines voice-over with images that play with the representation of the action from distinctive points of view. The most memorable is that of the only neutral eyewitness, played by José Isbert* in a brief but brilliant cameo, in which he suffers from an extreme stutter and thus produces a comic version of events the humor of which is built around his repetitions of words.

The film was extremely well-received upon its release, both by critics and the general audience. It led to a sequel, *La vida alrededor* [*Your Life around You*] (1959), which encountered numerous problems with the censors and was less favorably received by both critics and the Spanish audience.

BIBLIOGRAPHY
Angulo, Jesús, and Francisco Llinás (eds.). *Fernando Fernán-Gómez: el hombre que quiso ser Jackie Cooper.* San Sebastián: Ayuntamiento de San Sebastián, 1993.
Hidalgo, Manuel. *Fernando Fernán-Gómez.* Huelva: Festival de Cine Iberoamericano, 1981.

La vieja memoria [***The Old Memory***] **(1977: Jaime Camino*).** This film is Camino's third effort to explore the impact of the Civil War on contemporary Spanish consciousness. Working in a documentary format after the fictional narratives of *España, otra vez* [*Spain, Again*] (1968) and *Las largas vacaciones* del '36 [*The Long Summer Vacation of '36*] (1975), Camino still uses certain distinctive techniques of fiction-film editing to advance his thesis. At first the film appears to be simply a series of interviews shot between 1974 and 1976 with participants who were involved in both the Republican and the Nationalist side of the conflict. These include Dolores Ibarruri, "La Pasionaria," Federica Montseny, and Enrique Lister on the Republican side; David Jato, Raimundo Fernández Cuenca, and José María Gil Robles on the Nationalist side.

The interviews are, in turn, punctuated by newsreel footage of the period that is edited, as if to illustrate certain of the reminiscences of the participants. An equal number of supporters of the left and the right are presented, since it is not really Camino's objective to restage the ideological conflict that fueled the war and its aftermath. Rather, the filmmaker is interested in the fragility of memory that has kept those ideological passions alive some four decades later. To promote that theme, the audience is at times shown newsreel footage that blatantly contradicts the memories stated by individuals, or, more commonly, what appears to be the reaction shots of some participants as they hear the memories of others. In fact, most of the interviews were shot individually and later edited to simulate these diverging opinions, thereby underscoring the vitality of the rancors that continue to rage in the minds of an older generation.

The nature of this editing process, perhaps the most ingenious aspect of the film, provides the Spanish audience with the opportunity to reflect upon the conflicting memories that have shaped the political and social environment of Spain in the aftermath of the Civil War. Equally striking is Camino's construction of a chronology that continually stresses the centrality of Catalonia to the defense of the Spanish Republic, thereby adding yet another layer of recuperated memory to challenge implicitly the dictatorship's official view of the nature of the conflict. What ultimately emerges from *The Old Memory* is less an alternative retelling of recent national history than an interrogation into the personal and collective memories that, even by the time of the transition to democracy in the mid-1970s, still hold sway over many Spaniards. This conceptual project relates in basic ways to a series of other key films of the decade that confront the issue of the weight of popular cultural memory during the period of the Francoist dictatorship.

BIBLIOGRAPHY

D'Lugo, Marvin. "Catalan Cinema: Historical Experience and Cinematic Practice." *Quarterly Review of Film and Video* 13, nos. 1–3, (1991): 131–147.

Gubern, Román. *1936-1939: La guerra de España en la pantalla*. Madrid: Filmoteca Española, 1986.

Viridiana (1961: Luis Buñuel*). Buñuel's second film made in Spain is perhaps best remembered for the scandal it produced. Denounced by the Vatican newspaper, *L'Osservatore Romano*, it won the Golden Palm at the 1961 Cannes Film Festival. The Spanish government had originally supported *Viridiana* as the official Spanish entry at Cannes but later rescinded its endorsement. For nearly two decades *Viridiana* was therefore designated as a Mexican film.

The action is focused on Viridiana (Silvia Pinal), an orphaned postulant in a Spanish convent who, on the eve of taking her final vows, is coerced to make one last visit to her uncle Jaime (Fernando Rey*), who has paid for her support but whom she has not seen in years. Once at Jaime's country estate, the old man pressures his niece to marry him. When that fails, he drugs her and tries to rape her, but fails to carry through with his plan. The next morning she sets out to return to the convent, leaving her uncle in a state of agitation. Jaime hangs himself and leaves a will that divides the estate between Viridiana and Jaime's illegitimate son, Jorge (Francisco Rabal*).

When Jorge, an architect, arrives at the estate, he begins to plan all sorts of modernization. For her part, Viridiana wants to turn the estate into an asylum for beggars and the downtrodden. Thus the two cousins find themselves symbolically reenacting the tensions between a mystical and a modern Spain. After Viridiana is nearly raped by two of her beggars, she concedes to Jorge's point of view.

Inspired in part by the Benito Pérez Galdós novel about the excesses of religious fervor, *Angel Guerra*, Buñuel's script, written in collaboration with Julio Alejandro, emphasizes two pivotal themes that resound from his earlier films: the impossibility of individual denial of instinctual identity and the director's rejection of Catholicism's ideology of control of individual action and desire. The film's opening sequence underscores these themes. The scene begins with a tracking shot of the patio of a cloister, shot from behind one of the pillars. The camera reveals a group of small children, dressed in uniform, marching two by two, across the patio. In a single brief image Buñuel underscores his view of the all-embracing control that Catholicism has on its subjects. Throughout the rest of the film this same theme will be emphasized through images of the movement of feet and the lower torso of characters constrained by social and religious ritual.

Buñuel understood control in a double sense, both physical and ideological: as a submission of the body to the ritual rigors imposed by religious doctrine and also as an absorption of Christian dogma. Viridiana has been taught to suppress her natural sexual impulses and to attempt to lead a perfect Christian life, that is, to imitate the life of Christ. First Don Jaime, then the beggars, and, finally, Jorge, teach Viridiana to acknolwedge natural instinct and to reject the dangerous idealism of Catholicism.

Though deceptively simple in editing and most camera work, *Viridiana* nonetheless reveals a complex visual structure built around the repetition of a series of visual motifs. Prominent among these is a child's jump rope used by Rita, the daughter of Jaime's maid, Ramona (Margarita Lozano*). Jaime uses it to hang himself, and then it reappears in the hands of one of the beggars who restrain Viridiana while attempting to rape her. These repetitions underscore the process whereby everyday objects are often imbued with sacred and profane meanings. By far the most startling of those refigured images is Buñuel's profane reconstruction of da Vinci's *The Last Supper*, transformed into an orgy by the beggars and reenacted against the background music of Handel's *Hallelujah Chorus*.

BIBLIOGRAPHY

Aranda, J. Francisco. *Luis Buñuel: biografía crítica.* Barcelona: Editorial Lumen, 1969.

Fiddian, Robin W., and Peter W. Evans. *Challenges to Authority: Fiction and Film in Contemporary Spain.* London: Támesis, 1988.

***Volver a empezar* [*To Begin Again*] (1983: José Luis Garci*).** The principal significance of this, José Luis Garci's fifth film, is that it was the first Spanish motion picture to win an Oscar in the Best Foreign Film category (in 1972, Luis Buñuel's French-Spanish coproduction, *The Discreet Charm of the Bourgeoisie*, won). The film recounts the final days in the life of Antonio Miguel Albajara (Antonio Ferrandis*), a Spanish emigré to the United States who is now a fiction writer and university professor at Berkeley. Antonio returns to his native Gijón (Asturias) after having won the Nobel Prize for Literature, and there confides to one of his oldest friends, Roxú (José Bódalo*), now a physician, that he has been diagnosed with an incurable disease and has only a short time to live. Thus the nostalgic return is colored by Antonio's recognition that this will be the last time he will see his home and old friends.

Besides visiting with Roxú, a soccer enthusiast who toasts Antonio's youthful successes on the Gijón team, he reencounters Elena (Encarna Paso), the sweetheart of his youth. They recount their lives since they last saw each other and spend a night together at a country inn. Antonio returns to Berkeley to spend his final days teaching young people at the university.

The most striking formal and thematic feature of the film is the insistent background musical refrain of Cole Porter's "Begin the Beguine," a melody that rekindles fond memories for both Antonio and Elena and forms the nostalgic, sentimental aura that surrounds the entire narrative. Many of Garci's films have been harshly criticized for their intense sentimentality, and *To Begin Again* is no exception. To the director's credit, as some have noted, in a period in which Spanish filmmakers looking to Spain's past history for inspiration found only violence and political recriminations, Garci's view of that past celebrates a lyrical and highly personal vision. Also, Garci's script deftly captures a series of motifs of Spanish popular culture that helped make the film highly successful in its domestic market, even before the Oscar. These include a tender look at old age, a view of the national fascination with soccer, and a brief homage to King Juan Carlos as the arbiter of Spain's successful political transition to democracy.

BIBLIOGRAPHY

Caparrós-Lera, José María. *El cine español de la democracia: de la muerte de Franco al "cambio" socialista (1975–1989).* Barcelona: Anthropos, 1992.

García Fernández, Emilio C. *Historia ilustrada del cine español.* Barcelona: Planeta, 1985.

Directors, Producers, Cinematographers, and Critics

Alcaine, José Luis (Tetuán, 1938). After working in Tangiers in a color-photography laboratory, Alcaine entered the Escuela Oficial de Cine (EOC) in 1962 and graduated four years later with a speciality in cinematography. He made an inauspicious debut as the director of photography for Guillermo Ziener's *Javier y los invasores del espacio* [*Xavier and the Space Invaders*] (1967). This was followed by a long period of work on a series of forgettable films until Jaime Chávarri's* much praised debut film, *Los viajes escolares* [*School Vacation*] (1973). As a result of this film, Alcaine found himself invited to work on films by some of the most promising directors of the period, including the completion of Vicente Aranda's* *Cambio de sexo* [*Change of Sex*] (1976); Antonio Giménez Rico's* *Retrato de familia* [*Family Portrait*] (1976); *La vieja memoria* [*The Old Memory*]* (1977) and *La campanada* [*The Pealing of the Bells*] (1979, both by Jaime Camino*; Gutiérrez Aragón's* *Demonios en el jardín* [*Demons in the Garden*] (1982), and Víctor Erice's* *El sur* [*The South*]* (1983). This latter film was the spiritual sequel to Erice's *El espíritu de la colmena* [*Spirit of the Beehive*]* (1973) for which Luis Cuadrado* had been lauded for his brilliant photography; thus Alcaine's work was bound to be placed in the most difficult of comparisons. Though working with some of the visual play of shadows and light that had been Cuadrado's hallmark in the earlier film, Alcaine was able to forge a distinctive visual style for *The South* with a decided emphasis on the power of light over darkness.

By the middle of the 1980s, Alcaine had become a Spanish cinematographer of note, filming for some of the most outstanding works of Spanish cinema: Gutiérrez Aragón's* *La mitad del cielo* [*Half of Heaven*]* (1986); Vicente Aranda's* *La muchacha de las bragas de oro* [*Girl in the Golden Panties*] (1979), *El Lute* (1987), *El Lute II* (1988), and *Amantes* [*Lovers*]* (1990); Fernando Trueba's* *El sueño del mono loco* [*Twisted Obsession*] (1989), and

Belle Epoque (1992);* Carlos Saura's* *¡Ay, Carmela!*, (1990); Pedro Almodóvar's* *Mujeres al borde de un ataque de nervios* [*Women on the Verge of a
Nervous Breakdown*] (1988)* and *¡Atame!* [*Tie Me Up! Tie Me Down!*] (1989);
and Bigas Luna's* *Jamón, Jamón* (1992), *Huevos de oro* [*Golden Balls*] (1993),
and *La teta i la luna* [*The Tit and the Moon*] (1994). Of these stunning
collaborations that read as an abbreviated history of the best of recent Spanish
cinema, perhaps the most noteworthy of Alcaine's collaborations have been those
with Vicente Aranda, with whom he photographed a total of eight films, among
them, the most commercially successful of Aranda's career.

Alcaine won three Goya awards; these were awarded for his cinematography
in Trueba's *Twisted Obsession* (1989), *Belle Epoque* (1992), and Pilar Miró's*
El pájaro de la felicidad [*The Bird of Happiness*] (1993).

BIBLIOGRAPHY

Heredero, Carlos F. *El lenguaje de la luz: entrevistas con directores de fotografía del
cine español*. Alcalá de Henares: 24 Festival de Cine de Alcalá de Henares, 1994.
Llinás, Francisco. *Directores de fotografía del cine español*. Madrid: Filmoteca
Española, 1989.

Almodóvar, Pedro (Ciudad Real, 1949). Pedro Almodóvar is a self-taught
filmmaker who began his career in the late 1970s with a series of low-budget
short films shot in super 8. In 1980, he made his debut as a feature-length film
director with *Pepi, Luci Bom, y otras chicas del montón* [*Pepi, Luci, Bom, And
Other Girls Like That*],* produced by Pepón Coromina,* with additional financial
support from Almodóvar's close friends and actors in the film, Carmen Maura*
and Félix Rotaeta. This cult classic was followed two years later by *Laberinto
de pasiones* [*Labyrinth of Passion*] (1982), a film that shared many of the same
problems of incoherent script, poor acting, and poor technical elements as did
Pepi. Yet owing to Almodóvar's status as a counterculture figure of the Madrid
Movida (the "movement"), both films fared well with their limited distribution.

In 1985, with his fourth film, *¿Qué he hecho yo para merecer esto?* [*What
Have I Done to Deserve This?*], Almodóvar achieved a crossover success with
mainstream distribution as well as positive reviews resulting from its U.S. run.
This success brought him the support of a new producer, Andrés Vicente
Gómez,* and access to a more polished and visually sophisticated "look" in films
like *Matador* (1986), *La ley del deseo* [*Law of Desire*]* (1987) and *Mujeres al
borde de un ataque de nervios* [*Women on the Verge of a Nervous Breakdown*]*
(1988), which was nominated for an Oscar and proved to be one of the most
commercially successful films in Spanish history. Some of the credit for that new
"look" goes to Almodóvar's cinematographer, José Luis Alcaine.* But the
improvement in production values also marked a shift away from the style and
spirit of his early work, which was so deeply rooted in the youthful counterculture of Madrid.

From *Matador* on, Almodóvar's cinema began to show an increasingly more pronounced borrowing from Hollywood melodramas for his plots. The centerpiece of all of Almodóvar's films has been female characters, leading some to equate Almodóvar with the American director, George Cukor, known as a woman's director. With the exception of two films, *Entre tinieblas* [*Dark Habits*](1984), and *Matador* (1986), Carmen Maura was the central character of all of Almodóvar's films until 1988, when the two made an artistic break. Maura was then replaced by Victoria Abril,* who assumed the leading role in his next three films. In all of his works, Almodóvar gives increasing social power to female characters who have traditionally been marginalized within Spanish society. This reformulation of gender themes coincides with the larger project of Almodóvar's cinema: the demarginalization of gays, lesbians, and transsexuals, who gain centrality within the cinematic world evoked by Almodóvar. This refreshingly anti-establishment send-up of traditional conservative Spanish values may well account for much of the popular appeal of Almodóvar's cinema in Spain.

Beginning with *¡Atame!* [*Tie Me Up! Tie Me Down!*] (1989) these Spanish subtexts begin to disappear, till finally in *Kika* (1993) the story, save passing cultural references, seems unbound by any qualities that might distinguish it as a Spanish film. More recently, in *La flor de mi secreto* [*Flower of My Secret*] (1995), Almodóvar blended that international style with culturally-specific narrative elements that highlighted Spain's gradual integration within a new European culture.

BIBLIOGRAPHY
Smith, Paul Julian. *Desire Unlimited: The Cinema of Pedro Almodóvar*. London: Verso, 1994.
Vernon, Kathleen, and Barbara Morris (eds.). *Post-Franco, Postmodern: The Films of Pedro Almodóvar*. Westport, CT: Greenwood Press, 1995.

Amo, Antonio del (Valdelaguna, Madrid, 1911; Madrid, 1991). As one of the more promising young politically engaged documentary film-makers of the pre-Civil War 1930s, Antonio del Amo's artistic potential and career were profoundly frustrated by the Nationalist victory and the subsequent stabilization of the Franco regime. He began his contacts with Spanish film in his early twenties, writing film criticism during the early years of the Second Republic. His friendship with Luis Buñuel* during this period enabled del Amo to get a position on the shooting of Jean Grémillon's *La Dolorosa* [*The Pained Woman*] (1935). During the Civil War period he was put in charge of the film production unit assigned to the Lister Brigade, which defended the Republican cause. Because of this affiliation as well as his work on documentary films for the Spanish Communist Party, del Amo subsequently found himself in difficulties with the triumphant Nationalist regime.

He eventually was able to work himself into the commercial film industry but only in a secondary capacity, as directorial assistant for Rafael Gil,* Antonio Román,* and Ignacio Iquino.* Throughout the 1940s he devoted himself to scriptwriting as well as to the direction of documentary films. He made his debut as a commercial director in 1947 with *Cuatro mujeres* [*Four Women*], the first of a series of four melodramatic films he made between 1947 and 1950 that merely suggested his directorial competence.

Since his early days during the Republic, del Amo was an avid enthusiast of political cinema and by 1950 was actively seeking ways to practice the aesthetics of Italian Neorealism. The controversial success of José Antonio Nieves Conde's* *Surcos* [*Furrows*]* (1950) enabled him to attempt his own Neorealist project, *Día tras día* [*Day after Day*] (1951). Shot on location in a working-class district of Madrid, the film proved a critical more than a commercial success. It was followed, in turn, by two other films that critics often consider del Amo's best work, *Sierra maldita* [*The Cursed Hills*] (1954) and *El sol sale todos los días* [*The Sun Comes Out Every Day*] (1955). Even at their best, these films are marred by excessively melodramatic plots and frequent moralizing, especially in *Day after Day*, which deals with the theme of juvenile delinquency in the Madrid of the early 1950s.

Del Amo's fortunes changed in 1956 when, largely out of financial necessity, he directed the film that would launch the career of the child singing sensation, Joselito (José Jiménez Fernández), *El pequeño ruiseñor* [*The Little Nightingale*] (1956-1957). The commercial success of the film led to eight more musicals starring the child singer, with extraordinary results for both the director and his young star. Del Amo's films suddenly enjoyed unparalleled success throughout Europe and Latin America, enabling him to establish his own production company, Apolo Films, with its own studios outside Madrid, where he would produce and direct nineteen films over the next two decades. Nearly all of these films were of a rank commercial quality.

Along with his activities in the film industry, del Amo taught at the National Film School (IIEC) from its founding in 1947 till 1959. Under its reorganization as the Escuela Oficial de Cine (EOC), he taught film montage from 1965 to 1968. He also authored a number of books on film theory and history: *Historia universal del cine* [*Universal History of Cinema*] (1945); *El cine como lengua* [*Film As Language*] (1948); *La batalla del cine* [*The Battle of Cinema*] (1961); and *Estética del montaje* [*The Aesthetics of Montage*] (1972).

BIBLIOGRAPHY
Castro, Antonio. *El cine español en el banquillo*. Valencia: Fernando Torres, 1974.
Heredero, Carlos F. *Las huellas del tiempo: cine español 1951–1961*. Valencia: Filmoteca de la Generalitat Valenciana, 1993.

Aranda, Vicente (Barcelona, 1926). Coming from a working-class background, Aranda was employed in a variety of jobs before leaving Spain in 1949 for Venezuela, where he worked for a U.S. technical company. In 1956, he returned to his native Barcelona and became involved in film production. In his debut film, *Brillante porvenir* [*A Brilliant Future*] (1964), he shared directorial credits with Román Gubern*; he made his solo directorial debut the following year with *Fata Morgana*.* Conceived of and produced under the general rubric of the "Barcelona School" of filmmakers, *Fata Morgana* was an attempt of that group of film critics, writers, and intellectuals to propose a new Spanish cultural aesthetic that opposed the traditional imagery, thematics, and filmmaking style of Madrid-based directors. The film took inspiration for its visual style from television commercials and comic strips. Though a commercial failure in its original run, the film appears to have influenced other young directors in their filmmaking style, including Carlos Saura* and Iván Zulueta.*

Aranda's work over the next decade would reveal much of the same tension noted in *Fata Morgana*, namely a polarity between certain artistic pretensions and a visual style drawn from popular mass media. In these films Aranda worked within established film genres: science fiction, as in the case of *Las crueles* [*The Cruel Women*] (1969), and the erotic comedy in *Clara es el precio* [*Clara Is the Price*] (1973), with an eye toward revising and modernizing them. It is not, however, until his 1976 film, *Cambio de sexo* [*Change of Sex*], in which Aranda "discovered" Victoria Abril* as a teenage film actress, that the dominant chord of his film style and conception became clear. In this docudrama about a sex-change operation, Aranda worked with a potentially sensationalist theme of sexual identity, yet was able to maintain a certain dramatic distance and control that gives the film coherence and power.

The final element in the dominant Aranda style came in 1979 when he made a clever film adaptation of the popular novel by his fellow Catalán, Juan Marsé, *La muchacha de las bragas de oro* [*The Girl in the Golden Panties*]. Over the next fifteen years, Aranda established himself as Spain's foremost adaptor of popular novels into film. Unlike the more traditional adaptations that stressed their classical literary origins, his choices usually were guided by the centrality of an erotically defined female character, and a contemporary story emphasizing the force of milieu on the shaping of actions.

Following the commercially successful *Girl in the Golden Panties*, Aranda adapted two other popular contemporary Catalan novels, Manuel Vázquez Montalbán's political thriller, *Asesinato en el comité central* [*Assassination in the Central Committee*] (1982), which also starred Victoria Abril, and perhaps his most daring adaptation, a brilliant rewrite of Andreau Martín's noir detective novel, *Prótesis* [*Prothesis*], in which he transformed the male protagonist into a female, retitling the work *Fanny Pelopaja* (1983). It was not, however, until his adaptation of the famed Luis Martín-Santos novel, *Tiempo de silencio* [*Time of Silence*] (1985), which had a major cast headed by Imanol Arias* and Victoria Abril,* that the larger, profound design of Aranda's critical vision of Spain became apparent. Here, one sees clearly how Aranda's themes of sexuality are used as a register through which political and historical issues can be expressed. Though much criticized for his realistic approach to the narrational complexity of the Martín-Santos novel, *Time of Silence* was generally well-received by audiences. This film was followed by the two-part biographical film based on the events of the notorious bank robber, Eleuterio Sánchez, better known as "El Lute." (*El Lute I: Camina o revienta* [*Run Or Die*] [1987]; *El Lute II: Mañana seré libre* [*Tomorrow I Will Be Free*] [1988]).

Aranda achieved a good deal of international recognition for *Amantes* [*Lovers*]* (1990), a story originally planned as an episode for a Spanish television series but expanded to a period piece set during the black years of the dictatorship. The striking visual qualities of *Lovers*, especially the evocation of 1950s Madrid, were achieved through his productive collaboration with cinematographer, José Luis Alcaine* with whom Aranda has worked repeatedly for nearly twenty years.

Along with his sustained film career, Aranda has also from time to time ventured into television films including *El crimen del Capitán Sánchez* [*The Crime of Captain Sánchez*] (1985) and the more extensive *Los jinetes del alba* [*Horsemen of the Dawn*] (1990).

BIBLIOGRAPHY

Alvares, Rosa, and Belén Frías. *Vicente Aranda: el cine como pasión.* Valladolid: 36 Semana Internacional de Cine, 1991.

Guarner, José Luis, and Peter Besas. *El inquietante cine de Vicente Aranda.* Madrid: Imagfic, 1985.

Vera, Pascual. *Vicente Aranda.* Madrid: Ediciones JC, 1989.

Ardavin, César Fernández (Madrid, 1923). The nephew of filmmaker Eusebio Fernández Ardavín, he entered professional filmmaking as a member of the technical crew of a number of films in the late 1940s. Though specializing primarily in touristic shorts, a number of his dozen feature-length films were shown at prestigious international film festivals. The most famous of these, *Lazarillo de Tormes* (1960),* even won the grand prize, the Golden Bear, at the 1960 Berlin Film Festival. Though commercially successful at the time of their original release and even greatly praised by critics, his films have, since the end of the dictatorship, suffered the effects of a hostile critical revision. Ardavín's filmography is marked by a number of film adaptations of popular or classical literary works. Cinematically, these films are characterized by careful but cold technical efficiency, especially in terms of his use of lighting, at times tending toward a precious "artsy" quality, but with little else to distinguish it from other films of the period. Ardavín is credited with having directed Angela Molina* in her film debut, *No matarás* [*Thou Shalt Not Kill*] (1977).

BIBLIOGRAPHY

Heredero, Carlos F. *Las huellas del tiempo: cine español 1951–1961.* Valencia: Filmoteca de la Generalitat Valenciana, 1993.

Méndez-Leite von Haffe, Fernando. *Historia del cine español.* Vol 2. Madrid: Ediciones Rialp, 1965.

Armendáriz, Montxo (Olleta, Navarra, 1949). Armendáriz moved from a career as a university professor of electronics to filmmaking through a series of shorts on Basque topics: *Barregarien Dantza* (1979); *Ikuska 11* (1981); *Nafarroaka Ikukuskinak* [*Carboneras de Navarra* [*Carbon Workers of Navarre*] (1981). This latter short was to become the basis for his first feature-length film, *Tasio* (1984),* which traces the generational history of Navarese carbon-mound workers in a visual style that aproximates ethnographic cinema, but is clearly informed by traditional cinematic narrative. Produced by Elías Querejeta,* who also worked on the screenplay, *Tasio* won critical praise throughout Spain as evidence of a new and original filmmaker. It was followed two years later by a more conventional cinematic narrative, *27 horas* [*Twenty-Seven Hours*], which deals with the problems of drug addiction among Basque youths in San Sebastián.

In 1990, Armendáriz returned to the ethnographic style of his first feature with *Las cartas de Alou* [*Letters from Alou*],* which won first prize at the San Sebastián Film Festival as well as the best acting award for the film's protagonist, Mulie Jarju. *Letters From Alou* details the life and misfortunes of a young Senegalese man who comes to Spain as a farm worker but quickly encounters racial discrimination on both personal and institutional levels. Armendáriz's most recent film, *Historias del Kronen* [*Stories from the Kronen Bar*],* about alienated upper-class youth in Madrid, makes clear the general focus and style of the Basque filmmaker's work, namely an interest in the generational, familial, and social milieu of alienation within different sectors of contemporary Spanish society.

There is clearly a documentary sensibility informing Armendáriz's work. Yet at the same time, a highly personal quality of authorial style is evident as each work seeks to find the balance between the familial and the social as the sites of individual personal action and belief in modern Spanish society. Deriving from Armendáriz's earlier work in documentary shorts, his feature-length films, most strikingly *Tasio* and *Letters from Alou*, are shaped by the director's elaboration of his narratives from initial documentary videos that treat the same subject matter. This quasi-ethnographic approach to social problems has led to a certain criticism of the obvious didactic nature of his films.

BIBLIOGRAPHY
Pérez Manrique, José María. *Montxo Armendáriz: imagen y narración de libertad.* Burgos: Encuentro Internacional de Cine de Burgos, 1993.

Armiñán, Jaime de (Madrid, 1927). After receiving his law degree from the University of Madrid, Armiñán began writing for a number of popular Madrid magazines before he began to write seriously for the theater. After a period of commercial and critical success with his plays during the 1950s, he turned to television scriptwriting in 1959 and soon established himself as one of the most successful and prolific television writers. During the early 1960s he turned to screenwriting, contributing scripts most notably to José María Forqué,* one of the most commercially popular directors of the day. Among his script credits during this time are *El secreto de Mónica* [*Monica's Secret*] (1961), *El juego de la verdad* [*The Game of Truth*] (1963), and *El diablo bajo la almohada* [*The Devil under the Pillow*] (1967).

As the natural progression of his work in films, Armiñán moved into direction, filming his own scripts beginning in 1969 with *Carola de día, Carola de noche* [*Carol by Day, Carol by Night*], a contrived vehicle to help redirect the sagging career of the former child singing star, Marisol.* This was followed by the equally pedestrian *La Lola dicen que no vive sola* [*They Say that Lola Doesn't Live Alone*] (1970). Not until his third film, *Mi querida señorita* [*My Dearest Señorita*]* (1972), developed out of a collaboration with José Luis Borau,* did Armiñán achieve critical and popular success as a filmmaker. The film, starring the popular José Luis López Vázquez* in the dual roles of Adela, a sexually repressed provincial spinster, and Juan, the man Adela discovers she really is, was immensely popular in Spain and was nominated for the 1972 Oscar in the Best Foreign Film category.

My Dearest Señorita helped define a certain direction in Armiñán's work. Over the next twenty-five years he would attempt to focus on comedies of manners involving the personal crises of ordinary Spaniards, often stemming from their culturally deformed notions of their own sexual identity. These sexual themes insistently underscore the symptomatic nature of a fossilized Spanish culture. After *Un casto varón* [*A Chaste Youth*] (1973), Armiñán made *El amor del capitán Brando* [*The Love of Captain Brando*] (1974) a film that continued that serious interrogation of sexual and cultural identity.

During the post-Franco period, Armiñán sought ways to express both his political and social themes, but with varying degrees of success. *Nunca es tarde* [*Never Too Late*] (1977) recounts in parodic fashion the miraculous pregnancy of a woman in her eighties through her mystical identification with a young male neighbor whom she claims is the child's spiritual father. A more pointed narrative of sexual and political repression comes through in *Al servicio de la mujer española* [*At the Service of Spanish Womanhood*] (1978), which parodies with black humor the puritanical sexual values of Francoist culture that outlive the regime and continue to shape provincial life.

Armiñán's most acclaimed work of this period is *El nido* [*The Nest*]* (1980), which depicts the tragic consequences of the infatuation of an older widower (Héctor Alterio*) for an adolescent girl (Ana Torrent*). While seeming only to portray the details of the sexual infatuation between the older man and the young woman, the film exposes the dominance of Spanish women, like the young girl who fashions herself on Lady Macbeth, and the ambivalence of Spanish men who are controlled by matriarchal power. Ana Torrent won the Best Actress award at the Montreal Film Festival for her performance, and the film was also nominated for an Oscar that year; this was Armiñán's second nomination.

Armiñán's filmography over the next fifteen years remained notably slender, largely due to his return to television and his highly successful scripting of several dramatic series. Of the few films he made during this period, *La hora bruja* [*The Witching Hour*] (1985) is noteworthy for its strong dramatic performances by Francisco Rabal,* Concha Velasco,* and Victoria Abril* in an amorous narrative involving the activities of a lascivious traveling magician. *Al otro lado del túnel* [*The Other Side of the Tunnel*] (1994), presents a similar story of passion and old age, this time with the amorous pair constituted by Maribel Verdú* and Fernando Rey.*

BIBLIOGRAPHY
Crespo, Pedro. *Jaime de Armiñán: los amores marginales*. Huelva: Festival de Cine Iberoamericano, 1987.
Kinder, Marsha. *Blood Cinema: The Reconstruction of National Identity In Spain*. Berkeley: University of California Press, 1993.

Azcona, Rafael (Logroño, 1926). This most successful of Spanish screenwriters started his professional career in 1951 when he arrived in Madrid and began writing a series of short, satirical pieces that were eventually published in the famed weekly humor magazine, *La Cordoniz*. Over the years his contribution to the magazine would include articles, short stories, and anecdotes. He also wrote for the newspaper, *Pueblo*. By the mid-1950s he had managed to published several novels that were favorably reviewed by Madrid critics.

In 1958 Azcona made the acquaintance of Marco Ferreri,* the Italian filmmaker who had recently come to Spain as the business representative for a company selling panoramic motion-picture camera lenses. The two men discovered they shared a common cynical attitude and began collaborating on the script adaptation of Azcona's novel, *El pisito* [*The Little Flat*] (1958), a story inspired by Spain's endemic housing shortage. Their script called for the vivid images of a drab urban milieu to be used as the backdrop for a story of individuals hardened by the everyday struggles of Spanish life. In its transformation into a motion picture, *The Little Flat* appeared to be a scathing extension of the Spanish Neorealist film trends of the decade. But the film failed to attract any positive critical attention. It did, however, solidify Azcona's collaboration with Ferreri, which would involve seventeen films over the next twenty years, including *El cochecito* [*The Little Car*] (1960) and a series of highly popular Italian films, the most commercially successful of which is *La grande abbuffata* [*La Grande Bouffe*][*The Big Blow-Out*] (1973).

Over the next three decades, Azcona's career as a scriptwriter soared; he made a series of collaborations with some of the most esteemed and commercially successful Spanish filmmakers. He worked on seven with Luis García Berlanga,* including Berlanga's most acclaimed film, *Plácido* (1961), as well as all three parts of the commercial blockbuster series, *Escopeta nacional* [*National Rifle*] (1977), *Patrimonio nacional* [*National Patrimony*] (1981), and *Nacional III* [*National III*] (1982). He also coscripted the immensely popular, *La vaquilla* [*The Heifer*] (1985) with Berlanga. Azcona also collaborated on six films with

Carlos Saura,* five with Pedro Masó,* and four with José María Forqué.*

With a filmography of more than seventy film credits, including the script for the Oscar-winning Fernando Trueba* film, *Belle Epoque*,* the dominant features of Azcona's style are extremely well known: a striking penchant for choral scripts involving a multitude of characters in a single sequence; a corrosive black humor, often focused on physical deformities; a consistently harsh satirical view of Spanish cultural institutions and social practices; finally, a marked misogynist attitude that seems to feed into traditional Spanish patriarchal biases. These characteristics, put into service for some of the most creative and successful Spanish directors, makes Azcona Spain's most commercially successful scriptwriter, a reputation that has brought him international as well as national renown.

BIBLIOGRAPHY

Frugone, Juan Carlos. *Rafael Azcona: atrapados por la vida*. Valladolid: 32 Semana de Cine de Valladolid, 1987.
Riambau, Esteve (ed.). *Antes del apocalipsis: el cine de Marco Ferreri*. Madrid: Cátedra, 1990.

Baena, Juan Julio (Madrid, 1925). A member of the first generation of students to emerge from the recently established Instituto de Investigaciones y Experiencias Cinematográficas (IIEC), Baena received his diploma in cinematography in 1951. By the end of the decade he had begun to achieve prominence as a result of his striking Neorealist photography in the first two films for which he received screen credits: Carlos Saura's* debut film, *Los golfos* [*Hooligans*]* (1959) and Marco Ferreri's* *El cochecito* [*The Little Car*]* (1960). Though radically different in tone, both films display a stunning break from the mainstream of Spanish studio-based cinematography and an increasing reliance on contrasts of light and dark.

The striking effects of these two early collaborations with Saura and Ferreri would become the inspiration for the visual style of New Spanish Cinema of the mid-1960s, which Baena influenced through his own work on a number of important films of that movement. These included his work as director of photography for Francisco Regueiro's* *El buen amor* [*Good Love*] (1963), Saura's *Llanto por un bandido* [*Lament for a Bandit*] (1963), Miguel Picazo's* *La tía Tula* [*Aunt Tula*]*(1964), and Mario Camus's* *Con el viento solano* [*With a Wind from the East*] (1965). He was also the cinematographer for Juan Antonio Bardem's* *Nunca pasa nada* [*Nothing Ever Happens*]* (1963).

In 1968 Baena was named head of the recently reorganized national film school, renamed the Escuela Oficial de Cine (EOC), but his tenure there was marked by confrontation with students; the school was eventually disbanded and by the mid 1970s Baena had abandoned motion pictures to work exclusively in television productions.

BIBILOGRAPHY
Baena, Juan Julio. *"El cochecito." Temas de cine*, no. 6 (1960): 13–14. "Número especial dedicado a la película *El cochecito* invitado al Festival de Venecia."
Heredero, Carlos F. *Las huellas del tiempo: cine español 1951–1961*. Valencia: Filmoteca de la Generalitat Valenciana, 1993.
Llinás, Francisco. *Directores de fotografía del cine español*. Madrid: Filmoteca Española, 1989.

Baños, Ricardo de (Barcelona, 1892; Barcelona, 1939). This younger brother of the early silent film cameraman, Ramón de Baños, is generally considered one of the important pioneers of early silent cinema in Spain. He learned the basic skills of the medium in Paris at the Gaumont studios and returned to his native Barcelona in 1904 to make documentary films. By 1905 he was filming sequences from *zarzuelas* and synchronizing them with sound recordings.

In 1906, Baños became associated with the recently established production company, Hispano Films, and it was under their auspices that he produced the first screen version of Zorrilla's *Don Juan Tenorio*. (In 1921 he would remake the film in a decidedly more opulent form.) Collaborating closely with his brother, Ramón, Baños made a series of fiction films that were to become important commercial successes over the next decade. Of these, perhaps the most important is the very first screen adaptation of Jacinto Benavente's *La malquerida* [*Passion Flower*] (1914).

Two years later Baños founded Royal Films, the company through which he and his brother would make films for the rest of their professional careers. They continued to work throughout the silent period and made only one film in the sound period, *El relicario* [*The Shrine*] (1933). Though Baños is credited with having made only nineteen features between 1909 and 1933, the actual shorts and documentaries he shot number in the hundreds.

BIBLIOGRAPHY
Méndez-Leite von Haffe, Fernando. *Historia del cine español*. Vol. 1. Madrid: Ediciones Rialp, 1965.
Lasa, Joan Francesc. *Els germans Baños: aquell primer cinema català*. Barcelona: Generalitat de Catalunya, Departamento de Cultura, 1996.

Bardem, Juan Antonio (Madrid, 1922). The firebrand of the first generation of opposition filmmakers to come out of the recently established National Film School (Instituto de Investigaciones y Experiencias Cinematográficas) in the early 1950s, Bardem, along with his colleague and comrade in arms, Luis García Berlanga,* was among the first to openly challenge the status quo cinema that had developed in Spain in the aftermath of the Civil War. His talent lay not only in his critical positions regarding the state of Spanish cinema, but also in his ability to channel that critique into a series of often brilliant films.

Bardem's early career in filmmaking is marked by an impressive series of five films made between 1951 and 1956: *Esa pareja feliz* [*That Happy Couple*]*

(1951), made as a collaborative venture with Berlanga; *Cómicos [Comedians]**
(1953); *Felices Pascuas [Merry Christmas** (1954); *Muerte de un ciclista [Death
of a Cyclist]** (1955); and *Calle Mayor [Main Street]** (1956). These films
brought him to the attention of Spanish and European audiences who saw in him
not only a bright and promising filmmaker, but also a defiant auteur challenging
the hegemony of the Franco dictatorship from within. After this initial period of
success, Bardem became involved in an ambitious but ultimately flawed trilogy
of somber films about the Spanish heartlands. These included *La venganza [The
Vengeance]* (1957), *Sonatas*, a coproduction with Mexico (1959), and *A las cinco
de la tarde [At Five in the Afternoon]* (1960), this last film based on a play by
the opposition playwright, Alfonso Sastre.

During the mid to late 1950s, possibly the most successful phase of his career,
Bardem was involved in a number of efforts to revive an independent and
artistically viable Spanish cinema. In 1955, he was one of the organizers of the
famed "Salamanca Conversations on National Cinema," the goal of which was
to open a debate between the government and filmmakers with the aim of liberalizing the government's tight control of censorship. During these years he was
also a partner in the liberal production company, UNINCI, which coproduced
Carlos Saura's* first film, *Los golfos [Hooligans]** (1959), and was one of the
sponsors of Luis Buñuel's* controversial *Viridiana** (1961). The government's
response to the *Viridiana* scandal was to force the demise of the company.

It was not until his 1963 film, *Nunca pasa nada [Nothing Ever Happens]*,*
when Bardem returned to many of the now predictable political and cultural
critiques of his early period, that he was able to recoup some of that earlier
reputation. His career after this point, however, becomes rather checkered,
involving dubious projects, such as *Varietés* (1970), a musical remake of his own
Comedians with Sara Montiel,* and *La corrupción de Chris Miller [The
Corruption of Chris Miller]* (1972), a film intended to recharge the career of the
teenage actress and singer, Marisol.* By the end of the 1970s, Bardem returned
to ambitious political dramas such as *Siete días de enero [Seven Days in
January]* (1979), but his preeminent position as the principal political filmmaker
had been displaced by a younger generation of directors with more contemporary
political themes and more complex and sophisticated visual styles.

Bardem's most recent work made for Spanish television, is the biographical
film, *Lorca: muerte de un poeta [Lorca: Death of a Poet]* (1988), about the life
and death of Federico García Lorca.

BIBLIOGRAPHY
Egido, Luis G. *J.A. Bardem*. Huelva: Festival de Cine Iberoamericana, 1983.
Heredero, Carlos F. *Las huellas del tiempo: cine español 1951-1961*. Valencia: Filmoteca
      de la Generalitat Valenciana, 1993.

Bellmunt, Francesc (Barcelona, 1947). After a period of working on short
films, Bellmunt made a name for himself with the direction of two musical

documentaries in 1976, *La nova cançó* [*The New Song*] and *Canet Rock*, both of which introduced to a broad audience popular, youthful Catalan music. These two films were part of the larger effort to demarginalize and to stabilize Catalan culture. Over the next decade, Bellmunt would be viewed as a trailblazer who had tested the limits of the new freedoms of the post-Franco era.

La orgía [*The Orgy*], in 1978, for instance, proposed in a somewhat frivolous way the theme of new sexual freedom. The film is significant as the introduction of the *Comedia Catalana* (Catalan Comedy), a contemporary genre that focuses on the mores of a younger generation of urban and often cosmopolitan Barcelonians. It also marked the film debut of two young Catalan actors, Assumpta Serna* and Juanjo Puigcorbé,* who, over the next two decades, would become familiar faces to Spanish and European audiences.

La quinta del porro [*The Stoned Recruits*] (1980), Bellmunt's next film, was an ensemble comedy like *The Orgy*, this time dealing with the relation between Spanish youth and the unpopular government program of national military service. It was a hugely popular commercial hit throughout Spain but lacked any subtlety or profundity of characterization. Other Bellmunt films of the 1980s that similarly suggest the popular exploitation of topical themes include *Pa d'Angel* [*Pan de angel*] [*Angel Bread*] (1984), which comically deals with the contemporary struggle over religion in Spain, and *La radio folla* [*Crazy Radio*], a raucous and scatalogical comedy dealing with all-night radio shows and bikers in Barcelona. The upcoming Barcelona Olympic games, was the background for Bellmunt's next film, the international thriller, *El complot des anells* [*The Ring Plot*] (1988).

Though attempting to move beyond his base of a youthful Catalan audience and reach a broader Spanish public, Bellmunt's films are somewhat uneven in their development of plot and characters, and, except for their persistent settings in Barcelona, seldom touch themes that are of interest outside of Catalonia.

BIBLIOGRAPHY
Balló, Jordi, Ramón Espelt, and Joan Lorente (eds.). *Cinema català 1975–1986.* Barcelona: Columna, 1990.

Berlanga, Luis García (Valencia, 1921). Generally considered one of the two or three most original and popular Spanish filmmakers of the sound period, Berlanga is perhaps the only one to achieve sustained and resounding commercial successes while also being praised by critics and historians alike for the originality of his cinematic work. Abandoning his university studies to join the Blue Legion of the Spanish army to fight in the Soviet Union during World War II, he returned to Spain to become involved in film, first as the organizer of a *cine-club* in his native Valencia, then as a film reviewer for a local newspaper. In 1947 he enrolled in the recently founded National Film School (IIEC) in Madrid. It was here that Berlanga first came into contact with Juan Antonio Bardem,* with whom he would collaborate on his first feature-length film, the biting comedy, *Esa pareja feliz [That Happy Couple]** (1951). He also received the first critical exposure to Italian Neorealism at IIEC, which exerted a decisive influence in his early professional development.

Berlanga's output as a filmmaker is relatively modest, consisting of some seventeen films over a period of more than forty years. This is due primarily to the countless censorship problems he encountered with many of his film scripts. Yet a surprising number of the films he did manage to get past the censors are perceived by critics to be among the very best examples of Spanish black comedy.

Berlanga's films are usually divided into three key periods. The first runs from *That Happy Couple* (1951) through *Los jueves, milagro [Every Thursday, a Miracle]* (1958) and includes the immensely popular *Bienvenido Mister Marshall! [Welcome, Mister Marshall!]** (1953). This is a period marked by the clear influence of Neorealism in Berlanga's style. In *Every Thursday, a Miracle* he encountered perhaps his most trying censorial difficulties in which the producers hired a priest to rewrite the second half of the film so as to avoid potential negative criticism of the film's treatment of a false miracle as anti-Catholic. Though often biting in their treatment of Spanish social and political institutions, such as the Catholic Church and inefficient governmental bureaucracy, the films of this first period reveal a consistently sentimental and warm touch in Berlanga's treatment of his characters. The most striking example of that thread of tenderness is to be found in *Calabuch* (1956).

Berlanga's second period starts with his first collaboration with coscriptwriter, Rafael Azcona* in 1961 with *Plácido,** considered by many to be Berlanga's masterpiece, and extends through the end of the Franco dictatorship. In these films, tenderness gives way to an often savage black humor as in *El verdugo [The Executioner]** (1963), Berlanga's attack on the death penalty. The particularly vile form of Spanish execution, garrote, is satirized through the vicissitudes of a family dependent on the breadwinner's job as executioner.

In Berlanga's third period, films made since the dismantlement of the Franco dictatorship in the mid-1970s, with the continued collaboration of Azcona as scriptwriter, the focus is on the cultural mores of the period of the transition to democracy. During this period, he achieves some of his most astounding commercial successes, especially in the trilogy of ensemble comedies that begins with *Escopeta nacional [National Rifle]** (1977), and includes *Patrimonio nacional [National Patrimony]* (1980); and *Nacional III [National III]* (1982). These are followed in 1984 by one of the biggest commercial successes of Berlanga's entire career, *La vaquilla [The Heifer]*, based on a script that had been repeatedly turned down by the censors because it dared to treat themes related to the Civil War with levity and derision.

Besides his many achievements as a filmmaker, Berlanga taught courses in film direction at both the original National Film School (IIEC) as well as its subsequent reincarnation, the Escuela Oficial de Cine (EOC). In the early 1980s, he was named to head the *Filmoteca Española*, the National Film Archive, but eventually resigned from the position, arguing that he lacked the appropriate bureaucratic spirit.

BIBLIOGRAPHY

Gómez Rufo, Antonio. *Berlanga, contra el poder y la gloria.* Madrid: Temas de Hoy, 1990.

Hernández-Les, Juan, and Manuel Hidalgo. *El último austro-húngaro: conversaciones con Berlanga.* Barcelona: Editorial Anagrama, 1981.

Betriu, Francesc (Orgoño, Lérida, 1940). With an interest in both theater and film, Betriu entered the Escuela Oficial de Cine (EOC) in the early 1960s, following which he cofounded the production company IN-SCRAM, which specialized in the production of film shorts. In the early 1970s he assumed the editorship of the influential film magazine, *Fotogramas.* His debut as a director came in 1972 with his work on one part of the three-part film, *Corazón solitario* [*Lonely Heart*] (1972), which he followed in 1974 with his own film, *Furia española* [*Spanish Fury*]. That film faced severe problems with the Spanish censors who, after forcing revisions in the script, made even more cuts in the final film, delaying its release for over a year. Betriu's difficulties partially stemmed from his desire to cultivate a form of crude realism very close to the traditional Spanish *esperpento* or "grotesque," which clearly went against the tastes of the ultraconservative film censors.

In 1976 he made *La viuda andaluza* [*The Andalusian Widow*], a screen adaptation of the sixteenth-century erotic novel by Francisco Delicado, in which he similarly attempted to develop a sensationalist form of realism. A mordant comedy about role reversals between masters and servants, *Los fieles sirvientes* [*Faithful Servants*] (1980) suggested a new direction in Betriu's social thematics, but with little positive reaction from the critics. It was not until he began working conscientiously in film adaptations of modern literary works, specifically those relating to the traumatic Civil War, that Betriu's work began to find its critical audience. In *Plaça del Diamant* [*Diamond Square*] (1982), he adapted the popular Mercè Rodoreda novel into a television series, then edited it to a manageable two-hour length for release as a motion picture, with excellent critical and commercial results. This was followed in 1985 with a film adaptation of Ramón Sender's short novel, *Réquium por un campesino español* [*Requium for a Spanish Farmer*] (1985), which was similarly well received. Over the next decade Betriu divided his time between television and film productions, achieving only marginal success in the latter. His 1993 television adaptation of Juan Marsé's *Un día volveré* [*One Day I Will Return*], another period evocation of the post–Civil War period in Catalonia, was extremely well received and garnered special recognition at the Valladolid Film Festival that year.

BIBLIOGRAPHY

Balló, Jordi, Ramón Espelt, and Joan Lorente. *Cinema català 1975–1986.* Barcelona: Columna, 1990.

Bigas Luna, José Juan (Barcelona, 1946). Originally a graphic designer, cofounder of the Gris studio, which was dedicated to industrial design, Bigas made the transition to filmmaking largely through his own autodidactic energies. He first worked on a number of soft-porn shorts and made his debut as a director of feature-length films with *Tatuaje* [*Tattoo*] (1976), an adaptation of a Manuel Vázquez Montalbán detective novel. Although work on the film provided Bigas with firsthand experiential knowledge of the commercial medium, the film itself did not fare well commercially. Bigas would later describe *Tattoo* as neither a commercially viable work nor one that had any appeal to artistic communities. Two years later, with the help of his friend, the Catalan producer Pepón Coromina,* Bigas made the notorious *Bilbao* (1978),* one of the pivotal films of the early transition period, based on his own original story.

The tale of the sexually obsessed son of a Catalan factory owner and his effort to possess an idealized prostitute whom he has named Bilbao sets the stage for a disturbing view of the contemporary consumer pathology as understood within the context of a presumably modern Catalan urban space. The film possesses all the hallmarks of Bigas's later work: the narrative centrality of an obsessive sexual duo in which the female becomes the object of male pathological behavior; the link through theme and setting of a consumerist culture that leads the male to desire to possess the female as object; the insistent visual care that transforms even the most routine noir plot into a stunning visual interrogation of contemporary cultural icons and obsessions. *Bilbao* won wide attention at the 1978 Cannes Festival and garnered Bigas a reputation among European art filmmakers.

Bigas followed *Bilbao* with the equally disturbing *Caniche* [*It's a Dog's Life*] (1979), also set in a noir Barcelona. Bigas appeared determined to forge a career as an international and cosmopolitan rather than a "Spanish" filmmaker. To this end he went to Hollywood and in 1981 made *Reborn* [*Renacer*] with Dennis Hopper, a film about American television evangelists, but it proved a commercial failure. After his American disaster, Bigas would return to the American theme one more time with *Angoixa* [*Angustia*] [*Anguish*] (1987), a horror film-within-a-film that was an homage to Alfred Hitchcock. Though entirely filmed in Barcelona with American actors, *Anguish* gave the uncanny feel of having been filmed in an American suburban environment.

The real conceptual leap in Bigas's development came with a series of films developed in an allegorical key, beginning with *Lola* (1985) and followed by his Iberian trilogy of the early 1990s: *Jamón, Jamón** (1992); *Huevos de oro* [*Golden Balls*] (1993) and *La teta y la luna* [*The Tit and the Moon*] (1994). Here the erotic, visual, and commercial cultures that had earlier converged in *Bilbao* are given an allegorical touch, as each of the films focuses on the emerging redefinition of Spanish culture from a picturesque, folkloric world to an economically driven cultural space where women gain increasing power. Especially in his Iberian trilogy, Bigas presents the predicament of Spanish males as they find themselves torn between traditional culture and a reformulated

European society. In each of these films, as in his work generally, the unique blend of stunning visual elements and a narrative about modernizing Spanish culture contributes to Bigas's unique authorial signature.

BIBLIOGRAPHY
Espelt, Ramón. *Mirada al Món de Bigas Luna*. Barcelona: Editorial Laertes, 1989.
Weinrichter, Antonio. *La línea del vientre: el cine de Bigas Luna*. Gijón: Festival de Cine de Gijón, 1992.

Bodegas, Roberto (Madrid, 1933). After studying in Barcelona and Madrid, Bodegas worked at the telephone company while he tried to break into the film industry. He later worked as an unpaid apprentice on Sergio Leone's *The Colossus of Rhodes* (1960), then decided to go to Paris in the hopes of a becoming involved in a more artistically meaningful film career. There he worked as the technical assistant for a number of directors, including Fred Zinneman, Denis de la Pattellière, and Christian-Jacque. He also made the acquaintance of Christian de Challonge with whom he eventually collaborated on the script of *O salto* [*The Jump*] (1967), a French-Portuguese coproduction. Few aspiring Spanish directors of the period could boast of this kind of experience before directing their first films.

In the late 1960s, Bodegas met Spanish producer José Luis Dibildos,* who offered him his first directorial assignment for *Españolas en París* [*Spanish Girls in Paris*] (1970), and also enlisted the talents of José Luis Garci* to work on the script. Dibildos's plan was to develop a series of films that followed a *Tercera vía* or "Third Route," so called because it was seen as an alternative to the two principal film production strategies of the period: art-house fare or popular, mass consumption genre films. While attempting to bring to popular attention themes and concerns of contemporary Spanish life in a serious but not heavily intellectual way, the film projects that Dibildos proposed to Bodegas and later to Antonio Drove,* the other young talent associated with the movement, quickly revealed their limitations as standard genre fare. Presenting issues of the day, but seldom moving beyond the surface topicality, these Dibildos-Bodegas collaborations, especially the comic works, seemed to hark back to the folkloric comedies directed by Pedro Masó* and Pedro Lazaga in the previous decade.

Spanish Girls In Paris, a film about the lives of Spanish women forced by economic necessity to emigrate to Paris to find work, performed modestly at the box office but stirred critical attention, leading many to see Bodegas as the principal exponent of Third Route cinema. He followed this film with two other significant collaborations with Dibildos, *Vida conyugal sana* [*Healthy Married Life*] (1973) and *Los nuevos españoles* [*The New Spaniards*] (1974).

Attempting to distance himself from the Third Route, Bodegas next worked on two films with scripts by noted writers Rafael Azcona* and Juan Marsé. *La adúltera* [*The Adulteress*] (1975), a black farse in the Azcona style, and *Libertad* *provisional* [*Provisional Freedom*] (1976), a Marsé script about two socially marginalized characters, seemed like transparent efforts by Bodegas to rechannel something of the topical attraction of the Third Route into a more personal work; but both films received very mixed results from critics and audiences. It was also increasingly obvious that his directorial talents seemed painfully tied to the limitations of the scripts with which he was working. By the 1980s, Bodegas's career was in limbo. Two later films, *Corazón de papel* [*Paper Heart*] (1982) and *Matar al Nani* [*To Kill Nani*] (1988), were both suspense genre films, but failed to attract significant audiences.

BIBLIOGRAPHY
Monterde, José Enrique. *Veinte años de cine español (1973-1992): un cine bajo la paradoja.* Barcelona: Paidós, 1993.

Borau, José Luis (Zaragoza, 1929). Borau is one of a handful of contemporary Spanish filmmakers who consciously struggled to achieve and maintain an identity as a film author. He was born in Zaragoza in 1929 and received a degree in law from the University of Zaragoza. He began his professional contact with film as a movie critic for the regional newspaper, *Heraldo de Aragón.* Later he pursued his interest by enrolling in the National Film School (IIEC) where he specialized in film direction. He followed this with a series of shorts and commercials for Spanish television.

Borau made his film debut inauspiciously with genre films, a Western in 1963, *Brandy*, followed the next year with a thriller, *Crimen de doble filo* [*Double-Edged Crime*]. Despite his obvious efforts to personalize these films in the tradition of American film auteurs, in the emerging context of the New Spanish Cinema of the period, Borau was seen by most critics and audiences merely as a commercial director following the patterns of status quo, nonpolitical cinema. From 1962 until 1970 he taught screenwriting at the reorganized national film school (EOC). Having taught many of the principal filmmakers of the next generation—among them, Antonio Drove,* Manuel Gutiérrez Aragón," Pilar Miró,* and Iván Zulueta*—he would later receive the accolade, "teacher to a generation of filmmakers."

While still teaching at the film school, Borau attempted to interest other producers in his scripts, but to no avail. In 1967 he founded the production company, El Imán, in an effort to produce his own work and those of others whose film projects interested him. The first such production, in 1969, was *Un, dos, tres, al escondite inglés* [*Hide and Seek*], directed by Iván Zulueta,* followed in 1971 by Jaime de Armiñán's* *Mi querida señorita* [*My Dearest Señorita*], which Borau coscripted. The film was commercially successful in Spain and went on to be nominated for an Oscar in the Best Foreign Film category. In 1973 Borau scripted, produced, and directed the first film he considered entirely his own work, *Hay que matar a B* [*B Must Die*]. The film boasted an international cast, including Darin McGavin, Patricia O'Neill, and

Stéphane Audran. Though ostensibly a political thriller set in a fictitious Latin American country, *B Must Die* posed a vision of life in a politically fraught country that was clearly inspired by Francoist Spain.

In 1975 Borau achieved his greatest artistic success in *Furtivos* [*Poachers*]* which, among the key films of the political transition, is also one of the most commercially successful motion pictures in Spanish film history. This was followed the next year with his participation in coscripting and producing Gutiérrez Aragón's second feature film, *Camada negra* (1976: *Black Brood*).* In 1979 he developed another international coproduction, *La Sabina* with a cast of Spanish, British, and American actors. That same year, Borau moved to Los Angeles in order to fulfill his longtime dream of making a film in Hollywood.

Plagued by financial difficulties, he managed to complete *Río abajo* [*On The Line*] (1983) with a Spanish and American cast. The film was blocked from competing in the Berlin Film Festival, where it had been presented as the official Spanish entry, however, due to its "un-Spanish" look. *On The Line* was generally well received in Spain but failed to interest American distributors till 1988 and even then made a very poor showing in the American market.

Borau's seventh film, *Tata mía* [*My Nanny*] (1986), made in the style of Madrid comedies, was actually a deft allegory of the culture of the transition, focusing on the images and values of the past that continue to shape Spaniards' way of projecting their own future. One of the most distinctive aspects of the film was the way Borau implicitly underscored his historical theme by casting, in the three principal roles, actors who were emblematic of three different historical periods of popular Spanish comedy: Carmen Maura* plays Elvira, a former nun unprepared to face a world so different from her religious or familial past; her former childhood playmate, now an infantilized adult obsessed with seducing nurses, is played by Alfredo Landa;* and Elvira's former nanny, who has been brought to Madrid to help Elvira face the future, is played by Imperio Argentina.* Borau's homage to Imperio Argentina drew special praise from Spanish critics.

During the 1980s, Borau reluctantly dedicated his energies to television production and was coscriptwriter with Carmen Martín Gaite, as well as producer and director of the series, *Celia*, based on the children's stories of Elena Fortún. The series became the most-watched television film in Spanish media history.

BIBLIOGRAPHY
Heredero, Carlos F. *José Luis Borau: teoría y práctica de un cineasta.* Madrid: Filmoteca Española, 1990.
Kinder, Marsha. *Blood Cinema: The Reconstruction of National Identity in Spain.* Berkeley: University of California Press, 1993.
Sánchez Vidal, Agustín. *Borau.* Zaragoza: Caja de Ahorros de la Inmaculada, 1990.

Buchs, José (Santander, 1893; Madrid, 1973). Trained as a professional actor, Buchs first became involved in film as an actor interpreting a role in the adaptation of *Los intereses creados* [*The Bonds of Interest*] (1918), directed by the play's author, Jacinto Benavente. Intrigued by the technology of cinema, Buchs quickly mastered the technical aspects of film production and was placed under contract in 1919 with the Atlántida Production Company to finish directing three films that Julio Roesset had left incomplete. Over the next decade he made a total of some thirty films, a number of which were produced by the production company formed in partnership with José Forn.

The 1920s were the most significant period of Buchs's directorial career; during this time he produced the popular zarzuela, *La verbena de la paloma* [*Paloma Fair*] (1921). Reflecting his belief that Spanish cinema should devote itself to the adaptation of popular national cultural classics, the film was a huge success both in Spain and abroad. Other characteristic folkloric works by Buchs during the period included his *La reina mora* [*The Moorish Queen*] (1922) and *Una extraña aventura de Luis Candelas* [*Luis Candelas's Strange Adventure*] (1924).

By the end of the 1920s, Buchs had moved on from these folkloric works to more dramatic and historical films, such as *Prim* (1930) and *Carceleras* [*Women Jailors*] (1932). The latter, a melodrama, was the first Spanish film produced with full sound; it was a remake of his 1922 silent film. His difficulty in abandoning deep-set beliefs in folkloric and nationalistic themes and his troubles with developing a competitive style for his films gradually led to his marginalization within the film industry. Although Buchs continued to make films throughout the 1930s and 1940s and into the 1950s, his works were generally of a mediocre technical and artistic quality. Despite his later work in sound cinema, he is best remembered for his earlier phase, when, along with Florián Rey,* Benito Perojo,* Fernando Delgado,* and Eusebio F. Ardavín, he was part of a circle of filmmakers of the 1920s who helped shape the popular national flavor of Spanish cinema.

BIBLIOGRAPHY

García Fernández, Emilio C. *Historia ilustrada del cine español*. Barcelona: Planeta, 1985.
Méndez-Leite von Haffe, Fernando. *Historia del cine español*. Vol. 1. Madrid, Ediciones Rialp, 1965.

Buñuel, Luis (Calanda, Aragon, 1900-Mexico City, 1983). By far the most widely known and revered of all Spanish filmmakers, Buñuel's career spans a half century and four countries: Spain, France, Mexico, and the United States. Though much has been written about the presumed Spanishness of Buñuel's films, of the more than three dozen works that comprise his filmography, only four were actually made in Spain: *Tierra sin pan* [*Land without Bread*] (1932)*; *Viridiana* (1961),* *Tristana* (1970),* and *Cet obscur objet du désir* [*That Obscure Object Of Desire*] (1977). Four other films, *Don Quintín el amargao* [*Embittered Don Quintín*] (1935), *La hija de Juan Simón* [*Don Simón's Daughter*] (1935), *¿Quién me quiere a mí?* [*Who Loves Me?*] (1936), and

¡Centinela alerta! [Look Out, Sentry!] (1936), were at least partially directed by Buñuel in Spain, although he persistently denied any directorial credit for them. A closer examination of Buñuel's four acknowledged Spanish films, viewed in the context of his fifty year career, enables one to grasp some of the essential themes and cinematic strategies defined by critics worldwide as "Buñuelian."

Land without Bread, or *Las Hurdes,* as it is sometime known, is Buñuel's only incursion into documentary cinema. Yet such a classification may be deceptive since the film actually works as a parody of the patterns of conventional cinematic viewing, especially documentary and travelogue genres. Its ostensible subject matter is the discrepancy between the cultural richness of the Spanish province of Salamanca, which boasts Spain's oldest university, and the backwardness of the lives of the inhabitants of the nearby Hurdano region. Thematically the film works to discomfort its complacent bourgeois spectator through descriptions of the apparent hopelessness of the economic and social plight of many of the inhabitants. Although *Land without Bread* was shot as a silent film, with sound track later added, Buñuel's strategy of establishing a radical juxtaposition between sound and image is clearly established here. In particular, the clash between Brahms's Fourth Symphony and the horrific images of hunger, squalor, and death is notable.

Viridiana focuses its attack on the dogma of Christian charity by narrating the actions of a would-be perfect Christian, the innocent Viridiana, who wants to imitate the life of Christ by helping to feed, house, and educate a group of beggars. Buñuel's script, while following a realistic story, deftly poses an allegorical tale in which the various characters hold apparent symbolic meanings. If Viridiana comes to signify the dangerous innocence of the belief in Christian charity, she is situated between two extremes personified by the beggars and her cousin Jorge (Francisco Rabal), with whom she has jointly inherited her uncle's country estate. The beggars embody the notion of instinctual reality that cannot be denied by religious rhetoric; Jorge is the pragmatist who is not so naive as to believe he can change anything in society, but simply tries to better his own lot. The symbolic struggle between Viridiana and these two foils leads to a larger allegory about the Spain Buñuel has returned to after twenty-five years of exile, torn as it appears to be between the dogma of the past and the need to confront modernization.

Tristana emblemizes the deeply rooted Spanish cultural inspiration of Buñuel films. Though based on a minor novel by the nineteenth-century novelist, Benito Pérez Galdós, the film is cast as an international coproduction, with French actress Catherine Deneuve, Italian actor Franco Nero, and a supporting Spanish cast. Shot in Toledo, its narrational style suggests a modernist spirit, especially in the rapid cuts between scenes that had begun to appear in Buñuel's work with *Belle de Jour* (1967). As in that film, the cuts reflect the interplay of the characters' dreaming and waking states, thereby bringing the audience back to Buñuel's Surrealist period with its focus on the themes of desire and the unconscious. Focusing on the status of women in conservative Spain, the ultimate theme of *Tristana* is the false illusion of individual freedom, a theme that clearly transcends the particular national contexts of Buñuel's work and addresses an international audience.

That Obscure Object of Desire is, in many ways, a coda to Buñuel film career. Made when he was seventy-seven, the film reiterates a number of the key themes and formal qualities of his earlier works: unbridled desire made more intense by its social prohibition; the hypocritical nature of the predatory male characters; and the female's illusion of freedom. To these must be added the autobiographical theme of exile itself as the action moves between a Paris racked with a terorrism that suggests a contemporary update of the Surrealists' dream of social disruption, and a Spain caught in the clichés of touristic folklore and sexual enticement. The pursuit by Mateo (Fernando Rey*) of the elusive Conchita (played by two actresses, Carole Bourquet and Angela Molina, with a voice dubbed by a third actress) seems to embody the ambivalence of Buñuel's filmography, situated as it is between cultures and using that condition to forge a series of critical discourses into various cultures, patterns of representation, and patterns of perception. The film ends enigmatically by posing unanswerable questions for its audence about the nature of the action represented and the relation of such representations to the audience's own social world.

BIBLIOGRAPHY
Aranda, J. Francisco. *Luis Buñuel: biografía crítica.* Barcelona: Editorial Lumen, 1969.
Fuentes, Víctor. *Buñuel: cine y literatura.* Barcelona: Salvat, 1989.
Kinder, Marsha. *Blood Cinema: The Reconstruction of National Identity in Spain.* Berkeley: University of California Press, 1993.
Sánchez Vidal, Agustín. *Luis Buñuel: obra cinematográfica.* Madrid: Ediciones JC, 1984.

Burmann, Hans (Bod-Honnef, Germany, 1937). The son of the well-known scenic designer, Sigfried Burmann, Burmann was educated in Madrid and began working in the Spanish film industry at the age of sixteen. By the 1960s, he had become a highly experienced assistant cameraman for a variety of films, ranging from rank commercial films, such as works of Mariano Ozores and Pedro Lazaga, to more serious films: Miguel Picazo's* *La tía Tula* [*Aunt Tula*]* (1964), Fernando Fernán-Gómez's* *El extraño viaje* [*The Stange Journey*]* (1964), and various films by Mario Camus.*

Burmann made his debut as cinematographer for Ramón Fernández's popular *No desearás al vecino del quinto* [*Thou Shalt Not Covet Thy Neighbor on the Fifth Floor*](1970). He would later return to work with Fernández on nine other films over the next decade. More importantly, however, he became the preferred cinematographer for some of Spain's most important filmmakers, including Mario Camus, with whom he shot, among other films, *La colmena* [*The Beehive*] (1982), *Los santos inocentes* [*Holy Innocents*]* (1984), and *La Rusa* [*The Russian Woman*] (1987); Pilar Miró,* with whom he worked on *La petición* [*The Petition*] (1976), *El crimen de Cuenca* [*The Crime at Cuenca*]* (1979), and

Werther (1986); and Eloy de la Iglesia,* with whom he worked on *Colegas* [*Pals*] (1982) and *El pico* [*The Shoot*]* (1983).

Burmann's special talent is the versatility with which he is able to easily adjust his sense of visual design from an elegant period film containing subtle plays of shadows and light, such as Imanol Uribe's* *El rey pasmado* [*The Flustered King*]* (1991), to a contemporary comedy, such as Manuel Gómez Pereira's *¿Por qué lo llaman amor cuando quieren decir sexo?* [*Why Do They Call It Love When They Mean Sex?*] (1993). Precisely because of this skill, Burmann found himself one of the most sought after Spanish cinematographers of the 1980s and 1990s.

BIBLIOGRAPHY

Heredero, Carlos F. *El lenguage de la luz: entrevistas con directores de fotografía del cine español*. Alcalá de Henares: 24 Festival de Cine de Alcalá de Henares, 1994.

Llinás, Francisco. *Directores de fotografía del cine español*. Madrid: Filmoteca Española, 1989.

Camino, Jaime (Barcelona, 1936). Trained in law and music, Camino's earliest contacts with film came by way of film criticism published in the film journals *Indice* and *Nuestro cine*. His first film was a 16mm short entitled *Contraste* [*Contrast*], (1961) followed by a succession of others. His debut feature film, *Los felices sesenta* [*The Happy Sixties*] (1963), was an ironic look at the emerging image of European modernity on the Catalan Costa Brava. The film attempted to combine a European "look" in its visual style with a decidedly Catalan flavor, marked by the off-screen voice of the popular singer, Raimón; it was one of the first times since the Civil War that Spanish audiences could hear the Catalán language in a Spanish film. Though not a commercial success, *The Happy Sixties* announced one of the characteristic features of Camino's film work: an effort to combine cultural and political themes in a popular style.

In 1967, he directed *Mañana será otro día* [*Tomorrow Is Another Day*]; the script was written by fellow Catalan, Román Gubern,* and splendidly photographed by Luis Cuadrado.* The film was intended as a critique of the prominence of publicity in contemporary Catalan culture and used a visual style that again attempted to emulate European, particularly French New Wave, visual design. Despite such touches, the film failed commercially. The next year, in another collaboration with Gubern, joined now by Alvah Bessie, one of the notorious "Hollywood Ten" of the McCarthy era, Camino made *España, otra vez* [*Spain, Again*], openly developing the theme of the remembrance of the defeated of the Civil War. The film follows the return to Barcelona of an American participant in the International Brigade exactly thirty years after his departure. Though constrained by the censors' prohibitions, Camino was, nonetheless, able to pose a number of previously prohibited themes sympathetic to the Republican cause. *Spain, Again* was nominated for an Oscar in the Best Foreign Film category in 1968.

The success of *Spain, Again* led Camino to pursue Civil War themes in a number of docudramas and documentary films over the next two decades: *Las largas vacaciones del '36* [*The Long Summer Vacation of '36*] (1976), *La vieja memoria* [*The Old Memory*]* (1977), *El balcón abierto* [*The Open Balcony*] (1984), *Dragón Rapide* (1986),* and *El largo invierno* [*The Long Winter*] (1991). Though the timing of the release of *The Long Summer Vacation of '36*, shortly after Franco's death, brought the film major attention and a critics' award at the 1976 Berlin Film Festival, a more significant and conceptually more original work is the documentary, *The Old Memory*, made the following year. Consisting of a series of interviews with participants on both sides of the struggle who are called upon to recall their activities during the war, *The Old Memory* is edited to pose a dizzying compilation of newsreel footage that either confirms the narration or else questions the veracity of "old memories." As such, the film poses a brilliant interrogation of popular memory and history. Less complex and commercially less successful was Camino's *The Long Winter* (1991), which also dealt with Civil War themes.

Camino's other efforts to interrogate Spanish or Catalan cultural themes proved less successful from both artistic and commercial perspectives. *Un invierno en Mallorca* [*A Winter in Mallorca*] (1969), which retells a crucial episode in the lives of the famed pianist Fredric Chopin and writer George Sand, is marred by a low budget and uneven acting. *La campanada* [*Pealing of the Bells*](1979), one of Camino's most personal and dramatic films, which has a powerful performance by Juan Luis Galiardo,* similarly failed to reach a popular audience.

BIBLIOGRAPHY

Balló, Jordi, Ramón Espelt, and Joan Lorente (eds.). *Cinema català 1975–1986*. Barcelona: Columna, 1990.

Gubern, Román. *1936–1939: La guerra de España en la pantalla*. Madrid: Filmoteca Española, 1986.

Camus, Mario (Santander, 1935). Abandoning law studies to enter the National Film School (IIEC) in the mid-1950s, Camus began his professional film career working as a coscriptwriter on Carlos Saura's* first two features, *Los golfos* [*Hooligans*]* (1959), and *Llanto por un bandido* [*Lament For a Bandit*] (1963). In 1963 he made his own directorial debut with *Los farsantes* [*The Actors*] (1963). It was quickly followed by *Young Sánchez*, the story of an aspiring boxer, which bears considerable thematic similarities to *Hooligans* in its treatment of the economic struggles of a younger generation of Spaniards to achieve economic success through careers in sports. A critical more than a commercial success, *Young Sánchez* qualified Camus as one of the more promising members of the New Spanish Cinema that José María García Escudero, the director of the Ministry of Information's Film Office, was promoting. An equally promising Camus film, *Con el viento solano* [*With a*

Wind from the East] (1965), boasted appearances by Antonio Gades* and the legendary Imperio Argentina.*

Over the next decade, Camus developed a somewhat irregular career as a director of both serious films, such as *Los pájaros de Baden-Baden* [*The Birds Of Baden-Baden*] (1975) and rank commercial works, such as the debut musical drama of pop singer, Raphael, *Cuando tú no estás* [*When You're Not Here*] (1966). He was one of the first important filmmakers to accept a major television project—the ten-part epic adaptation of the nineteenth-century Benito Pérez Galdós novel, *Fortunata y Jacinta* (1979), followed in 1983 with *Los desastres de la guerra* [*The Disasters of War*], which presented episodes in the life of the Spanish painter, Francisco de Goya.

Camus's work does not begin to achieve serious and sustained authorial coherence until the 1980s, the decade in which he was sufficiently established to be able to scrupulously select his film projects. The majority of these were literary adaptations, such as his two most important films of the this period, *La colmena* [*The Beehive*] (1982) from the popular novel by Camilo José Cela, which won the Gold Bear at the Berlin Film Festival, and the extraordinary artistic and commercial success, *Los santos inocentes* [*Holy Innocents*]* (1984), which won the major acting award at the 1985 Cannes Festival for its two leading actors, Francisco Rabal* and Alfredo Landa.*

These two adaptations underscore Camus's special talents: a striking ability to develop relatively faithful screen adaptations from important literary sources, and an ability to bring together talented stage and film actors in a well-balanced dramatic ensemble. Yet his later adaptation of García Lorca's *La casa de Bernarda Alba* [*The House of Bernarda Alba*] suffered from the predictability of these very qualities: Critics found the film ponderous and inflated. Returning to more cinematic material, in 1993 he received the Spanish critics' award for *Sombras en una batalla* [*Shadows in a Battle*], a film that combines melodrama with a story of political intrigue.

Returning to scriptwriting for his friend, Pilar Miró,* Camus scripted two of Miró's important films of the 1990s: *Beltenebros* (1991), and *El pájaro de la felicidad* [*The Bird Of Happiness*]* (1993). More recently, he attempted to expand his range as a scriptwriter/director with the ill-fated comic drama, *Amor propio* [*Self-Esteem*] (1994) starring Verónica Forqué.*

BIBLIOGRAPHY

Caparrós-Lera, José María. *El cine español de la democracia: de la muerte de Franco al "cambio" socialista (1975–1989)*. Barcelona: Anthropos, 1992.

Frugone, Juan Carlos. *Oficio de gente humilde . . . Mario Camus*. Valladolid: Semana de Cine de Valladolid, 1984.

Chávarri, Jaime (Madrid, 1943). Chávarri entered the Escuela Oficial de Cine (EOC) in 1968, already having completed a law degree. He abandoned his formal film studies in his second year, moving into film criticism and writing for *Film*

Ideal while devoting himself to making feature-length films in super 8. He collaborated with Iván Zulueta* in the latter's series for Spanish television, *Ultimo grito* [*The Last Cry*], and subsequently scripted *Un, dos tres . . . al escondite inglés* [*Hide And Seek*] (1969). Over the next several years he worked on the technical crew of a number of films and contributed one segment to the collective film, *Pastel de sangre* [*Blood Pie*] (1971). His first directorial assignment for a feature-length film was *Los viajes escolares* [*School Trip*] (1974), a complex autobiographical film that focuses on the ambience of a dysfunctional family. While acknowledging Chávarri's distinctive talents in developing characters and narrative, critics commented on the obscure symbolism of the film, which weakened its appeal to audiences.

Two years later, Chávarri continued that same theme of the dysfunctional family in a radical new format, a powerful and unconventional documentary on the family of the deceased Francoist poet, Leopoldo Panero, *El desencanto* [*Disenchantment*]* (1976). The film is one of the truly brilliant documentaries of Spanish cinema, not only stripping bare the hypocrisy of the Francoist family, but capturing the visceral relations forged out of the patriarchal tyranny in the poet's three sons and widow.

Chávarri followed this tour de force with another highly original film, *A un dios desconocido* [*To an Unknown God*] (1977), which dramatizes the self-interrogation of a lonely gay man (Héctor Alterio*) in contemporary Madrid as he ponders his life, moving from the memories of the mythic figure of Federico García Lorca to his own contemporary existence as a professional magician. Again marked by a notable ambiguity in narration, the film, coscripted with producer, Elías Querejeta,* also contains some of the most impressive imagery of Spanish film of the period, a result of the excellent collaboration between Chávarri and his cameraman, Teo Escamilla.* *To an Unknown God* won prizes for the director and the leading actor at the 1977 San Sebastián festival.

A later collaboration with Querejeta, *Dedicatoria* [*A Dedication*] (1980), probed questions of political and ethical compromise. Juan Oribe (José Luis Gómez*) is a journalist whose interrogation of his comrade, Luis Falcón, a political prisoner, leads him to discover the incestuous relation between Falcón and his daughter, the same woman with whom Juan is having sexual relations. Like earlier Chávarri films, *A Dedication* was praised for its uncompromising thematics and artistry but failed to make a strong showing at the box office.

By the early 1980s, Chávarri had embarked on a series of film adaptations of diverse fictional works which lent a seeming randomness and lack of focus to his development as a filmmaker. In 1983 he directed the opulent adaptation of the Lorenç Villaronga novel, *Bearn o la sala de las muñecas* [*Bearn or the Doll's Room*], and followed that with a screen version of Fernando Fernán-Gómez's* Civil War play, *Las bicicletas son para el verano* [*Bicycles Are for Summer*] (1984). In the following years, Chávarri's most commercially successful film was the musical drama set in the 1930s, *Las cosas del querer* [*The Things of Love*] (1989).

BIBLIOGRAPHY
Hernández-Les, Juan, and Miguel Gato. *El cine de autor en España.* Madrid: Castellote,
     1978.

Chomón, Segundo De (Teruel, 1871; Paris, 1929). Although the vast majority
of his more than one hundred and fifty short films have been lost, Chomón is
recognized today as one of the true pioneers of early Spanish cinema, often
called the Spanish Méliès, because of his array of visual innovations in early
silent fiction films. Film historians have argued that Méliès more appropriately
might have been dubbed the French Chomón, so great was the Spaniard's
innovative range in the cinema of the first decade of the twentieth century.
     He arrived in Paris in 1895 when the Lumière's exhibition of the cinematic
apparatus first was being shown publicly. He soon went to work for Méliès and
the Pathé brothers, stencil-tinting plates for   special effects for their films.
Having mastered techniques of cinematic special effects, he returned to Barcelona
as the offical Pathé representative, where he established his own studio and began
to produce a variety of documentary and fictional films. During this period he
designed some of the most creative special effects of cinema anywhere to be
found. His films of this period included *Choque de trenes* [*Train Wreck*] (1902)
and *Gulliver en el país de los gigantes* [*Gulliver in the Land of the Giants*]
(1903), two films that reveal Chomón's skill at producing special effects for
realistic as well as fantastic narration.
     His fame for innovative special effects led Chomón back to Paris in 1905
where he again collaborated with the Pathés on productions until 1909. During
this period he was reputed to have directed some sixty-five short films. He
returned once again to Barcelona where over the next four years he managed to
direct from his own studio some forty-eight more films. In 1912 he was
contracted by Italia Films in Turin where he worked on the silent-film epic,
Cabiria (1914), which was directed by Giovanni Pastrone, but contained a
number of lavish sequences of technical dexterity supervised by Chomón himself.
The first moving camera (for *Cabiria*) attributed to Pastrone, was actually
Chomón's invention. Working with other famous filmmakers of the day, he
returned to Paris where he spent the rest of his life.
     Of his vast filmography, *El hotel eléctrico* [*The Electric Hotel*](1905), is
Chomón's definitive masterpiece. The film is described as a machine-age comedy
that employs the technique of *pixilation*, frame-by-frame photography used to
produce the effect of objects in autonomous motion.

BIBLIOGRAPHY
Méndez-Leite von Haffe, Fernando. *Historia del cine español.* Vol. 1. Madrid: Ediciones
     Rialp, 1965.
Sánchez Vidal, Agustín. *El cine de Segundo de Chomón.* Zaragoza: Caja de Ahorros de
     la Inmaculada, 1992.

Colomo, Fernando (Madrid, 1946). Attracted to motion pictures from an early age, Colomo was shooting shorts in super 8 by the age of sixteen. He first completed a degree in Architecture, then entered the Escuela Oficial de Cine (EOC) with a specialty in decoration. With money earned from his architectural jobs, he made his first 16mm film, *Mañana llega el presidente* [*The President Arrives Tomorrow*] (1972), a blend of fiction and documentary about the state visit of Argentine president, Héctor Cámpora, to Spain. After completing his film degree, he worked as a scriptwriter and eventually established his own production company, La Salamandra, which would produce all of his feature-length films.

Colomo's first feature-length film, the commercially successful *Tigres de papel* [*Paper Tigers*]* (1977), was warmly received by the critics. Establishing Carmen Maura* as a promising young star, the film was an intimate yet light, comic look at the contradictory impulses of exemplary members of a Spain's youthful progressive urban population. Colomo's script, which placed his characters in a seemingly spontaneous set of situations, helped establish the *Nueva Comedia Madrileña*, "New Madrid Comedy," of which Colomo and later Fernando Trueba* would be the chief exponents during the 1980s.

While continuing the line of urbane Madrid comedies with *¿Qué hace una chica como tú en un sitio como éste?* [*What Is a Girl Like You Doing in a Place like This?*] (1978) and *Estoy en crisis* [*I'm in Crisis*] (1982), he experimented with varying degrees of success with more established cinematic formats, such as the detective genre (*La mano negra* [*The Black Hand*] [1980]) and science fiction (*El caballero del dragón* [*The Dragon Knight*] [1985]). His principal successes, however, have remained Madrid comedies, among which the most noteworthy and commercially successful ones have been films that deftly exploit the confusion of sexual and social mores in contemporary liberal Spanish society, such as *La vida alegre* [*The Happy Life*] (1987) and *Alegre ma non troppo* (1994).

BIBLIOGRAPHY

Caparrós-Lera, José María. *El cine español de la democracia: de la muerte de Franco al "cambio" socialisita (1975-1989)*. Barcelona: Anthropos, 1992.

Hernández-Les, Juan, and Miguel Gato, *El cine de autor en España*. Madrid: Castellote, 1978.

Coromina, Pepón (Josep Coromina Farreny) (Barcelona, 1946, Barcelona, 1987). This enterprising Catalan producer began studying economics at the University of Barcelona, but abandoned his studies in order to go into business for himself, first with a line of youthful fashion, eventually as a film producer. His first production was the flawed adaptation of Juan Marsé's *La oscura historia de la prima Montse* [*The Dark Story of Cousin Montse*] (1977), directed by Jordi Cadena. When the film made a surprisingly strong commercial showing, Coromina decided to establish his own production company, Fígaro Films, through which he was able to produce some nineteen motion pictures over the next decade. Some of these film projects were clearly motivated by Coromina's desire to support an emerging Barcelona-based Catalan cinema, as was the case with Bigas Luna's* *Bilbao** (1978), *Caniche* [*It's a Dog's Life*] (1979), and later *Angoixa* [*Angustia*] [*Anguish*] (1987), or Francesc Betriu's* *La plaça del diamant* [*Diamond Square*] (1982) adapted from the novel by the famed Catalan writer, Mercè Rodoreda, and cofinancied by Catalan television. Others were simply astute choices to support the work of non-Catalan directors in films with non-Catalan-speaking actors. These include important films by Eloy de la Iglesia* (*El diputado* [*The Deputy*] [1978], and *Navajeros* [*Knife Fighters*] [1980]) and Pedro Almodóvar's* first film, *Pepi, Luci, Bom, y otras chicas del montón* [*Pepi, Luci, Bom, and Other Girls like That*]* (1980). The subject-matter of a number of these films either is linked to Catalan culture or focuses on socially marginal characters and groups. Thus, Coromina's principal contribution to Spanish cinema was his pivotal activity in helping to diversify the look of Spanish films and to support the larger project of social demarginalization in the immediate aftermath of the defunct Franco regime.

BIBLIOGRAPHY

Hopewell, John. *Out of the Past: Spanish Cinema after Franco.* London: BFI Books, 1986.

Font, Domenèc, Joan Batlle, and Jesús Garay. "Entrevista con Pepón Coromina," *La mirada: textos sobre cine*, no. 4, Año 1 (October 1978): 28–29.

Cuadrado, Luis (Toro, Zamora, 1934; 1980). Abandoning studies at the University of Madrid Medical School to enter the Escuela Oficial de Cine (EOC), Cuadrado graduated in 1962 with a degree in cinematography. He joined Elías Querejeta's* production team and made his film debut as director of photogaphy in 1965 with Antonio Eceiza's* *De cuerpo presente* [*Lying in State*]. Over the next decade, and as a result of the international success of the Querejeta productions, Cuadrado would receive both national and international recognition as a highly innovative and creative director of photography, principally through his participation in the creative production team assembled by Querejeta. His major screen credits in this period include the first seven of Carlos Saura's* films produced by Querejeta, beginning with *La caza* [*The Hunt*]* (1965) and running through *La prima Angélica* [*Cousin Angelica*] (1973); and Víctor Erice's *El espíritu de la colmena* [*Spirit of the Beehive*]* (1973). He also photographed Armiñán's *Mi querida señorita* [*My Dearest Señorita*]* (1971), José Luis Borau's *Hay que matar a B* [*B Must Die*] (1973) and *Furtivos* [*Poachers*]* (1975), as well as early films by Vicente Aranda* and Manuel Gutiérrez Aragón.*

During the ten-year period of 1965–1975, Cuadrado was generally perceived as the most talented and innovative of Spanish cinematographers. The dominant visual style of many but not all of the films he made during this period had a dark and shadowy quality, said to be inspired by the paintings of Goya and seventeenth-century painters such as Murillo. These qualities are particularly conspicuous in Saura's *Peppermint Frappé* (1967) and Erice's *Spirit of the*

Beehive, as well as Borau's *Poachers*. By 1975, at the height of his talent and international renown, Cuadrado's eyesight began to fail and he was replaced on Ricardo Franco's *Pascual Duarte** by his assistant cinematographer, Teo Escamilla.*

BIBLIOGRAPHY
Barroso, Jaime. "Homenaje a Luis Cuadrado." *Contracampo*, nos. 10–11, Año 2 (March–April 1980): 14–30.
Hernández-Les, Juan. *Elías Querejeta: un productor singular*. Bilbao: Ediciones Mensaje-ro, 1986.
Llinás, Francisco. *Directores de fotografía del cine español*. Madrid: Filmoteca Española, 1989.

Cuerda, José Luis (Albacete, 1947). Abandoning his law studies in his third year at the University of Madrid, Cuerda began working in Spanish state television in 1968 and became affiliated with the group of film critics, writers, and actors who would form the so-called Argüelles School. Between 1969 and 1974 Cuerda became part of Spanish Television's news division, producing more than five hundred news reports and short documentaries. While still working for state television, he made a number of cultural and dramatic films, one of the most striking of which is *Mala racha* [*A Bad Time*] (1985).

In 1982, Cuerda made his debut as a commercial film director with *Pares y nones* [*Odds and Evens*] a comedy that clearly fit into the model of the Madrid Comedy of his colleagues, Fernando Trueba* and Fernando Colomo.* In 1987 he made what would be his most commercially successful and artistically satisfying film, *El bosque animado* [*The Enchanted Forest*]. The film, based on a novel of the same title by the noted Spanish writer of the 1920s and 1930s, Wenceslao Fernández Flores, boasted an excellent script by Rafael Azcona,* as well as a distinguished ensemble cast headed by Alfredo Landa.* The following year, Cuerda scripted and directed his most personal film, *Amanece, que no es poco* [*Waking Up, Which Is No Small Feat*]. The film is characterized by Cuerda's own ironic sense of humor. His subsequent work, often of a highly topical nature, such as *Tocando fondo* [*Hitting Bottom*] (1993), was marred by a forced humor and fared poorly with Spanish audiences.

BIBLIOGRAPHY
Torres, Augusto M. *Diccionario del cine español*. Madrid: Espasa Calpe, 1994.

Delgado, Fernando (Madrid, 1891; Madrid, 1950). Son of playwright Sinesio Delgado, Fernando abandoned law studies for acting, making his theatrical debut in 1909. In 1916 he debuted in films and two years later he began working with Jacinto Benvente in film productions. Delgado directed his first film in 1924, *Los granujas* [*The Rascals*] and continued to direct eight more films before the end of the silent era, the most creative period of his career. His most praised and commercially successful films of this period were *Las de Méndez* [*Méndez's*

Women] (1927), *¡Viva Madrid, que es mi pueblo!* [*Long Live Madrid, It's My Town!*] (1928), and *El gordo de Navidad* [*First Prize in the Christmas Lottery*] (1929).

With the advent of sound, Delgado temporarily stopped working in film, only to return in 1934 with the comedy, *Doce hombres y una mujer* [*Twelve Men and a Woman*]. His biggest commercial success of this period was the first sound version of the bullfighting film, *Currito de la Cruz* [*Currito of the Cross*] (1936). Production of his next film, *El genio alegre* [*The Happy Spirit*], was interrupted by the outbreak of the Civil War, and not completed until 1939; doubles were used for the film's principal actors, who had been Republican sympathizers during the war. At the war's end, Delgado renewed his directorial career with some six additional films; he finally retired in 1947. Critics generally agree that despite Delgado's transition to sound productions, his most creative work remains his films of the late silent era.

BIBLIOGRAPHY
Fernández Cuenca, Carlos. *La obra de Fernando Delgado*. Madrid: Circe, 1949.
Gubern, Román. *El cine sonoro de la II República (1929–1936)*. Barcelona: Editorial Lumen, 1977.

Dibildos, José Luis (Madrid, 1929). Having completed his studies in law, Dibildos's interest in film led him to the motion picture industry in which he debuted as a scriptwriter in 1950 with Pedro Lazaga's *Hombre acosado* [*Hunted Man*]. Over the next years, Dibildos worked with the prolific playwright Alfonso Paso on a number of scripts, the best of which is generally considered to be Juan Antonio Bardem's* *Felices Pascuas* [*Merry Christmas*] and Antonio del Amo's* *Sierra maldita* [*Cursed Hills*], both made in 1954.

In 1956 Dibildos established his own production company, Agata Films, through which over the next three decades he would produce more than forty films. His specialty during the rest of the 1950s was the genre of "Italian comedies," that is, comedies with a narrative emphasis on sexual twists. Having established his presence as a producer of note through a series of commercially successful films, in the early 1960s Dibildos attempted to expand and solidify his financial base through a number of international coproductions. These were all costumed, historical films produced with pretensions of epic grandeur and boasting international casts. They included Carlos Saura's* second film, *Llanto por un bandido* [*Lament For a Bandit*] (1963), Christian-Jacque's *El tulipán negro* [*The Black Tulip*] (1964), and Abel Gance's version of *Cyrano de Bergerac* (1964).

By the mid 1960s, however, after several commercial flops, Dibildos returned to coscripting and producing comedies, some of which would be directed by Fernando Merino, José María Forqué,* and Javier Aguirre. By 1970, he had developed a new strategy for what he saw as socially progressive comedy, termed by the critics *tercera vía* or Third Route, in which traditional light comedies were set against the backdrop of topical social issues and events. The term "Third Route" derived from the assumption that such films would somehow mediate between the extremes of serious art cinema on the one hand, and low popular comedy on the other.

Working with José Luis Garci* on these scripts, Dibildos enlisted two young directors for this new genre: Roberto Bodegas* directed *Españolas en París* [*Spanish Girls in Paris*] (1970); *Vida conyugal sana* [*Healthy Married Life*] (1973), and *Los nuevos españoles* [*New Spaniards*] (1974). Antonio Drove* directed *Tocata y fuga de Lolita* [*Lolita's Toccata and Fugue*] (1974), and *Mi mujer es decente dentro de lo que cabe* [*My Wife Is Decent as Far as That's Possible*] (1974). Though Third Route films offered limited possibilities, given the increasingly strident expressions of dissident cinema in the last five years of the dictatorship, they did provide important professional experience to young directors and help launch Roberto Bodegas and José Luis Garci's career. By the middle of the 1970s, however, Dibildos had returned to his more traditional comedies, this time collaborating with Pedro Lazaga.

Of the films that Dibildos produced over the final ten years of his professional career, the most important, indeed, the most outstanding of his entire career, was Mario Camus's* *La colmena* [*The Beehive*] (1982), an adaptation of Camilo José Cela's novel of postwar Madrid. With an impressive ensemble cast, the film won the Golden Bear for best film at the 1982 Berlin Film Festival. Dibildos's final production was the 1986, *A la pálida luz de la luna* [*In the Pale Moonlight*] directed by José María González Sinde.

BIBLIOGRAPHY
Caparrós-Lera, José María. *El cine político visto después del franquismo*. Barcelona: Dopesa, 1978.
Monterde, José Enrique. *Veinte años de cine español (1973-1992): un cine bajo la paradoja*. Barcelona: Paidós, 1993.

Drove, Antonio (Antonio Drove Shaw) (Madrid, 1942). Abandoning his studies in electrical engineering to enter the Escuela Oficial del Cine (EOC), Drove graduated in 1967 with a short film, *Caza de brujas* [*Witch Hunt*], which was later banned by the Francoist censors. He worked for a time in Spanish television and as a coscriptwriter with Mario Camus* (*La leyenda del Alcalde de Zalamea* [*The Legend of the Mayor of Zalamea*] [1972], Gonzalo Suárez* (*Al diablo con amor* [*To the Devil with Love*] [1973] and José Luis Borau* (*Hay que matar a B* [*B Must Die*] [1973]. In 1974 he was contracted by José Luis Dibildos* to direct two films, *Tocata y fuga de Lolita* [*Lolita's Toccata and Fugue*] and *Mi mujer es muy decente dentro de lo que cabe* [*My Wife Is Decent as Far as That's Possible*], as part of Dibildos's effort to develop a *tercera vía* or Third Route for Spanish films, which was aimed at a liberal, contemporary audience somewhere between the presumed extremes of mass consumption movies and art-house fare. Both films dealt with aspects of contemporary sexual mores in the final days of the dictatorship and were mildly successful at the box office. He went on to make a third example of the genre, *Nosotros que fuimos tan felices* [*We Who Were So Happy*] (1976) which was produced by Alfredo Matas.*

While these films indicated Drove's ability to work with some measure of creativity within the commercial film industry, his more personal adaptation of modern novels better reflects his much praised talents within the Spanish film community. *La verdad sobre el caso Savolta* [*The Truth about the Savolta Case*]* (1978) is a screen adaptation of the Eduardo Mendoza novel about a thwarted factory strike in Barcelona in the early part of the century. *El túnel* [*The Tunnel*] (1987) is based upon the Argentine novel by Ernesto Sábato. Thematically, the two films are radically different: *Savolta* is a political study of the false illusions of liberal movements in Spain that are eventually thwarted by the dictatorship of Primo de Rivera in 1923; *The Tunnel*, like the novel on which it is based, is an existentialist narrative about individual alientation and a frustrated struggle for communication. Yet stylistically both works share a common quality in their often brilliant elaboration of a mise-en-scène with a striking play of light and shadows that shows the influence of American film noir as well as German Expressionism. At Sábato's insistence, *The Tunnel* was shot in English with an international cast, with only Fernando Rey* in a secondary role to suggest the Spanish origin of the production.

BIBLIOGRAPHY
Hopewell, John. *Out of the Past: Spanish Cinema after Franco*. London: BFI Books, 1986.
Torres, Augusto M. *Diccionario del cine español*. Madrid: Espasa Calpe, 1994.

Ducay, Eduardo (Zaragoza, 1926). Interested in film since his youth, Ducay joined Orencio Ortega Frisón and Antonio Serrano in founding the Zaragoza Cine-Club in 1945. In Madrid, he studied film direction at the recently established Instituto de Investigaciones y Experiencias Cinematográficas (IIEC) and was a prominent voice in the generation of Juan Antonio Bardem* and Luis García Berlanga,* who fought to reshape Spanish film in the 1950s. Ducay began to write film criticism for the most important film magazine of the 1950s, *Objetivo*, and was one of the cosponsors for the important Salamanca Conversations on National Cinema in May of 1955. After the magazine was dissolved as part of the government's crackdown on intellectual dissent, Ducay moved on to the prestigious liberal literary and cultural periodical, *Insula*, where he headed the film review section.

During the late 1950s, in keeping with his position in support of a rebirth of Spanish film, and as a strong advocate of Neorealism, he participated in the formation of Epoca Films, which was set up to produce Marco Ferreri's* Neorealist depiction of life on Madrid streets, *Los chicos* [*The Boys*] (1959). By the end of the 1950s he was working as an influential critic as well as in film production in the script department of Moro Studios.

He later went on to produce some of the landmark Spanish films of the 1970s and 1980s, including Luis Buñuel's* *Tristana** (1970), Francisco Regueiro's* *Padre nuestro* (1985), and José Luis Cuerda's* highly successful *El bosque animado* [*The Enchanted Forest*] (1987).

BIBLIOGRAPHY

Heredero, Carlos F. *Las huellas del tiempo: cine español 1951–1961*. Valencia: Filmoteca de la Generalitat Valenciana, 1993.

Eceiza, Antonio (San Sebastián, 1935). After receiving his law degree, Eceiza entered the National Film School (IIEC) in 1958. Over the next four years, he contributed critical and theoretical articles to a number of the principal film journals of the day, including *Cinema Universitario, Film Ideal*, and *Nuestro Cine*. Though he never completed his film degree, by the early 1960s he was collaborating on scripts, among them Juan Antonio Bardem's* *Los inocentes* [*The Innocents*] (1962), filmed in Argentina, as well as Vittorio Cottafavi's *Los cien caballeros* [*The One Hundred Gentlemen*] (1965). He scripted two shorts with Elías Querejeta,* *A través de San Sebastián* [*Through San Sebastián*] (1961) and *A través del fútbol* [*Through Soccer*] (1963). Over the next seven years, it would be Querejeta's own production company that produced four of Eceiza's films. The first three films—*El próximo otoño* [*Next Autumn*] (1963); *De cuerpo presente* [*Lying in State*] (1965), based on a novel of the same title by Gonzalo Suárez;* and *Ultimo encuentro* [*Final Encounter*] (1966)—were criticized for a rigid and inflexible sense of social realism. Vicente Molina-Foix notes that *Las secretas intenciones* [*Secret Intentions*] (1969), produced by Querejeta and based on a script by Rafael Azcona,* was artistically a more interesting work involving fantasy and neurosis. *Secret Intentions* also boasts cinematography by Luis Cuadrado* and an international cast, including French actor Jean Louis Trintignant. Yet, despite these strengths, the film proved a commercial failure.

For political reasons Eceiza was forced to leave Spain in 1973, moving first to Paris, then to Mexico where he filmed *Mina, viento de libertad* [*Mina, the Wind of Liberty*] (1976), and *El complot mongol* [*The Mongol Conspiracy*] (1977). He returned to Spain in the late 1970s and, after shooting a number of shorts in Euskera, the Basque language, he made *Días de humo* [*Days of Smoke*] (1989), which dealt with the theme of political conflicts in the Basque country.

Eceiza's early films, shot under the Querejeta rubric, were linked with the promotion of New Spanish Cinema, but although they appeared to espouse the critical realism that was the fervor of dissident filmmaking of the day, they failed to attract any sizeable audience.

BIBLIOGRAPHY

Molina-Foix, Vicente. *New Cinema in Spain*. London: BFI, 1977.
Rodero, José Angel. *Aquel "nuevo cine español" de los '60*. Valladolid: 26 Semana Internacional de Cine de Valladolid, 1981.

Elías, Francisco (Huelva, 1890; Barcelona, 1977). One of Spain's pioneers in sound film, Elías started working in the motion pictures industry at the age of eighteen as an editor for silent film intertitles in Paris, first for Gaumont and later for the Eclair company. In 1914 he became Eclair's representative in Barcelona; shortly thereafter he established his own company, Manufactura del Film. By 1916 he was established in New York with his own company, Elías Press Inc., which produced intertitles in Spanish for American newsreels until the end of the silent period. During this time he began making his own short films and learning more of the technical side of filmmaking.

In 1928 Elías returned to Spain to make his first feature films using the new Phono-film system. *El misterio de la Puerta del Sol* [*The Mystery of the Puerta del Sol*], the first Spanish film shot entirely with sound, turned out to be a commercial failure due to the poor quality of sound equipment. Elías quickly moved on to Paris where he directed three French films. He returned to Barcelona where, along with Camille Lemoine and José María Guillén García, he founded Estudios Orphea, the first production center in Spain constructed for the filming of sound motion pictures. In the years leading up to the Civil War Elías directed four films in these studios—all of unexceptional quality, according to critics of the time.

During the Civil War, Elías was a partisan of Franco. As a result of his political affiliation, he was forced to flee Republican Barcelona and spent ten years in Mexico, from 1938 to 1948, where he directed some eight films. In 1954 Elías founded Amílcar Films, through which he directed his last feature film, *Marta*, in 1954.

Though Elías was known through the sound period as a director, contemporaries and film historians generally agree that his principal contribution to Spanish cinema was less in the area of artistic development, where he was an unexceptional director, than in his promotion and support of sound film during the critical period of the Second Republic.

BIBLIOGRAPHY
Gubern, Román. *El cine español en el exilio: 1936–1939*. Barcelona: Editorial Lumen, 1976.
Pérez Gómez, Angel, and José L. Martínez Montalbán. *Cine español 1951–1978: diccionario de directores*. Bilbao: Editorial Mensajero, 1978.

Erice, Víctor (Carranza, Vizcaya, 1940). Erice is one of the outstanding voices of a generation of filmmakers who appear most strikingly touched by the Civil War and its aftermath. A student of the reorganized national film school (EOC), he contributed to a variety of film journals in the 1960s, the most important of these being the leftist inspired *Nuestro Cine*. During the late 1960s, Erice made a number of shorts and received coscript credit for several important films of the period, including Miguel Picazo's* *Oscuros sueños de agosto* [*Dark Dreams of August*]. In 1970, Elías Querejeta* gave Erice the opportunity to direct one of the three episodes of *Los desafíos* [*The Challenges*], for which he won the

Concha de Plata at the San Sebastián film festival. Three years later, Erice made his first feature-length film, *El espíritu de la colmena* [*Spirit of the Beehive*], again produced by Querejeta.

In *Spirit of the Beehive*, Erice demonstrates the force of an elliptic visual style that depends very little on dialogue, but engages the viewer in an intense scrutiny of the iconic value of images. The story is set in a small Castilian village in 1940, and focuses on the experiences and perspective of Ana (Ana Torrent*), a girl of seven or eight, who is torn between the pervasive sense of isolation of the community around her that is mirrored by the alienation of her parents (Fernando Fernán Gómez* and Teresa Gimpera*) from each other and from their two daughters. The monotony and loneliness of Ana's world is shattered with the arrival of a stranger in the town, whom Ana takes to be the incarnation of the monster in James Whale's *Frankenstein*, recently screened in the village. Ana's confusion between the world of movies and her own world sets up much of the visual tension of the film.

Known as an eccentric and demanding director with a highly original personal vision, Erice did not direct another film for ten years. The 1983 *El sur* [*The South*], based on a story by Adelaida García Morales, appears to be a spiritual update to *Beehive*. It deals with the loneliness of a teenage girl growing up in a dysfunctional family in Castile in the 1950s and with the mysterious relationship between father and daughter.

In 1992, again nearly a decade later after his previous film, Erice made his third feature-length film, the quasidocumentary, *El sol de membrillo* [*Quince-Tree Sun*],* which chronicles the attempts by the artist, Antonio López, to paint a still life of a quince tree in his garden during the autumn of 1991. The story of the artist's failed attempt is set against the backdrop of local and international events that lead the audience to interrogate the modes of representation in contemporary culture as well as the nature of national identity. The film won a special prize at the 1992 Cannes Festival.

The authorial style of Erice's three feature-length films is characterized by a complex interplay of narrative and visual elements that engage the audience's reflection on the nature of visual representation itself. All three films are notable for a paucity of dialogue, and self-referential plots that bring the audience to note the problems of cinematic representation.

BIBLIOGRAPHY
Arocena, Carmen. *Víctor Erice*. Madrid: Cátedra, 1996.
Kinder, Marsha. "The Children of Franco in the New Spanish Cinema." *Quarterly Review of Film Studies* 8, no. 2 (Spring 1983): 57–76.
Marías, Miguel, and Felipe Vega, "Una conversación con Víctor Erice," *Casablanca* nos. 31–32, (July–August 1983): 59–70.

Escamilla, Teo (Sevilla, 1940). Escamilla began his professional career first as a newspaper photographer; he later worked as a Arocena television cameraman, then finally as an asistant cameraman on films. During a ten-year period, he worked in this position on key films by Jaime de Armiñán* (*Mi querida señorita* [*My Dearest Señorita*]* [1971]), José Luis Borau* (*Hay que matar a B* [*B Must Die*] [1973] and *Furtivos* [*Poachers*]* [1975]), as well as Víctor Erice* (*El espíritu de la colmena* [*Spirit of the Beehive*]* [1973]). During these years, while working on Elías Querejeta* productions, Escamilla became a close friend and disciple of Querejeta's principal photographer, Luis Cuadrado,* working under him on important films by Carlos Saura* such as *La madriguera* [*The Bunker*] (1968), and *Jardín de las delicias* [*Garden of Delights*] (1970).

When Cuadrado's failing eyesight worsened on the shooting of Ricardo Franco's* *Pascual Duarte** (1975), producer Querejeta asked Escamilla to replace Cuadrado as the principal cinematographer for the film. Having learned much of what he knew about the use of light and shadows in cinematography from Cuadrado, Escamilla would be called upon not only to replace Cuadrado in some of the most important and highly praised Querejeta films but, also to develop his own visual style, evolving as Querejeta's directors evolved throughout the late 1970s. This evolution in style is recorded in a prodigious number of films that consist of all of Carlos Saura's projects from 1975 through 1989, including *El amor brujo* [*Love, the Magician* (1986), for which he won a Goya for best photograhy. Other films made during the height of the Querejeta film operation that Escamilla worked on are Jaime Chávarri's* *El desencanto* [*Disenchantment*]* (1976), *A un dios desconocido* [*To an Unknown God*] (1977), and *Dedicatoria* [*A Dedication*] (1979); and Manuel Gutiérrz Aragón's* *Sonámbulos* [*Sleepwalkers*] (1977), *Maravillas* [*Marvels*] (1980), and *Feroz* [*Ferocious*] (1984). Of his work in the 1980s, especially noteworthy are his luminous lighting and striking camera work in José Luis Borau's* *Tata mía* [*My Nanny*] (1987).

Escamilla's own skills as a director were much in evidence in the quasidocumentary on bullfighting, *Tú, solo* [*You Alone*] (1983), which combines his early dedication to documentary photography with the visual style he had developed on fiction films during the 1970s.

BIBLIOGRAPHY
Heredero, Carlos F. *El lenguaje de la luz: entrevistas con directores de fotografía del cine español*. Alcalá de Henares: 24 Festival de Cine de Alcalá de Henares, 1994.
Gutiérrez-Solana, Ignacio. "Teo Escamilla: Contra el estilo." *Casablanca*, no. 9 (September 1981): 31–38.

Escrivá, Vicente (1913, Valencia). Beginning his professional career in journalism, Escrivá directed Spanish National Radio's programming for Latin America in the immediate post–Civil War period. As the author of several novels and collections of essays, he won the National Literature Prize in 1947. The following year he turned to film, working initially as a script collaborator on José Luis Sáenz de Heredia's* religious drama, *La mies es mucho* [*Bountiful Harvest*] (1948). The film's success led him to become further involved in the film industry, initially as one of the cofounders of ASPA Films, and then as a scriptwriter in the late 1940s and first half of the 1950s for some of the most popular of quasi-religious and political genre films of the day. These included José Antonio Nieves Conde's *Balarrasa* (1950) and Rafael Gil's *La señora de Fátima* [*The Lady of Fatima*] (1951), *Sor Intrépida* [*Sister Intrepid*] (1952), *La guerra de Dios* [*God's War*] (1953), *El beso de Judas* [*Judas's Kiss*] (1953), and *Murió hace quince años* [*He Died Fifteen Years Ago*] (1954).

Given Escrivá's subsequent career in both scriptwriting and directing, film historians tend to view this stage of his success as reflecting an astute sense of the contemporary movie trends rather than any abiding religious conviction. By the end of the decade, he was producing as well as scripting a prodigious number of popular films. In 1959, he directed his first film, *El hombre de la isla* [*The Man of the Island*], followed two years later by *Dulcinea* (1962), both of which failed commercially although the comedies he was scripting and producing continued to be highly successful at the box office. This discrepancy soon led Escrivá to try directing more traditional Spanish comedies, a genre in which he clearly excelled.

By the end of the 1960s, Escrivá had moved into light erotic comedies that insistently emphasized the oversexed nature of long-repressed Spanish males. The most commercially successful of these was *El verde empieza en los Pirineos* [*Green Begins in the Pyrenees*] (1973). Even with the dismantlement of the dictatorship, Escrivá continued to flourish. His adaptation of the sixteenth-century Francisco Delgado erotic novel, *La lozana andaluza* [*The Andalusian Beauty*] (1976), clearly reflected Escrivá's ability to assess audience tastes and to cater to them. His films of the 1980s similarly reflect his skill at exploiting film trends, as is noted in his Spanish version of the American hit *Kramer vs. Kramer* transformed into *Esperando a Papá* [*Waiting for Daddy*] (1980).

One of the most commercially successful of Spanish filmmakers, Escrivá reflects the tendency toward commercial opportunism of a certain sector of the Spanish film industry. The practitioners of this approach toward popular cinema were able to maintain a domestic market during the latter half of the Franco dictatorship and the early transition period, but it has since largely disappeared because of the same impulse of Spanish television to provide easy topical entertainment with little concern for artistic merit.

BIBLIOGRAPHY
Pérez Gómez, Angel, and José L. Martínez Montalbán. *Cine español 1951–1978: diccionario de directores.* Bilbao: Editorial Mensajero, 1978.

Fernán-Gómez, Fernando (Lima, Peru, 1921). One of Spain's most prolific actors (more than 150 film credits in a period of 50 years), Fernán-Gómez has also written, directed, and staged a number of original works for the theater and film. His somewhat irregular career as a director began in 1953 with *Manicomio* [*Asylum*], which he produced himself. Over the next four decades he directed some twenty-three films, the majority of which he scripted himself, and in a number of which he starred as well. His film production is uneven because of the hectic pace of his commitments as an actor in theatrical and film productions.

The significant corpus of Fernán-Gómez's films is a small portion of his total output, which captures the underlying ironic vision of Spanish life and, in a number of instances, plays off his own autobiographical experiences in both the theater and film, predominently in a comic tone. His first commercial success was *La vida por delante* [*Your Life before You*]* (1958), the story of the struggles of a newly-wed couple in the Madrid of the 1950s. Inspired by the Juan Antonio Bardem*-Luis García Berlanga* collaboration, *Esa pareja feliz* [*That Happy Couple*]* (1951), in which Fernán-Gómez played a role not unlike the character he portrays here, the film glows with comic inventiveness—especially in the use of visual gags, and plays with editing and sound track. A similar vein of visual inventiveness is evident in *El extraño viaje* [*The Strange Journey*]* (1964), which was based on an idea from Berlanga and partially scripted by Fernán-Gómez. Blocked from a normal premiere and distribution, *The Strange Journey* was only "discovered" by film buffs and critics nearly a decade later, at which time it was praised for its brilliant and sardonic humor in telling a series of comic incidents that revolved around the mysterious disappearance of three people from a small Castilian town.

Of much less formal invention is the autobiographical *El viaje a ninguna parte* [*Journey to Nowhere*] (1986), which tells the multiple stories of an itinerant theatrical troupe touring the Spanish provinces in the 1940s. Inspired by a variety of similar works of the 1950s and 1960s (Bardem's 1954 *Cómicos* [*Comedians*]; Camus's 1963 *Los farsantes* [*The Actors*]), *Journey to Nowhere* distinguishes itself by its light humor and impressive acting performances by both Fernán-Gómez and the young Gabino Diego* in the role of the actor's son.

Although known primarily for his comic inventions, Fernán-Gómez's *El mar y el tiempo* [*The Sea and Time*] (1989) shows a more dramatic side to his writing and directorial talents in this nostalgic tale set in the 1960s and evoking the bittersweet memories of political exile. In works such as these, which draw heavily on Fernán-Gómez's already familiar presence in other media, the director-actor-writer offers Spanish audiences a highly personal cinema, unique in Spanish film culture.

BIBLIOGRAPHY

Angulo, Jesús, and Francisco Llinás (eds.). *Fernando Fernán-Gómez: El hombre que quiso ser Jackie Cooper*. San Sebastián: Ayuntamiento de San Sebastián, 1993.

Contracampo. No. 35 (Spring 1984): 6–82. Special issue devoted to Fernando Fernán-Gómez.

Ferreri, Marco (Marc'Antonio Ferreri Bismark) (Milan, 1928; 1997). Though born in Italy, where he has made the overwhelming majority of his films, Marco Ferreri actually began his directorial career in Spain. Through his first three films, he made a significant contribution to the development of Spanish cinema in the 1960s.

Abandoning studies in veterinary science for a career in journalism, Ferrreri gravitated toward the Italian film industry and film publicity in his early twenties. He founded the film magazine *Documento Mensile*, which, though it lasted less than a year, featured articles by Visconti, De Sica, Antonioni, and other major Italian filmmakers. Trained in filmmaking through his work as a production assistant in films by Lattuada, Antonioni, Fellini, and Zavattini, by 1955 Ferreri found himself representing a motion picture optical company in Madrid. Here he met and began a productive friendship with the Spanish novelist, Rafael Azcona.*

In 1958, Ferreri codirected *El pisito* [*The Little Flat*] with Isidoro Ferry, with a script by Azcona adapted from the writer's own novel. Set in the period of severe housing shortages in Madrid, the film was marked by a grotesque blend of black humor that would characterize much of the subsequent Ferreri-Azcona collaboration. Less biting but no less grim was Ferreri's next film, *Los chicos* [*The Boys*] (1959), which traced the daily lives of a group of youths in a Madrid neighborhood. The film gave clear evidence of the force of Neorealism that marks all three of Ferreri's early works. The least appreciated of his three Spanish films, *The Boys* nonetheless laid the groundwork for the most elaborate part of the trilogy, *El cochecito* [*The Little Car*] (1960), a black comedy based on another Azcona novel and embued with the Neorealist penchant for location views of Madrid.

Common thematic as well as stylistic qualities mark the three films, specifically, the conflicts between men and women and the individual's relation to consumerist society. In *The Little Flat*, Rodolfo (José Luis López Vázquez*) is willing to marry a woman in her eighties in order to inherit her apartment and marry his true love, Petrita (Mary Carrillo*). In *The Little Car*, the aging Don Anselmo (José Isbert*) becomes so possessed with the idea of owning his own motorized car that when his son refuses him the money for the purchase, he poisons his entire family to be able to buy the car. In both works, the narrative, built upon the frustrated desires of characters deformed by an emerging consumerist society, enables the filmmaker to document the social environment that produces grotesque individual actions.

The influence of Ferreri's three films in Spain, especially their blending of an Italian Neorealist visual style with the black humor of the Spanish grotesque *esperpento*, clearly influenced the emerging generation of opposition filmmakers in the 1960s. Films like Berlanga's *El verdugo* [*The Executioner*]* (1962) and Fernando Fernán-Gómez's *El extraño viaje* [*The Strange Journey*]* (1963), show the influence of the Ferreri-Azcona style.

After returning to Italy, Ferreri continued to work with Rafael Azcona on the majority of his films, the most critically and commercially successful of which was *La grande abbuffata* [*La grande bouffe*] [*The Big Blow-Out*] (1973).

BIBLIOGRAPHY
Frugone, Juan Carlos. *Rafael Azcona: atrapados por la vida*. Valladolid: 32 Semana de Cine de Valladolid, 1987.
Riambau, Esteve (ed.). *Antes del apocalipsis: el cine de Marco Ferreri*. Madrid: Cátedra, 1990.

Fons, Angelino (Madrid, 1935). Abandoning his studies at the University of Murcia, Fons entered the National Film School (IIEC), graduating with a specialty in directing in 1960. Closely associated with Carlos Saura* during that director's first decade of professional filmmaking, Fons collaborated on a number of Saura's scripts during the early 1960s, receiving screen credits for *La caza* [*The Hunt*]* (1965), *Peppermint Frappé* (1967), and *Stress es tres, tres* [*Stress Is Three, Three*] (1968), as well as Francisco Regueiro's* *Amador* [*Lover*] (1965). He made his own directorial debut in 1966 with *La busca* [*The Search*] (1966), a modern-day adaptation of a novel by Pío Baroja marked by a sense of critical realism reminiscent of Miguel Picazo's* *La Tía Tula* [*Aunt Tula*]* (1964). The film was extremely well received and, as a result, Fons basked in critical adulation for a number of years as one of the most promising of the young filmmakers of the generation of New Spanish Cinema of the second half of the 1960s. *The Search* was followed two years later by the mediocre musical, *Cantando a la vida* [*Singing to Life*] (1968).

In 1969, Fons began a collaboration with the producer, Emiliano Piedra,* directing a weak adaptation of the Pérez Galdós novel, *Fortunata y Jacinta* (1969), with the producer's wife, Emma Penella,* in the lead. This was followed by *La primera entrega* [*The First Delivery*] (1971), with even less favorable critical results. Fons directed another Galdós adaptation the following year, *Marianela* (1972), but it was becoming increasingly apparent to critics and audiences that the promise shown in his first film had largely dissipated. Even a collaboration with Carmen Martín-Gaite, in an adaptation of one of her stories, *Emilia . . . parada y fonda* [*Emilia*] (1976), scripted by the novelist herself, did little to alter the apparent downward course of Fons's filmmaking career. By the early 1980s, Fons was directing cheap comic sexploitation films such as *El Cid cabreador* [*The Vexing Cid*] (1983).

BIBLIOGRAPHY
Higginbotham, Virginia. *Spanish Film Under Franco*. Austin: University of Texas Press, 1988.
Rodero, José Angel. *Aquel "nuevo cine español" de los '60*. Valladolid: 26 Semana Internacional del Cine de Valladolid, 1981.

Forn, Josep Maria (Barcelona, 1928). One of the strongest advocates of Catalan regional cinema in the 1970s, Josep Maria Forn began working in a much more conventional and mainstream Spanish film industry. In 1948, while still working as a studio apprentice, he directed the literary journal, *Panorama Literario*. He continued to work on the technical crew of a number of popular films of the period, including Julio Salvador's *Apartado de Correos 1001* [*Post Office Box 1001*] (1950) and Francisco Rovira-Beleta's *Hay un camino a la derecha* [*There's a Road on the Right*] (1953). Forn gradually worked his way up to the position of assistant director, debuting as a director in 1955 with *Yo maté* [*I Killed*].

Having been shaped by the conventions of Spanish commercial cinema of the day, Forn's work on this genre piece did not announce the arrival of a new film author. Even with the formation of his own production company, Teide Films, his primary interest remained conventional and commercial film fare. Over the next decade, Forn's work on nine other films only seemed to suggest that he was a competent but predictably commercial film artisan.

In 1966, he made *La piel quemada* [*Burnt Skin*], based on his own script, which, for the first time, indicated a break in his work. The story of the travels and travails of the family of migrant workers from Murcia who come to the Catalan Costa Brava in search of work in the local building trade becomes an interrogation of Catalan cultural identity and, as such, one of the first films since the end of the Civil War to approach this theme. It was followed three years later by *La respuesta* [*The Response*], which tried for a similarly daring approach to the emergence of a new and defiant generation of politically progressive Catalans. The film was severely mutilated by the censors and only received a public screening in 1976 after Franco's death. By then, Forn's political theme had become dated.

These two films, however, revealed Forn's concern for promoting the sense of Catalan cultural identity through cinema. In collaboration with Jaime Camino* and Antoni Ribas*, he helped to found the Instituto de Cinema Català and in 1979 scripted, directed, and produced perhaps his most explicitly Catalanist film, *Companys: Procés a Catalunya* [*Companys: Catalonia on Trial*], a hagiographic biography of the last president of Catalonia during the Civil War period. Given the limited appeal of the regionalist thematic, as well as Forn's uncritical view of Companys's life, the film found only a narrow regional audience. Forn's principal importance within Spanish cinema lies in his dedication to the concept of a distinctive cinematic and cultural tradition for the Catalonian autonomous region, and his development of strategies both in film production and government administration to further that cause.

BIBLIOGRAPHY

Balló, Jordi, Ramón Espelt, and Joan Lorente (eds.). *Cinema català 1975–1986*. Barcelona: Columna, 1990.

Batlle, Joan, and Ramón Sala. "Entrevista con Josep Maria Forn." *Contracampo* no. 7, Año 1 (December 1979): 13–19.

D'Lugo, Marvin: "Catalan Cinema: Historical Experience and Cinematic Practice." *Quarterly Review of Film and Video* 13, nos. 1–3 (1991): 131–147.

Forqué, José María (Zaragoza, 1923; Madrid, 1995). Forqué abandoned professional studies in architecture for a career in theater, working first at the university theater in Zaragoza, where he eventually became a stage director. His interest in film during this period led him to work on a dozen shorts. With Pedro Lazaga, he codirecting his first commercial feature-length film, *María Morena*, in 1951. That same year he directed *Niebla y sol* [*Fog and Sun*], his first solo directorial assignment. His career over the next thirty-five years would include some fifty-three films as well as a number of serialized dramas for Spanish television.

Forqué's first five films represent an apprenticeship phase in which he grew in both confidence and skill, but with very undistinguished results. In 1956, he achieved his first resounding success with *Embajadores en el infierno* [*Ambassadors in Hell*], based on a popular short story of the day that described the odyssey of Spanish soldiers of the Blue Legion who were taken prisoners in Russia during World War II. The following year he began a trilogy of films based on scripts by the noted Spanish playwright, Alfonso Sastre. The first of their collaborations was *Amanecer en Puerta Oscura* [*Dawn in Puerta Oscura*], a period film based on the exploits of nineteenth-century Andalusian bandits. The film won the Silver Bear at the 1957 Berlin Film Festival and was extremely well-received by Spanish audiences.

Forqué's next two films in the series fared poorly, even though the last of the three, *La noche y el alba* [*The Night and the Dawn*] (1958) was praised by critics as a noteworthy psychological study. The economic failures of these latter films led Forqué to seek out more commercially secure projects, which, in turn, led him to direct one of the most critically acclaimed and commercially successful comedies of his career: *Maribel y un señor de Murcia* [*Maribel and a Gentleman from Murcia*] (1960). Based on the popular stage success by Miguel Mihura, the film's strong reception made it easier for Forqué to continue in a comic vein throughout most of the 1960s. Of his films of this period, critics often single out *Atraco a las tres* [*Hold-Up at 3:00 P.M.*] (1963), a spoof of the genre of the perfect bank robbery gone amuck. Besides a clever script, the film boasts an excellent ensemble cast, including "Cassen,"* José Luis López Vázquez,* and Rafaela Aparicio.*

In 1967, Forqué established his own production company, Orfeo Films, which produced most of his subsequent productions. Following popular moviegoers' tastes, by the 1970s, Forqué was making erotic comedies of increasingly less artistic or critical interest. He went on to direct a number of serialized dramas for television, the most impressive of which was his collaboration with Adolfo Marsillach,* *Ramón y Cajal* (1982), based on the life of the noted physician and scientist.

BIBLIOGRAPHY

Heredero, Carlos F. *Las huellas del tiempo: cine español 1951–1961*. Valencia: Filmoteca de la Generalitat Valenciana, 1993.

Franco, Jesús (Madrid, 1930). Perhaps the most prolific of all Spanish filmmakers of the sound era, Franco boasts more than two hundred film titles to his credit, many of them under the pseudonyms he adopted over a thirty-four year career in Spain, France, West Germany, Holland, Portugal, Switzerland, and the United States: Jess Frank, Robert Zinnermann, David Khunne, Clifford Brown, Frarik Hollman, and Toni Falt.

Franco began studying law at the University of Madrid and music at the Royal Conservatory of Madrid. He later entered the National Film School (IIEC) with a specialization in direction, but halted his studies to go to Paris where he enrolled in filmmaking courses at the Institute des Hautes Etudes Cinématographiques (IDHEC). Upon his return to Madrid, he worked as technical assistant on films by Juan Antonio Bardem,* Luis García Berlanga,* Joaquín Luis Romero Marchent, León Klimovski, and others. He also collaborated on film scripts for a number of directors before making his own first short in 1957, *Arbol de España* [*The Tree of Spain*].

Franco made his commercial debut in 1959 with *Tenemos 18 años* [*We're Eighteen Years Old*], followed the next year by *Labios rojos* [*Red Lips*], two light comic films. Between 1959 and 1966, Franco made twelve films, most of which were popular terror films designed to cater to a Spanish audience. Beginning in 1966, he started to make international coproductions, almost exclusively within established genres, such as detective and police thrillers (*La muerte silba un blues* [*Death Whistles the Blues*]: [1962]; *Cartas boca arriba* [*The cards Face Up*] [1966]), terror films (*Bésame, monstruo* [*Kiss Me, Monster*] [1968]; *Fu-Manchu y el beso de la muerte* [*Fu-Manchu and the Kiss of Death*] [1977], and later soft core films (*Shining Sex* [1976]; *La chica de las bragas transparentes* [*The Girl in the Transparent Panties*] [1980]). Directed under pseudonyms, and distributed in languages other than Spanish, very few of these films were shown in Spain, leaving Franco in the curious position of being one of Spain's most prolific filmmakers and yet virtually unknown to Spanish audiences, except through a few titles.

BIBLIOGRAPHY
Aguilar, Carlos, and Ramón Freixas (eds.) *Dezine.* no. 4 (November 1991) Special issue dedicated to Jesús Franco.
Pérez Gómez, Angel, and José L. Martínez Montalbán. *Cine español 1951–1978: diccionario de directores.* Bilbao: Editorial Mensajero, 1978.

Franco, Ricardo (Madrid, 1949). After abandoning his university studies, Franco began his training as a filmmaker by assisting his uncle, Jesús Franco.* He wrote, produced, and directed *El desastre de Annual* [*The Massacre at Annual*] (1970), the intimate portrait of a decadent family trapped in the memory of the defeat of the Spanish Army in Morocco in 1921. Shot in 16mm, the film was denied a commercial release during the years of the dictatorship. *Pascual Duarte** (1975), adapted from the famed Camilo José Cela novel, catapulted Franco to both national and international prominence. The film's complex and elliptical script was the product of a collaborative enterprise with producer Elías Querejeta* and scriptwriter Emilio Martínez-Lázaro.* But the power of Franco's directing is evident in the fact that the film's lead actor, José Luis Gómez,* received the Best Acting award at the 1976 Cannes Film Festival.

Franco followed *Pascual Duarte* with a highly personal film, *Los restos del naufragio* [*The Remains from the Shipwreck*] (1978), which he scripted, directed, and starred in as Mateo, a man seeking refuge from a failed romance by entering a retirement home. Mateo makes friends with Pombo (Fernando Fernán-Gómez*), a retired theater director. Together, the two construct a series of imagined adventures rooted in large part in the appeal of genre films. Franco's subsequent film work, in fact, *El sueño de Tánger* [The Dream of Tangiers] (1986) and *Berlin Blues* (1988), are themselves homages to genre films, the adventure film and the musical, respectively.

In 1994, after working in Spanish television for a number of years, Franco returned to film with *Después de tantos años* [*After So Many Years*], a continuation of *El desencanto* [*Disenchantment*]* (1976), the powerful documentary originally made nearly two decades earlier in which Jaime Chávarri* interviewed members of the family of Francoist poet, Leopoldo Panero. Though much less taut than the Chávarri film, *After So Many Years* still provides some stunning insights into the process of political and cultural change in the years of the transition from dictatorship to democracy in Spain.

BIBLIOGRAPHY

García Fernández, Emilio C. *Historia ilustrada del cine español*. Barcelona: Planeta, 1985.
Hopewell, John. *Out of the Past: Spanish Cinema after Franco*. London: BFI Books, 1986.

Garci, José Luis (Madrid, 1944). A self-taught cinephile, Garci has had a varied career in film, clearly delineated in three stages: film critic, screenwriter, and finally, director. He began in the early 1960s as a reviewer for various film magazines such as *Signos, Cinestudio,* and *Reseña,* winning an award in 1968 from the Círculos de Escritores Cinematográficos for his movie criticism. In 1969 he became involved in scriptwriting, receiving his first screen credits for Antonio Giménez-Rico's* *El cronicón* [*The Chronicle*] (1970).

Between 1972 and 1977 he scripted five more films, becoming especially identified with José Luis Dibildos's* efforts to develop a *tercera vía* or Third Route. Garci became skilled in this genre for progressive social themes that were intended to serve an audience addressed in neither elite art cinema nor the base popular style of most Spanish comedies. During these years, Garci's most important scripts included Pedro Olea's* *No es bueno que el hombre esté solo* [*A Man Shouldn't Be Alone*] (1973), Roberto Bodegas's* *Vida conyugal sana* [*Healthy Married Life*] (1973) and *Los nuevos españoles* [*New Spaniards*] (1974), and Antonio Drove's* *Tocata y fuga de Lolita* [*Lolita's Toccata and*

Fugue] (1974). During this same period, Garci also wrote scripts for Spanish television.

The third phase of his film career began in 1977 with his shift to directing films, often with his own script. His first directorial credit was for *Asignatura pendiente* [*Pending Examination*]* from a script by González Sinde. The film was to become one of the emblematic expressions of the generation of Spaniards who, having suffered the period of transition from dictatorship to democracy, felt themselves in social as well as political limbo. A simple story of an amorous seduction by the film's hero, José Sacristán,* is shaped around a series of topical references to a generation of Spaniards born in the immediate post–Civil War period whose frustration and nostalgias are embodied in the film's protagonists. As striking as is the thematic focus of *Pending Examination*, Garci's detractors have often noted the way the film seeks to imitate the patterns of visual-narrative construction of Hollywood films. An insistence on extravagant establishing shots and a rigorous emulation of Hollywood shot/reverse-shot construction of scenes suggest a blatant imitation of the "look" of Hollywood cinema of the period.

Garci was able to develop *Pending Examination* around the lessons of the Third Route. The formula worked as well in his next film, *Solos en la madrugada* [*Alone at Dawn*] (1978), which also starred José Sacristán. In these films, and especially in his next film, *Las verdes praderas* [*The Green Prairies*] (1979), a heavily sentimental side to Garci's film style was becoming recognizable.

An apparent change of pace came with *El crack* [*The Crack*] (1980), which took elements of American noir cinema, especially the figure of the hard-boiled detective, and gave them a Spanish flavor. One of Garci's most striking achievements in *The Crack* is the way he transforms Alfredo Landa,* the principal comic figure of Spanish films of the 1960s, into a highly convincing Bogart-style detective. The formula worked so well that two years later Garci made a sequel in *El crack II*.

The pinnacle of Garci's career seemed to be reached the next year with his super sentimental *Volver a empezar* [*To Begin Again*]* (1983), which cleverly addressed the foreign clichés of Spaniards returning after the Civil War. The film was the first Spanish motion picture to win the Oscar as Best Foreign Film. Garci's work since *To Begin Again* has been characterized by two dominant qualities that defined much of his earlier work as well: an admiration for Hollywood films apparent in filming and editing style, and a tendency of overstated sentimentality. *Sesión continua* [*Double Feature*] in 1984 and *Asignatura aprobada* [*Examinations Approved*] (1987) give emphasis to the former tendency. *Canción de cuna* [*Cradle Song*] (1994), a film adaptation of the sentimental Gregorio Martínez Sierra play, which won for Garci the award for Best Direction at the Montreal Film Festival, exemplifies the latter.

BIBLIOGRAPHY
Garci, José Luis. *Morir de cine*. Oviedo: Caja de Ahorros de Asturias, 1990.

García Sánchez, José Luis (Salamanca, 1941). With professional degrees in law and sociology from the University of Madrid, García Sánchez entered the National Film School (EOC) but never completed his degree there due to the political expulsions of the Francoist period. For a time he worked as an assistant director for films by Carlos Saura* and Basilio Martín Patino,* but gradually moved to scriptwriting. He collaborated on Manuel Gutiérrez Aragón's* first feature-length film, *Habla mudita* [*Speak Little Dumb Girl*] (1973), as well as Francesc Betriu's* *Corazón solitario* [*Lonely Heart*] (1972) and *Furia española* [*Spanish Fury*] (1974), among others. His debut as a director came in 1972 with *El Love feroz* [*Fierce Love*], after which he made *Colorín colorado* [*And They Lived Happily Ever After*] (1976).

These directorial efforts were the testing ground for García Sánchez's first major artistic and commercial success, *Las truchas* [*Trout*] (1977), as demonstrations of the effort to uplift the much debased Spanish comedy of the final decade of the Franco dictatorship. The film was clearly viewed as an inspired satire of the decaying political and social milieu of Spain during and immediately after the dictatorship. *Trout* also crystallized a visual/narrative style of satire in García Sánchez's works that would become increasingly more savage over the next two decades. After codirecting a documentary on Dolores Ibarruri ("La Pasionaria"), *Dolores* (1980), also marked by its black humor, he teamed up with the famed master of Spanish black humor, Rafael Azcona,* for scripts of his film, *La corte de Faraón* [*The Pharaoh's Court*] (1985).

The collaboration continued with *Pasodoble* (1988), although García Sánchez was clearly moving into a new phase of his career. This was evidenced by his ambitious adaptation of Ramón María Valle-Inclán's *Divinas palabras* [*Holy Words*] (1987), a complex play by a dramatist whose sensibility for the grotesque seemed a perfect match for his own. Continuing with anti-Francoist themes, he made *La noche más larga* [*The Longest Night*] (1991), a historical treatment of the last major series of political executions carried out under the dictatorship. Narrated as a flashback from the contemporary period (1991), the film offers an important link between the traumatic national past and the seemingly tranquil historical present. A much more problematic film was his second adaptation of a Valle-Inclán work, this time the complex novel, *Tirano Banderas* (1993). Working with a huge international cast and his own adaptation of the novel, García Sánchez produced a film that once again underscored his characteristic mordant skill at political caricature and ensemble structure, but nonetheless proved a failure among both critics and audiences.

BIBLIOGRAPHY

Monterde, José Enrique. *Veinte años de cine español (1973–1992): un cine bajo la paradoja.* Barcelona: Paidós, 1993.

Gelabert, Fructuoso (Barcelona, 1874; Barcelona, 1955). One of the true pioneers of Spanish cinema, Gelabert was a trained mechanic who was also an aficionado of photography when he became interested in the Lumière Brothers' invention in 1897. He constructed his own version of the motion picture projector and that same year shot the first Spanish fictional film, a short entitled *Riña de café* [*Cafe Brawl*], for which he was scriptwriter, producer, director, and actor. It would be followed by a series of actuality films such as *Salida del público de la iglesia parroquial de Sans* [*Departure of People from the Church at Sans*] (1898), and *Visita de Doña María Cristina y Don Alfonso XII a Barcelona* [*The Visit of their Highnesses María Cristina and King Alfonso XII to Barcelona*] (1899). That same year he began developing an interest in special effects, as noted in his film, *Choque de dos transatlánticos* [*Collision of Two Transatlantic Steamers*] (1899). The striking quality of some of these early films, besides their value as the earliest evidence of filmmaking in Spain, is Gelabert's inspiration in the *sainete*, an immensely popular theatrical form focusing on the comedy of Spanish customs. *Cafe Brawl* is a vivid example of this genre and appears to underscore the preferences by Spanish audience for moving pictures that imitated preexisting cultural forms of entertainment.

Throughout the silent period Gelabert would not only continue to function in multiple roles as producer, director, and scriptwriter for the prodigious number of short films he made, but, as a technician, he would also construct equipment and create his own studios and laboratories for film production. His massive work divided into both reportage and fiction films. He worked throughout the silent period but abandoned filmmaking in 1928, precisely at the moment of the advent of sound. Of his enormous output, only a small portion remains.

BIBLIOGRAPHY
Fernández Cuenca, Carlos. *Fructuoso Gelabert, fundador de la cinematografía española*. Madrid: Filmoteca Española, 1957.
Francesc, Joan. *El món de Fructuós Gelabert*. Barcelona: Generalitat de Catalunya, Departamento de Cultura, 1988.
Porter i Moix, Miquel. *Historia del cinema català* (1895–1968). Barcelona: Editorial Taber, 1969.

Gil, Rafael (Madrid, 1913; Madrid, 1986). One of the most honored Spanish film directors during the years of the Franco dictatorship, Gil's career seems to have been clearly shaped by the ideological ups and downs of Francoist culture. He began his professional contact with motion pictures when he was in his early twenties, writing film reviews for a number of Madrid newspapers. In 1935, he published his first book of film criticism, *Luz de cinema* [*Cinema's Light*]. It was about this same time that he became interested in motion picture production and began working on 16mm documentary films. With the outbreak of the Civil War, he was recruited by Antonio del Amo* for a production unit that made documentary films for the Republican government. At the war's end, he apparently switched allegiances and started writing film reviews for Francoist publications. In 1941, he was contracted by CIFESA, the distribution company beginning to branch into the area of fictional film production. *El hombre que se* *quiso matar* [*The Man Who Tried to Kill Himself*] (1941) was the first of some seventy films Gil directed before his death in 1986.

The 1940s, and especially the time Gil spent under contract with CIFESA, was the richest period of his film work. His first hit, *Huella de la luz* [*Trace of Light*] (1943) was followed by *El clavo* [*The Nail*] (1944). Other majors films of this period include *El fantasma y doña Juanita* [*The Ghost and Doña Juanita*] (1944), *Tierra sedienta* [*Parched Land*] (1946), *Reina santa* [*Holy Queen*] (1947) and *Don Quijote de la Mancha* (1947). These films show an eclectic range from contemporary comedies and melodramas to costumed epics, with a heavy emphasis on period decor and settings.

In 1951, Vicente Escrivá,* who had recently won national acclaim as the scriptwriter of a number of quasi-religious films, invited Gil to direct *La señora de Fátima* [*The Lady of Fatima*]. Therein began the second major phase of Gil's filmmaking career, a six-year collaboration under the rubric of Escrivá's production company, Aspa, devoted to a further exploitation of pseudoreligious sentimental films. Gil's principal works of this period include *Sor Intrépida* [*Sister Intrepid*] (1952), *La guerra de Dios* [*God's War*] (1953), *El beso de Judas* [*Judas's Kiss*] (1953), *El canto del gallo* [*The Cock's Song*] (1955), and *Un traje blanco* [*A White Suit*] (1956).

Despite the success of these films, there was an apparent falling-out with Escrivá, and in 1957 Gil established his own production company, Coral Films, in an effort to return to the broad-based popularity of his forties work. This final phase of his career, extending up to the early 1980s, is marked by a wide thematic and genre range, as well as an increasingly calculated effort to capitalize on passing cultural trends. His most notable efforts of this period were a number of literary adaptations, including his remake of his own first film, *The Man Who Tried To Kill Himself* (1971); an Unamuno short story, *Nada menos que todo un hombre* [*Nothing Less than a Whole Man*] (1972); and *El abuelo* [*The Grandfather*] (1972), an adaptation of a Pérez Galdós novel that tried to capitalize on the recent success of Buñuel's *Tristana** (1970). Gil ended his filmmaking career with a series of adaptations of reactionary social novels by Fernando Vizcaíno Casas: . . . *y al tercer año resucitó* [. . . *And in the Third Year He Rose*] (1979); *Hijos de papá* [*Papa's Children*] (1980), and *De camisa vieja a chaqueta nueva* [*From Old Shirt to New Jacket*] (1982). His last films underscore the total lack of connection with social reality Gil's career had suffered since the end of the dictatorship.

BIBLIOGRAPHY
García Fernández, Emilio C. *Historia ilustrada del cine español*. Barcelona, Planeta: 1985.
Castro, Antonio. *El cine español en el banquillo*. Valencia: Fernando Torres, 1974.
Méndez-Leite von Haffe. *Historia del cine español*. 2 vols. Madrid: Ediciones Rialp, 1965.

Giménez-Rico, Antonio (Burgos, 1939). With a law degree from the University of Valladolid, Giménez-Rico directed the film club at the University of Burgos and went on to write movie criticism for the film magazine, *Cinestudio*. He began his apprenticeship in film production in 1963, working as an assistant director for films by Vittorio Cottafavi and Eugenio Martín, among others. In 1966 he made his debut as a director of the children's film, *Mañana de domingo* [*Sunday Morning*], from which followed a number of uneven comedies including *El hueso* [*The Bone*] (1968) and the failed *¿Es usted mi padre?* [*Are You My Father?*] (1970).

In 1970 he began working intensely in state television for a period of six years before returning to motion pictures in 1976 with *Retrato de familia* [*Family Portrait*], an adaptation of Miguel Delibes's novel, *Mi idolatrado hijo Sisí* [*My Idolized Son, Sisí*]. Dealing with members of a provincial family during the Civil War, the film is considered by many to be Giménez-Rico's best film. It enabled him to go on to make *Al fin, solos, pero . . .* [*At Last, Alone, But . . .*] (1977), which critics and audiences found disappointing. He moved back to television drama but made the highly acclaimed documentary film, *Vestida de azul* [*Dressed in Blue*] (1983), which combines a series of interviews with transsexuals with dramatized fictional scenes. This was followed two years later with another adaptation of a Delibes novel, *El disputado voto del Señor Cayo* [*The Disputed Vote of Mr. Cayo*] (1986), which dealt with life in a Castilian village during the all-important post-Franco elections of 1977.

Though Giménez-Rico continued to work in films, his later work, including the antimilitarist comedy, *Soldadito español* [*Spanish Soldier Boy*] (1988), coscripted with Rafael Azcona,* *Cuatro estaciones* [*Four Seasons*] (1991) and *Tres palabras* [*Three Words*] (1993), failed to impress critics or audiences.

BIBLIOGRAPHY
Kinder, Marsha. *Spanish Cinema: The Politics of Family and Gender*. Los Angeles: Spanish Ministry of Culture and USC School of Cinema and Television, 1989.
Pérez Gómez, Angel, and José L. Martínez Montalbán. *Cine español 1951–1978: diccionario de directores*. Bilbao: Editorial Mensajero, 1978.

Gómez, Andrés Vicente (Madrid, 1943). This most influential producer of Spanish films of the post-Franco period began his contact with film by working for American production companies shooting films in Spain in the 1960s. He also worked with Elías Querejeta* during this same period and began to produce films in the late 1960s, including James Hill's *Black Beauty* (1968), Gonzalo Suarez's* *La loba y la paloma* [*The Wolf and the Dove*] (1973), and the controversial production of Antonio Drove's* *La verdad sobre el caso Savolta* [*The Truth About the Savolta Case*]* (1979). During the 1970s, Gómez also stepped in to finish the production of Orson Welles's *F for Fake* (1973). This formative period of his career as producer clearly placed Gómez in a context to influence a distinctive, more universal, high quality Spanish cinema than was the norm during the Franco years.

In the mid-1980s, when he became the head of the Iberoamericana Production Company, he spearheaded the production of a series of films that would radically transform the complexion of Spanish cinema. These began with Fernando Trueba's* *Sé infiel y no mires con quién* [*Be Unfaithful and Don't Worry With Whom*] (1985), followed by Trueba's *El año de las luces* [*The Year of Light*]* (1986) and *El sueño del mono loco* [*Twisted Obsession*] (1989). Besides guiding Trueba's development, Gómez supported a number of Carlos Saura's* films of the second part of the 1980s (*El Dorado* [1988], *La noche oscura* [*Dark Night*] [1989], and *¡Ay, Carmela!* [1990]), Pedro Almodóvar's* *Matador* (1986), and Bigas Luna's* *Jamón Jamón** (1992) and *Huevos de oro* [*Golden Balls*] (1993).

BIBLIOGRAPHY
Torres, Augusto M. *Diccionario del cine español*. Madrid: Espasa Calpe, 1994.

Grau, Jorge (Barcelona, 1930). Grau began working as a bellboy in the Gran Liceo Theater in Barcelona where he first discovered his enthusiasm for theater. He went on to study acting at the Theater Institute, later working as a theatrical actor, then as a director. He then became a scriptwriter for Radio España in Barcelona. Also a painter, Grau exhibited his works in Spanish galleries from 1952 to 1956. In 1956, he made his debut as a film actor in Josep Maria Forn's* *La rana verde* [*The Green Frog*]. The following year he received a scholarship to study filmmaking at the prestigious Centro Sperimentale in Rome. Upon his return to Spain, he worked as an assistant to a number of important Spanish and international directors, including Sergio Leone, José Luis Sáenz de Heredia,* and Luis García Berlanga.* By the early 1960s he had amassed extensive credits as the director of short films.

Grau's first feature-length film for which he received director's credit was his *Noche de verano* [*Summer Night*] (1962), a film that reflected the influence of Antonioni's narrative style. Grau received the first award for new directors for this film, through José María García Escudero's New Spanish Cinema subsidy plan. This period of Grau's career coincides with the government's promotion of New Spanish cinema and includes films such as *Una historia de amor* [*A Love Story*] (1966) and *La cena* [*The Dinner*] (1969), which appealed to an increasingly more limited art-house audience.

During the early 1970s, in an effort to make more commercial fare, Grau made a trilogy of horror films, *Ceremonia sangrienta* [*Bloody Ceremony*] (1972), *Pena de muerte* [*Death Sentence*] (1973), and *No profanar el sueño de los muertos* [*Don't Profane the Dream of the Dead*] (1974). These blatantly commercial works led him to a successful collaboration on four films with producer José Frade over the next four years. The most commercially notable of these was *La trastienda* [*The Backroom*] (1975). Although the film's treatment of the traditional running of the bulls in Pamplona set the background, what really secured its commercial appeal was the inclusion of the first frontal female nude scene in Spanish cinema.

Grau's subsequent work of the 1980s moved back from these tendencies to exploitative commercialism toward a more personal perspective in films such as *Coto de caza* [*Game Preserve*] (1983), which, though filled with vivid scenes of violence, reflect a more personal thematic. Besides his film work, Grau has also published various books on film themes and, during the 1960s and 1970s, taught at the Escuela Oficial de Cine (EOC).

BIBLIOGRAPHY
Pérez Gómez, Angel, and José L. Martínez Montalbán. *Cine español 1951–1978: diccionario de directores.* Bilbao: Editorial Mensajero, 1978.
Torres, Augusto M. *Diccionario del cine español.* Madrid: Espasa Calpe, 1994.

Gubern, Román (Barcelona, 1934). With a law degree, Gubern began his contacts with motion pictures through his writing of film criticism in the 1950s (*Cinema Universitario, Nuestro Cine, Triunfo*). Though he would continue as the foremost and most prolific Spanish author of serious books on Spanish and world cinema, his interest in film became more direct in 1964 when he made his debut as a scriptwriter and codirector with Vicente Aranda* *Brillante porvenir* [*A Brilliant Future*]. Gubern was more closely identified with his fellow Barcelonian, Jaime Camino,* over the next two decades, scripting Camino's *Mañana será otro día* [*Tomorrow Is Another Day*] (1967), *España, otra vez* [*Spain, Again*] (1968), *Un invierno en Mallorca* [*A Winter in Mallorca*] (1969), *La vieja memoria* [*The Old Memory*]* (1977), *La campanada* [*Pealing of the Bells*] (1979), *Dragón Rapide* (1986), and *El largo invierno* [*The Long Winter*] (1991).

Gubern's most enduring contribution to film culture in Spain, however, has been his extensive research activity including *El cine sonoro de la II República* [*Sound Film in the Second Republic*] (1977), *El cine español en el exilio* [*Spanish Cinema in Exile*] (1978), *Un cine para el cadalso* [*A Cinema for the Gallows*] (1976), coauthored with Domènec Font; *Raza: el ensueño del General Franco* [*Race: General Franco's Dream*] (1977), the monumental *La guerra de España en la pantalla* [*The Spanish Civil War on Screen*] (1986), and the exhaustive *Benito Perojo: pionerismo y supervivencia* [*Benito Perojo, Pioneerism and Survival*] (1995).

Gutiérrez Aragón, Manuel (José Manuel Gutiérrez Sánchez) (Torrelavega, Santander, 1942). Born in the mountainous region of northern Spain that would from time to time be the lush, poetic site of a number of his films, Gutiérrez Aragón studied in the Faculty of Philosophy and Letters at the University of Madrid in the early 1960s before entering the recently reorganized national film school (EOC), graduating in 1970. After making a number of film shorts, he worked as a scriptwriter on Francesc Betriu's* *Corazón solitario* [*Lonely Heart*] (1972). He would later collaborate on the scripts for Jaime Camino's* *Las largas vacaciones del '36* [*The Long Summer Vacation of '36*] (1975), and José

Luis Borau's* *Furtivos* [*Poachers*] (1975).*

Gutiérrez Aragón debuted with his first feature-length credit as a director in 1973 with *Habla mudita* [*Speak Little Dumb Girl*] (1973), produced by Elías Querejeta,* which won the Silver Bear at the 1974 Berlin Film Festival. The next year he collaborated on the script and direction of Borau's *Poachers* (1975). This was followed by the first part of what would eventually represent a trilogy of political films about Spanish fascism, *Camada negra* [*Black Brood*]* (1977), coscripted and produced by Borau. Set in the Madrid of the immediate post-Franco period, the film uses elements of fairy-tale narration to evoke the culture of fascist violence and terrorism rooted in a right-wing family. The film won Gutiérrez Aragón his second Silver Bear at the 1977 Berlin Film Festival, this time for Best Film.

Black Brood was followed by a unique expression of magical realism in *Sonámbulos* [*Sleepwalkers*] (1978). *Sleepwalkers* is a haunting depiction of the images of violence and conflict that mark the same political environment as *Black Brood*, but it is set in a variety of more complex cultural spaces: the Spanish National Library, a performance of Strindberg's *Ghost Sonata*, and a house used as a hideout for political terrorists. The film gives clear evidence of Gutiérrez Aragón's particular authorial skills in creating striking and memorable poetic images.

In sharp contrast to the urban settings of the first two parts of the trilogy, *El corazón del bosque* [*Heart of the Forest*] (1978) takes place in the lush rural Cantabrian region of the director's childhood. It tells the story of the last of the *maquis*, or resistence fighters, against Franco. Despite the difference of locale from his early urban films, *Heart of the Forest* also partakes of the poetic, fairy-tale structures that inform the other two parts of the trilogy.

Though by the 1980s Gutiérrez Aragón had clearly established himself as one of Spain's most creative and innovative filmmakers, he was not immune from commercial and artistic failures. At least two of his films of this period, *Feroz* [*Wild*] (1983), and *La noche más hermosa* [*The Most Beautiful Night*] (1984), failed at the box office. In sharp contrast to these flops, two other films of this period, *Demonios en el jardín* [*Demons in the Garden*] (1982) and *La mitad del cielo* [*Half of Heaven*]* (1986), both produced by Luis Megino,* proved to be among his most commercially successful films. Along with *Maravillas* [*Marvels*] (1980), these three films constitute something of a second trilogy, an apparent effort to trace the history of the Spanish family over the Francoist and early post-Francoist period. Each is marked by the presence of strong female characters who dominate the narrative (Cristina Marcos in *Marvels*; Ana Belén* and Angela Molina* in *Demons*; Angela Molina and Margarita Lozano* in *Half of Heaven*). Such characters—and the often poetic, mystical view of their social environment that they evoke—derive from Gutiérrez Aragón's earlier works; they offer a powerful rereading of modern Spanish history.

After *Half of Heaven*, Gutiérrez Aragón's film productions have been sporadic and generally not of the same critical force as his earlier works. *Malaventura*

[*Misfortune*] (1988) was a critical and commercial failure and *El rey del río* [*King of the River*] (1993) proved only a limited success. The director received much greater critical reaction for his six-hour television dramatization of the first book of Cervantes's *Don Quijote* in 1991. In addition to his work in film and television, Gutiérrez Aragón holds the distinction of being the first film director to become president of Spain's prestigious Sociedad General de Autores (General Society of Authors).

BIBLIOGRAPHY
Payán, Miguel Juan and José Luis López. *Manuel Gutiérrez Aragón*. Madrid: Ediciones JC, 1985.
Torres, Augusto M. *Conversaciones con Manuel Gutiérrez Aragón*. Madrid: Editorial Fundamentos, 1985.

De la Iglesia, Eloy (Zaraus, Guipúzcoa, 1944). Unable to gain entrance to the National Film School because he was too young, Eloy de la Iglesia began studying Philosophy at the University of Madrid, but soon abandoned it to direct children's theater. His first effort in filmmaking was a series of adaptations of three children's stories, *Fantasía 3* [*Fantasy 3*] (1966), made when he was only twenty-two years old. While doing required military service, he wrote the script of his second film, *Algo amargo en la boca* [*Something Bitter-Tasting*] (1967), which, with the help of Ana Diosdado, was revised and produced. But both *Something Bitter-Tasting* and de la Iglesias's next film, *Cuadrilátero* [*Quadrilateral*] (1969), encountered censorship problems and fared poorly at the box office. It was not until his fourth film, *El techo de cristal* [*The Glass Ceiling*] (1970) that de la Iglesia's film work received any kind of commercial success. Though artistically undistinguished, this police genre film, replete with erotic motives and special effects to intensify its suspense, started de la Iglesia on the road to what appeared to be conventional commercial filmmaking.

In the years after Franco's death, a marked strain of erotic themes began to enter de la Iglesia's films in works like *Juego de amor prohibido* [*Games of Forbidden Love*] (1975) and *La otra alcoba* [*The Other Alcove*] (1976). Gay themes became prominent in *Los placeres ocultos* [*Hidden Pleasures*] (1976), *El sacerdote* [*The Priest*] (1977) and, most daringly, in *El diputado* [*The Deputy*] (1978). These films were clearly an effort to address a popular audience in a direct and unpretentious style on a series of topical social themes that had been proscribed by the now-defunct censorship system. His formula for success involved nonprofessional actors, topical themes, a modest budget, and usually on-location shooting. Though de la Iglesia enjoyed extraordinary commercial success during the late 1970s and well into the 1980s, his films were regularly panned by critics.

In the late 1970s, his collaboration with scriptwriter Gonzalo Goicoechea on films dealing with the problem of the drug culture of urban youth led to a series of phenomenal box-office successes and some grudging acknowledgment by

Spanish critics of de la Iglesia's talent in evoking seedy urban milieus. *Navajeros* [*Knife Fighters*] (1980), *Colegas* [*Pals*] (1982), *El pico* [*The Shoot*]* (1983), and *El pico II* (1984) established de la Iglesia as one of the most commercially successful Spanish directors of the first decade of the transition to democracy. *The Shoot*, in particular, is often praised for its complex handling of themes of sexual and social politics within the context of Basque regional identity.

Though his later *La estanquera de Vallecas* [*The Kiosk Vendor from Vallecas*] (1986) continued that commercial success, the film was not well received by Spanish critics.

BIBLIOGRAPHY

Hopewell, John. *Out of the Past: Spanish Cinema after Franco*. London: BFI Books, 1986.

Smith, Paul Julian. *Laws of Desire: Questions of Homosexuality in Spanish Writing and Film 1960-1990*. Oxford: Clarendon Press, 1992.

Iquino, Ignacio F. (Ignacio Ferrés Iquino) (Tarragona, 1910; Barcelona, 1994). One of the most prolific film directors of the sound period in Spain, Iquino has to his directorial credit over eighty films covering a period of fifty-three years. Only a small portion of these, perhaps no more than four titles, are memorable for their special artistic qualities or view of Spanish social themes. Together, however, his films constitute a corpus of work that helped shape popular cinema in Spain for nearly a half century, while offering important actors and directors their start in commercial filmmaking.

Iquino was born into an artistic environment. His father was the composer Ramón Ferrés; his mother the actress, Teresa Iquino. By the time he was twenty-five, Iquino was an accomplished violinist, painter, sculptor, stage designer, and playwright who had studied stage design in Paris and already had his own photography studio in Barcelona. All of these varied skills were, however, only preparation for what would eventually be his principal love, motion pictures. His interest in film led him to establish his own production company, Emisora Films, in 1934 in order to produce and direct his first film, *Al margen de la ley* [*On the Edge of the Law*] (1935), a historical retelling of a notorious train robbery during the Primo de Rivera dictatorship. His career was temporarily halted by the outbreak of the Civil War, but by the war's end Iquino was under contract with CIFESA, directing a number of sentimental comedies.

Among his early successes were *¡El difunto es un vivo!* [*The Deceased Is Alive!*] (1941), *El pobre rico* [*The Poor Rich Man*] (1942) and *Boda accidentada* [*The Eventful Wedding*] (1942). These successes led him to revive his own company and to turn out at a vertiginous rate a series of low-budget films. By 1950, far and away the most prolific Spanish director of the decade, Iquino had already written, directed, and produced another twenty-five films. Most of these were repetitive genre films, often using the same actors and same sets in narratives that were thematically indistinguishable from one another. Of this first phase of his career, the most striking films were *El tambor de Bruch* [*Bruch's Drum*] (1948), a patriotic costumed drama, and *Brigada criminal* [*Criminal Division*] (1950), said to have established the police investigation film as one of the popular genres of the next decades.

The 1950s would see a gradual decline in the quality of Iquino's work as he quickened his already fast pace of cheap productions; he took on the role of producer and only sporadically directed films himself. The most important of his films of the decade, and the last of major significance in its own right, is *El Judas* [*The Judas*] (1953), the first film since the Civil War to be exhibited in both Castilian and Catalan language versions. Partaking of the popular pseudoreligious film genre of the period, *The Judas* tells the story of the impact on members of a small Catalan community when one of their number is called upon to play the role of Judas in the Holy Week Passion Play.

After *The Judas*, Iquino's career appears to be have been guided only by commercial interests, including the children's genre films of the 1950s, spaghetti westerns made in the 1960s under the pseudonym of Nick Nostro, and soft-core pornographic films in the 1970s. Most film critics and historians concede the unique status of Iquino during the crucial decade of 1942–1952. His successes at CIFESA and his work up to and including the production of *The Judas* form a significant body of popular genre films that clearly responded to the tastes and needs of Spanish audiences during the aftermath of the Civil War.

BIBLIOGRAPHY

García Fernández, Emilio C. *Historia ilustrada del cine español*. Barcelona, Planeta, 1985.
Pérez Gómez, Angel, and José L. Martínez Montalbán. *Cine español 1951–1978: diccionario de directores*. Bilbao: Editorial Mensajero, 1978.

Llobet-Gracia, Lorenzo (Sabadell, Barcelona, 1911; Barcelona, 1976). Llobet-Gracia was the director and screenwriter of only one film, *Vida en sombras* [*Life in the Shadows*]* (1948). But it has been lavishly praised for its extraordinary cinematic self-reference by film historians since the film was first rediscovered by Ferrán Alberich in the late 1970s. *Life in the Shadows* also contains a heavy dose of autobiography, as it traces the life of photographer-filmmaker Carlos Durán (Fernando Fernán-Gómez*) from his birth—literally in a movie theater, through pre–Civil War Spain, to the postwar years in Barcelona.

Like his fictional character, Llobet was fascinated by photography and cinema in his youth and made his debut with a documentary reportage of the International Exposition of Barcelona in 1929. From this point on in his life, Llobet dedicated himself exclusively to amateur film, founding a local cine-club, *Les amics del Cinema* [Friends of Cinema]. In the early 1940s, he came into contact with Carlos Serrano de Osma* and Pedro Lazaga, both of whom were already involved in writing film criticism. During this period, Llobet made the contacts through which he hoped to make his first film. It was finally achieved in part under the auspices of Castilla Films, but also largely financed through Llobet's own monies. Actors such as Fernán-Gómez and some of the technical crew came from the circle of those who had worked with Serrano de Osma.

Once completed, the film received the lowest category of distribution classification, effectively destroying the possibility of a first-run commercial release. Llobet spent the next several years reediting it to improve the film's category, but without success. After the death of his son, he was hospitalized, and after his release never again attempted anything on the scale of *Life in the Shadows*. Because of the various reeditings of the film and the changing of its commercial title, it was lost until its rediscovery in the early 1980s, at which time scholars and film historians alike were stunned by the film's highly sophisticated treatment of cinematic self-referentiality as well as its thematic daring.

BIBLIOGRAPHY
Alberich, Ferrán. *Bajo el signo de la sombra.* Madrid: Filmoteca Española, 1984.
Méndez-Leite, Fernando. *Historia del cine español en 100 películas.* Madrid, Jupey, 1975.

Lucia, Luis (Luis Lucia Mingarro) (Valencia, 1914, Madrid, 1984). Lucia was one of the most prolific and commercially successful of Spanish filmmakers of the Franco era. His forty films, made over a period of three decades, are less a reflection of individual talent than of skilled craftsmanship geared to the popular tastes of successive generations of audiences in search of largely escapist cinema.

Trained as a lawyer, Lucia showed no particular interest in film until after the Civil War. Unable to find employment, he approached a family friend, Vicente Casanova, the founder of the major film distribution company, CIFESA, who agreed to take Lucia on as legal advisor for the firm as it began to branch into the area of film production. Between 1940 and 1943, Lucia gradually worked his way from the legal department into the production side of the company, first preparing a script of *El hombre que se quiso matar* [*The Man Who Tried to Kill Himself*] (1941), which became Rafael Gil's* first directorial credit for CIFESA. In 1943 he made his own directorial debut in an espionage film, *El 13-13*. Despite the low quality of the film, it did well commercially and Lucia was given an assignment directing his first comedy, *Un hombre de negocios* [*A Businessman*] (1945). As with his next film, *Dos cuentos para dos* [*Two Stories for Two People*] (1947), Lucia seemed to thrive on mediocre genre films that fared relatively well commercially but reflected nothing more than a merely competent director.

His next film, one of the famous historical costume epics for which CIFESA was to become well known, *La princesa de los Ursinos* [*Princess of the Ursinos*] (1947), was a prestige success for him and solidified his reputation as a consummate director of popular film fare. Lucia excelled in all the important film genres of the period. His *Currito de la cruz* [*Currito of the Cross*] (1948) is a highly successful blend of the bullfight film with the pseudoreligious genre. His remake of Florián Rey's *La hermana San Sulpicio* [*Sister St. Sulpicio*] (1954) and *Molokai* (1959), a film about Father Damian and his leper colony further exploited that pseudoreligious vogue. *De mujer a mujer* [*From Woman to Woman*] (1949) masterfully exploits the female melodrama, while *Cerca de la ciudad* [*Near the City*] (1952) borrows freely from the conventions of Frank Capra comedies.

At the end of the 1950s, Lucia became identified with a new genre, films that featured a singing child star, in which he managed to launch the careers of three of the most prominent female singers of the next two decades. *Un rayo de luz* [*A Ray of Light*] (1960), began the film career of the then twelve-year-old singing star, Marisol.* The film eventually became part of a popular trilogy. In 1962 Lucia's film *Canción de juventud* [*Song of Youth*] was used as a vehicle to launch the film career of Rocío Dúrcal.* Three years later, Ana Belén* made her screen debut as a singing teenager in *Zampo y yo* [*Zampo and Me*] (1965).

Lucia's career as one of Spain's foremost popular filmmakers continued through 1973 and was consistently aimed at popular audiences in search of entertainment. His greatest strength as a director—his skill at adjusting to a variety of popular genres over decades—would eventually become the principal criticism leveled against his work by his detractors.

BIBLIOGRAPHY

Castro, Antonio. *El cine español en el banquillo*. Valencia: Fernando Torres, 1974.
García Fernández, Emilio C. *Historia ilustrada del cine español*. Barcelona: Planeta, 1985.
Pérez Gómez, Angel, and José L. Martínez Montalbán. *Cine español 1951–1978: diccionario de directores*. Bilbao: Editorial Mensajero, 1978.

Mariscal, Ana (Ana María Rodríguez Arroyo Mariscal) (Madrid, 1923; Madrid, 1995). Mariscal is known primarily for her highly successful career as a stage and film actress whose greatest period of popularity was in the 1940s. She established her own production company in 1952, Bosco Films, through which she subsequently produced eleven motion pictures, all of which she directed. She had become interested in filmmaking previously; in 1946 she shot a documentary short, *Misa en Compostela* [*Mass at Santiago de Compostela*]. Her first feature-length film, *Segundo López* (1952), showed an effort to embrace the Neorealist style, but the film proved a commercial disappointment even though it received strong praise from Spanish critics. It would be five years before Mariscal made another film, *Con la vida hicieron fuego* [*Ablaze with Life*] (1957), a political work about the Civil War, which fared equally poorly at the box office.

These failures apparently moved Mariscal into a much more conscious effort to conform to the commercial demands of the Spanish market. Of the nine films she made between 1959 and 1968, only her 1963 adaptation of Miguel Delibes's novel, *El camino* [*The Road*], breaks with that tendency, as it presents the lives of adolescents in a small Castilian village. Generally considered by critics to be a solid work, the film was a dismal commercial failure.

The interest generated by Mariscal's work as a director is less a function of any striking qualities in her films, which are considered to be at best unexceptional, than by the extraordinary fact that she was the first woman to attempt to break the all-male monopoly of filmmaking in Francoist Spain. Indeed, her only female predecessor in Spanish filmmaking is Rosario Pi, whose work is restricted to the pre–Civil War period.

BIBLIOGRAPHY
Domínguez, Ramón María. *Miguel Delibes: la imagen escrita*. Valladolid: 38 Semana Internacional de Cine, 1993.
Martin-Márques, Susan. *Spanish Women Filmmakers*. Unpublished manuscript.

Marquina, Luis (Barcelona, 1904; Madrid, 1980). Son of the noted dramatist Eduardo Marquina, some of whose historical dramas he would adapt to the screen, Luis was trained as an industrial engineer. He soon became interested in the new field of sound engineering for motion pictures. Studying the various sound systems of French and German film studios, he returned to Madrid in 1934 where he worked for a short time in the CEA studios, in which his father had a financial interest. That same year Marquina was recruited by Luis Buñuel,* then executive producer of the recently established Filmófono Studios, where he was given the opportunity to direct his first feature film, *Don Quintín, el amargao* [*Embittered Don Quintín*] (1935). By 1936, Marquina had directed his second feature-length film, *El bailarín y el trabajador* [*The Dancer and the Worker*], an adaptation of a play by Jacinto Benavente, said by a number of critics to be the best comic work of his career.

Marquina spent the Civil War years in Argentina where he codirected *La chismosa* [*The Gossip*] (1938) and scripted Francisco Mugica's Argentine film, *Así es la vida* [*Such Is Life*] (1939). At the war's end, he went to Italy where he directed films under contract with the Spanish company, CIFESA. Returning to Spain that same year, he began a career as a film director in earnest, turning out two films in 1942, and one each in 1943 and 1944. Among these early post–Civil War films, *Malvaloca* (1942), a remake of an earlier silent film adaptation of a play by the Alvarez Quintero brothers, is generally considered to be his best and most characteristic film of the 1940s. Developing his own adaptation of the play, Marquina worked with two of the leading dramatic stars of the day, Amparito Rivelles* and Alfredo Mayo,* to emphasize the melodrama of a story already excessive in its melodramatic subject matter. The film proved one of his biggest commercial hits.

Marquina continued to enjoy great commercial success during the 1940s, directing films by some of the major stars of the day, including Ana Mariscal* (*Vidas cruzadas* [*Crossed Lives*] [1943]), Conchita Piquer (*Filigrana* [*Filagree*] [1949]), and Fernando Fernán-Gómez* (*El capitán Veneno* [*Captain Poison*]

[1950]).

During the 1950s, Marquina's interests and talents shifted more and more toward production, although he continued to direct films as well. In 1955 he founded the production company D.I.A. and, over the next two decades, produced some twenty films.

Most Spanish film historians note the general lack of artistic qualities in Marquina's work as a director, usually pointing to *The Dancer and the Worker* (1936), *Malvaloca* (1942), and *Captain Poison* (1950) as his strongest works. His commercial success, however, seemed to be based on his skill in reflecting and enriching the form of escapist popular cinema of the first two decades of the Franco dictatorship.

BIBLIOGRAPHY
Méndez-Leite, Fernando. *Historia del cine español en 100 películas.* Madrid: Jupey, 1975.

Martínez-Lázaro, Emilio (Madrid, 1945). As a schoolmate of Antonio Drove* and Enrique Brasó, Martínez-Lázaro was invited to participate in the short-lived film magazine, *Griffiths*, and later *Nuestro Cine*. He subsequently studied physical sciences at the University of Madrid but continued to be drawn toward film culture. In the late 1960s, he started making film shorts and became identified with the group of young, self-taught filmmakers known as the Argüelles School who were shooting shorts in 16mm. After winning the Espiga de Oro prize at the Valladolid Festival for his short, *Camino del cielo [Heavenly Road]*, in 1970, he went on to direct the sketch, *Victor Frankenstein*, as part of the composite film, *Pastel de sangre [Blood Pie]* (1971).

During the first part of the 1970s, Martínez-Lázaro directed dramatic programs for Spanish television while he wrote scripts for horror films under the pseudonym of Lazarus Kaplan. He was recruited to work on the script of Ricardo Franco's* *Pascual Duarte** (1975). The film's producer, Elías Querejeta,* gave him the opportunity to direct his first feature-length film, *Las palabras de Max [Max's Words]* (1976), a brooding film about an eccentric man's solitude and his relationship with his daughter. The film, one of the very few Querejeta productions of this period that appears unrelated to politics, went on to win the Golden Bear at the 1976 Berlin Film Festvial. This stunning success led Martínez-Lázaro to become his own producer, dedicating himself to cultivating a personal style of comedies.

During the 1980s, he scripted and directed an uneven series of such works, including *Sus años dorados [Golden Years]* (1980), *Todo va mal [Everything's Going Badly]* (1984), and *Lulú de noche [Lulu By Night]* (1985) Two of his later films, *Amo tu cama rica [I Love Your Rich Bed]* (1990), and *Los peores años de nuestra vida [The Worst Years of Our Lives]* (1994), efforts to update the Madrid comedies of the late 1970s by addressing a newly emerging, sophisticated youth, proved to be minor popular successes.

BIBLIOGRAPHY
Hernández-Les, Juan and Miguel Gato. *El cine de autor en España*. Madrid: Castellote, 1978.
Hopewell, John. *Out of the Past: Spanish Cinema after Franco*. London, BFI Books, 1986.

Masó, Pedro (Madrid, 1927). This scriptwriter, producer, and director is one of the "self-made men" of Spanish film. He is responsible for some of the most commercially successful popular films of the 1960s and 1970s. He began his career in 1943 at the age of sixteen as an extra at the recently opened Chamartín Studios, where he worked as a page for José Luis Sáenz de Heredia.* Abandoning aspirations to become an actor after a number of appearances in minor roles, Masó moved through the whole range of jobs related to the artistic production of films, culminating in 1953 with his credits as a screenwriter. From that point on, he would regularly script all of the films he produced and/or directed, often in collaboration with Rafael Salvia, as in *Aquí hay petróleo* [*There's Oil Here*] (1955). *Manolo, guardia urbano* [*Manolo, Urban Guard*] (1956), and *Las chicas de la cruz roja* [*The Girls from the Red Cross* (1958); or with Vicente Coello, as in *Atraco a las tres* [*Stick-Up at 3:00 P.M.*] (1962), *Vacaciones para Ivette* [*Vacation for Yvette*] (1964); or with Antonio Vich in *La gran familia* [*The Big Family*] (1962), *La familia. . . y uno más* [*The Family. . . And One More*] (1965), and *Un millón en la basura* [*A Million in the Trash*] (1967). Masó's forte was light comedy and he coscripted some of his best comedies for other directors, such as for Rafael Salvia's *The Girls from the Red Cross*, Fernando Palacios's family series, and José María Forqué's* *Stick-Up at 3:00 P.M.*

In the decade of the 1970s, Masó turned to producing and, in a period of some ten years, his name appeared as producer of more than forty films. By the mid-1960s, he had teamed with comic director Pedro Lazaga, to make *La ciudad no es para mí* [*The City's Not For Me*] (1965). Together they made more than twenty films over the coming years, all of which were topical comedies often of minimal technical quality; but they were perfect reflections of the broad popular Spanish tastes of the period.

Masó's career as a director began in 1971 and ran a full decade before he abandoned cinema for television. This period included films of topical subjects, such as *Experiencia prematrimonial* [*Premarital Experience*] (1972) and *Una chica y un señor* [*A Young Girl and a Gentleman*] (1973). Though the themes were contemporary in these seventies films, their treatment was a throwback to his earlier style of comedy. Masó finished off the decade with several immensely popular comedies based on Rafael Azcona* scripts: *La miel* [*Honey*] (1979); *La familia, bien gracia* [*The Family's Fine, Thank You*] (1979), and *El divorcio que viene* [*Divorce Is Coming*] (1980). Like most of his earlier work as a scriptwriter and producer, these films reflected a popular vein of Spanish comedy, with little effort towards serious artistic expression but a fine connection with popular Spanish tastes.

BIBLIOGRAPHY
Pérez Gómez, Angel, and José L. Martínez Montalbán. *Cine español 1951–1978: diccionario de directores.* Bilbao: Editorial Mensajero, 1978.

Matas, Alfredo (Barcelona, 1920). In 1960 Matas founded Jet Films, the company that produced Luis García Berlanga's* critically acclaimed *Plácido* (1961), which was nominated for an Academy Award the following year. Jet Films went on to produce the first two films by Francisco Regueiro,* *El buen amor* [*Good Love*] (1963) and *Amador* [*Lover*] (1965), both of which found problems with the censors. Jet Films was soon to be disbanded, but in the 1970s Matas returned to film production under the rubric of INCINE, becoming one of the most powerful and influential film producers of the next two decades. His activities in film production eventually led him to become actively involved in both distribution and exhibition of the films he produced.

Matas's screen credits include such key films of the 1970s and 1980s' as Luis Buñuel's* final film, *Ese oscuro objeto del deseo* [*That Obscure Object of Desire*] (1977), Pilar Miró's* controversial, *El crimen de Cuenca* [*The Crime at Cuenca*]* (1979), Jaime Chávarri's* *Bearn, o la sala de las muñecas* [*Bearn, or the Doll's Room* (1983), and *Las bicicletas son para el verano* [*Bicycles Are for Summer*] (1983), as well as five Berlanga films. These include the entire "National Rifle" trilogy, as well as *Tamaño natural* [*Life-Size*] (1973) and *La vaquilla* [*The Heifer*] (1984). Among his other signficant activities related to Spanish film was his tireless work during the mid 1980s in helping establish the Spanish Academy of Motion Picture Arts and Sciences.

BIBLIOGRAPHY
Torres, Augusto M. *Diccionario del cine español.* Madrid: Espasa Calpe, 1994.

Medem, Julio (San Sebastián, 1958). Medem began writing film criticism in his native San Sebastián and later contributed to the film magazines *Casablanca* and *Cinema 2002*. In the mid-1970s, he began to direct film shorts in super 8, and went on to direct the 35mm shorts, *Patas en la cabeza* [*Kick in the Head*] (1985) and *Las seis en punto* [*Six O'clock Sharp*] (1987). His debut as a director of feature-length films with *Vacas* [*Cows*]* (1992) brought enthusiastic praise from all quarters, suggesting the arrival of an exciting new filmmaker.

One aspect of this epic historical tapestry that caught critical attention was Medem's deft handling of subjective representations of three generations of a Basque family caught in political and personal struggles. The inventive style combines surrealist imagery with a historical narration to produce a magical and poetic style. *Cows* stands as one of the most original "first films" of recent Spanish history, winning its director a 1993 Goya for the Best New Filmmaker of the year.

Cows was followed in 1993 by *La ardilla roja* [*The Red Squirrel*], a contemporary suspense film in which the theme of amnesia and the search for one's identity enabled Medem once again to experiment with subjective camera work in highly inventive ways. The film won the Director's Fortnight Prize at that year's Cannes Film Festival. Though less well-received by the critics than *Cows*, *The Red Squirrel* made a strong box-office showing in Spain. Medem's third feature film, *Tierra* [*Land*] (1996), employed the same subjective camera techniques that, by this point, had become a stylistic signature in his films in order to transform an otherwise conventional story of life in rural northern Spain into a haunting dreamlike narrative. Similar to the artistic development of both of his earlier films, *Land* places special emphasis on the power and mystery of natural settings as a critical mise-en-scène in the shaping of characters' actions and moods.

BIBLIOGRAPHY

Smith, Paul Julian. *Vision Machines: Cinema, Literature and Sexuality in Spain and Cuba, 1983-1993*. London: Verso, 1996.

Vincendeau, Ginette (ed.). *Encyclopedia of European Cinema*. New York: Facts on File, 1995.

Megino, Luis (Madrid, 1940). After completion of his studies in film production at the national film school (EOC), Megino became one of the founders of Inscran, a production company specializing in film shorts. Under the rubric of Inscran, Megino was in charge of the film projects that would constitute the first professional film work of Francesc Betriu,* Antonio Drove,* José Luis García Sánchez,* and Manuel Gutiérrez Aragón.* After working on the feature-length productions of Jaime de Armiñán's* *Mi querida señorita* [*My Dearest Señorita*]* (1971), Francesc Betriu's *Corazón solitario* [*Lonely Heart*] (1972), José Luis Borau's* *Hay que matar a B* [*B Must Die*] (1973), and Bernardo Fernández's *Contra la pared* [*Against the Wall*] (1975), Megino decided to establish his own independent production company, LUIS MEGINO P.C. He produced two consecutive films by García Sánchez, *Colorín colorado* [*And They Lived Happily Ever After*] (1976) and *Las truchas* [*Trout*] (1977), the latter film becoming a resounding critical and commercial success, winning the Golden Bear at the 1977 Berlin Film Festival.

About the same time, Megino began working with Gutiérrez Aragón, not only as the producer of his films, beginning with *El corazón del bosque* [*The Heart of the Forest*] (1978), but also as scriptwriter for some six films of the seven Gutiérrez Aragón made over the next decade. These included *Maravillas* [*Marvels*] (1980); *Demonios en el jardín* [*Demons in the Garden*] (1982); *La noche más hermosa* [*The Most Beautiful Night*] (1984); *La mitad del cielo* [*Half of Heaven*]* (1986), and *Malaventura* [*Misfortune*] (1988). By the mid-1980s, Megino rivaled Elías Querejeta* as Spain's foremost independent producer. As with Querejeta's relationship with Carlos Saura* and Jaime Chávarri,* Megino's collaboration with Gutiérrez Aragón, in both scripting and the development of film projects, combined a keen critical eye for themes and narratives that reflect national culture and an astuteness about the commercial promotion of these films.

This is most noticeable in both *Demons in the Garden* and *Half of Heaven*, Gutiérrez Aragón's most commercially successful and possibly richest works of the period of political transition.

BIBLIOGRAPHY
Torres, Augusto M. *Conversaciones con Manuel Gutiérrez Aragón*. Madrid: Editorial Fundamentos, 1985.

Mira, Carles (Valencia, 1947; Valencia, 1993). Mira studied political science at the University of Madrid while also enrolled at the national film school (EOC) but was expelled from the latter for having participated in a student strike. His interest in theater led to his working as an assistant to the noted director, José Luis Gómez,* in a number of productions. He began making film shorts in 1973, winning awards at festivals in Huesca and Valladolid.

Mira's own irreverent antitraditionalist, anti-Francoist views became pronounced in the series of feature-length films he began making with his 1978 *La vida portentosa del Padre Vicente* [*The Marvelous Life of Father Vincent*], an idiosyncratic biographical film about the life and miracles of a Valencian saint. The film raised cries of protest in ecclesiastical circles and announced the essentially irreverent nature of Mira's later films.

In the 1980s he directed six feature-length films that reflected a spirit of hedonism, which he identified with Valencian culture, and a disdain for traditional Castilian or Francoist values. This view is especially clear in his *Con el culo al aire* [*Caught With Your Pants Down*] (1980) whose plot involves a young man placed in a religious asylum after a brief sexual encounter with a prostitute. The sane inmates must masquerade as Catholic inspirational figures in order to be cured. In this way, Mira cleverly contrasts the hero's natural sexual instincts with the repressive institutions of Castilian culture.

A similar theme, juxtaposing Francoist culture with a more sensual Mediterranean or Valencian tradition, abounds in *Jalea real* [*Royal Jelly*] (1981) and *Que nos quiten lo bailao* [*No One Can Take Away Our Good Times Together*] (1983). Mira's efforts to join his Mediterranean themes with his interest in theater led to *Karnabal* [*Carnival*] (1985) a highly theatrical but ultimately failed fantasy film performed by the theatrical company, *Els Comediants*. Given his insistence upon the superiority of regional, especially Valencian culture, over Castilian tradition, Mira was able to benefit from the vogue of regional, especially Catalan, cinema of the 1980s. His films, however, were less explicitly tied to the political agenda often identified with Antoni Ribas* and Josep Maria Forn.* He sought, instead, a reassessment of non-Castilian culture.

BIBLIOGRAPHY
Balló, Jordi, Ramón Espelt, and Joan Lorente. *Cinema català 1975–1986*. Barcelona: Columna, 1990
Hopewell, John. *Out of the Past: Spanish Film after Franco*. London: BFI Books, 1986.

Miró, Pilar (Madrid, 1940). After studying law and journalism, Miró entered the Escuela Oficial de Cine (EOC), specializing in screenwriting. Beginning in the 1960s, she spent more than a decade working in Spanish television, where she directed over three hundred programs. In 1965 she collaborated with Manuel Summers* in the scripting of his film, *El juego de la oca* [*Snakes and Ladders*], but it was not until 1976 that she would debut with her first directorial credit, *La petición* [*The Petition*], an adaptation of a story by Emile Zola. The film was suppressed by the censors for its blunt treatment of sexual relations.

Three years later, Miró directed her most controversial film, *El crimen de Cuenca* [*The Crime at Cuenca*]* (1979), a historical re-creation of the wrongful imprisonment and torture of two peasants by the Spanish Civil Guard in the second decade of this century. This was to become her most commercially successful film, in part due to the controversy surrounding the film's graphic depiction of torture by members of the Civil Guard, a symbolic expression of a long-simmering grievance against Francoist state violence.

Despite the fact that the 1978 Spanish constitution guaranteed freedom of artistic expression, the Spanish Civil Guard, claiming historical privilege, ordered the director and her producer, Alfredo Matas,* jailed for libel against the organization. The situation was further complicated by the fact that a copy of the film had already been sent abroad as the official Spanish entry to the Berlin Film Festival. The charges against the filmmaker were eventually transferred to a civil court and dropped.

In the midst of the swelling public controversy over *The Crime at Cuenca*, Miró coscripted and directed one of her most personal films, *Gary Cooper que estás en los cielos* [*Gary Cooper Who Art in Heaven*] (1980). Paralleling aspects of her own life, Miró's heroine, Andrea Soriano (Mercedes Sampietro*), a television director, reaches a personal crisis as she faces life-threatening surgery. Sampietro would become, over the next decade, the cinematic alter-ego for Miró in other films that explore female sensibility, namely *Werther* (1976) and her strongest personal film, *El pájaro de la felicidad* [*The Bird of Happiness*] (1993), which deals with a similar narrative of a professional woman's emotional crisis.

Miró's film style joins polar opposites: powerful political dramas, such as *The Crime at Cuenca* and *Beltenebros* (1991), the narrative of a political assasination gone wrong, and introspective films that focus on the self-interrogation of women in the midst of emotional crises. The uniqueness of Miró's cinema lies principally in this latter group of films that interrogates the emotional dimension of the social liberation of Spanish women in post-Franco society.

As Director General of film for the Socialist Ministry of Culture (1982–1986), Miró developed a radical approach to film subsidies and worked energetically to promote Spanish film for foreign markets. Later, she assumed a similar position in Spanish state television.

BIBLIOGRAPHY

Pérez Millán, Juan Antonio. *Pilar Miró: directora de cine.* Valladolid: Semana Internacional de Cine, 1992.

Molina, Josefina (Córdoba, 1936). After completing her university studies in political science, Molina founded an experimental theater group in 1962 in her native Córdoba. Two years later, she began working in Spanish state television as a technicial assistant to Pilar Miró.* By 1968 she had begun directing her first television documentaries for the series *Aquí España* [*Here, Spain*] and *Fiesta*. During the period of her apprenticeship in television, Molina also pursued studies at the Escuela Oficial de Cine (EOC), completing her degree in 1969 as the first woman in the history of the film school to receive a degree in film direction.

Between the completion of her degree and her debut as a professional filmmaker four years later, she directed more than forty dramatic programs for state television. Her debut as a film director was with *Vera, un cuento cruel* [*Vera, a Cruel Story*] (1973) a tepid gothic horror story. After directing a stage adaptation of the popular Miguel Delibes novel, *Cinco horas con Mario* [*Five Hours With Mario*] (1979), she scripted and directed an interesting cinema verité film involving the play's leading actress, Lola Herrera, and her real-life estranged husband, Daniel Dicenta, *Función de noche* [*Evening Performance*]* (1980). The film, which bared many of the intimate details of the couple's life, underscored certain feminist themes related to the legacy of Francoist culture on the social formation of Spanish women.

Though Molina previously had dealt with certain women's issues in her television dramas (an adaptation of Ibsen's *The Doll House*, a documentary on *La mujer y el deporte* [*Women and Sports*]), her film work began to focus on stories that concentrated specifically on the status of women within Spanish society. One of her most successful works in this context was her highly praised television docudrama, *Teresa de Jesús* (1984), a biography of the sixteenth-century writer. Other works emphasizing the presence of strong female characters in a variety of historical contexts include her uneven historical drama, *Esquilache* (1988), *Lo más natural* [*The Most Natural Thing*] (1990), and *La Lola se va a los puertos* [*Lola Goes to the Ports*] (1993). Though focusing on the status of women, Molina's cinema is not doctrinaire, but rather leads audiences to consider the nature of social constructions of sexual identity.

BIBLIOGRAPHY
Torres, Augusto M. *Diccionario del cine español*. Madrid: Espasa Calpe, 1994.

Neville, Edgar (Madrid, 1899; Madrid, 1967). Born into a wealthy family, Neville was educated in Switzerland and Madrid. With degrees in philosophy and letters as well as in law, he began his professional career in the diplomatic corps assigned to the Spanish Consulate first in Washington and later in Los Angeles. It was in Los Angeles where he made his first serious contacts with the film industry, eventually working for MGM where he was in charge of Spanish dialogue for their films. During his Hollywood sojourn, he learned much about scriptwriting, which would become a major asset when he began working on his own feature-length films in the early 1940s. When he returned to Madrid in 1931, Neville was able to make a number of commercially popular comic shorts, including a series of parodies of contemporary documentary newsreels. He made his debut in feature-length productions in 1935 with *El malvado carabel* [*Ship of Evil*], an adaptation of the Wenseslao Fernández Flores novel. The following year, he directed his own adaptation of the Carlos Arniches play, *La señorita de Trevélez* [*Miss Trevélez*].

During the Civil War, Neville supported the Nationalist cause and made a number of documentaries on behalf of the Francoists, including *La ciudad universitaria* [*University City*] and *Las juventudes de España* [*Spanish Youth*], both made in 1938. At the war's end, he went to Rome where he directed two feature films that were clearly fascistic in inspiration: *Carmen Fra I Rossi*, known in Spain as *Frente de Madrid* [*Madrid Front*] (1939) and *Santa María*, known in Spain under the title, *La muchacha de Moscú* [*The Girl from Moscow*] (1941).

Returning to Spain in 1942, Neville accepted a number of directing assignments for popular films largely distanced from his earlier propagandistic work. Of these the most notable are a trilogy of popular mysteries set in striking Madrid environments: *La torre de los siete jorobados* [*The Tower of the Seven Hunchbacks*] (1944); *Domingo de carnaval* [*Carnival Sunday*] (1945), and *El crimen de la Calle de Bordadores* [*Crime on Bordadores Street*] (1946). In 1945 he also made a light comedy, *La vida en un hilo* [*Life on a String*], which for many critics is his very best and most representative film work. Witty and well structured like the best of Hollywood screwball comedies, the film is constructed on the flimsiest of premises.

Though the period of Neville's greatest popular commercial successes was the 1940s, two of his later films of the 1950s are worthy of special note. The first is *El último caballo* [*The Last Horse*] (1950), a bittersweet comedy starring Fernando Fernán-Gómez,* which was thought be the inspiration for the early films of Luis García Berlanga.* Neville's 1952, *Duende y misterio del flamenco* [*Magic and Mystery of Flamenco*] (1952), a documentary historical view of flamenco song and dance was presented with voice-over commentaries by Fernando Rey.* The film is among the first Spanish motion pictures to move beyond many of the usual touristic clichés of flamenco genre films.

BIBLIOGRAPHY
Méndez-Leite von Haffe. *Historia del cine español*. Vol 2. Madrid: Ediciones Rialp, 1965.
Pérez Perucha, Julio. *El cinema de Edgar Neville*. Valladolid: 27 Semana Internacional de Cine de Valladolid, 1982.

Nieves Conde, José Antonio (Segovia, 1915). Nieves Conde began his long association with Spanish film as a movie critic for the Madrid daily *Pueblo* in the early 1940s, later writing for the film magazine, *Primer Plano*. During this same period, he worked as Rafael Gil's* directorial assistant from 1941 until 1946 when he directed his first film, *Senda ignorada* [*Unknown Path*] (1946), the first of a trilogy of police genre films. The others in the series were *Angustia* [*Anguish*] (1947) and *Llegada de noche* [*Night Arrival*] (1949). Nieves Conde's work in these genre films, while competent, did not suggest anything more than a merely adequate filmmaker, a criticism that would follow him for much of the rest of his career over the next twenty-five years.

In 1950 he directed his biggest commercial success, *Balarrasa*, scripted and produced by Vicente Escrivá.* The film reflects its producer's propensity, at this point in his career, to exploit the genre of quasi-religious films. The film's commercial success enabled Nieves Conde to direct his next film, one of the legendary works of Spanish cinema, *Surcos* [*Furrows*]* (1951). Tracing the fortunes of a peasant family who, as a result of Franco's failed agricultural economy, move to Madrid, the film expands obvious stylistic elements of Neorealist cinema to present a critique of corrupt urban culture. Though marred by its melodramatic plotting and the impossibility of elaborating on the reasons for the family's exodus from the provinces, *Furrows* nonetheless reveals a powerful realist image of Spanish urban life, never before shown so vividly in Spanish films.

Nieves Conde's later films barely approach the evocative power of *Furrows*. Rather, they fluctuate between genre films of intrigue and those that pose social themes but in a restricted style imposed by the Spanish censors. An example of the former group is *Los peces rojos* [*Red Fish*] (1955), while *Todos somos necesarios* [*We're All Necessary*] (1956) presents a mild social theme. Hoping to capitalize on the anti-Communist fervor of the day, he made *La legión de silencio* [*The Legions of Silence*] (1955), but the weak commercial and critical response to the film moved him to return to the critical vision of urban life in *El inquilino* [*The Tenant*] (1957). This time, however, the imposition of censorial cuts, including the suggestion of a new ending for the film, thwarted his efforts and doomed the film to commercial as well as critical failure.

The difficulties of the production of *The Tenant* led the director to seek less troublesome film subjects, with the result that his filmography declined notably from this point on. The thirteen features he directed during the 1960s and 1970s in no way approach the power of his most important film, *Furrows*, nor the commercial appeal of his films of the 1940s or 1950s. This last phase of Nieves Conde's career is characterized by films such as *El diablo también llora* [*The Devil Also Cries*] (1963), a weak police melodrama that attempts to recapture some of his earlier genre film achievements but with little commercial success. His last film was *Mónica, corazón dormido* [*Monica, Sleeping Heart*] (1977).

BIBLIOGRAPHY
Heredero, Carlos F. *Las huellas del tiempo: cine español 1951–1961*. Valencia: Filmoteca de la Generalitat Valenciana, 1993.

Kinder, Marsha. *Blood Cinema: The Reconstruction of National Identity in Spain.* Berkeley: University of California Press, 1993.

Olea, Pedro (Bilbao, 1938). Olea studied at the Escuela Oficial de Cine (EOC) and contributed to the leftist film journal, *Nuestro Cine*, in the early 1960s. During the same period he began to make 8mm and 16mm films, finally entering television production by the decade's end. After a number of feature-length films that proved less than solid commercial successes, Olea finally achieved a popular hit with *No es bueno que el hombre esté solo* [*A Man Shouldn't Be Alone*] in 1972. This film enabled him to develop a series of striking film projects in the 1970s that were some of the most daring and original works of any Spanish filmmaker of the decade. These films included *Tormento* [*Torment*] (1974), an adaptation of a nineteenth-century Pérez Galdós novel; *Pim, pam, pum . . . ¡fuego!* [*Bang, Bang . . . You're Dead!*]* (1975), an evocation of immediate post–Civil War Madrid; and *Un hombre llamado flor de otoño* [*A Man Named Autumn Flower*] (1978), a re-creation of the milieu of 1920s Barcelona in which a respectable lawyer by day performs as a female impersonator in a cabaret by night.

Each of these films is a period piece, presenting prototypal characters in powerful evocations of distinct historical moments in modern Spanish history. Stylistically, these works suggest a political and cultural seriousness that both predates and is more coherent than the later "retro" historical style that was to dominate much Spanish production in the 1980s. Olea's 1992 film, *El maestro de esgrima* [*The Fencing Master*], attempts to return to that style, but the obvious limits of budget and script weakened the critical reception of the film.

In 1984, Olea made *Akelarre* [*Witch's Sabbath*], a film that brought him back to his Basque roots. Previously, he had made a short *Ikuska 2* (*Gernika*), on a Basque theme, but with the financial support now provided by the Basque regional government, he was able to complete a series of film and television projects during the 1980s that clearly derived from his desire to situate his film work within a regional cultural setting. These include *Bandera negra* [*Black Flag*] (1986) and *El día en que nací yo* [*The Day I Was Born*] (1991).

BIBLIOGRAPHY
Angulo, Jesús, Carlos F. Heredero, and José Luis Rebordinos (eds.). *Un cineasta llamado Pedro Olea.* San Sebastián: Filmoteca Vasca, 1993.

Orduña, Juan de (Madrid, 1907; Madrid, 1974). Born into an aristocratic family, Orduña was attracted to theater at an early age. He made his debut as an actor in 1923 and in 1925 was coaxed into appearing in his first motion picture, *La casa de la Troya* [*The House of La Troya*], directed by a young Florián Rey.* The two became friends and Rey eventually persuaded Orduña to try his hand at directing. Orduña's appearance in Benito Perojo's* *Boy* (1926), catapulted him to the status of the most popular romantic Spanish actor of the day. Successfully making the transition to sound cinema, he appeared in a steady stream of films up to the outbreak of the Civil War. The most popular of these was Florián Rey's* *Nobleza baturra* [*Rustic Gallantry*]* (1935).

At the war's end, Orduña directed a series of shorts, including *Ya viene el cortejo* [*The Cortege Passes By*] (1940), which brought him to the attention of Vicente Casanova, the owner of the Valencian production company, CIFESA. Casanova offered him a job directing, therein opening up Orduña's second film career as one of the two principal film directors of the first decade of the postwar period. Beginning with *Porque te vi llorar* [*Because I Saw You Cry*] (1941), a saccharine love story told against the backdrop of the Civil War, Orduña directed a series of films that had the poorly disguised objective of aggrandizing the recently ended war and establishing a romantic idyll around the emotional and physical sacrifices the war had produced. These included one of the most popular films of this bellicose genre, *¡A mí la legión!* [*The Legion's for Me!*]* (1942). Orduña next moved on to the popular comedy genre with *Deliciosamente tontos* [*Delightfully Daffy*] [1943] and *Ella, él y sus millones* [*She, He, and His Millions*] (1944), both of which helped establish Amparo Rivelles's* status as the preeminent female star of the early 1940s.

In 1948, Orduña embarked on his most ambitious production to date, the historical epic, *Locura de amor* [*The Madness of Love*],* a film that would prove to be the most commercially popular film of the decade. Noteworthy for its lavish sets and massive cast, as well as its excessive melodramatic style, the film was the star vehicle for an actress who, until then, had been a virtual unknown, Aurora Bautista.* As the mad queen Juana, Bautista would begin a cycle of powerful female roles developed under Orduña's direction that would run over the next fifteen years. In 1950 he again cast her in two strong female roles in historical films: *Pequeñeces* [*Trifles*] and the patriotic epic, *Agustina de Aragón*. Though much criticized for the melodramatic excesses of this style of film, Orduña could look to the popular sucess of a seemingly endless series of prestigious hits that bore his name throughout much of the 1950s. The most characteristic of these were historical epics clearly linked to the xenophobic historical tendencies of the regime, such as *Alba de América* [*Dawn in America*] and *La leona de Castilla* [*The Lioness Of Castile*], both made in 1951.

After a series of film adaptations of novels, in the mid-1950s Orduña made what would be the most commercially successful film of his career: *El último cuplé* [*The Last Song*]* (1957). He cast an actress with whom he had worked during the 1940s, Sara Montiel,* in the lead role of the singer whose career is depicted from youth to old age. With the success of the film, Orduña would take credit for transforming Montiel into Spain's biggest movie star of the decade.

The Last Song was clearly the pinnacle of Orduña's career. Though he continued to make films, some eleven motion pictures and a cycle of thirteen complete *zarzuelas* for Spanish television, he would never enjoy the same popularity as he had with that film. By the 1960s he was generally ignored and derided by critics who saw his works as a vestige of an earlier, debased tradition of filmmaking.

BIBLIOGRAPHY
Heredero, Carlos F. *Las huellas del tiempo: cine español 1951–1961*. Valencia: Filmoteca de la Generalitat Valenciana, 1993.
Méndez-Leite, Fernando. *Historia del cine español en 100 películas*. Madrid: Jupey, 1975.

Patino, Basilio Martín (Salamanca, 1930). Patino first became deeply involved in film culture during his years of university study at the conservative University of Salamanca where he helped to found the Cine-Club Universitario of Salamanca and coedited *Cinema Universitario*. Under the auspices of the magazine, Patino was able to help organize the "Salamanca Conversations on National Cinema" in May of 1955, the first such gathering of professionals and students of film of all political persuasions to be held during the Franco regime. After the government's retaliation against the seemingly dissident meeting, the magazine was closed down and Patino moved to Madrid where he entered the national film school (IIEC).

He graduated from the film school in 1960 but, unable to find work in the Spanish film industry, he turned to publicity filmmaking to earn a living. The experience of working on publicity shorts provided him an excellent education in editing and montage techniques that would shape the course of his subsequent career in filmmaking. While working on publicity films, he also taught scriptwriting at the newly reorganized Escuela Oficial de Cine (EOC), at the same time developing a number of script projects of his own inspiration.

One of these was a script that interested ECO films and would develop into Patino's first feature film, *Nueve cartas a Berta* [*Nine Letters to Bertha*]* (1965). The film is a scathing critique of the closed-minded intellectual milieu of contemporary Spain as revealed through the narrative of a university student at Salamanca who writes to the daughter of a Republican exile in London. What sets the film apart from others of similar thematic focus is Patino's dazzling use of freeze-frame and montage effects to underscore his themes. Despite the fact that the film won the Concha de Plata at the San Sebastián Film Festival, distributors had very little faith in its commercial prospects. When it was finally released three years after its completion, the film showed a remarkably strong box-office response throughout Spain.

Patino's next film, *Del amor y otras soledades* [*Of Love and Other Solitudes*] (1969), starred Lucía Bosé* in a story that seemed to be a commercial exploitation of the actress's recent separation from the Spanish torero, Luis Miguel Dominguín. Continuing to explore the dynamics of editing, in 1971 Patino made one of the most popular Spanish films of all time, the documentary *Canciones para después de una guerra* [*Songs for after a War*].* A compilation of newsreel footage running from the Civil War through the late 1950s, the film purported to depict the evolution of popular music of the period. In fact, it was a clever exploration of popular cultural memory blocked by the decades of official censorship in Spain.

A more restrained documentary style marked Patino's next film, *Queridísimos verdugos* [*Beloved Executioners*] (1973), a series of interviews with state executioners, which again revealed the director's anti-Francoist social thematics. In 1976 he made *Caudillo*, more in the spirit of *Songs for after a War*. Although purporting to be a biography of Franco, its irreverent focus included cuts of comic-strip renditions of the dictator's exploits as a young soldier.

Reluctant to adapt to a merely commercial cinema, Patino made only two films in the post-Franco period, *Los paraísos perdidos* [*The Lost Paradises*] (1985) and *Madrid* (1987), each of which appeared as a self-conscious reflection of the world of Patino's early films. *The Lost Paradises* picks up the thread of the lives of the two characters from *Nine Letters to Bertha*, with Berta returning to Salamanca to attend her mother's funeral. Just as the focus of his first film had been a view of Salamanca in the midst of Francoism, *The Lost Paradises* presents life in the university town in the early years of the socialist government's return. *Madrid* also proved to be a personal retrospective movie by Patino as it juxtaposed a visual montage of newsreels depicting the Spanish capital during the Civil War against contemporary images of the vibrant city. Unlike his earlier montage films, however, *Madrid* attempted to frame the montages by a narrative line. Despite its brilliant visual qualities, however, *Madrid* was largely ignored by audiences.

BIBLIOGRAPHY
Company, Juan M., and Pau Esteve. "Habla Patino." *Dirigido Por*, no. 38 (November 1976): 27–29.
Lara, Fernando. "*Canciones para después de una guerra.*" *Revista de Occidente* (October 1985): 92–101.

Perojo, Benito (Madrid, 1894, Madrid, 1974). Along with Florián Rey,* Perojo was the major Spanish commercial filmmaker of the pre-Civil War sound period in Spain. His film career, however, covers a much broader period from the silent to the sound period. Recent extensive research by Román Gubern* shows the full extent of Perojo's film career, which includes over fifty films made between 1913 and 1950 in Spain, France, Germany, Italy, Argentina, and the United States. These include five films made in France between 1918 and 1923 where Perojo expanded his expertise in film direction; Spanish language versions of films originally produced in French, also made in France (1930); *Mamá*, shot during a sojourn in Hollywood, and five films made in Germany and Italy during the Civil War period of hostilities. Between 1942 and 1948 Perojo also made eight films in Argentina. Even after giving up directing films in 1950, he remained active in filmmaking, producing more than forty films before his death in 1974.

The significance of Perojo's rich career lies principally in two interrelated areas: his efforts to modernize and innovate Spanish film production during the 1920s and 1930s based on his extensive work in France and the United States, and his achievement of a striking, popular authorial style that crystallized in a series of musical comedies made during the first decade of the sound period. His most impressive successes and the films that best reflect the combination of these qualities run the gamut from *El negro que tenía un alma blanca* [*The Black Who Had a White Soul*] (1926), later remade as a sound film in 1934, to *Los hijos de la noche* [*Children of the Night*] (1939). These films were rooted in prevailing cultural themes such as race and class. They were marked by evidence of Perojo's increasing dexterity in filmmaking strategies for more and more complex group sequences. Of these, perhaps the most memorable, although not the most technically accomplished, was his 1935 adaptation of the popular *zarzuela*, *La verbena de la paloma* [*Paloma Fair*],* which begins with a famous trolley car sequence. The sequence involved a large cast performing an ensemble musical number shot with a variety of camera movements and cuts from a turn-of-the-century trolley to the interiors of houses along the route. In later films, especially *Children of the Night*, his last major epic endeavor of this scale, Perojo sought to find the means to construct a similar kind of spectacle that would somehow compare with the advanced state of Hollywood filmmaking. The films he made between *Paloma Fair* and *Children of the Night*, shot in both Berlin and Rome, bear evidence of his mastery of that elegant and popular style.

Though his work as a director runs to 1950, including a six-year period of productions in Argentina, his principal critical successes end in 1944 with the Argentinian production, *La casta Susana* [*The Chaste Susan*].

BIBLIOGRAPHY
Gubern, Román. *Benito Perojo: pionerismo y supervivencia*. Madrid: Filmoteca Española, 1994.

Pi, Rosario. (Barcelona, 1899; Madrid, 1968). Little is known of the early biography of Spain's first woman director, other than the fact that she was born into a wealthy Catalan family and was involved in the fashion business in her native Barcelona during the late 1920s before becoming actively interested in motion pictures. In 1931 she cofounded the production company, Star Films with the Mexican, Emilio Gutiérrez Bringas, and the Spaniard, Pedro Ladrón de Guevara. The company produced the first feature film of Edgar Neville,* *Yo quiero que me lleven a Hollywood* [*I Want Them to Take Me to Hollywood*] (1931). The commercial success of *I Want Them to Take Me to Hollywood* made it possible for Pi's production company to prosper over the next several years. She contracted Benito Perojo* for *El hombre que se reía del amor* [*The Man Who Laughed at Love*] (1932) and supported Fernando Delgado's first sound film, *Doce hombres y una mujer* [*Twelve Men and a Woman*] (1934), which was scripted by Pi herself.

Pi made her own debut as Spain's first woman film director in 1936 with *El gato montés* [*The Mountain Cat*], adapted by her from the Manuel Penella *zarzuela* of the same title. Though following the apparent model of the *españoladas*, folkloric dramatic and cinematic works that focus on the stereotypes of gypsies and bullfighters, Pi's version of *The Mountain Cat* attempts a number of modifications in this genre that emphasize the social status of women. Probably due to the film's tragic ending and its release during the bellicose period leading up to the outbreak of the Civil War, the film did not do well commercially, despite strongly positive critical reviews.

Pi's second film, *Molinos de viento* [*Wind Mills*] (1936), is also based on material adapted from a *zarzuela*, this time by Pablo Luna and Luis Pascual Frutos. Unlike her earlier film, *Wind Mills* is set in Holland, not Spain. Much of it was shot during the bombings of Barcelona, which may account for the film's modest appearance. It was not released in Spain until the war's end and did poorly. Pi left Spain during the war and resided in Italy through much of the 1940s. Her failure to find backing for film projects in the 1960s stopped her short in the effort to rekindle her career as a filmmaker. She died in 1968.

Interest in Pi's status as the first prominent woman in the directorial and production side of Spanish cinema has led scholars to evaluate not only the three films in which she had script credits, but also the early productions of Star Films, her production company, as an early expression of Pi's own feminist aesthetic.

BIBLIOGRAPHY
Caparrós-Lera, José María. *Arte y política en el cine de la II República (1931-1939)*. Barcelona: Ediciones 7 1/2, 1981.
Gubern, Román. *El cine sonoro de la República: 1929-1936*. Barcelona: Editorial Lumen, 1977.
Irazábal Martín, Concha. *Alice, sí está: directoras de cine europeas y norteamericanas 1896–1996*. Madrid: horas y HORAS, 1996.

Picazo, Miguel (Jaén, 1927). Picazo earned a degree from the National Film School (EOC) in 1960 with a practice film entitled *Habitación de alquiler* [*Rented Room*]. He went on to teach courses in the newly restructured Escuela Oficial de Cine (EOC) and eventually was able to direct his first film, *La tía Tula* [*Aunt Tula*]* (1964). An updated adaptation of the well-known novel by Miguel de Unamuno, *Aunt Tula* was widely praised both for the power of Aurora Bautista's* performance in the title role and for Picazo's scathing critique of the oppressively puritanical environment of provincial life in Spain. Such social criticism had been, for over a decade, one of the tolerated modes of opposition expression through which filmmakers could channel their attacks on Francoist ideology and still avoid censorial cuts. With generally positive reviews and a strong box-office showing, the film was to bring Picazo to the forefront of the New Spanish Cinema. The film had been promoted by José María García Escudero, the recently appointed director of the film section of the Franco administration's Ministry of Information and Tourism.

Despite this success, Picazo delayed nearly three years before directing his next film, *Oscuros sueños de agosto* [*Dark Dreams of August*] (1967), a film marred by censorial cuts and the untimely death of the film's producer, which hampered commercial distribution. Picazo waited another nine years to direct a third film. He devoted his creative energies to scripting and directing a series of short films for Spanish television, including children's films and adaptations of literary works. When he returned to directing in 1976, it was through a pair of films that seemed to reflect his preferred themes of religious spirituality and the depravations of rural life. The first theme is found in an odd, historical film, *El hombre que supo amar* [*The Man Who Learned How to Love*] (1976), based on the life of the curate, Juan de Dios. Despite the impressive financial backing of the religious order of the Brothers of San Juan de Dios, who had originally commissioned the film and who supported its general distribution in Spain, *The Man Who Learned How to Love* did not fare well commercially. Picazo's fourth film, *Los claros motivos del deseo* [*The Clear Motives of Desire*], about adolescent life in the provinces, fared no better at the box office. Thus Picazo returned to his television work and by the early 1980s he had managed to script and direct nearly sixty projects.

His erratic film career includes a fifth pivotal title, *Extramuros* [*Outside the Walls*] (1985), adapted from the novel of the same name by Jesús Fernández Santos. The film features Aurora Bautista in a role that seems to have developed from her acclaimed performance as the sexually repressed spinster in *Aunt Tula* Here she is the tyrannical mother superior of a convent of sexually represed nuns whose authority is challenged by two younger women, played by Mercedes Sampietro* and Carmen Maura.* In *Outside the Walls*, the striking elements of Picazo's film style are manifested once again: a subtle appreciation for the entrapment of individuals in psychological as well as social confinements; a strong thematics of sexual repression; finally, the masterful direction of actresses.

BIBLIOGRAPHY
Pérez Gómez, Angel, and José L. Martínez Montalbán. *Cine español 1951–1978: diccionario de directores.* Bilbao: Editorial Mensajero, 1978.

Piedra, Emiliano (Madrid, 1931, Madrid, 1991). One of the creative forces in film production in the years 1960–1990, Piedra became enamored with motion pictures at an early age and found himself involved in work related to films long before he became a producer. His first job, at the age of sixteen, was as an assistant with a film distribution company. During the 1940s he worked as a traveling projectionist, traveling throughout Castile on weekends to show films in isolated rural communities. He later established a company that built 16mm motion-picture projectors.

Piedra entered the film distribution business in the 1950s and by 1961 had produced his first feature, *Canción de cuna* [*Cradle Song*] directed by José María Elorrieta. He followed this two years later with *La boda* [*The Wedding*], a Spanish-Argentine coproduction directed by Lucas Demare. The crowning achievement of his early career was his development and support of Orson Welles's film, *Chimes at Midnight* (1967), a work that brought a measure of international renown to the Spanish film industry. *Chimes* is an adaptation of various scenes from Shakespeare's plays involving Falstaff, directed by and starring Orson Welles, with a cast that included John Gielgud and Jeanne Moreau.

In 1967 Piedra married film actress Emma Penella,* for whom he produced a series of films in which she appeared in leading roles. These included a screen adaptation of the Pérez Galdós novel, *Fortunata y Jacinta* (1969) and *La primera entrega* [*The First Delivery*] (1969), both directed by Angelino Fons,* and *La regenta* [*The Regent's Wife*] (1974), directed by Gonzalo Suárez.* Piedra's other activities during this period included the construction of a multiplex film house in Madrid (Cines Luna) and the international distribution of films produced by Elías Querejeta.*

In 1980, Piedra persuaded Carlos Saura* to film a dance adaptation of Antonio Gades's* flamenco ballet, *Bodas de sangre* [*Blood Wedding*] (1980), based on the Federico García Lorca play of the same title. The project initiated a collaboration among the producer, the choreographer, and the filmmaker that would last another five years and include two more films, *Carmen* (1983), one of the biggest international commercial successes of Spanish cinema, and *El amor brujo* [*Love, the Magician*] (1986), an adaptation of Manuel de Falla's flamenco ballet.

Piedra's final project was a six-hour adaptation of Cervantes's *Don Quijote* made for Spanish television, directed by Manuel Gutiérrez Aragón* and starring Fernando Rey* and Alfredo Landa.* This filmed version of the Cervantine masterpiece perfectly embodies the formula that guided some of the best of Piedra's productions over the preceding three decades: a talented and well-known cast brought together for the adaptation of a major Spanish literary or cultural work, produced on a epic scale with a clear eye to international as well as national audiences.

BIBLIOGRAPHY

Various Authors. *Emiliano Piedra*. Alcalá de Henares: 13 Festival de Cine de Alcalá de
    Henares, 1983.
Galán, Diego. *Emiliano Piedra: un productor*. Huelva: Festival de Cine Iberoamericano,
    1990.

Portabella, Pere (Figueras, Gerona, 1929). This important liberal film producer and scriptwriter of the late 1950s and early 1960s came from a well-to-do Barcelona family; he moved to Madrid with the intention of studying chemistry. However, he soon found himself more interested in the arts than in the sciences. He made contact with prominent vanguard painters, Antoni Tapiès, Antonio Saura, and Eduardo Chillida. In 1959 Portabella set up his own production company, Films 59, which in a short span of three years produced three of the key films of the period: Carlos Saura's* debut film, *Los golfos* [*Hooligans*]* (1959), the Marco Ferreri*–Rafael Azcona* hit, *El cochecito* [*The Little Car*]*

(1960), and Luis Buñuel's* notorious return to Spanish film production, *Viridiana** (1961). The political scandal that followed *Viridiana*'s success at the Cannes Film Festival and its denunciation by the Vatican newspaper, *L'Osservatore Romano*, led to the dissolution of Portabella's company.

Films 59 had been part of Portabella's conscious effort to challenge the system of official film culture of the day. Though the immediate series of projects he envisioned was halted through government coercion, he worked over the next two decades to find progressively more politically militant ways to counter the dominant modes of Spanish film culture. In the mid-1960s, he contributed to the script of Francesco Rosi's *El momento de la verdad* [*The Moment of Truth*] (1965), a docudrama about bullfighting. From scriptwriting Portabella moved into film direction with the highly innovative *No compten amb els dits* [*Don't Count on Your Fingers*] (1967), which utilized the language of film commercials. Portabella's efforts to establish a creative area for Spanish art cinema on the margins of conventional commercial film productions are clearly reflected in two later films, *Vampir-Cuadecuc* [*Cuadecuc, the Vampire*] (1970) and *Umbracle* (1972), in which he collaborated with the noted Catalan vanguard poet and playwright, Joan Brossa.

Nocturno 29 [*Nocturne 29*] (1970), starring Lucía Bosé,* was his first commercially released film and was followed by two other feature-length films, *Informe general* [*General Report*] (1977), a documentary involving interviews with prominent politicians on the eve of the general elections of 1978, and *Puente de Varsovia* [*Warsaw Bridge*] (1989).

The close link between political and aesthetic issues in Portabella's films is perhaps best noted in the series of 16mm documentaries he shot on subjects ranging from Catalan art—such as a biography of Joan Miró—to issues of political militancy—such as *El sopar* (1974), which consists of an extended interview with five ex-political prisoners as they sit around a dinner table. Though his activities related to the politics of cinema span more than three decades, the period of Portabella's maximum influence was clearly the years of Films 59, 1959–1961.

BIBLIOGRAPHY
Heredero, Carlos F. *Las huellas del tiempo: cine español 1951-1961*. Valencia: Filmoteca de la Generalitat Valenciana, 1993.
Molina-Foix, Vicente. *New Cinema in Spain*. London: BFI, 1977.

Querejeta, Elías (Hernani, Guipúzcoa, 1935). A member of the Real Sociedad de San Sebastián soccer team, his interest in film led him to work at UNINCI, the independent production company that coproduced Luis Buñuel's* notorious return to Spanish cinema, *Viridiana** (1961). Querejeta then collaborated with Antonio Eceiza* on two short documentaries, *A través de San Sebastián* [*Through San Sebastián*] (1960), and *A través del fútbol* [*Through Soccer*] (1961). After working on the production of Jorge Grau's 1962 film, *Noche de* *verano* [*Summer's Night*], he established his own production company in 1963. Over the next three decades, Querejeta would produce some of the finest and most polemical Spanish films. His efforts to improve the technical and artistic quality of Spanish cinema are especially noteworthy.

Querejeta organized a small, highly talented production team that included Primitivo Alvaro as head of production, Pablo G. del Amo as editor, Luis Cuadrado* and later Teo Escamilla* as cinematographers, and Luis del Pablo as resident composer for Querejeta films. Together, this team forged what critics would call the "Querejeta look," a highly polished visual style characterized by striking film editing, high-quality sound, and a sense of narrative construction designed to appeal to international as well as domestic audiences.

Through Querejeta's support, filmmakers such as Jaime Chávarri,* Manuel Gutiérrez Aragón,* and Ricardo Franco* made their debut films. Querejeta's first production was Carlos Saura's* third film, *La caza* [*The Hunt*]* (1965), which won the Silver Bear at the 1966 Berlin Film Festival and signaled to European and American audiences the emergence of a powerful opposition cinema in Spain. Over the next seventeen years, Querejeta would be the exclusive producer for Saura's films, which would total thirteen before their collaboration ended in 1982 after *Dulces horas* [*Sweet Hours*].

Closely aligned with the opposition politics of Saura's films, Querejeta also supported Víctor Erice's film work. Though much less prolific than Saura, Erice debuted with one episode from Querejeta's three-part film, *Los desafíos* [*The Challenges*] (1970). He made two other films under Querejeta's rubric, *El espíritu de la colmena* [*Spirit of the Beehive*]* (1973), which won the Concha de Oro (the highest award at the 1973 San Sebastián Film Festival) and *El sur* [*The South*]* (1983), before they ended their professional relationship.

Beginning in 1975, Querejeta began working as a script collaborator for the films of a number of the directors he supported, most notably for Ricardo Franco's *Pascual Duarte** (1975) and Jaime Chávarri's *A un dios desconocido* [*To an Unknown God*] (1977). Up to the early 1980s, many of the productions he developed focused on the cultural politics of oppposition to the dictatorship and the regressive mentality that still lingered in the years of transition. In 1984, he sought a new direction for his production company and found it in the emerging career of Montxo Armendáriz,* whose films touched issues of Basque regional culture as well as the crisis of Spain's youth. Querejeta produced Armendáriz's first four feature films: *Tasio** (1984), *27 horas* [*Twenty-Seven Hours*] (1986), *Las cartas de Alou* [*Letters from Alou*]* (1990) and *Historias del Kronen* [*Stories from the Kronen Bar*]* (1995).

BIBLIOGRAPHY

Hernández-Les, Juan. *El cine de Elías Querejeta: un productor singular*. Bilbao: Editorial Mensajero, 1986.

D'Lugo, Marvin. *The Films of Carlos Saura: The Practice of Seeing*. Princeton, NJ: Princeton University Press, 1991.

Regueiro, Francisco (Valladolid, 1934). A professor of commercial studies, a talented cartoonist, and a draughtsman, Regueiro wrote a humor column in the leading newspaper of his native city before moving to his interest in film. In the late 1950s, he entered the Escuela oficial de Cine (EOC), from which he graduated in 1963 with a specialty in direction. Though dedicating himself principally to filmmaking, he also continued a diverse set of other artistic impulses, winning the Sésamo prize for one of his short stories and opening a number of expositions of his paintings.

In 1963 he made his debut with *El buen amor* [*Good Love*], one of the earliest films identified with the New Spanish Cinema. The film, which narrates the relationship of a student couple, was well received by those critics who wished to support any glimmer of fresh new cinematic direction; yet the film was largely ignored by the public. The three films Regueiro directed over the next seven years proved equally disappointing from both critical and commercial perspectives. After problems with the censors in *Amador* [*Lover*] (1965), he made *Si volvemos a vernos* [*Smashing Up*] (1967), a collaboration with Elías Querejeta,* Regueiro's producer, which dealt with political and racial themes. It too failed to excite the critics. This was followed by *Me enveneno de azules* [*I'm Poisoning Myself with the Blues*] (1969), and *Cartas de amor a un asesino* [*Love Letters to an Assassin*] (1973), two films that similarly proved critical disappointments. Up to this point, Regueiro's career appeared to follow the pattern of other recent graduates of the national film school who were unable to sustain their imaginative works beyond a single, initial success.

Regueiro's career broke from that pattern in the mid-1970s, however, as he found a degree of commercial success in genre films, *Duerme, duerme, mi amor* [*Sleep, Sleep, My Love*] (1974) and *Las bodas de Blanca* [*Blanca's Wedding*] (1975), two films of notable black humor.

After a ten-year absence during which time he devoted himself to painting, Regueiro reemerged in 1985 with a series of films that brought him his first broad commercial and critical successes. *Padre nuestro* (1985) boasts a superb cast headed by Fernando Rey,* Francisco Rabal,* and Victoria Abril,* and a script by Angel Fernández-Santos, with whom Regueiro had earlier collaborated on the script of *Blanca's Wedding*. This was followed by *Diario de invierno* [*Winter Diary*] (1988), which features another stunning performance by Fernando Rey, and *Madregilda* (1993), which boasts one of the most talked-about performances of the 1990s, Juan Echanove's* impersonation of General Franco.

These latter films, aided in large measure by Fernández-Santos's screenplays, reveal a balance between an abrasive and cynical view of characters, very often with strong allegorical connotations, and an emotional tenderness that enables particular actors, such as Rey and Echanove, to deliver memorable performances.

BIBLIOGRAPHY
Barbáchano, Carlos. *Francisco Regueiro*. Madrid: Filmoteca Española, 1989.

Rey, Florián (Antonio Martínez de Castillo) (La Almunia de Doña Godina, Zaragoza, 1894; Alicante, 1962). The man who would become one of the major filmmakers of pre–Civil War Spanish cinema began with professional aspirations in law, but quickly abandoned his studies at the University of Zaragoza in favor of a career as a journalist at the age of sixteen, eventually writing for major Madrid newspapers. It was at this point that he assumed the pseudonym that would remain with him for the rest of his life.

At the age of twenty-six Rey began an acting career first in theater, then in silent films, appearing in motion pictures directed by José Buchs.* In 1924 he costarred with Juan de Orduña* in Buchs's *La casa de La Troya* [*The House of La Troya*]. Out of their friendship came the plan for the two men to set up their own independent production company, Goya Films. That same year Rey directed his first motion picture, an adaptation of the Spanish *zarzuela*, *La revoltosa* [*The Mischievous Girl*]. The film's success led to an offer from Atlántida Films to become their house director. Over the next three years, Rey directed seven more films ranging from realist dramas to folkloric *zarzuelas*. In 1927, he cast a young singer, Magdalena Nile, popularly known as Imperio Argentina,* in the title role of *La hermana San Sulpicio* [*Sister Saint Sulpicio*], a comic love story based on a Palacio Valdés novel. The film was a resounding success and established the pair of Rey-Argentina as a creative force in Spanish cinema. Together they made a total of fifteen films over the next decade.

During the final years of the 1920s, Rey directed a variety of films, the most impressive being the last great Spanish silent epic, *La aldea maldita* [*The Cursed Village*]* (1930). Upon its completion, Rey's producers suggested that the film be synchronized with sound and so he and Argentina went off to Paris, where the film was later premiered to generally glowing reviews. During his Paris sojourn, Rey was contracted by Paramount to direct the Spanish version of four Hollywood films. In 1933, now married to Argentina, the couple returned to Madrid where Rey shot *Sierra de Ronda* [*The Ronda Mountains*] before embarking on a series of films that would produce his and Argentina's greatest popular success.

The first of the series was *El novio de mamá* [*Mama's Suitor*] (1934), a frivolous musical comedy that fared extremely well commercially, followed by a remake of his and Argentina's earlier silent film, *Sister Saint Sulpicio* (1934), their first collaboration for the CIFESA production company. The film proved an even greater success than the earlier silent version. Their next two films, *Nobleza baturra* [*Rustic Gallantry*]* (1935) and *Morena clara* [*The Light-Skinned Gypsy*] (1936) were resounding commercial successes, recognized, along with Benito Perojo's *La verbena de la Paloma* [*Paloma Fair*] (1935), as the artistic height of Spanish cinema of the Republican period.

The particular quality of these films comes from their rendering of folkloric environments populated by charming characters drawn from popular stereotypes and skillfully portrayed by consummate and well-directed actors. The striking evocation of Aragonese rural life in *Rustic Gallantry*, for instance, at times verges on ethnographic cinema. In sharp contrast, the stylized choral and solo musical numbers in *The Light-Skinned Gypsy* provide a highly original lyrical evocation of Andalusian stereotypes. Both films found extraordinarily universal acceptance throughout a Spain otherwise divided politically by the Civil War.

During the war, Rey and Argentina accepted an invitation from the German government to shoot films in Berlin. They made German and Spanish versions of two films over the next two years: the highly successful adaptation of the Prosper Mérimée story of Carmen, *Carmen, la de Triana* [*Carmen, the Girl from Triana*]* (1938), and *La canción de Aixa* [*The Song of Aixa*] (1939), which proved an artistic disappointment.

By this point, Rey's professional and personal relationship with Argentina had dissolved and at the end of the Civil War he returned to Spain, where he continued to make films, often in imitation of his earlier triumphs. But even when these films were a popular success, such as *La Dolores* (1939), a folkloric musical in which the noted Andalusian singer, Conchita Piquer, replaced Argentina, Rey was never able to recapture the level of artistic achievement of his earlier work. Although he made some eighteen films over the next eighteen years, his talents were clearly in decline. He retired from filmmaking in 1956 and died some six years later.

BIBLIOGRAPHY
Caparrós-Lera, José María. *Arte y política en el cine de la República (1931-1939)*. Barcelona: Editorial 7/12, 1981.
Fernández Cuenca, Carlos. *Recuerdo y presencia de Florián Rey*. San Sebastián: Festival Internacional de Cine, 1962.
Sánchez Vidal, Agustín. *El cine de Florián Rey*. Zaragoza: Caja de Ahorros de la Inmaculada, 1991.

Ribas, Antoni (Barcelona, 1935). With degrees in law and political science, Ribas began writing plays and eventually became interested in filmmaking. His professional training consisted of an extensive period of apprenticeship to such noted directors as Antonio Isasi, Rafael Gil,* Luis César Amadori, and Ramón Torrado. He made his debut as a film director in 1968 with *Las salvajes del puente San Gil* [*The Savage Women of the San Gil Bridge*], followed by two commercial flops, *Medias y calcetines* [*Stocking and Socks*] (1970), and *La otra imagen* [*The Other Image*] (1973).

With the Franco dictatorship at an end, Ribas openly embraced Catalan nationalist themes. He joined Jaime Camino* and Josep Maria Forn* in founding the Institut de Cinema Catalá (Catalan Film Institute) to help promote the development of a distinctive regional cinema in Catalonia. In 1975 he scripted, produced, and directed *La ciutat cremada* [*Burnt City*]* (1975), perhaps the most widely praised example of Catalanist regional cinema. The success of that film was followed eight years later by the inflated, three-part, six-hour *¡Victoria!* [*Victory!*] (1983). Both films explore historical upheavals that involved the expression of Catalan self-determination in early parts of this century, and each involves a huge cast. Both works clearly propose a revision of official history regarding the nature of Catalan social movements and their relation to a problematic notion of Spanish national cultural identity.

The much praised *Burnt City* follows the fortunes of a single Barcelona family and those associated with them during the *semana trágica* (Tragic Week) of 1909 when a general strike led to confrontation with the central government troops. The film was well received throughout Spain and abroad, in part garnering sympathy as an expression of vindication for the Catalan martyrs of the Francoist dictatorship. When Ribas attempted to repeat this same formula of a huge historical epic with *Victory!*, this time dealing with the general strike of 1917, the film failed commercially both in Catalonia and elsewhere. In part, this reflects a general resistance to the themes of regional autonomy in the early 1980s. Also, Ribas's uncompromising insistence on the details of regional history proved simply uninspiring to all but stalwart regionalists.

Recuperating from the financial disaster of *Victory!*, Ribas directed two radically different films: the whimsical *El primer torero porno* [*The First Porno Bullfighter*] (1985) and the more serious *Dalí* (1989). Despite the unevenness of his subsequent career, Ribas's success with *Burnt City* proved a unique moment in Spanish film history because of the film's striking cinematic conception and its cultural politics, which appeared to strike a sympathetic chord with audiences throughout Spain.

BIBLIOGRAPHY

Balló, Jordi, Ramón Espelt, and Joan Lorente (eds.). *Cinema català 1975-1986.* Barcelona: Columna, 1990.
Hopewell, John. *Out of the Past: Spanish Cinema after Franco.* London: BFI Books, 1986.

Román, Antonio (Antonio Fernández García de Quevedo) (Orense, 1911). Abandoning his studies in pharmacy at the University of Madrid in 1931, Román began writing movie commentaries for a number of Madrid film publications. At about the same time, his interest in motion pictures led him to begin shooting amateur 16mm films. In 1934 he turned to professional documentary filmmaking with a number of presumably touristic shorts, such as *Del Alhambra al Albaicín* [*From the Alhambra to Albaicín*] and *La ciudad encantada* [*The Enchanted City*]. From 1939 through 1941, Román was the film critic for *Radiocinema*. He finally abandoned his work as a critic to devote himself completely to feature-length film production.

His first film, *Escuadrilla* [*Squadron*] (1941), was an effort to capitalize on the popularity of war films of the immediate post–Civil War period. He had, in fact, already collaborated on the scripting of José Luis Sáenz de Heredia's* *Raza* [*The Race*]* (1941). Throughout the 1940s, Román would share the limelight, along with Sáenz de Heredia and Rafael Gil,* as the most important trio of directors producing the canon of quasi-official triumphalist cinema of the period.

Exemplary of this genre are Román's *Boda en el infierno* [*Wedding in Hell*] (1942) and *Los últimos de Filipinas* [*Martyrs of the Philippines*]* (1945); the latter was one of the most commercially successful films of the decade as well as a major propagandistic triumph.

The success of these films led Román to abandon for the time his effort to develop a name as a comic director. His earlier comic detective films, *Intriga* [*Intrigue*] (1944) and *La casa de la lluvia* [*The Rain House*] (1944), had been commercial flops. Now he sought out those film projects that were assured commercial successes—imitations of established popular genre films and particularly projects that might be obvious contenders for special state subsidies as films of "special interest." Román, in fact, managed to garner three such special subsidies, one each for *Lola Montes* (1944), a historical biography; *Martyrs of the Philippines* (1945); and his re-creation of the popular Lope de Vega honor play, *Fuenteovejuna* (1947).

Despite these achievements, by the decade's end popular tastes and Román's fortunes were changing. His efforts to work in melodrama (*La vida encadenada* [*Chained Life*] [1948] and *Pacto de silencio* [*Pact of Silence*] [1949]) proved commercially unsuccessful and suggested the limitations of Román's skills as both a scriptwriter and a director. Though his career continued another two decades with some sixteen films, his directorial work was generally considered in decline. Critics often cite *La fierecilla domada* [*The Tamed Vixen*] (1955), an adaptation of Shakespeare's *Taming of the Shrew*; *Madrugada* [*Dawn*] (1957); and *Los clarines del miedo* [*The Trumpets of Fear*] (1958) as exceptions to the general rule of Román's waning talents. Yet, the evidence of his fall from artistic and popular favor was inexorable. For instance, one of his last films, *Ringo de Nebraska* [*Ringo from Nebraska*] (1966), is a mediocre imitation of the then popular spaghetti westerns.

BIBLIOGRAPHY

Méndez-Leite von Haffe, Fernando. *Historia del cine español*. Vol. 2. Madrid: Ediciones Rialp, 1965.

Pérez Gómez, Angel, and José L. Martínez Montalban. *Cine español 1951–1978: diccionario de directores*. Bilbao, Ediciones Mensajero, 1978.

García Fernández, Emilio C. *Historia ilustrada del cine español*. Barcelona: Planeta, 1985.

Rovira Beleta, Francisco (Barcelona, 1912). With his university studies interrupted by the Civil War, Rovira Beleta pursued his artistic bent by producing animated films. At the war's end he was recruited by Vicente Casanova as a scriptwriter for the CIFESA production company, where he later worked as a contract assistant director on productions directed by Luis Lucia* and Juan de Orduña.* After working on some nine films over a period of seven years, in 1948 Rovira Beleta was given full directorial authority over his first film, *Doce horas de vida* [*Twelve Hours of Life*]. He made two more mediocre films over the next two years as a form of practice apprenticeship before his first major commercial success, *Hay un camino a la derecha* [*There's a Road to the Right*] (1953). Marked by the outer trappings of the then popular Neorealist style, the film was to be the first of a trilogy of social dramas featuring characters caught in difficult economic straights who become involved in robberies. *El expreso de Andalucía* [*The Andalusian Express*] (1956) and *Los atracadores* [*The Robbers*] (1961) concluded the series and displayed the brash directness of Rovira Beleta's style, which inevitably produced difficulties with the Spanish film censors, especially in the case of *The Robbers*.

During his CIFESA years, he was also involved in a series of sports documentaries under the generic title of *Deportes y figuras* [*Sports and Sports Figures*]. His interest in Neorealism and sports led him to try to combine the two in a film about soccer players, *Once pares de botas* [*Eleven Pairs of Boots*] (1954), but the film proved a commercial disappointment.

By the mid-1960s, Rovira Beleta was looking for ways to move beyond mere status quo cinema with artistically serious works that would not provoke difficulties with the censors. His resolution was a series of films inspired by Andalusian and gypsy themes. In 1963 he produced and directed, *Los tarantos*, a modern flamenco retelling of the Romeo and Juliet story set on the streets of Barcelona. Though it did not fare especially well in Spain, it was nominated for an Oscar in the Best Foreign Film category, only the third time a Spanish film had been so recognized. Rovira Beleta was buoyed by the possibility of cultivating a serious international cinematic connection for a Spanish film. In 1967, he directed *El amor brujo* [*Love, the Magician*] (1967), a flamenco ballet based on Manuel de Falla's musical text. As in *Los tarantos*, the film starred the gifted young flamenco dancer, Antonio Gades.* Again, his efforts were rewarded by an Oscar nomination.

Over the next two decades Rovira Beleta divided his time between projects for Spanish television and a few films. These latter efforts, such as *No encontré rosas para mi madre* [*I Didn't Find Roses for My Mother*] (1972) and *La espada negra* [*The Black Dagger*] (1976), were not well received by either critics or audiences.

BIBLIOGRAPHY
Castro, Antonio. *El cine español en el banquillo*. Valencia: Fernando Torres, 1974.
Heredero, Carlos F. *Las huellas del tiempo: cine español 1951–1961*. Valencia: Filmoteca de la Generalitat Valenciana, 1993.

Sáenz De Heredia, José Luis (José Luis Sáenz de Heredia y Primo de Rivera) (Madrid, 1911; Madrid, 1992). One of the major figures of Spanish commercial filmmaking of the post–Civil War period, Sáenz de Heredia's film career coincided in large part with the fortunes of the Franco dictatorship, although only a few of his films could be said to be specifically political.

Abandoning studies in architecture, he began his film career in the mid 1930s, first as a scriptwriter for *Patricio miró a una estrella* [*Patricio Saw a Star*]

(1934), a film produced by his close friend Serafín Ballesteros. The film impressed Luis Buñuel* who, at that time, had just assumed the position of executive producer of Filmófono and recruited Heredia to direct *La hija de Juan Simón* [*Juan Simón's Daughter*] and *¿Quién me quiere a mí?* [*Who Loves Me?*], both made in 1935. Heredia later credited Buñuel with having taught him to direct films, although the only quality that the two directors seemed to share was an appreciation for popular themes and narrative styles.

At the war's end, Heredia was chosen to direct the Nationalist epic, *Raza* [*Race*]* (1941), scripted by Franco, which catapulted the young director to a position of prestige in the film world of post–Civil War Spain. Because of his work on *Race*, he was generally viewed as the "official" director of the regime, yet his films of the 1940s, his richest period of filmmaking, show a remarkable range of popular forms not all of which are so easily reduced to expressions of the Nationalist ideology. Note in particular *El destino se disculpa* [*Destiny Apologizes*] (1944), a light comedy in the screwball genre that displays innovative narrational devices. Other striking films of this period include *El escándalo* [*The Scandal*] (1943) and *Mariona Rebull* (1947), both period melodramas that proved highly successful at the box office.

His most commercially popular film is his best work is *Historias de la radio* [*Radio Stories*]* (1955), a light comedy that inadvertently captures the cultural poverty of the Franco years. The story traces three sets of characters who are contestants on a radio quiz show. *Radio Stories* reflects Heredia's special talent in directing actors. In particular, the film features one of José Isbert's* best comic performances. Though he had progressively distanced himself from political and propagandistic films over the years, in 1964 Heredia was called upon to make a film that would be part of the twenty-fifth anniversary of Franco's rule. The film, *Franco, ese hombre* [*Franco, That Man*] (1964), served to remind audiences of the degree to which Heredia's career had been linked to the fortunes of the dictatorship.

He continued to make films throughout the 1960s and into the mid-1970s, but the quality of his work declined markedly as audiences moved away from the type of escapist works that were his principal talent. Tellingly, his last film, *Solo ante el streaking* [*Alone before Streaking*] (1975), was made in the final year of the Franco dictatorship.

BIBLIOGRAPHY

Méndez-Leite von Haffe, Fernando. *Historia del cine español*. Vol. 2. Madrid: Ediciones Rialp, 1965.

Vizcaíno Casas, Fernando. *De la checa a la meca: una vida del cine*. Barcelona: Planeta, 1988.

Saura, Carlos (Huesca, 1932). Along with Luis Buñuel* and Pedro Almodóvar,* Saura is one of the most internationally acclaimed Spanish filmmakers. A professional photogapher before completing the course of studies in the Instituto de Investigaciones y Experiencias Cinematográficas (IIEC) in 1955, in his early years he was more interested in photography and documentary films than narrative cinema. His 1957 documentary, *Cuenca*, was commissioned by the provincial government of Cuenca in the hopes of promoting local industry. Saura's vision of Cuenca, however, was more by way of an intensely critical interrogation of traditional Castilian culture. Though stylistically distinct from that first documentary, Saura's subsequent film work was to share a common conceptual affinity with *Cuenca*.

His first three feature-length films, *Los golfos* [*Hooligans*]* (1959), *Llanto por un bandido* [*Lament for a Bandit*] (1963), and *La caza* [*The Hunt*]* (1965), all focus on male camaraderie and the violence out of which such social groupings are forged. *The Hunt*, Saura's first film produced in collaboration with Elías Querejeta,* won the Silver Bear at the 1966 Berlin Film Festival. With Querejeta's help, Saura developed a distinctive cinematic signature over the next seventeen years and thirteen films. The thrust of much of this work was a critical denunciation of Francoist culture and an increasingly more aggressive treatment of the theme of the Civil War.

During the last five years of the dictatorship, Saura directed three films that took progressively more confrontational views of the ideological impact of Francoism. *Jardín de las delicias* [*Garden of Delights*] (1970), *Ana y los lobos* [*Ana and the Wolves*] (1972), and *La prima Angélica* [*Cousin Angelica*]* (1973) used a range of symbolic characters as well as elliptical editing to circumvent censorial problems in their delineation of the effects of decades of repressive ideological indoctrination of Spaniards. Since by this point in his career Saura had achieved wide international recognition as a defiant, oppositional filmmaker, the regime was at a loss to respond to these films without further enhancing Saura's status as a martyr. Finally, the censorship boards merely intensified their tight review of each film before approving its release.

Saura's *Cría cuervos* [*Raise Ravens*] (1975), one of the key films of the transition to democracy, was actually shot before Franco's death. The film details the travails of a young girl (Ana Torrent*) who reflects on the oppressive world of her family during the later Franco years as she tries to imagine a future distinct from her past. The film was one of Saura's and Querejeta's strongest commercial hits.

After Franco's death and the dismantlement of the censorship system, Saura turned to more intimate, personal films, the most strikingly original of these being *Elisa vida mía* [*Elisa, My Life*]* (1977). In the early 1980s, Saura began a productive collaboration with Emiliano Piedra,* who produced a trilogy of dance films in which Saura collaborated with the flamenco choreographer, Antonio Gades.* Of the three, *Carmen** (1983), proved to be one of the most commmercially successful in Spanish film history. Though these films also sought to underscore the structures of social containment that shape Spanish identity, they were ultimately viewed outside of Spain simply as expressions of Spanish art cinema. In later years, Saura's commercial career floundered, but he made a strong comeback in 1991 with *¡Ay, Carmela!* which, for the first time, was completely set in the Civil War period. In the 1990s, Saura dedicated himself to films related to flamenco themes, including *Sevillanas* (1992), and *Flamenco* (1994).

BIBLIOGRAPHY

D'Lugo, Marvin. *The Films of Carlos Saura: The Practice of Seeing.* Princeton, NJ: Princeton University Press, 1991.
Sánchez Vidal, Agustín. *El cine de Carlos Saura.* Zaragoza: Caja de Ahorros de la Inmaculada, 1988.

Serrano De Osma, Carlos (Madrid, 1916; Alicante, 1984). Fascinated by film culture as a teenager during the period of the Second Republic, Serrano later joined the film production team of the Communist party, where he worked on documentary films. After the war, he directed industrial shorts for various governmental agencies and began writing film reviews. He was instrumental in the formation of the original national film school, the Instituto de Investigaciones y Experiencias Cinematográficas (IIEC), where he taught film direction for over twenty years.

His own career as a director of feature-length films began in 1947 with *Abel Sánchez*, based on the novel of the same title by Miguel de Unamuno and inspired by the aesthetic theories of the *Telúrico* circle of Barcelona. This group of avant-garde filmmakers was interested in ways to develop a film culture in Spain on the par of recent European art cinema. Serrano's film was a radical experiment in that direction that emphasized visual and lighting elements over the essentials of a sustained narrative line. It failed both commercially and with the critics. Despite this, Serrano's producers offered him a second project, *Embrujo* [*Bewitched*] (1947). The film was a surrealist rendition of the well-established genre of flamenco dance films, starring the principal flamenco dance couple of the period, Lola Flores* and Manolo Caracol. Despite the attraction of these stars, this film also failed commercially.

A more traditional project was offered to Serrano next: a screen adaptation of the nineteenth-century novel by feminist Emilia Pardo Bazán, *La sirena negra* [*The Black Siren*] (1947). But Serrano's insistence on experimenting with the use of chiaroscuro as developed in Orson Welles' *The Magnificient Ambersons*, led to a much criticized baroque visual quality to the film. Despite the failure to produce a commercially viable film, Serrano de Osma was able to make four more feature-length films, including a screen version of the Wagner opera, *Parsival* (1951), codirected with Daniel Mangrane.

In all of his film work, and despite the marked failure for any of his films to connect with a popular audience, Serrano de Osma stands as a relatively rare example of the efforts to forge an aesthetically legitimate cinematic tradition in early Francoist Spain.

BIBLIOGRAPHY
Castro, Antonio. *El cine español en el banquillo.* Valencia: Fernando Torres, 1974.
Pérez Perucha, Julio. *Carlos Serrano de Osma.* Valladolid: 28 Semana Internacional de
    Cine, 1983.

Suarez, Gonzalo (Oviedo, 1934). Suárez began studies in French philology at
the University of Madrid but soon abandoned them for involvement in university
theater groups, appearing in acting roles beginning in 1953. After a sojourn in
Paris he returned to Spain, writing for Barcelona newspapers under the
pseudonym of Martín Girard. By 1963 Suárez had given up this career to devote
himself more fully to fiction writing while gradually branching into film writing
and later directing.

His first formal contact with film was in 1965 when he collaborated on the
script of Vicente Aranda's* *Fata Morgana**. The next year he produced, wrote,
and directed two 16mm shorts, *Ditirambo vela por nosotros* [*Ditirambo Is
Keeping Vigil over Us*] and *El horrible ser nunca visto* [*The Horrible Unseen
Being*], based upon his own stories. In 1967, he wrote, produced, and directed
his first feature-length film, *Ditirambo*, developing the enigmatic character from
his previous film short. The film was a strong critical success. Owing to its
experimental visual and narrative style, as well as to Suárez's earlier collaboration with Aranda, the film was linked in the press with the Barcelona School
of filmmakers. Like members of the Barcelona School, Suárez was indeed
looking for the means through which to express a more poetic reality than was
common fare in the largely realist cinema of Spain in the 1960s. His emphasis
on images often at the expense of coherent narrative plotting, such as in *El
extraño caso del doctor Fausto* [*The Strange Case of Doctor Faustus*] (1969),
proved a commercial drawback for Suárez's films. Dialogue, while poetic, was
often enigmatic; the exotic settings of these films similarly limited their popular
appeal.

The struggle to accommodate the self-conscious film auteur with the demands
of an inflexible, commercially driven cinema brought Suárez to a critical impasse
in his career with *Aoom* (1970), a never-released film that was eventually
destroyed. In an effort to adjust to the market demands of commercial cinema
of the day, he turned to popular genre films such as *Morbo* [*Disease*] (1971) and
Al diablo con el amor [*To the Devil with Love*] (1972), but they too proved to
be disappointingly limited efforts to appeal to a more mainstream audience. He
followed these in 1974 with *La regenta* [*The Regent's Wife*] (1974), a screen
adaptation of Leopoldo Alas's nineteenth-century naturalist novel. It was followed two years later with *Beatriz* (1976), from a short story by Ramón María
Valle-Inclán, and *Parranda* (1977), from a novel by Eduardo Blanco Amor. The
critical and commercial response to these "literary" projects, however, proved
equally disappointing.

Gradually, Suárez came to correct the much criticized "literariness" of his
films. *La reina zanahoria* [*Queen Carrot*] (1978) and subsequently *Epílogo*

[*Epilogue*] (1984) suggest a deepening understanding of the ways literary motives may be developed cinematically. Though the themes of writing and literary creativity remained a constant over the next fifteen years, the appeal of his works for general audiences grew and stabilized in the 1980s. In *Remando al viento* [*Rowing with the Wind*] (1988), for example, a Spanish-Norwegian coproduction with a largely British cast, Suárez developed a new variation on the Frankenstein theme as he focused on Mary Shelley's creative powers. *Don Juan en los infiernos* [*Don Juan in Hell*](1991) and *La reina anónima* [*The Anonymous Queen*] (1992) showed a similar dexterity in blending literary and visual motifs. *El detective y la muerte* [*The Detective and Death*] (1994) mirrors the essential motif of the pursued detective that was the focus of his first feature-length film. Yet in the later film, Suárez developed a curious blend of gothic ambience and a film noir narrative that suggested a more controlled self-consciousnenss.

BIBLIOGRAPHY

Castro, Antonio. *El cine español en el banquillo*. Valencia: Fernando Torres, 1974.
Hernández Ruiz, Javier. *Gonzalo Suárez: un combate ganado con la ficción*. Alcalá de Henares: Festival de Cine, 1991.

Summers, Manuel (Manuel Summers Rivero) (Seville, 1935; Madrid, 1993). The son of painter Francisco Summers and nephew of the noted caricaturist, Serni, Summers began his professional studies in law, then switched to fine arts; he finally graduated from the national film school (IIEC) in 1959 with a practice film, *El viejecito* [*The Little Old Man*]. During his training as a director, he contributed cartoons and jokes to a Madrid newspaper and humor magazines, including *La cordoniz*, the popular antiestablishment satirical publication. Working in television in a variety of technical positions, he made his first feature-length film, *Del rosa al amarillo* [*From Pink to Yellow*],* in 1963. The film was generally well received by audiences, and lavishly praised by critics, winning five awards at the 1963 San Sebastián Film Festival.

The success of *From Pink to Yellow* led Summers to *La niña del luto* [*The Girl in Mourning*] (1964) and *El juego de la oca* [*Snakes And Ladders*] (1965), two personal films with striking similarities to his first film, neither of which, however, was commercially successful. His fourth film, *Juguetes rotos* [*Broken Toys*] (1966), about the problems of three celebrity figures—a boxer, a bull fighter, and a master of ceremonies whose careers move them from public adulation to oblivion—is considered by some critics to have been his most original film. During this first phase of his career, Summers was viewed by many to be a promising talent for the much heralded New Spanish Cinema the government was promoting. But the commercial failure of his personal films quickly led him to abandon his plans for a career as a serious film author and to develop more commercial projects.

In the late 1960s he directed a number of Alfredo Landa* comedies that were indeed strong commercial successes. In 1971, he made *Adios, cigueña, adios*

[*Good-Bye Stork, Good-Bye*], a commercial hit that returned to the themes of adolescent love and sexuality. This, in turn, spawned a series of three other films with the same collaborative team: *El niño es nuestro* [*The Baby is Ours*] (1975), *Ya soy mujer* [*I'm Already a Woman*] (1976), and *Mi primer pecado* [*My First Sin*] (1976). The cycle ended a decade later with *Me falta un bigote* [*Half My Moustache Is Missing*] (1986). During the intervening years, Summers appears to have lost most of his critical support as he made films that catered to a progressively lower estimation of popular Spanish tastes for humor. Regarding films such as *To er mundo é gueno* [*Everybody's Good*] (1982) and *To er mundo é mejor* [*Everybody's Better*] (1983), critics regularly chided Summers for his socially reactionary themes. His last two films, *Sufre mamón* (1987) and *Suéltate el pelo* [*Let Your Hair Down*] (1988), efforts at pop musicals, were commercial failures.

BIBLIOGRAPHY
Castro, Antonio. *El cine español en el banquillo*. Valencia: Fernando Torres, 1974.
Hopewell, John. *Out of the Past: Spanish Film after Franco*. London: BFI Books, 1986.

Trueba, Fernando (Fernando Rodríguez Trueba) (Madrid, 1955). After completing his studies at the Faculty of Information Sciences at the University of Madrid, Trueba became the film critic of the influential daily, *El País* He went on to found the film magazine, *Casablanca*, but it soon became clear that his goal was to become a filmmaker. After a series of shorts, Trueba completed his first feature-length film in 1980: *Opera prima* [*First Work*]* or *A Cousin in Opera*), one of the key films of the *Nueva Comedia Madrileña* (New Madrid Comedy), a sophisticated blend of progressive filmmaking of the late seventies and the urbane comedies of Woody Allen. The film, which Trueba coscripted with his leading male actor, Oscar Ladoire,* became one of the critical successes of the early 1980s. Its unabashed embrace of a Hollywood cinephile outlook was read as an unequivocal rejection of the brooding and introspective political cinema that had marked much Spanish filmmaking of the early years of the post-Franco transition period.

Over the next several years Trueba worked as a coscriptwriter for Fernando Colomo's* *La mano negra* [*The Black Hand*] (1981), Ladoire's debut film, *Contratiempo* [*Delay*] (1981), and his own *Mientras el cuerpo aguante* [*While the Body Lasts*] (1982) and *Sal gorda* [*Coarse Salt* or *Get Lost, Fatty*] (1983). These latter two films were viewed critically as the dissipation of Trueba's promising talent. It was not until he began a fruitful collaboration with producer, Andrés Vicente Gómez,* beginning with his film adaptation of an English comedy, *Sé infiel y no mires con quién* [*Be Unfaithful and Don't Bother with Whom*] (1985), that Trueba began to achieve broad popularity. The film turned out to be one of the biggest box-office hits of the year.

With Gómez's support, Trueba began moving away from his earlier focus on Madrid comedies with *El año de las luces* [*The Year of Light*] (1986), for which he shared screen credits with the famed scriptwriter, Rafael Azcona.* Though the film follows the pattern of Azcona's well-known ensemble film formula for savage critiques of life under the Franco regime, Trueba was experimenting with new ways of moving beyond the standard clichés of Spanish popular cinema. The formula of a European comedy set in a rustic world in which politics and young love intermingle would come to fruition only with his Oscar-winning *Belle Epoque* (1992),* also coscripted by Azcona. Before the international artistic and commercial success of that film, however, Trueba was to make one crucial flop which constituted a total disavowal of Spanish themes, settings, and characters. This was *El sueño del mono loco* [*Twisted Obsession*] (1989), a thriller set in Paris and involving an international cast, including the American actor, Jeff Goldblum, and the English actress, Miranda Richardson.

He returned to his Spanish material with *Belle Epoque*, which was only the second Spanish film to win the Oscar for Best Foreign Film. Three years later, however, he returned once again to what was now clearly a persistent dream of making an American film by shooting *Two Much* (1995) in English in Miami. Unlike the earlier *Twisted Obsession*, *Two Much* included a Spanish actor, Antonio Banderas,* as one of the leads, with other Spanish actors, such as Gabino Diego,* in supporting roles. Although the film, starring Melanie Griffith, did well in its Spanish-language version in Spain, it failed commercially in the American market.

BIBLIOGRAPHY
Alegre, Luis. *Besos robados: pasiones de cine.* (Zaragoza: Xordica, 1994).

Uribe, Imanol (San Salvador, El Salvador, 1950). Born of Basque parents in El Salvador, Uribe was sent back to Spain to study in religious schools at the age of seven. From an early age Uribe declared his desire to become a movie director, finally fulfilling that wish in 1974 when he graduated from the Escuela Oficial de Cine (EOC). In 1976 he joined Fernando Colomo* and Miguel Angel Díez to form the production company, Zeppo Films. Before Zeppo broke up the following year, Uribe was involved in the scripting and production of *Ez*, a documentary short that dealt with what was then perceived as the radical thematic of popular resistance to the building of nuclear reactors in the Basque Country.

Ez was to lead Uribe to the development of his first feature-length film, the documentary, *El proceso de Burgos* [*The Trial at Burgos*] (1979), which dealt with a similarly "radical" Basque thematic. Originally proposed by Fernando López Letona, the project involved a documentary retelling of the notorious 1970 trials in Burgos of Basque militants. In order to receive a license to film, Uribe had to establish a new production company, a cooperative called Cobra Films.

The Trial at Burgos constituted a new kind of political cinema in Spain, one dealing with pressing contemporary issues and suggestively close to militant cinema. Because of the obvious sympathy with which the members of ETA were treated, the film could not be released until 1981 when it received a mixed and polemical response from critics and audiences.

That same year Uribe completed *La fuga de Segovia* [*The Flight from Segovia*], a fictional retelling of the actual escape of members of ETA from a jail in the Castilian city of Segovia. It too provoked a polemical response from the government and audiences alike. By this point, Uribe's dedication to the thematics of contemporary Basque culture was obvious. In the early 1980s he was active in the formation of the short-lived *Asociación de Cineastas Vascos* (Association of Basque Film-makers), aimed at promoting a tangible presence for Basque cinema.

In 1983, he made the film that brought him his widest recognition as a Basque director, *La muerte de Mikel* [*The Death of Mikel*]. So polemical was the identification of the film with the cause of Basque autonomy that when it won the grand prize at that year's San Sebastián film Festival, Spanish television would not announce the film's title, only referring to it as "the film by Uribe." Such political response ironically confirmed the film's thematic premise, which was a denunciation of intolerance on both the left and the right. A combination of a taut dramatic structure, a thematic core that paired sexual marginalization with regional political themes, and the presence in the title role of the popular young actor, Imanol Arias,* led the film to become the most commercially successful Basque film up to that time.

Uribe's films since *The Death of Mikel* have been somewhat irregular. A genre film *Adiós, pequeña* [*Good-Bye Little Girl*] (1986), set in the Basque Country, made a weak box-office showing. Yet the atypically elaborate, costumed period comedy, *El rey pasmado* [*The Flustered King*]* (1991), adapted from a novel by Gonzalo Torrente Ballester, proved a popular commercial and artistic success, winning a number of Goya awards. His 1993 political thriller involving Basque terrorists in Madrid, *Días contados* [*Running Out of Time*], returned to Uribe's earlier Basque thematic but with very little of the political force of his earlier films. As in the previous *The Death of Mikel, Running Out of Time* revealed Uribe to be one of the few filmmakers able to balance a commitment to regional cultural themes with the commercial demands of a broad national and international film market.

BIBLIOGRAPHY
Angulo, Jesús, Carlos F. Heredero, and José Luis Rebordinos (eds.). *El cine de Imanol Uribe: entre el documental y la ficción*. San Sebastián: Filmoteca Vasca, 1994.

Vajda, Ladislao (Budapest, Hungary, 1906; Barcelona, 1965). The son of the noted Hungarian playwright, theatrical director, and film writer of the same name, Vajda was pushed by his father into film training, beginning with technical aspects of filmmaking. By the time he directed his first film, at the beginning of the sound era (in 1932), he had already worked on the technical aspects of a long series of films. During the following years he directed films in England, France,

Portugal, Switzerland, and Germany, finally arriving in Spain in 1942.

With his extensive experience, Vajda seemed to have a special talent for light comedy, directing his first Spanish production that year, *Se vende un palacio* [*A Palace for Sale*] (1942). In the 1940s he made seven more films in Spain. Though technically adequate, these films suffered from flimsy plots. It was not until the 1950s, with films such as *Carne de horca* [*Flesh for the Gallows*] (1953), about nineteenth-century Andalusian bandits, and his popular trilogy that starred the child star, Pablito Calvo, that Vajda hit his stride in Spanish cinema. In 1952 he received the Cross of Isabel la Católica from the Spanish government for his contribution to Spanish cinema. Two years later he became a Spanish citizen.

Although Vajda won a variety of awards for his films, including a prize at Cannes and Venice for *Flesh for the Gallows* and *Marcelino, pan y vino* [*Marcelino, Bread and Wine*]* (1954), it was primarily through the latter film that he achieved extensive international recognition. The film became the first part of the trilogy starring Pablito Calvo, which included *Mi tío Jacinto* [*My Uncle Jacinto*] (1956) and *Un angel pasó por Brooklyn* [*An Angel Passed through Brooklyn*] (1957).

BIBLIOGRAPHY
Heredero, Carlos F. *Las huellas del tiempo: cine español 1951–1961*. Valencia: Filmoteca de la Generalitat Valenciana, 1993.
Pérez Gómez, Angel, and José L. Martínez Montalbán. *Cine español 1951–1978: diccionario de directores*. Bilbao: Editorial Mensajero, 1978.

Zulueta, Iván (San Sebastián, 1943). One of the most unique of Spanish filmmakers, Zulueta studied design in Madrid and New York before entering the Escuela Oficial de Cine (EOC) in 1964. Upon completion of his degree in 1967, he had already completed two shorts, *Agata* (1966) and *Ida y vuelta* [*Round-Trip*] (1967), reflecting his interest in tales of the fantastic. In 1969 with the help of his supporter from EOC, José Luis Borau,* he directed his first feature-length film, *Un dos tres, al escondite inglés* [*Hide and Seek*], produced by Borau's recently established production company, El Imán. The film, a pop musical comedy, was in the spirit of Richard Lester's *The Knack* and *A Hard Day's Night*, with a neglible plotline that worked as the pretext for the introduction of a series of songs performed by a youthful and exuberant troupe of singers, edited with the whimsical style of the Lester comedies of the early 1960s.

It would be ten years before Zulueta would direct another commercial film, largely as the result of his own decision to involve himself in the popular mystical movements and drug culture of the 1970s. During this same period he made a huge number of super 8 shorts, in the "home movie" format, none of which has been commercially released. When he did return to make his only other commercial film to date, it was the complex, equally antiestablishment *Arrebato* [*Rapture*] (1979), which failed commercially but eventually became a cult classic among younger Spanish audiences. The film plays self-consciously with the cinematic medium in ways that pick up on the film-within-the-film structures of Lorenzo Llobet Gracia's* *Vida en sombras* [*Life in the Shadows*]* (1948) and prefigures Víctor Erice's* *El sol de membrillo* [*Quince-Tree Sun*]* (1992). It would be another full decade after *Rapture* before Zulueta would return to commercial production with a film made for Spanish television, *Párpados* [*Eyelids*] (1989), in every way as complex and disturbing as the earlier *Rapture*.

Throughout the years 1975–1990, Zulueta's talents in graphic design were much in evidence, for he created posters for the films of a number of his friends. These included Borau's *Furtivos* [*Poachers*]* (1975), Gutiérrez Aragón's* *Maravillas* [*Marvels*] (1980), and various of the early films of Pedro Almodóvar.*

BIBLIOGRAPHY
Heredero, Carlos F. *Iván Zulueta: la vanguardia frente al espejo*. Acalá de Henares: Festival de Cine, 1989.

Actors and Actresses

Abril, Victoria (Madrid, 1959). Though she studied classical dance throughout her childhood, Victoria Abril's film career did not begin until she decided to test for a minor part in Francisco Lara Polop's *Obsesión* [*Obsession*] (1974). Therein followed a series of minor roles over the next two years in films by Richard Lester (*Robin and Marianne* [1975]), Miguel Picazo* (*El hombre que supo amar* [*The Man Who Knew How to Love*] [1976]), and Juan Antonio Bardem* (*El puente* [*The Long Week-End*] [1976]). But her career did not begin to take shape until an improbable appearance in Vicente Aranda's* docudrama, *Cambio de sexo* [*Change of Sex*] (1976), in which she played the leading role of an adolescent male who undergoes a sex change operation. This was followed by Abril's appearance in a number of Aranda's films, including the commercial hit, *La muchacha de las bragas de oro* [*The Girl in the Golden Panties*] (1979); as well as *Asesinato en el comité central* [*Assassination in the Central Committee*] (1982); *Tiempo de silencio* [*Time of Silence*] (1985); *El crimen del Capitán Sánchez* [*The Crime of Captain Sánchez*] (1985); *El Lute I: camina o revienta* [*El Lute: Run or Die*] (1987), and *Amantes* [*Lovers*]* (1991).

Abril's career showed signs of stabilizing around a distinctive and highly original cinematic persona in the 1980s. The range of her dramatic talents began to emerge with her performance in Josep Anton Salgot's *Mater amatísima* [*Beloved Mother*] (1980), in which she played the unmarried mother of an autistic child whom she refuses to institutionalize. For the first time, her performance depended more on her acting abilities than on her physical attributes. Though always closely identified with a strong sexual persona, Abril's roles called increasingly for complex psychological characterizations, which the young actress clearly was able to deliver. These performances led to a number of striking roles in international films, especially in France (Robin Davis's *J'ai épousé une ombre* [*I Married a Shadow*] [1982]; Denis Amar's *L'Addition* [*The*

Bill] [1983]).

Abril's greatest international exposure, however, came from Spanish films by Pedro Almodóvar* and Aranda. The controversial *¡Atame! [Tie Me Up! Tie Me Down!]* (1989), in which she played a drug-addicted porn movie star, was followed by her powerful portrayal of a ruthless femme fatale in Aranda's international hit, *Amantes [Lovers]* (1991). During the early 1990s, she appeared in two other major Almodóvar hits, *Tacones lejanos [High Heels]* (1991) and the controversial *Kika* (1993). By this time, Victoria Abril had clearly established herself, along with Carmen Maura,* as one of the two Spanish actresses who best embodied Spanish cinema both to the outside world as well as to Spanish audiences.

Alterio, Héctor (Buenos Aires, Argentina, 1929). Trained professionally for the Argentine theater, Alterio received various awards for his acting in his native country. In the early 1960s he began to divide his professional time between film and theater, appearing in films by some of Argentina's most important directors, including Manuel Antín (*Don Segundo Sombra* [1969]), Leopoldo Torre Nilsson (*Los siete locos [Seven Mad Men]* [1972]), and Héctor Oliveira (*La Patagonia rebelde [Rebellious Patagonia]* [1973]). In 1974, while attending the San Sebastián Film Festival, he learned that his name was on an Argentine terrorists' death list. He therefore went into political exile in Spain, which would open up a new career avenue in the following decades.

In 1976 he appeared in Carlos Saura's* *Cría cuervos [Raise Ravens]* and Ricardo Franco's* *Pascual Duarte.** These appearances were followed in fairly rapid succession by other key films of the period of political transition, such as Jaime Chávarri's *A un dios desconocido [To an Unknown God]*, José Luis García Sánchez's* *Las truchas [Trout]*, José Luis Garci's* *Asignatura pendiente [Pending Examination]*,* and Luis García Berlanga's* *Escopeta nacional [National Rifle]*,* all made in 1977. By the end of the decade Alterio had established himself as an excellent character actor in a variety of roles and regularly had appeared in important films by Pilar Miró* (*El crimen de Cuenca [The Crime at Cuenca]** [1979]), Jaime de Armiñán* (*El nido [The Nest]** [1980]), and Carlos Saura (*Antonieta* [1983]).

Even after Argentina's return to democracy in 1983, Alterio continued to appear in Spanish films and a number of Hispano-Argentine coproductions. These included María Luisa Bemberg's *Camila* (1982) and *Yo, la peor de todas [I, The Worst of All]* (1990), as well as other films by Spanish filmmakers, such as Jaime de Armiñán's *Mi general [My General]* (1986), Gonzalo Suárez's* *Don Juan en los infiernos [Don Juan in Hell]* (1991) and *El detective y la muerte [The Detective and Death]* (1994).

A versatile character actor, Alterio's performances have ranged from unsympathetic figures such as the uncaring father of Ana Torrent in Carlos Saura's *Raise Ravens* and a similarly brutish husband in Luis Puenzo's *La historia oficial [The Official Story]* (1985) to the sensitive homosexual magician in Jaime Chávarri's *To an Unknown God* (1977) and the sexually obsessed widower in Jaime de Armiñán's *The Nest* (1980). Though he has appeared in comic works such as Luis García Berlanga's *National Rifle* and Fernando Colomo's *¿Qué hace una chica como tú en un sitio como éste?* [*What Is a Girl like You Doing in a Place like This?*] (1978), his real strength lies in the depth of emotion he is able to develop in brooding and often taciturn characters, who often erupt into violent figures.

Aparicio, Rafaela (Málaga, 1906). One of the most beloved of Spanish actresses, Aparicio has appeared in over one hundred films and countless television programs, and has maintained more than a half century of regular contact with the comic theater, beginning in pre–Civil War Madrid with a series of *zarzuelas*. This extensive range of performances helped to give her powerful name-recognition as a notable character actress in both theater and film.

Short and rotund, with a quick wit and a distinctive Andalusian lilt to her speech, she has played a limited range of roles that run from meddling maids to meddling grandmothers, with only slight variations. Despite such a narrow repertory, some of Spain's most prestigious filmmakers have called upon her regularly to enhance their films with roles especially written for her talents. These include Carlos Saura* (*Ana y los lobos* [*Ana and the Wolves*] [1972], *Mamá cumple cien años* [*Mama Turns 100*] [1979]), Fernando Fernán-Gómez* (*El extraño viaje* [*The Strange Journey*] [1964],* *El mar y el tiempo* [*The Sea and Time*] [1989]), Víctor Erice* (*El sur* [*The South*] [1983]),* and Francisco Regueiro* (*Padre nuestro* [1985]). Though individual performances have seldom garnered festival prizes for Aparicio, she was recognized by her profession with a special lifetime achievement Goya (the equivalent of an Oscar) in 1987, and was recipient of the prestigious Premio Nacional de Cinematografía, which is usually awarded to directors.

Argentina, Imperio (Buenos Aires, Argentina, 1906). Born Magdalena Nile del Río, of a theatrical family, she studied dance in Málaga and made her theatrical debut in Buenos Aires at the age of twelve. Adopting the nickname "Petite Imperio" to distinguish her from the Spanish dancer, Pastora Imperio, she toured South America, returning to Spain in 1926. That same year, the promising young filmmaker, Florián Rey,* discovered Imperio for his silent version of the popular Armando Palacio Valdés novel, *La hermana San Sulpicio* [*Sister Saint Sulpicio*] (1927), in which she played the title role of a beguiling but undisciplined young nun.

With the advent of sound, her career brought her and Rey to the Paramount studios at Joinville, outside of Paris, where she was cast in the Spanish version of a number of films originally made in English. Of these the most memorable was *Su noche de boda* [*Her Wedding Night*] (1931) codirected by Rey and Louis Mercanton. She married Rey in 1934 and returned to Spain to star in a number of films produced by the fledgling CIFESA studio, which would bring her her greatest popularity.

The first of these was Rey's sound remake of *Sister Saint Sulpicio* in which Argentina costarred with the comic actor and singer, Miguel Ligero.* The film was an enormous commercial success and established her as the sweetheart of Spanish popular audiences. This was followed with the two films that represent the height of that stardom: *Nobleza baturra* [*Rustic Gallantry*] (1935)* and *Morena clara* [*The Light-Skinned Gypsy*]* (1936). In each, she was paired with Ligero, although the two films are radically different. *Rustic Gallantry* was set in rural Aragon and, though it contained songs, was really a somber tale of a deformed honor code. The more whimsical *The Light-Skinned Gypsy* was clearly a film tailored to show off Argentina's considerable comic and singing talents. Designed as an opulent Andalusian musical, it is built upon the comic identities of Argentina and Ligero as thieving gypsies whose run-in with a serious Sevillano judge, Manuel Luna,* leads to romance.

These films provided Argentina her greatest popularity. She was said to have been revered by audiences on both Republican and Nationalistic sides during the Civil War, although her allegiances, like those of her director-husband, were indisputably with the Francoists. In 1938, in fact, she made another one of her great popular successes, *Carmen, la de Triana* [*Carmen, The Girl from Triana*],* shot in Berlin, once again playing off her established persona as a high-spirited gypsy character. Though she continued to make films through much of the 1940s, her career never regained the general popularity of the mid 1930s.

In later years, Argentina returned to film for a limited number of appearances, the two most important being in Mario Camus's* *Con el viento solano* [*With a Wind from the East*] (1965) and José Luis Borau's* *Tata mía* [*My Nanny*] (1986), in which she played the title role and even sang a song from *Rustic Gallantry*.

Arias, Imanol (Riaño, León, 1956). As a child Arias's family moved to the Basque Country where he began university studies in electronics but soon abandoned it for theater. Arriving in Madrid at the age of nineteen, he was able to obtain a series of small parts on Spanish television, but it was not until he was noticed by theatrical director and actor, Adolfo Marsillach,* and trained in the Centro Dramático Nacional, that his career started to develop. Arias's earliest major film work as the romantic but obsessed hero in Humberto Solás's ill-fated Cuban epic, *Cecilia* (1981), and his subsequent appearance as the priest in *Camila* (1983), the Argentine film directed by María Luisa Bemberg, painfully reveal his inexperience before the camera.

In 1982, he played a lead role in Pedro Almodóvar's* *Laberinto de pasiones* [*Labyrinth of Passion*] as well as one of the ensemble roles in Mario Camus's* *La colmena* [*The Beehive*]. These experiences apparently helped to loosen up his acting style, for by the following year when he appeared in Manuel Gutiérrez Aragón's* much praised *Demonios en el jardín* [*Demons in the Garden*] and the equally well received *La muerte de Mikel* [*The Death of Mikel*]* (1983) by

Imanol Uribe,* it was apparent that Arias was developing into a strong acting talent. Despite the eccentric nature of these roles (in *Demons* he played an egotistical, fascist soldier; in *Mikel* a homosexual involved in the Basque separatist movement), he was still widely regarded as primarily an attractive romantic male star with obvious power at the box office.

It was not, however, until his appearance in the title role of Vicente Aranda's biographical films based on the exploits of Eleuterio Gutiérrez, "El Lute," *El Lute I: camina o revienta* [*Run or Die*] (1988) and *EL Lute II: Mañana seré libre* [*Tomorrow I Will Be Free*] (1988), that Arias achieved major recognition for his acting talents. He won the best male acting award that year at the San Sebastián Film Festvial. Though his choices of films from this point on appear somewhat erratic, including light comedy as well as melodrama, he has been able to sustain a reputation as a serious actor in a variety of roles; his appearance in Aranda's *El amante bilingüe* [*The Bilingual Lover*] (1992) confirmed that talent. Returning to the director with whom he made his commercial breakthrough, he appeared in 1995 as the indifferent husband of Marisa Paredes in Pedro Almodóvar's *La flor de mi secreto* [*The Flower of My Secret*].

Banderas, Antonio (Málaga, 1960). Originally trained in theater, in his early twenties he came to Madrid and made his film debut in Pedro Almodóvar's second film, *Laberinto de pasiones* [*Labyrinth of Passion*] (1982), playing the role of a Middle Eastern terrorist. Two years later he appeared in Carlos Saura's* flawed *Los zancos* [*Stilts*] (1984) as a young theatrical artist whose wife is involved in a brief affair with an older man. It was not, however, until Almodóvar's *Matador* (1986), in which Banderas was given a more central role that his popularity began to rise. The following year, he played a lead role as the gay lover in Almodóvar's *La ley del deseo* [*Law of Desire*] (1987), and, along with the director, began attracting a wide international following, especially in the United States. This was solidified in somewhat different kinds of roles in two subsequent Almodóvar films, *Mujeres al borde de un ataque de nervios* [*Women on the Verge of a Nervous Breakdown*]* (1988), and *¡Atame!* [*Tie Me Up! Tie Me Down!*] (1989), both of which received wide and, in the latter case, controversial publicity in the United States.

Though Banderas continued to appear in several Spanish films, most prominently in Vicente Aranda's *Si te dicen que caí* [*If They Tell You that I Died*] (1990), his career shifted to American films, including weak but significant performances in Arne Glimcher's *Mambo Kings*, Jonathan Demme's Oscar-winning *Philadelphia*, Roberto Rodríguez's first major film, *Desperado* (1995) and Neil Jordan's *Interview with a Vampire* (1995). His acting talents have often seemed limited, and clearly quite stretched in his American films; yet he continues to enjoy a reputation as one of the few Spanish actors of recent years to make a successful crossover to American and international films. The majority of these, however, tend to play off his celebrity persona as the stereotypical Hispanic male, oversexed and predatory.

Bardem, Javier (Madrid, 1969). Grandson of famed film director, Juan Antonio Bardem,* Javier is one of the best known of the generation of younger actors who made their debuts in Spanish film in the late 1980s, signaling the emergence of a more youth-oriented cinema. Bardem's striking physical appearance made for easy casting in roles as a tough, street-smart youth with a powerful sexual persona, first in a minor role in Bigas Luna's controversial *Las edades de Lulú* [*The Ages of Lulú*] (1990), followed by a similar role in Vicente Aranda's *El amante bilingüe* [*The Bilingual Lover*] (1992), and culminating in one of the most commercially successful Spanish films of the early 1990s, Bigas Luna's *Jamón, Jamón* (1992) in which he portrayed a character driven as much by his sexual appetite as by his desire for material success.

Bardem's powerful performance in the film led to a series of roles that further built upon his well-established persona. These included the next film of Bigas Luna's Iberian trilogy, *Huevos de oro* [*Golden Balls*] (1993), roles in the Imanol Uribe* political thriller, *Días contados* [*Running out of Time*] (1994), and Gonzalo Suárez's* poetic film noir, *El detective y la muerte* [*The Detective and Death*] (1994). As a drug addict in the Uribe's film, Bardem demonstrated a dramatic range that suggests that he is moving beyond the narrow sexual sterotype of his earliest film work. In Manuel Gómez Pereira's *Boca a boca* [*Mouth to Mouth*] 1966, he even parodies that persona as he plays an actor forced to imitate the Antonio Banderas* stereotype for American film producers.

Barranco, María (Málaga, 1961). After abandoning medical studies in her native Málaga, María Barranco switched to acting, later coming to Madrid where she debuted in a revival of Pedro Muñoz Seca's play, *La venganza de don Mendo* [*The Vengence of Don Mendo*]. She eventually moved into films with a string of secondary roles. She was catapulted into prominence by her beguiling comic performance as Carmen Maura's girlfriend in Pedro Almodóvar's* smash hit comedy, *Mujeres al borde de un ataque de nervios* [*Women on the Verge of a Nervous Breakdown*]* (1988). The success of her performance and of the film led to a series of largely comic roles in films by Spain's most popular and commercially successful directors. These included roles in Jaime Chávarri's* *Las cosas del querer* [*The Things of Love*] (1989), Bigas Luna's* *Las edades de Lulú* [*The Ages of Lulú*] (1990), Almodóvar's *¡Átame!* [*Tie Me Up! Tie Me Down!*] (1990), Imanol Uribe's* *El rey pasmado* [*The Flustered King*] (1991), and Julio Medem's* *La ardilla roja* [*The Red Squirrel*] (1993). As in her crossover performance in *Women on the Verge*, Barranco's comic persona characteristically plays off an appearance of innocence and vulnerability exaggerated by her Andalusian accent.

Bautista, Aurora (Valladolid, 1925). After theatrical training in Barcelona, she made her dramatic debut in a production of Jacinto Benavente's *La malquerida* [*Passion Flower*] in 1944 in Barcelona. While appearing in a Spanish-language production of Shakespeare's *A Midsummer Night's Dream* in Madrid, she was discovered by Juan de Orduña* who was then casting for roles in the CIFESA historical epic, *Locura de amor* [*The Madness of Love*]* (1948). Bautista was offered the title role and an exclusive contract to work under Orduña's direction. Owing to the extraordinary popular success of *The Madness of Love*, Orduña continued to cast Bautista in a series of historical costume dramas in which her excessively declamatory style of acting seemed appropriate. In 1950, she appeared in the title role of Orduña's *Agustina de Aragón* as well as in his adaptation of the nineteenth-century melodramatic novel, *Pequeñeces* [*Trifles*], both of which were well received.

Though by the mid-1950s Bautista had shifted to less colorful roles, her acting style seemed to be fixed in the rigid style of her earliest popular triumphs. In 1962 she starred in her last historical epic under Orduña's direction, as the caricaturesque embodiment of the title character in *Teresa de Jesús*. The film's scenario was by this time merely an anachronistic reminder of the kind of cultural ideology of the late 1940s that had made Bautista's career possible in the first place.

In 1964, she made the most radical shift of her film career by playing the title role of the spinster aunt in Miguel Picazo's* modern adaptation of Miguel de Unamuno's *La tía Tula* [*Aunt Tula*].* The film and her performance were generally praised, although it was clear to critics that the film was the exact ideological opposite of Bautista's earlier roles. Here the very controlled and obsessive behavior that had once seemed so stilted became part of the film's indictment of the repressive environment of Spanish rural life. Bautista, ironically, won her third major acting prize from the Sindicato Nacional de Espectáculos for the performance, following awards she had earlier received for *The Madness of Love* and *Agustina de Aragón*. Though her career after *Aunt Tula* floundered in mediocre scripts throughout the sixties and seventies, in 1985 she reappared in a powerful performance as the mother superior in Picazo's adaptation of Fernández Santos's *Extramuros* [*Outside the Walls*].

Belén, Ana (Madrid, 1950). At the age of fourteen Ana Belén made her screen debut in Luis Lucia's* *Zampo y yo* [*Zampo and Me*] (1965), a commercial failure that derailed the prospects of converting the young actress into an updated version of Lucia's earlier teenage starlets, Marisol* and Rocío Dúrcal.* Persevering in her desire for a serious acting career, Belén joined the Teatro Estudio de Madrid under the direction of Miguel Narros, who would develop her talents in a series of strong dramatic performances in classical Spanish theater. After a series of minor roles in popular films, she received strong critical recognition when she appeared in two films in 1974, Jaime de Armiñán's* *El amor del Capitán Brando* [*The Love of Captain Brando*] and Pedro Olea's* *Tormento* [*Torment*]. Her reputation as a serious actress was confirmed with performances in two Manuel Gutiérrez Aragón* films, *Sonámbulos* [*Sleepwalkers*] (1977) and *Demonios en el jardín* [*Demons in the Garden*] (1982).

One of the earliest examples of her ability to reach a wide audience was her

1979 epic television film, *Fortunata y Jacinta*, directed by Mario Camus* in which she received highly favorable reviews for her performance as Fortunata. Appearances in Camus's *La colmena* [*The Beehive*] (1982) and in his subsequent film adaptation of her stage success as Adela in Federico García Lorca's *La casa de Bernarda Alba* [*The House of Bernarda Alba*] (1987) solidified her growing reputation for strong and resolute females in situations of adversity. Though she has appeared in musical films and comedies, (García Sánchez's* *La corte de Faraón* [*The Court of the Pharaoh*] and Fernando Trueba's* *Sé infiel y no mires con quien* [*Be Unfaithful and Don't Worry with Whom*] [both in 1985], her principal reputation in film lies in her performance of straight dramatic roles. In 1991 she attempted to make the shift from acting to directing with *Como ser mujer y no morir en el intento* [*How to Be a Woman and not Die Trying*], but the film was resoundingly rejected by critics and audiences alike.

Bódalo, José (Córdoba, Argentina, 1916; Madrid, 1985). Born in Argentina into an acting family, Bódalo studied medicine at Salamanca. When his family moved to Caracas, Venezuela, due to the Civil War, he quickly changed careers and became involved in radio and later theater. He returned to Spain in 1947 and began appearing in films as well as theatrical productions. He played a secondary role in Juan de Orduña's 1948 *Locura de amor* [*The Madness of Love*]* and over the next four decades appeared in countless screen and television dramas in Spain, almost always as a colorful supporting actor.

In the early 1980s, Bódalo began to receive wider attention for his portrayals of cynical characters in José Luis Garcí's* *El crack* [*The Crack*] (1980) and *El crack II* (1983). He also appeared in Garci's Oscar-winning film, *Volver a empezar* [*To Begin Again*]* (1983), in which he played the childhood friend of the protagonist, Antonio Ferrandis.

Bosé, Lucia (Milan, Italy, 1931). After winning the Miss Italia beauty contest, Bosé began a screen career in 1950, appearing in Giuseppi De Santis's *Non c'é pace tra gli ulivi* (1950), which quickly established her as one of the bright young starlets of Italian cinema. She went on to appear in a series of Italian films, most notably two by Michelangelo Antonioni: *Cronaca di un amore* [*Story of a Love Affair*] (1950) and *La signora senza camelie* [*The Lady without the Camellias*] (1952). Later she appeared in a number of French films, including Luis Buñuel's* French-produced *Cela s'appelle l'aurore* [*They Call It Dawn*] (1955). That same year, she came to Madrid to appear in Juan Antonio Bardem's* Spanish-Italian coproduction, *Muerte de un ciclista* [*Death of a Cyclist*].* The film, one of the key works of opposition political cinema during the second decade of the Franco dictatorship, was an international success which helped to solidify Bosé's film career. After the filming, she married the famed torero, Luis Miguel Domínguin, and subsequently retired from the film industry.

Bosé returned to film acting in 1967, virtually forming a different career. She balanced her European film performances with those in Spanish works, appearing in a variety of eccentric roles in Spanish films, often by young directors not yet fully established. These included roles in *No somos de piedra* [*We're Not Made of Stone*] (Manuel Summers,* 1967), *Del amor y otras soledades* [*Of Love and Other Solitudes*] (Basilio Martín Patino,* 1969), *Un invierno en Mallorca* [*A Winter in Mallorca*] (Jaime Camino,* 1969), *Los viajes escolares* [*School Trips*] (Jaime Chávarri,* 1973), and *El niño de la luna* [*The Little Boy in the Moon*] (Agustín Villaronga, 1988). Though known primarily for her striking beauty during the early part of her career, in later years Bosé developed as an accomplished character actress in a series of offbeat films.

Bosé, Miguel (Panamá, 1956). Son the Italian actress, Lucia Bosé,* and the legendary Spanish bullfighter, Luis Miguel Dominguín, Bosé was catapulted into the public eye at an early age. A publicity effort to develop his persona as a precocious adolescent movie star along with his sister, Paola, failed, but he did regain momentum as a serious actor with his appearance in a featured role in Antonio Giménez Rico's* *Retrato de familia* [*Family Portrait*] (1976). He began to develop a parallel career in popular music, becoming in a short time one of the youthful idols of popular Spanish music. During the early 1980s, he continued this double track, though he seemed more interested in Italian film projects than in Spanish ones. It was, in fact, not until the early 1990s, with his appearance in two radically different roles in major Spanish films that Bosé was able to secure his general popularity with Spanish audiences. His appearance in a serious dramatic role in Josefina Molina's* *Lo más natural* [*The Most Natural Thing*] (1990) followed the next year by a much publicized performance in a multiple role—that of a female impersonator in Pedro Almodóvar's *Tacones lejanos* [*High Heels*] (1991)—assured Bosé a solid national and international audience.

Calvo, Armando, (San Juan, Puerto Rico, 1919). This son of the noted comic stage and screen actor, Juan Calvo, was born while his family was on tour in Puerto Rico. Educated in Spain, he made his theatrical debut at the age of seven. He abandoned his secondary school studies to begin a formal theatrical career at the age of fifteen. His first film appearance was in José Luis Sáenz de Heredia's* *Patricia miró a una estrella* [*Patricia Looked at a Star*](1934).

Calvo's film career, which spans more than four decades, is divided into three distinct periods. The first runs from the end of the Civil War to his stellar performance in 1945 in Antonio Román's* *Los últimos de Filipinas* [*Martyrs of the Philippines*].* During these early postwar years, Calvo played a series of romantic leads in both plays and films. Between 1945 and 1957 he appeared in some thirty-five films in Mexico, a number of which were eventually distributed in Spain. The bulk of these were melodramatic roles in which Calvo assumed a more mature version of his previous romantic persona. He returned to Spain in 1957, costarring with Sara Montiel* in Juan de Orduña's* *El último cuplé* [*The Last Song*].* By the early 1960s, however, he increasingly appeared in secondary roles in less prestigious genre films. These included spaghetti westerns and pseudo–James Bond films. His last film appearance was a minor role in José María Forqué's* *El canto de la cigarra* [*Song of the Cicada*] in 1980.

Carrillo, Mary, (Toledo, 1919). Carrillo began acting professionally at the age of sixteen; she received popular and critical acclaim in the title role of Benito Perojo's* *Marianela* (1940). Yet subsequently her career faltered for many years, because of a series of weak roles in less that totally successful commercial films. Her career was revitalized in 1958 by her performance as Petrita, the strong-willed fiancée of Rodolfo (José Luis López Vázquez*) in Marco Ferreri's black comedy, *El pisito* [*The Little Flat*].* Therein followed a series of nearly three dozen appearances in character roles over the next thirty years for some of the outstanding directors of recent decades (Angelino Fons,* Jose Luis García Sánchez,* Mario Camus,* José Luis Borau,* Fernando Colomo,* and Agustín Villaronga). She also appeared in the popular Spanish comedies of Pedro Masó* and Pedro Lazaga.

The distinctive signature of Mary Carrillo's acting style is most evident in her performances as strong-willed, often ruthless, upper-class matrons. Perhaps her most memorable roles are from an unlikely pair of films of the early 1980s: She played the uncaring Marquise in Mario Camus's* powerful *Los santos inocentes* [*Holy Innocents*]* [1983], and she appeared in a similar role, done almost tongue in cheek, as the Marquise in Pedro Almodóvar's *Entre tinieblas* [*Dark Habits*] (1984). Though never achieving the status of lead actress in this second phase of her career, Carrillo's name has become closely identified with a particular range of powerful character performances.

Casaravilla, Carlos (Montevideo, Uruguay, 1900; Valencia, 1981). Born of Spanish emigré parents in Uruguay, Casaravilla's family eventually moved to Buenos Aires where he began training for a career in the theater. After a period of stage success in Argentina, Casaravilla moved to Spain in 1932. He made his first film appearance in 1934 in *¡Viva la vida!* [*Long Live Life!*] but his film career was interrupted by the Civil War. He spent the war years in Argentina and returned to Spain definitively in 1942.

During the next decade he played a number of romantic male leads in Spanish films. But it wasn't until the 1950s that his talent was fully realized, in films directed by Juan Antonio Bardem*: *Cómicos* [*Comedians*]* (1953), *Muerte de un ciclista* [*Death of a Cyclist*]* (1955),* and *Sonatas* (1959). In Bardem's films, Casaravilla's true dramatic range could at last be seen. His tour de force performance as a cowardly art critic turned blackmailer, Rafa, in *Death of a Cyclist* presaged the evil characters in which he later would specialize. The techniques he developed in his most memorable role, that of the perverse blindman in César Ardavín's* *Lazarillo de Tormes,* were to become the hallmark of his character acting in a variety of other films. His film career, spanning some fifty years, includes nearly eighty films, among them a number of minor appearances in international coproductions made in Spain, such as Nicholas Ray's *55 Days at Peking* (1963) and Burt Kennedy's *Return of the Magnificent Seven* (1966).

Castro, Estrellita (Sevilla, 1914; Madrid, 1983). A child star in her native Seville by the age of ten, Castro's talents lay principally in the performance of Andalusian songs and dances. She made her film debut as the lead in the popular 1935 folkloric hit, *Rosario la cortijera* [*Rosario, the Country Girl*], in which she created a stage persona strikingly reminiscent of Imperio Argentina* of the same period. She soon teamed up with director Benito Perojo* for a series of similar films all shot during the Civil War in foreign studios. Films such as *Mariquilla Terremoto* [*Mariquilla, the Bombshell*], *Suspiros de España* [*Sighs of Spain*], and *El barbero de Sevilla* [*The Barber of Seville*], all made in 1938, helped establish Castro's star status and indelible persona as one of the principal figures of Spanish folkloric musical comedy cinema. At the end of the war, her box-office popularity declined and she abandoned film for theater, returning to it intermittently over the next three decades in a series of mediocre films. Despite these later forays, the most memorable period of her fourteen-film career was that of her early, folkloric work.

Chaplin, Geraldine (Los Angeles, 1944). Chaplin came to Spain to make her film debut in David Lean's *Doctor Zhivago* (1965). The following year she was approached by the Spanish producer, Elías Querejeta* who was seeking an actress with an international reputation to costar in *Peppermint Frappé* (1967), the Carlos Saura* film he was producing. Chaplin accepted the complex role, which required her to play three separate but interrelated characters in the tale of sexual repression in provincial, Catholic Spain. Extremely well received by Spanish audiences, the film paved the way for a series of seven more films produced by Querejeta and directed by Saura over the next twelve years.

In Saura's films, Chaplin often played the part of a foreigner whose very presence is a challenge to and a critique of traditional conservative, Francoist culture (*Ana y los lobos* [*Ana and the Wolves*] [1973], *Mamá cumple cien años* [*Mama Turns 100*] [1979]). Or else she was cast as a highly creative individual misplaced or marginalized within traditional Spanish society (*Cría cuervos* [*Raise Ravens*] [1975]; *Elisa vida mía* [*Elisa, My Life*] [1977]*). In these latter films, and following a stylistic penchant Saura had developed from *Peppermint Frappé*, Chaplin assumed dual roles, playing mother and daughter in both films. Though not well appreciated by Spanish critics, who often complained about her pronunciation of Spanish, Chaplin received plaudits from foreign critics and audiences alike. As well as appearing in Saura films, Chaplin has appeared in a number of works by other Spanish filmmakers, such as Enrique Brasó's *In memoriam* (1977).

Closas, Alberto (Barcelona, 1921; Madrid, 1994). Born in Barcelona, Closas emigrated with his family to Buenos Aires because of the Civil War. In Argentina, he studied drama and joined Margarita Xirgu's theatrical company. He later organized his own company and toured South America with productions of plays of his fellow Spanish exile, Alejandro Casona. In 1943 Closas made his debut in a Chilean film, José Bohr's *El renegado de Pichitún [The Renegade of Pichitún]*. Over the next twelve years, he appeared in twenty-four films, the majority of them Argentine.

In 1955 Closas returned to Madrid for his Spanish film debut as the morally pained protagonist, Juan, in Juan Antonio Bardem's* *Muerte de un ciclista [Death of a Cyclist]*.* Over the next three decades, he appeared in more than forty films, many of them light, popular comedies under the direction of some of the most popular commercial filmmakers of the period (Luis César Amadori, José Antonio Nieves Conde,* Pedro Masó*). Closas excelled in the role of a sophisticated, romantic lead in the style of Cary Grant. Amadori's *La muchachita de Valladolid [The Proper Young Lady from Valladolid]* (1958) is typical of these as he plays the role of a romantically-inclined bachelor ambassador.

In later years, he appeared in the commercially successful series of "family" films directed first by Fernando Palacios: *La gran familia [The Big Family]* (1962), *La familia . . . y uno más [The Big Family . . . and One More]* (1965), and continued by Pedro Masó's* *La familia bien, gracias [The Family's Fine, Thank You]* (1979). In the 1980s, he continued to appear in films, usually in secondary roles, while also performing regularly in theatrical productions and on Spanish television. Two of his last film appearances were Gonzalo Heralde's *Ultimas tardes con Teresa [Last Afternoons with Teresa]* (1983) and Josefina Molina's* *Esquilache* (1988).

Cruz, Penelope (Madrid, 1970). Cruz was discovered by Bigas Luna* and catapulted to stardom by his highly successful *Jamón, Jamón** in which she played a factory girl torn between the factory owner's son by whom she is pregnant and a local stud with an earthy appeal. Promoted as a "Spanish beauty," Cruz went on to play one of Fernando Fernán-Gómez's* sexually appealing daughters in the Oscar-winning Fernando Trueba* film, *Belle Epoque.** In such roles, Cruz has come to embody a newer version of the sexually alluring Spanish female that in previous decades had been played out by Victoria Abril and Angela Molina.

Díaz-Gimeno, Rosita (Madrid, 1911; New York City, 1986). Abandoning her studies in medicine for theater, Díaz-Gimeno joined Gregorio Martínez Sierra's theatrical company and toured Latin America and France with them. She made her film debut in 1931 in Spanish-language versions of English films produced by Paramount—first in Hollywood, and later in France. She became one of the major film stars of the Republican period when she appeared in a succession of four films directed by Benito Perojo,* all of which became impressive popular commercial successes (*El hombre que se reía del amor* [*The Man Who Laughed at Love*] [1932], *Susana tiene un secreto* [*Susana Has a Secret*] [1933], *Sierra de Ronda* [*The Ronda Mountains*] [1933], and *Se ha fugado un preso* [*A Prisoner Has Escaped*] [1933]). Díaz-Gimeno's forte was that of the attractive heroine in light comedic works such as Louis King's *Angelina o el honor de un brigadier* [*Angelina, or a Soldier's Honor*] (1935), a frothy costume comedy shot in Spanish in Hollywood with a script by Jardiel Poncela.

While working on the filming of Fernando Delgado's* *El genio alegre* [*The Happy Spirit*] in 1936, during the early days of the Civil War, she was taken prisoner by the Nationalists. Eventually escaping to France, she returned to Spain to help fight on the Republican side. When the film was eventually completed, her named was deleted from the credits, owing principally to her marriage to Juan Negrín, the last president of the Republic. After the war, she emigrated to New York where she took up U.S. citizenship. Devoting herself primarily to theater, she did appear in a number of Mexican films; the most prominent of these was Emilio Fernández's screen adaptation of Juan Valera's *Pepita Jiménez* (1947).

Diego, Gabino (Madrid, 1966). Diego was discovered at the age of seventeen by Jaime Chávarri* during tryouts of more than two hundred teenagers for a leading role in the film version of Fernando Fernán-Gómez's* play, *Las bicicletas son para el verano* [*Bicycles Are for Summer*] (1983). He followed his film debut with a period of intense training in acting, voice, and guitar in preparation for a serious film career. When he appeared three years later in Fernán-Gómez's *El viaje a ninguna parte* [*The Journey to Nowhere*] (1986), Diego gave a thoroughly convincing and highly stylized performance of the inept and vulnerable son of the actor-father, Fernán-Gómez. The performance distinguished him from a talented ensemble cast and won him critical raves. It also set the pace for his later roles as a taciturn, vulnerable, at times comic, and yet innately intelligent and sensitive young man.

His performance in Carlos Saura's* 1990 film, *¡Ay, Carmela!*, as a mute shell-shocked youth won him a Goya. The following year he played the title role in Imanol Uribe's* *El rey pasmado* [*The Flustered King*]* in which he was called on again to portray a character defined externally by costume and circumstance but whose underlying personality transcended those definitions, often through a striking grimace and his powerful stare.

More recent and contemporary roles, such as the misunderstood and gawky youth turned stand-up comic in Manuel Gómez Pereira's *Los peores años de nuestra vida* [*The Worst Years of Our Life*] (1994), reveal even more of Diego's acting range.

Diego, Juan (Bermujos, Sevilla, 1942). Diego made his theatrical debut in a Spanish-language production of *Waiting for Godot* in 1957, followed by appearances on Spanish television in the 1960s, first as a nonspeaking extra, later in small supporting roles. By the end of the 1960s, he was appearing in important roles in television dramas as well as motion pictures. Among the latter, his appearances in Eloy de la Iglesia's* *Algo amargo en la boca* [*Something Bitter-Tasting*] (1968) and José Luis García Sánchez's* *Colorín colorado* [*They All Lived Happily Ever After*] (1976) are particularly noteworthy.

Diego began to specialize in eccentric character roles, which eventually led to a series of striking dramatic performances in the 1980s that brought him to broad public attention. Perhaps the most important of these roles was that of the pompous and vicious Señorito Iván in Mario Camus's* award-winning *Los santos inocentes* [*Holy Innocents*]* (1983). This performance was followed by a number of other noteworthy character roles in critically acclaimed and commercially successful films of the following years, including *De tripas corazón* [*Gutsy*] (Julio Sánchez Valdés, 1984); *Los paraísos perdidos* [*Lost Paradises*] (Basilio Martín Patino,* 1985), and *La corte de Faraón* [*The Pharoah's Court*] (José Luis García Sánchez,* 1985). It was not, however, until his stunning imterpretation of Francisco Franco in Jaime Camino's* *Dragón Rapide* (1986), that Diego received general recognition for his extraordinary dramatic talents. In Camino's controversial film, Diego offered the first sustained dramatic presentation of the late Spanish dictator with what many Spanish critics viewed as an uncanny physical and gestural likeness to Franco.

Though subsequent dramatic roles in the late 1980s and the 1990s capitalized on Diego's special versatility for near total transformation of his physical and verbal presence to fit particular roles, not all of his performances were of the same high artistic caliber. Among the most striking performances in lead roles were his portrayal of two historical personages: the mystic poet Juan de la Cruz in Carlos Saura's* *La noche oscura* [*The Dark Night*] (1988); and the ship-wrecked protagonist in the Spanish-Mexican coproduction of *Cabeza de Vaca* (1990), directed by Nicolás Echeverría. Diego continues to appear in secondary roles as well, often delivering striking performances as part of ensemble productions, such as his roles in Bigas Luna's* *Jamón, Jamón* (1992)* and José Luis García Sánchez's *Tirano Banderas* (1993).

Durán, Rafael (Madrid, 1911; Seville, 1994). Trained as a stage actor, Durán first became involved in motion pictures as a dubber for MGM in Madrid, then he worked his way into acting in motion pictures. His second screen credit, Gonzalo Delgrás's *La tonta del bote* [*A Perfect Fool*] (1939), was so well received that it quickly led to his pairing with Josita Hernán in a series of CIFESA films. Of these, the most successful were Rafael Gil's* *Eloísa está debajo de un almendro* [*Eloísa Is under an Almond Tree*] (1943) and Juan de Orduña's* *Tuvo la culpa Adán* [*It Was Adam's Fault*] (1944). Their last appearance together was in Gonzalo Delgrás's *Un viaje de novios* [*A Honeymoon Trip*] (1947). Durán was also successfully paired with Conchita Montes* in José Luis Sáenz de Heredia's* *El destino se disculpa* [*Destiny Apologizes*] (1945).

By the mid-1940s, Durán had established himself as a suave romantic leading male actor, ideal for light Spanish comedies; in Rafael Gil's* *El clavo* [*The Nail*] (1944) he showed his ability to take on more dramatic roles. By the end of the decade, however, the moment of his popularity with Spanish audiences had passed. He was relegated to secondary roles in often mediocre films for the next decade and a half, until he finally ended his screen career in the mid-1960s.

Dúrcal, Rocío (María Angeles de las Heras Ortiz) (Madrid, 1945). Discovered by the producer Luis Sanz in a contest designed to promote young singers, Dúrcal was easily transformed into a new version of the teenage starlet, Marisol,* appearing in a series of films that transparently mimicked the Deanna Durbin Hollywood musicals of the late 1930s. Her first film, Luis Lucia's *Canción de juventud* [*Song of Youth*] (1962), became an extraordinary success and served to formalize a minigenre of Dúrcal musicals (*Rocío de la Mancha* [*Rocío from La Mancha*] [1962], *La chica del trébol* [*The Cloverleaf Girl*] [1963], and *Tengo diecisiete años* [*I'm Seventeen Years Old*] [1964]). Moving into theatrical appearances, she continued her highly successful career in film musicals throughout the rest of the decade.

In the early 1970s, Dúrcal attempted to alter her screen persona by appearing in more dramatic roles, such as in Angelino Fons's* adaptation of the Benito Pérez Galdós novel, *Marianela* (1972), and the Spanish-French coproduction, *Díselo con flores* [*Say It with Flowers*] (Pierre Grimblar, 1974). After her controversial appearance in Enrique Martí Maqueda's tale of lesbian love, *Me siento extraña* [*I Feel Strange*] (1977), Dúrcal ended her film career and devoted herself exclusively to her professional singing.

Echanove, Juan (Madrid, 1961). Abandoning law studies for theater, Echanove made his film debut in the political thriller, *El caso Almería* [*The Almería Case*] (Pedro Costa, 1983). He immediately achieved critical recognition for his distinctive physical presence, which reminded critics of either a Spanish Charles Laughton, for his heavy musculature, or an Iberian Peter Lorre. His appearance in Antonio Mercero's highly successful television series, *Turno de oficio* (1985), brought him even wider acclaim. In 1986, Echanove's stellar performance as the sexually obsessed Matías in Vicente Aranda's* *Tiempo de silencio* [*Time of Silence*] solidified his status as one of the most promising and unique of Spanish character actors. Over the next decade he played in a variety of film roles ranging from light comedy (Fernando Colomo's* *Miss Caribe* and *Bajarse al moro* [*Going Down to Morroco*], both in 1988) to powerful dramatic interpretations (José Luis García Sánchez's* *Divinas palabras* [*Holy Words*] [1987]), to what many critics consider his definitive triumph as a character actor, his appearance in Francisco Regueiro's* *Madregilda* (1993), in which he gave an uncanny interpretation of Francisco Franco. Despite the lavish praise given for Echanove's acting talents, critics regularly note his tendency toward self-parody in some of his less controlled performances. In the role of the sympathetic newspaper editor in Pedro Almodóvar's* *La flor de mi secreto* [*Flower of My*

Secret] (1995), Echanove's performance displayed a more nuanced and subtle range of emotions than previously. This development suggests a conscious effort on his part to redirect his acting style to exhibit a more self-assured and understated presence.

Elorriaga, Xabier (Maracaibo, Venezuela, 1944). Born of Basque parents in exile in Venezuela, Elorriaga was educated in Chile, where he studied for but never completed a degree in engineering. In 1969 he arrived in Spain and settled in Bilbao where he began graduate studies in law. During this period, he made his debut in the Basque acting group, Kriselu, but eventually moved to Barcelona where he studied for a journalism degree. He taught at the University of Bellaterra but soon abandoned that career when he made his debut as one of the leading characters in Antoni Ribas's* historical epic, *La ciutat cremada* [*Burnt City*]* (1975).

His work in the Ribas film led to a series of other important parts over the next decade in films with a decided political or ideological bent. These included roles in Jaime Chávarri's* daring *A un dios desconocido* [*To an Unknown God*] (1977), *Toque de queda* [*Curfew*] (Iñaki Núñez, 1978), *Companys: proceso a Cataluña* [*Companys: Catalonia on Trial*] (Josep Maria Forn,* 1979), and two films by Imanol Uribe* (*Fuga de Segovia* [*Flight from Segovia*], 1982, and *La muerte de Mikel* [*The Death of Mikel*], 1983). Elorriaga's particular political affiliation with Basque film and culture took expression in his work in dubbing films into Euskera and eventually his direction of the short film, *Zergatik panpox?* (1986).

Elorriaga's dramatic talents have not always been well appreciated by Spanish reviewers who have often criticized him for a stiff and formal delivery. That lack of ease in dramatic roles is perhaps most effectively utilized in his performance as Peter, the British historian, in José Luis Borau's* *Tata mía* [*My Nanny*] (1987), in which the part calls for precisely a comic rendition of a stuffy and pedantic English historian researching the Spanish Civil War. By the end of the 1980s, Elorriaga began distancing himself from Spanish film to devote his energies to Basque television.

Fernán-Gómez, Fernando (Lima, Peru, 1921). The son of professional actors, much of Fernán-Gómez's youth was spent touring South America with his parents in repertory productions. He returned to Spain at the end of the Civil War and quickly gained popularity as a comic *galán*, or male romantic lead, in the theater. He made his film debut in 1943 in the CIFESA production of *Cristina Guzmán* directed by Gozalo Delgrás, the first of some 150 films in which he would appear over the next five decades. During the late 1940s and early 1950s, Fernán-Gómez made some twenty-seven films, the majority of which, made for mainstream popular cinema, reinforced his comic persona. A small number of these films were key works by some of the most important filmmakers of the period (Carlos Serrano de Osma,* Lorenzo Llobet-Gracia,* and Juan Antonio Bardem*). Certain of these films, such as Llobet-Gracia's* *Vida en sombras* [*Life in the Shadows*]* (1948), offered him the opportunity to show off his dramatic range.

In 1952 Fernán-Gómez turned to directing with *Manicomio* [*Asylum*]. Though his career as a director is somewhat erratic, several key titles of the 1950s and 1960s are the product of his cinematic inventiveness. Of his prodigious activity as a screen actor, a number of performances over five decades have been repeatedly singled out as outstanding. These include José Antonio Nieves Conde's* *Balarrasa* (1950), Víctor Erice's *El espíritu de la colmena* [*Spirit of the Beehive*]* (1973), Carlos Saura's *Ana y los lobos* [*Ana and the Wolves*] (1973), Juan Estelrich's *El anacoreta* [*The Anchorite*] (1976), and Carlos Saura's *Los zancos* [*Stilts*] (1984). Throughout his long career, Fernán-Gómez has managed to achieve the difficult balance between light, comic roles and a number of strikingly serious, brooding characters. His performances have been acknowledged through a series of national and international acting awards, including prizes at the Venice and Berlin film festivals and the Spanish National Film Prize in 1989, which is awarded for lifetime achievement.

Ferrandis, Antonio (Paterna, Valencia, 1921). Professionally trained as an elementary school teacher, Ferrandis maintained an avid interest in theater and in 1950 began to devote himself exclusively to stage acting. By the mid-1950s he was appearing in films but mostly in secondary roles as compared to the "first actor" status he enjoyed with the María Guerrero company. A deeply resonant voice gained him a certain prominence in television productions. With featured roles in Mario Camus's* *Con el viento solano* [*With a Wind from the East*] (1965) and Vicente Aranda's* *Fata Morgana** (1966), Ferrandis began to dedicate more energy to his film career. In 1974, his performances in Jaime de Armiñán's* *El amor del capitán Brando* [*The Love of Captain Brando*] and Roberto Bodegas's* *Los nuevos españoles* [*The New Spaniards*] were recognized by an award from the Círculo de Escritores Cinematográficos. In 1976, he played a leading role in Antonio Giménez-Rico's* *Retrato de familia* [*Family Portrait*], which established him as a serious leading actor.

From time to time over the next two decades Ferrandis would achieve leading-role status, for instance as the dying Nobel laureate, Antonio, in José Luis Garci's* Oscar-winning *Volver a empezar* [*To Begin Again*]* (1983), and as the ill-fated defender of Republican forces in Barcelona at the time of the outbreak of the Civil War in José Luis Madrid's *Memorias del General Escobar* [*Memoirs of General Escobar*] (1984). Yet he continued to appear primarily in secondary featured roles, such as his performance in Francesc Betriu's* *Réquiem por un campesino español* [*Requiem for a Spanish Farmer*] (1985). Indeed, in many of the roles in which Ferrandis appeared over the fifteen years following *To Begin Again*, he was cast according to his well-established screen persona as a warm-hearted, avuncular figure. This typecasting occurred despite the obvious evidence in his earlier films of a versatile dramatic actor.

Flores, Lola (María de los Dolores Flores Ruiz) (Jérez de la Frontera, 1925; Madrid, 1995). Performing flamenco song and dance publicly since her early childhood, Flores made her professional debut in her native Jérez at the age of fifteen, the same year she began appearing in minor roles in films. In 1944 she formed a professional flamenco troupe with Manolo Caracol and together they achieved broad popular success. This fame brought Flores to the attention of filmmaker Carlos Serrano de Osma,* who proposed that the team appear in his exotic flamenco musical film, *Embrujo* [*Enchantment*] (1947). Together the dance team appeared in three more films: *Jack el negro* [*Jack the Black*] (Julián Duvivier, 1950), *La niña de la venta* [*The Girl from the Inn*] (Ramón Torrado, 1951), *La estrella de Sierra Morena* [*The Star of Sierra Morena*] (Ramón Torrado, 1952).

With her star status well established, Flores dissolved her association with Caracol and embarked on her own dance and film career. This included an ambitious tour of Mexico, Cuba, and Argentina, as well as a some twenty films over the next two decades. Most of these were of folkloric and flamenco genres, capitalizing on her ever-popular stage persona. Of these films, perhaps the most significant titles are *Morena clara* [*The Light-Skinned Gypsy*], Luis Lucia's* 1954 remake of the famed Florián Rey* film of the 1930s that had been the pinnacle of Imperio Argentina's* film career; Luis Saslavsky's *El balcón de la luna* [*The Balcony of the Moon*] (1962), in which she costarred with flamenco legends Carmen Sevilla* and Paquita Rico; and one of her most successful nonfolkloric films, *Una señora estupenda* [*An Incredible Lady*] (Eugenio Martín, 1967). In these films, as well as in her weaker dramatic appearances, such as Victor Barrera's suspense melodrama, *Los invitados* [*The Guests*] (1986), the particular merits of the story or production were usually eclipsed by Flores's appearance and her near mythic status as one of Spain's most popular performers of this century.

Flores González, Josefa (*See* Marisol).

Forqué, Verónica (Madrid, 1955). Daughter of famed director-producer of the Francoist period, José María Forqué,* Verónica made her screen debut in a tiny role in Jaime de Armiñán's* *Mi querida señorita* [*My Dearest Señorita*]* (1971) and then continued to appear in a series of minor roles in films directed by her father throughout the rest of the decade. She also appeared in films made by other well-known directors of the period, notably *Las truchas* [*Trout*] (José Luis García Sánchez*), and *La guerra de papá* [*Papa's War*] (Antonio Mercero), both made in 1977. But it was not until her role as Crystal, the prostitute with a heart of gold, in Pedro Almodóvar's* *¿Qué he hecho Yo para merecer esto?* [*What Have I Done to Deserve This?*] (1985) that she achieved stardom.

That same year she appeared in Fernando Trueba's* *Sé infiel y no mires con quién* [*Be Unfaithful and Don't Worry with Whom*], one of the most commercially successful films of the decade. Her now highly developed comic style, marked by a huge grin and a high-pitched, squeaky voice, became easily identifiable marks of Forqué's screen persona. The following year, her performance in Trueba's next hit, *El año de las luces* [*The Year of Light*] (1986), revealed a wider range to her acting talents than had her previous films. For her performance as the director of a children's hospice in immediate post–Civil War Spain, Forqué won a Goya award. In 1987 she appeared in another hit comedy, Fernando Colomo's* *La vida alegre* [*The Happy Life*], playing the head of a clinic for venereal diseases married to the minister of Public Health, which won her her second Goya.

Despite efforts to break out of the now clichéd persona she had constructed for herself, such as the dramatic role in Basilio Martín Patino's* *Madrid* (1987), her greatest popular successes remained in the realm of screwball comedy. In 1993 she played the title role in Almodóvar's controversial *Kika*, in which, for the first time, Forqué was given the principal role. The next year she appeared in a dramatic lead in Mario Camus's* bittersweet comedy, *Amor propio* [*Self-esteem*] (1994) which was largely ignored by both the Spanish public and critics.

Gades, Antonio (Antonio Esteves Rodenas) (Elda, Alicante, 1936). The son of Catalans, Gades spent his early youth in a variety of odd jobs until 1953 when he was discovered by the famed dancer, Pilar López. He remained with López's dance troupe until 1960 when he was contracted as choreographer for the Opera of Rome. A vocal opponent of the Franco regime, Gades spent much of the next decade and half in Italy and France, first affiliated with the Rome Opera, then later working for Milan's renowned La Scala Opera company.

Gades made his screen debut in 1963 in Francisco Rovira Beleta's* *Los tarantos*, a gypsy retelling of the Romeo and Juliet story that enabled him to show off his dancing skills. Three years later he appeared in a secondary dramatic role in Mario Camus's* *Con el viento solano* [*With a Wind from the East*] (1966). That was followed by a more ambitious project by Rovira Beleta in the spirit of the earlier *Los tarantos*, a film adaptation of the Manuel de Falla ballet, *El amor brujo* [*Love, the Magician*]. This was a role he would repeat nearly twenty years later in a remake directed by Carlos Saura.* During the 1970s, Gades balanced his professional dance career with erratic incursions into film. One of the more interesting of these was Mario Camus's *Los días del pasado* [*Days of the Past*] (1977). Gades had asked Camus to make the film, the story of a *maquis*, a resistance fighter against the dictatorship, as a vehicle for himself and his wife, Pepa Flores, (the former child star, Marisol*). Though Gades's acting remained largely wooden, Flores delivered what may be the most powerful performance of her own erratic acting career. In 1978 Gades was named director of the Ballet Nacional de España but resigned after two years to form his own company.

His international theatrical reputation as a dancer and innovative flamenco choreographer was already well established before he met film director Carlos Saura in 1980. At the instigation of producer Emiliano Piedra,* Saura was urged to make a film version of Gades's dance adaptation of the Federico García Lorca play, *Bodas de sangre* [*Blood Wedding*] (1980). The film became a modest international success, highly praised by critics but, as a dance film, of limited appeal to general audiences. Piedra encouraged Gades and Saura to continue their collaboration, which they did over the next four years with *Carmen** (1983) and the remake of *El amor brujo* [*Love, the Magician*] in 1986. In each of these films Gades played the lead role, mixing a dramatic performance with his own stylized version of Andalusian or flamenco dance. *Carmen* was a huge international success and was nominated for a 1983 Oscar in the Best Foreign Film category.

Galiardo, Juan Luis (San Roque, Cádiz, 1940). Abandoning his studies in economics and agronomy at the University of Madrid to enroll in the National Film School (EOC) where he trained as an actor, Galiardo made his film debut in the leading role in Julio Diamante's *El arte de vivir* [*The Art of Living*] (1965). Over the next sixteen years he appeared in more than fifty motion pictures, becoming one of the most popular romantic lead actors of Spanish film. Though the majority of the films in which he appeared were of a rank commercial nature, his performances in Carlos Saura's* *Stress es tres, tres* [*Stress is Three, Three*] (1968), Vicente Aranda's* *Clara es el precio* [*Clara Is the Price*] (1974), and two films by Jaime Camino,* *Mañana será otro día* [*Tomorrow Is Another Day*] (1966) and *La campanada* [*Pealing of the Bells*] (1980), suggest a more versatile range of acting. In these latter roles, Galiardo played against his appearance of a merely romantic figure and began to suggest characters with inner turmoil, culminating in *Pealing of the Bells* in which he portrayed a man in the midst of a mid-life crisis.

In 1981, Galiardo went to Mexico where he lived for five years, appearing in secondary roles in Mexican films as well as in popular television dramas. Returning to Spain in 1986, he continued his acting career but also became involved in film production. Of the many serious dramatic roles he accepted in this third phase of his career, the most striking was his interpretation of the drunken and mutilated General Millán Astray in Francisco Regueiro's* *Madregilda* (1993), a performance that not only went against the general image of his earlier screen persona, but revealed Galiardo's ability to assume an eccentric range of character roles.

Gaos, Lola (Valencia, 1921; Madrid, 1993). One of the most prominent of a handful of outstanding character actresses produced by Spanish cinema, Lola Gaos's film career, with rare exception, was marked by a series of altogether too facile character roles as witches, maids, or mere villagers. This was due largely to her plain features and distinctively rough voice. Exceptions to that pattern, however, were roles in two Luis Buñuel* films, and a Borau* film, works of sufficient merit to secure her a place in Spanish film history.

Trained in the theater, and having spent part of her youth touring in theater companies in Latin America, Gaos did not return to Spain until 1945. In 1951 she made her film debut in a small but memorable cameo in Juan Antonio Bardem* and Luis García Berlanga's* *Esa pareja feliz* [*That Happy Couple*]* (1951) doing a parody of Aurora Bautista's* histrionic queen from Juan de Orduña's* recent *Locura de amor* [*The Madness of Love*]* (1948). It was not until 1961, however, after a decade of negligible film roles, that she appeared as Enedina in Luis Buñuel's *Viridiana.* In that role she urinates on the tableau parody of da Vinci's *The Last Supper* during the beggars' orgy scene. She appeared, again in an abbreviated role, in Luis García Berlanga's *El verdugo* [*The Executioner*]* (1963). It was, however, not until Buñuel's return to Spain in 1970 to shoot *Tristana* that Gaos was to get her chance for a truly memorable role. Recalling her performance a decade earlier, Buñuel expanded the role of the maid, Saturna, as Tristana's confidant. The result was an extraordinary part as the earthy but shrewish maid to Catherine Deneuve's Tristana.

On the basis of this role, Borau cast her as the central figure of the devouring mother, Martina, in his masterpiece, *Furtivos* [*Poachers*]* (1975), the only film in which she was to achieve full star status. Despite her tour de force performance and the incredible popularity of the film, in later years Gaos failed to receive the public appreciation or the quality of roles her obvious talents merited.

Gimpera, Teresa (Igualada, Barcelona, 1936). Discovered in her teens by the photographer, Leopoldo Pomés, who quickly converted her into a popular commercial model widely known as "Gim," Gimpera became the symbol in the 1960s of the commercial and publicity culture that was sweeping Francoist Spain in the first wave of consumerism since the end of the Civil War. Ironically, she made her screen debut in a film that made pointed fun of that culture and of her very status in it. In Vicente Aranda's* futuristic science-fiction film, *Fata Morgana* (1966), she played a somewhat autobiographical part of a popular model named Gim whose image is plastered on walls throughout the modernist city. She is pursued by teenagers and is the object of an assassin's plot. The film, often categorized as the major work of the Barcelona School of filmmaking, led to Gimpera's appearance in a film by another member of the group: *Una historia de amor* [*A Love Story*] (Jorge Grau, 1966). Gimpera's career quickly moved from marginal art cinema of the period to rank commercial films as she completed over forty motion pictures by the end of 1973. Most of these were either forgettable Spanish comedies directed by Pedro Lazaga,* or else genre films, usually horror or suspense films made as Spanish-Italian coproductions. The one exception to this pattern, and perhaps her most distinguished work, was Víctor Erice's* *El espíritu de la colmena* [*Spirit of the Beehive*]* (1973), in which she played the mother of seven-year old Ana Torrent.*

By the late 1970s, Gimpera's career had taken a decisive turn downwards as she appeared with more and more regularity in soft-core porn films. Though she ended her film career in the late 1970s, she still appeared from time to time in some serious films, such as Antonio Mercero's adaptation of a Miguel Delibes novel, *La guerra de papá* [*Papa's War*] (1977), Antoni Ribas's* ill-fated second epic, *¡Victoria!* [*Victory!*] (1983), and José Luis Garci's* *Asignatura aprobada* [*Examination Completed*] (1988). These performances reminded audiences that Gimpera's dramatic talents were based on more substantial qualities than merely her physical attractiveness.

Gómez, José Luis (Huelva, 1940). After studying acting in West Germany and Paris, Gómez began an impressive acting career that led him from Austria to Poland to Brazil. He finally returned to Spain in 1972. Having already become a well-established name in theater, he made his film debut in 1975 in the title role of the Ricardo Franco* film, *Pascual Duarte*,* an adaptation of the famed Camilo José Cela novel. His electrifying performance, combined with a script that was perhaps the most violent filmed in Spain up to that point, brought a notoriety that catapulted Gómez into the popular spotlight during the early post-Franco years. He followed *Pascual Duarte* with a series of other prestigious films, which included Manuel Gutiérrez Aragón's* *Sonámbulos* [*Sleepwalkers*] (1977), Carlos Saura's* *Los ojos vendados* [*Blindfolded Eyes*] (1978), and Jaime de Armiñán's* *Nunca es tarde* [*Never Too Late*] (1978). Through the scrupulous selection of film scripts that involved powerful dramatic roles for him, Gómez was able to develop a career as one of a handful of serious Spanish actors whose name lent prestige to the films with which he was associated.

During the two decades following *Pascual Duarte*, he continued to balance his theatrical career with a limited number of appearances in demanding film roles, including important films by Gonzalo Suárez* (*Remando al viento* [*Rowing with the Wind*] [1987]) and Pilar Miró* (*Beltenebros* [1991]).

González, Agustín (Madrid, 1930). González became interested in theater while studying at the University of Madrid. After appearing in university productions, he abandoned his studies in 1952 to devote himself to an acting career. He made his screen debut in a secondary role in Juan Antonio Bardem's* *Felices Pascuas* [*Merry Christmas*] (1954) and his television debut in 1958 in dramas directed by Jaime de Armiñán* and Adolfo Marsillach.* In 1958 he also began to appear regularly in secondary roles in a variety of films. His career as a screen actor spans some four decades and includes more than 130 films ranging from comic to dramatic roles.

Given his striking physical appearance, a pronounced bald head, an often stern expression, and a distinctive voice, González has specialized in often negative characters, though not necessarily villains. Rather, he is able to play, for instance, a figure of authority, a military officer, a functionary, or a slave to ritual or routine in either a comic or a serious key. Among the most striking performances in a career that has involved working with many of the most important Spanish filmmakers of the period are his role as the diffident Civil Guard officer in Jaime de Armiñán's* *El nido* [*The Nest*]* (1980) and the obsequious desk clerk in José Luis Garci's* *Volver a empezar* [*To Begin Again*]* (1982). He won Best Actor honors at the Karlov-Vary Film Festival for his performance in Jaime Cháva-rri's* *Las bicicletas son para el verano* [*Bicycles Are for Summer*] (1983).

Guillén, Fernando (Barcelona, 1932). Trained as a stage actor, Guillén began his film career in a walk-on role in José María Forqué's* *Un día perdido* [*A Lost Day*] (1954). Over the next three decades he appeared in more than two dozen films, mostly in secondary roles in which his face became familiar to Spanish audiences as a competent and versatile supporting actor but one who apparently lacked any real star persona. This situation changed completely with Guillén's appearance as the cynical detective in Pedro Almodóvar's smash hit, *La ley del deseo* [*Law of Desire*] (1987). This was followed by Guillén's first major lead role in Almodóvar's next film, *Mujeres al borde de un ataque de nervios* [*Women on the Verge of a Nervous Breakdown*]* (1988). His performance as Iván, the elusive actor, movie dubber, and lover of three different women introduced him to international audiences and enabled him to make a major career change.

Guillén continued to appear in roles that were comparable to his previous work, such as Eloy de la Iglesia's* *La estanquera de Vallecas* [*The Kiosk Vendor from Vallecas*] (1986) and Imanol Uribe's* *La luna negra* [*Black Moon*] (1989). But his talents were clearly more tested and his performances revealed a striking dramatic range in works such as Carlos Saura's* *La noche oscura* [*Dark Night*] (1989) and Gonzalo Suárez's* *Don Juan en las infiernos* [*Don Juan in Hell*] (1991) and *El detective y la muerte* [*The Detective and Death*] (1994).

Gutiérrez Caba, Emilio (Valladolid, 1942). The scion of one of the major Spanish acting families, son of Emilio Gutiérrez and Irene Caba, young Emilio entered professional theater in the early 1960s. He made his film debut in a small role in Luis César Amadori's popular comedy, *Como dos gotas de agua* [*Like Two Drops of Water*] (1964). The following year he was catapulted to critical aclaim through appearances in two of the most important films of the emerging New Spanish Cinema: Carlos Saura's* cross-over film, *La caza* [*The Hunt*]* and Basilio Martín Patino's* *Nueve cartas a Berta* [*Nine Letters to Berta*]*. In the former he played a relatively small but important role while in the latter film he was the lead character. In each film, Gutiérrez Caba's role was limited to playing a representative figure of a Spanish generation shaped by the cultural repression of the dictatorship. These roles called less on his acting range than on a certain appearance of type, which led to the impression that this popular young actor was somehow limited in his acting talent.

Although reduced to secondary roles in films over the next three decades, he maintained an active career on the Spanish stage. Among his most notable film performances were those in Pilar Miró's* first film, *La petición* [*The Petititon*] (1976); a cameo in Mario Camus's* ensemble film, *La colmena* [*The Beehive*] (1983), and the alcoholic psychiatrist in Pedro Almodóvar's* first international hit, *¿Qué he hecho Yo para merecer esto?* [*What Have I Done to Deserve This?*] (1985).

Hinojosa, Joaquín (Madrid, 1951). This versatile actor with diverse training in all aspects of theater made his screen debut in 1975 in an important secondary role in Ricardo Franco's* *Pascual Duarte*.* He played "El Estirao," a performance that, by virtue of its violent, taciturn quality, would become one of the hallmarks of Hinojosa's screen persona over the next decade. In 1977 he revealed his versatility, appearing in three quite distinct roles in important films by key directors of the period of political transition. In Gutiérrez Aragón's* *Camada negra* [*Black Brood*],* he played the part of a member of a fascist family that commits various acts of violence although maintaining membership in a church choir. In Carlos Saura's* *Elisa vida mía* [*Elisa, My Life*]* he played a self-centered lawyer who is incapable of understanding the emotional needs of his wife (Isabel Mestres) or the spiritual yearnings expressed by his father-in-law (Fernando Rey*). In *Tigres de papel* [*Paper Tigers*]*, Fernando Colomo's* debut film, he played the role of a hypocritical liberal, separated from his wife (Carmen Maura*) but still emotionally attached to her.

While continuing to be involved in professional theater during the 1980s, Hinojosa appeared in important screen adaptations of literary works, such as Miguel Angel Díez's *Luces de Bohemia* [*Bohemian Lights*] (1985) and Vicente Aranda's* *Tiempo de silencio* [*Time of Silence*]* (1985), in both of which he reverted to his best-known screen persona of the taciturn, violent figure.

Isbert, José (Madrid, 1886; Madrid, 1966). Trained to become a professor of commerce, Isbert showed an early inclination for theater. He made his debut at the age of nineteen at the famed Teatro Apolo in Madrid and later joined the Teatro Lara as its principal actor, where he remained for sixteen years. In 1935 he formed his own theatrical company.

Though he appeared in silent films as early as 1912, and had worked in France at the Paramount Studios at Joinville, dubbing films into Castilian, Isbert's film career did not begin in earnest until the post–Civil War period. Between 1940 and his death in 1966, he appeared in more than one hundred motion pictures; he was one of the most popular and well-loved comic supporting actors in Spanish film of that period. His raspy voice and distinctive physical appearance were used to tremendous comic effect by nearly all of the major directors of the postwar period. Isbert's enduring reputation as one of Spain's great comic actors, however, is based largely on a series of bravura comic performances of the 1950s and 1960s. Foremost among these are four performances. The first is his rendition of the bungling mayor of the Castilian village in García Berlanga's* *Bienvenido, Mister Marshall!* [*Welcome, Mister Marshall!*]* (1953). The second, one of his most popular roles (in José Luis Sáenz de Heredia's* *Historias de la radio* [*Radio Stories*]* [1955]) is that of an inventor who rushes through Madrid dressed up as an eskimo in order to win the cash prize in a radio contest. The third is Isbert's very believable rendition of a retired old man who kills off his family in order to obtain a motorized cart (Marco Ferreri's black comedy, *El cochecito* [*The Little Car*]* [1960]). The fourth is his last screen appearance, in which he played the retired executioner, Don Amadeo, who arranges for his son-in-law to replace him as executioner for the state so that the younger man may also obtain a state-subsidied apartment (Luis García Berlanga's *El verdugo* [*The Executioner*]* [1963]).

The particular quality of Isbert's screen persona that so endeared him to audiences may well have been the very ordinariness of the characters he portrayed. Though often bungling and fixated on a single idea or goal, his characters seem drawn from the real foibles of real people.

Ladoire, Oscar (Madrid, 1954). Ladoire is a member of a generation of students who came out of the University of Madrid's Faculty of Information Sciences at the end of the 1970s and helped shape the emerging *Nueva Comedia Madrileña* ("New Madrid Comedy"), one of the striking new genres of the 1980s. Ladoire participated in the founding of the film magazine, *Casablanca*, and achieved prominence in the lead role in Trueba's first feature-length film, *Opera prima* [*First Work*]* (1980). He won the best acting award for that role at the Venice Film Festival and went on to script, direct, and star in his own first film the following year, *A contratiempo* [*Delay*] (1981), with indifferent results. His presence as an eccentric, almost Woody Allen–type character in Trueba's films gave Ladoire a short-term aura as the ideal young *progre* or politically progressive character. With his break from Trueba after the failure of *Sal gorda* [*Coarse Salt* or *Get Lost, Fatty*] (1982), however, he went on to an uneven series of films with a variety of directors as diverse as Manuel Gutiérrez Aragón* (*La noche más hermosa* [*The Most Beautiful Night*] [1984]), Fernando Fernán-Gómez* (*El viaje a ninguna parte* [*The Journey to Nowhere*] [1986]), and Bigas Luna* (*Las edades de Lulú* [*The Ages of Lulú*] [1990]).

Ladoire's second attempt to achieve an authorial success came in the 1987 *Esa cosa con plumas* [*That Strange Thing with Feathers*] in which he again directed and starred, but the film proved a commercial and critical failure. Having debuted in 1980 with much fanfare, by the decade's end he was appearing as a self-parody of his own film persona in Mariano Ozores's *Disparate nacional* [*National Joke*] (1989).

Lampreave, Chus (Madrid, 1930). Lampreave's early film career includes small roles in three important black comic masterpieces of the late 1950s and early 1960s: Marco Ferreri's* *El pisito* [*The Little Flat*]* (1958) and *El cochecito* [*The Little Car*]* (1960), and Luis García Berlanga's* *El verdugo* [*The Executioner*]* (1962). During the 1970s she continued to appear in small supporting roles in films by important filmmakers, such as Jaime de Armiñán's* *Mi querida señorita* [*My Dearest Señorita*]* (1971) and *El amor del Capitán Brando* [*The Love of Captain Brando*] (1974). It was not, however, until her success in Berlanga's *La escopeta nacional* [*National Rifle*]* (1977) and its two sequels that she achieved status as a distinctive character actress with a recognizable screen persona. This led to her appearances as one of the regulars in a number of Pedro Almodóvar* comedies: *Laberinto de pasiones* [*Labyrinth of Passion*] (1982); *Entre tinieblas* [*Dark Habits*] (1984); ¿*Qué he hecho Yo para merecer esto?* [*What Have I Done to Deserve This?*] (1985); *Matador* (1986), and *Mujeres al borde de un ataque de nervios* [*Women on the Verge of a Nervous Breakdown*]* (1988). At the same time she made important appearances in Fernando Trueba's* *Sé infiel y no mires con quién* [*Be Unfaithful and Don't Bother with Whom*] (1985) and *El año de las luces* [*The Year of Light*] (1986).

The striking feature of Lampreave's comedic style is the development of a grotesque, impertinent, or daffy character, a persona whose zany possibilities she developed to the fullest in the comedies of Pedro Almodóvar.

Landa, Alfredo (Pamplona, 1933). Landa completed his primary education in San Sebastián, where he developed an interest in theater and became associated with the university theater group (TEU) while studying law. He appeared in forty plays in that group before moving to Madrid in 1958 where he worked as a film dubber while trying to develop a professional career in acting. He made his theatrical debut in Madrid in 1961 in the comic *La felicidad no lleva impuesto de lujo* [*Happiness Doesn't Carry a Luxury Tax*] and quickly established himself as a comic actor. The following year he made his film debut with a leading role in José Maria Forqué's* *Atraco a las tres* [*Stick-Up at Three P.M.*]. Though he continued to appear in theatrical works, Landa began one of the most prolific film careers of the sound period, appearing in over a hundred films in a period of twenty years.

His career is generally divided into three distinct stages. In the first, the years 1961–1969, he appeared in secondary comic roles in artistically insignificant films. The exceptions during this period were appearances in Luis García Berlanga's* *El verdugo* [*The Executioner*]* (1963), *Ninette y un señor de Murcia* [*Ninette and a Gentleman from Murcia*] (Fernando Fernán-Gómez,* 1965), and *De cuerpo presente* [*Lying in State*] (Antonio Eceiza,* 1967). His second period began with his appearance in Ramón Fernández's *No desearás al vecino del quinto* [*Thou Shalt Not Covet Thy Neighbor on the Fifth Floor*] (1970), one of the most commercially successful Spanish productions of all times, which ushered in an avalache of Spanish comedies of the 1970s that were fixated on the consumerist fever of the period and sprinkled with mildly erotic themes. Landa's incredible popularity in such works defined a subgenre, called *Landismo* in recognition of the way his comic persona defined these films. During the late 1970s, Landa gradually shifted to serious roles in sentimental and melodramatic films, including José Luis Garci's* *Las verdes praderas* [*The Green Prairies*] (1978) and Juan Antonio Bardem's* *El puente* [*The Long Weekend*] (1978). But the definitive end of *Landismo* came with Landa's stunning portrayal of Germán Areta, a hard-boiled detective of the Humphrey Bogart film noir tradition, in Garci'a *El crack* [*The Crack*] (1981).

Landa's screen persona in the 1980s was one that had clearly matured from the image that he had developed during the two preceding decades. The transformation was especially pronounced in the two Germán Areta films, as well as Mario Camus's* *Los santos inocents* [*Holy Innocents*]* (1983), for which Landa shared the Best Actor award with Francisco Rabal* at the Cannes Film Festival.

Despite his successes in powerful, dramatic roles, Landa continued to appear in the 1980s and 1990s in films that exploited his skills in slapstick as well as in sentimental light comedy. His role in, for instance, Berlanga's *La vaquilla* [*The Heifer*] (1985) and Ricardo Palacios' *Biba la banda* [*Long Live the Gang!*] (1987) were of a comedic nature. On the other hand, his roles in *El bosque animado* [*The Enchanted Forest*] (José Luis Cuerda, 1987), *Tata mía* [*My Nanny*] (José Luis Borau,* 1987), and *Canción de cuna* [*Cradle Song*] (José Luis Garci,* 1994), reveal a more dramatic range in Landa's acting talents.

Ligero, Miguel (Madrid, 1897; Madrid, 1968). From the age of twelve Ligero peformed in professional theatrical productions, predominantly in comic works. In 1917 he achieved the status of *primer galán*, leading male romantic actor, in the Enrique Lacasa Theater Company. Throughout the 1920s he participated in a number of theatrical tours of Latin America, principally in light comic works, *zarazulas* and *sainetes*. He returned to Spain in 1926 to make his silent film debut in Arturo Caballo's *Frivolinas*. By 1930 he was working at Paramount's Joinville studio outside of Paris, making the Spanish version of English-language sound films. He was brought to Hollywood by Fox Studios the following year to perform the same task, but by 1933 he had returned to Madrid to make *Susana tiene un secreto* [*Susan Has a Secret*], the first of a series of eight films he appear in under the direction of Benito Perojo.

In 1934, he began appearing in films directed by the other great filmmaker of the Republican years, Florián Rey.* His first performance in a Rey film was a comic role in *El novio de mamá* [*Mama's Suitor*] (1934), followed in rapid succession by Rey's *La hermana San Sulpicio* [*Sister Saint Sulpicio*] (1934), in which he was teamed for the first time with Imperio Argentina,* the top film actress of the day. He next appeared in *Nobleza baturra* [*Rustic Gallantry*]* (1935) and *Morena clara* [*The Light-Skinned Gypsy*]* (1936), as well as Benito Perojo's *La verbena de la Paloma* [*Paloma Fair*]* (1936)—three of the most commercially popular films of the Republican period.

Alternating comic successes between directors Perojo and Rey, Ligero was a recognized national celebrity by the time of the outbreak of the Civil War. His specialty was an exaggerated form of theatrical humor, complete with broad facial mugging. During the period of Civil War hostilities, he followed Perojo first to Berlin to make *El barbero de Sevilla* [*The Barber of Seville*] and *Suspiros de España* [*Sighs of Spain*], both in 1938, then to Rome to make *Los hijos de la noche* [*Children of the Night*] (1939).

Ligero's career as a consummate comic actor continued in the post–Civil War period; between 1939 and 1950 he appeared in a total of thirteen more films. His status as a comic lead diminished with the years, although he continued to play minor comic roles up to the time of his death. Two of his most significant roles of the latter period of his career were in the Luis Lucia 1954 remake of *The Light-Skinned Gypsy* and José Luis Sáenz de Heredia's remake of *Paloma Fair* in 1963, in which Ligero re-created what had long since become his signature role of Don Hilarión.

López, Charo (María del Rosario López Piñuelas) (Salamanca, 1943). While studying at the University of Salamanca, López became involved in university theater productions (TEU). After completing her studies at the Faculty of Philosophy and Letters, she moved to Madrid and worked under the direction of Miguel Narros at the Compañía del Teatro Español. She made her film debut in Gonzalo Suárez's* eccentric thriller, *Ditirambo* (1967). Over the years she would appear in a total of five more Suárez films: *El extraño caso del doctor Fausto* [*The Strange Case of Doctor Faustus*] (1969), *La regenta* [*The Regent's Wife*] (1974), *Parranda* [*Binge*] (1977), *Epílogo* [*Epilogue*] (1984), and *Don Juan en los infiernos* [*Don Juan in Hell*] (1991). During the 1970s and early 1980s, López appeared in nearly thirty films, most of which were typical comedies and genre films of the period and of little artistic pretension.

In 1982, after her appearance on Spanish television in Rafael Moreno Alba's dramatic series, *Los gozos y las sombras* [*Pleasures and Shadows*], which raised López to the status of a national celebrity, she began to appear in more important films and in roles of more stature. These included Mario Camus's* *La colmena* [*The Beehive*] (1982), for which she received the Best Actress Award at the Berlin Film Festival; Camus's *La vieja música* [*The Old Music*] (1985); Vicente Aranda's* *Tiempo de silencio* [*Time of Silence*] (1985); Josefina Molina's* *Lo más natural* [*The Most Natural Thing*] (1990); and Gonzalo Suárez's* popular *Don Juan en los infiernos* [*Don Juan in Hell*] (1991). As a reflection of the degree of celebrity and audience recognition López had achieved by the early 1990s, Pedro Almodóvar used her for a brief cameo, without screen credit, as the suicidal mother in the opening moments of his 1994 film, *Kika*.

López Vázquez, José Luis (Madrid, 1922). While still a university student López Vázquez began to work as an extra in Spanish films of the early 1940s. He then switched to theater, making his professional debut in 1946 in the prestigious María Guerrero Theater Company where he appeared in a number of Spanish Golden Age dramas. He returned to film in 1951 with a minor role in the Juan Antonio Bardem*–Luis García Berlanga* collaborative film, *Esa pareja feliz* [*That Happy Couple*]*. He then dedicated himself with progressively more intense energy to a career in films, accepting roles often indiscriminately in both serious and mere exploitative works. By the end of the 1950s, López Vázquez had appeared in some thirty-five films, most of which were simple, popular comic roles. Of this first decade of his screen career, his most important performances were in films by Luis García Berlanga (*Novio a la vista* [*Boyfriend in Sight*] [1953]; *Los jueves, milagro* [*Every Thursday, a Miracle*] [1958]; *Plácido* [1961]) and Marco Ferreri* (*El pisito* [*The Little Flat*]* [1958]; and *El cochecito* [*The Little Car*]* [1960].)

The 1960s saw a major expansion of López Vázquez's popularity in comedy films, for he appeared in some sixty-six motion pictures by the end of that decade. While the majority of these played off a well-established comic persona, especially in the immensely popular Pedro Lazaga* and Mariano Ozores comedies, he also made important moves toward serious dramatic acting. For many critics of the period, López Vázquez's lead performance as a sexually repressed middle-aged bachelor in Carlos Saura's* *Peppermint Frappé* (1967) was a revelation. By 1970, when he starred in Saura's *Jardín de las delicias* [*Garden of Delights*] as the infirmed Antonio Cano, he was already acknowledged as a consummate actor with a wide range of acting styles. The following year he appeared in one of the most demanding roles of his career, that of Adela, a fortyish spinster who discovers that she is really a man in Jaime de Armiñán's* spoof on sexual repression during the Franco years, *Mi querida señorita* [*My Dearest Señorita*].*

López Vázquez went on to play the lead in Saura's *La prima Angélica* [*Cousin Angelica*]* (1973), one of the most praised performances of his entire career. He was called upon to play the part of an emotionally stunted middle-aged man who feels himself still a child as he relives the painful memories of having been separated from his parents during the Civil War. Other important roles during this period included that of an alienated book editor in Gutiérrez Aragón's debut film, *Habla mudita* [*Speak, Little Dumb Girl*] (1973).

Though his versatility as an actor had become widely recognized by the mid-1970s, he continued to be offered and to accept roles in popular comedies; in these, he began to fall into a self-parody of his own earlier comic persona. Some of these appearances, such as his roles in all three parts of Berlanga's *Escopeta nacional* [*National Rifle*]* series and in José Luis García Sánchez's* *La corte de Faraón* [*The Pharoah's Court*] (1985), were critically well received, but others, such as his appearance in Luis Delgados's *Profesor Eroticus* (1981), were dismissed as mere sexploitation comedies.

Despite such an uneven development in a career that includes roles in nearly two hundred films, López Vázquez remains one of the emblematic actors of the modern Spanish cinema. He appeared in some of the key dramatic and comic films over a period of four decades.

Lozano, Margarita (Tetuan, 1931). Lozano's film career began in the early 1950s with appearances in a variety of motion pictures that ranged from serious films, such as Fernando Fernán-Gómez's* directorial debut, *Manicomio* [*Asylum*] (1953), to commercial potboilers, such as several films by Antonio Isasi. Her career fortunes changed radically as a result of her appearance in César Ardavín's* award-winning *Lazarillo de Tormes** (1959) and in Luis Buñuel's* notorious *Viridiana** (1961) as the maid, Ramona. The prestige associated with this latter film enabled Lozano to sustain an active career over the next decade. She made a variety of film appearances in works by well-established box-office names such as Juan de Orduña* (*Teresa de Jesús* [1962]), and Francisco Rovira Beleta* (*Los tarantos* [1963]). She also appeared in works of a more serious fledging group of filmmakers, such as Jaime Camino* (*Los felices sesenta* [*The Happy Sixties*] [1963]), Mario Camus* (*Los farsantes* [*The Actors*] [1963],) and Francisco Regueiro* (*Amador* [*Lover*] [1964]).

Her appearance in Sergio Leone's spaghetti western, *A Fistful of Dollars* (1967), put her into contact with a number of Italian directors, including Pier Paolo Passolini (*Porcile* [1969]) and the Taviani Brothers (*Night of the Shooting Star* [1981], *Good Morning, Babylon* [1987]). In 1986, she made her triumphant return to Spanish cinema in the rich and suggestive role of the grandmother in Manuel Gutiérrez Aragón's* *La mitad del cielo* [*Half of Heaven*].* Since then, however, Lozano has made only brief appearances in Spanish films. She has appeared in European films directed by the Taviani brothers and in Spanish television films such as Juan Antonio Bardem's* *Lorca, muerte de un poeta* [*Lorca, Death of a Poet*] (1992).

Luna, Manuel (Sevilla, 1898; Madrid, 1958). Attracted to theater from an early age, Luna made his theatrical debut at fifteen in the Anita Ferri Theater Company. His first film appearance was in José Sobrado's *Santa Isabel de Ceres* [*Saint Elizabeth of Ceres*] in 1923. It was not, however, until the mid-1930s and his appearance in some of the major successes directed by Florián Rey* and starring Imperio Argentina* that Luna achieved wide renown. He was cast as one of Argentina's vying lovers in *Nobleza baturra* [*Rustic Gallantry*]* (1935), the love-smitten lawyer who falls for the gypsy played by Argentina in *Morena clara* [*The Light Skinned Gypsy*]* (1936), and Antonio Vargas Heredia, the doomed bullfighter, again in love with the Argentina character in *Carmen, la de Triana* [*Carmen, the Girl from Triana*] (1938).*

Luna's success as a powerful dramatic presence, due in no small part to his striking appearance and prominent, penetrating eyes, continued into the 1940s. He modulated his fairly set persona as the ill-fated romantic lead with a new series of negative roles in which he played disagreeable, villainous characters. Notable among these are Adolfo Aznar's *Con los ojos del alma* [*With the Eyes of the Soul*] (1943), Antonio Román's* *Fuenteovejuna* (1947), and Juan de Orduña's* *La leona de Castilla* [*The Lioness of Castile*] (1951). During the 1940s, the peak of his career, he appeared in over thirty films, including some of the most popular works directed by the most important directors of the day. These included a lead in Juan de Orduña's *¡A mí, la legión!* [*The Legion's for Me!*]* (1942) and *Locura de amor* [*The Madness of Love*]* (1948), José Luis Sáenz de Heredia's* *El escándalo* [*The Scandal*]* (1943), and Florián Rey's* *La nao capitana* [*The Captain's Ship*] (1947). By the 1950s Luna's roles had noticeably depreciated from leads to important secondary acting roles. Even within this apparent decline, owing largely to the actor's age, Luna figured prominently in a series of important historical epic films of the 1950s, including Orduña's *Agustina de Aragón* [*Agustina of Aragón*] (1950), *La leona de Castilla* (1951), and *Alba de América* [*Dawn in America*] (1951).

Mariscal, Ana (Ana María Rodríguez Arroyo Mariscal) (Madrid, 1923; Madrid, 1995). The sister of the stage actor, Luis Arroyo, Mariscal was discovered by film director, Luis Marquina,* who contracted her for a major secondary role in *El último húsar* [*The Last Hussar*] (1940). Mariscal's success in the film led to another secondary female lead in José Luis Sáenz de Heredia's* *Raza* [*Race*]* (1941), arguably the most important film of the early post–Civil War period. The fame and popularity of her performance as the chaste sweetheart of José Churruca (Alfredo Mayo*) in this film scripted by Franco led to a continuous series of romantic roles for her throughout the 1940s and early 1950s, establishing Mariscal as a major star. During this same period she was actively pursuing her talents on the stage of the National Theater and other prestigious theatrical companies.

As her popularity diminished in the early 1950s, Mariscal sought other outlets for her dramatic talents. In 1952 she established her own production company, Bosco Films, through which she financed eleven films that she directed, making her the first of a prominent group of Spanish women filmmakers of the post–Civil War period. In 1954, with the commercial failure of her first production, *Segundo López* (1952), Mariscal decided to move to Argentina. She lived there for two years, performing on the stage and in films, and wrote her first television drama. Returning to Spain in 1956, she taught at the National Film School (IIEC), a post she held until 1961. At the same time she appeared in a variety of films, including some that she directed herself.

After the commercial failure of her first two directorial works, Mariscal switched to more proven commercial formulas and was able to achieve a measure of box-office success, although these films were also met by critical indifference. Mariscal's film credits as an actress number more than fifty and span four decades. Her primary successes, however, remain in the series of largely melodramatic works in which she appeared in the first decade following the end of the Civil War.

Marisol, (Josefa Flores González) (Málaga, 1948). Josefa "Pepa" Flores, later to become known as the child phenomenon, "Marisol," was first noticed by producer Manuel Goyanes when she appeared on a televised musical pageant of regional songs and dances from her native Málaga. He became determined to transform the twelve-year old singer and dancer into a Spanish Shirley Temple. Marisol's first three films seemed to confirm Goyanes's vision. Luis Lucia's* *Un rayo de luz* [*A Ray of Light*] (1960), *Ha llegado un ángel* [*An Angel Has Arrived*] (1961), and *Tómbola* (1962), all light musical comedies, in the Shirley Temple style, proved astoundingly successful in both Spain and Latin America.

However, the fact of Flores's physical development shortly required certain transformations of her screen persona from perky child star to amorous adolescent. This necessarily altered the formula that had previously been so successful. The Marisol genre continued to work until the end of the 1960s, when, in order to accomodate her appearance of a young woman, she was situated in a series of progressively less wholesome narrative situations. The weakening commercial success of films such as *Las cuatro bodas de Marisol* [*Marisol's Four Weddings*] (1967) and *Solos los dos* [*Two Alone*] (1968), both directed by Luis Lucia, led to a radical transformation of the Marisol persona toward a more eroticized character in the late 1960s and early 1970s.

She joined forces with the famed director, Juan Antonio Bardem,* whose career was also sagging, to work on two films intended to demonstrate Marisol's dramatic potential and to provide Bardem with a popular commercial success. *La corrupción de Chris Miller* [*The Corruption of Chris Miller*] (1972) dealt with the traumatic effects of rape on an adolescent girl, and *El poder del deseo* [*The Force of Desire*] (1975) situated Flores in a police genre film. Both efforts failed to achieve either their critical or commercial goals. One of her more accomplished dramatic roles, however, was in Mario Camus's* political drama of the *maquis*, or anti-Francoist resistent fighters, *Los días del pasado* [*Days of the Past*] (1977). The film had been designed as a favor for her husband, Antonio Gades,* the flamenco dancer turned film actor, who had asked Camus to make a film that would be vehicle for the couple. Camus's script chronicles the separation and reencounter between Flores, a rural school teacher, and her lover, Gades, who is in hiding in the mountains. Flores's performance is possibly the most accomplished of her short dramatic acting career.

By the end of the 1970s, she had completely distanced herself from the original child-singing star persona, yet was unable to find the films to sustain a career as a serious film actress. When she appeared in brief musical numbers in two parts of Carlos Saura's* flamenco trilogy, *Bodas de sangre* [*Blood Wedding*] (1980) and *Carmen** (1983), it was under her adult stage name, Pepa Flores.

Marsillach, Adolfo (Barcelona, 1928). A major figure in Spanish theater and television as an actor and director, Marsillach has also maintained a regular presence in Spanish cinema over more than forty years. After working in theater in Barcelona during his youth, he joined Madrid's prestigious María Guerrero Theater Company in 1952, debuting in the important Antonio Buero Vallejo drama, *En la ardiente oscuridad* [*In the Burning Darkness*] (1951). By 1956 he had formed his own theatrical company.

Marsillach's film debut was in José Luis Sáenz de Heredia's* *Mariona Rebull* (1946) and throughout the 1950s he appeared in a number of films in secondary roles. In 1959, he played the lead role of Ramón y Cajal in León Klimovsky's biographical film, *Salto a la gloria* [*Jump to Glory*], a dramatized version of the life of the famed Spanish physician and investigator, which brought him his first major success as a film star. He would later repeat that role in José María

Forqué's* television movie, *Ramón y Cajal* (1981). Following his role in *Jump to Glory*, he appeared in the lead role in Forqué's popular comic success, *Maribel y la extraña familia* [*Maribel and the Strange Family*] (1960), a screen adaptation of the popular Miguel Mihura play.

While maintaining parallel careers in television and theater throughout the 1960s and 1970s, he continued to appear in films, attempting his own unsuccessful move to directing in an adaptation of Ramón María Valle-Inclán's *Flor de santidad* [*The Flower of Sanctity*] (1972). His notable screen acting roles throughout the decade, however, offset that failure. These included performances in Gonzalo Suárez's* *La regenta* [*The Regent's Wife*] (1974), Antoni Ribas's* *La ciutat cremada* [*Burnt City*]* (1976) and Jaime de Armiñán's* *Al servicio de la mujer española* [*At the Service of Spanish Womanhood*] (1978), one of his most powerful dramatic performances in which he played an emotionally stunted, vindictive man scarred by the sexual repression of the Franco years.

Though Marsillach has over thirty films to his credit, his appearances increasingly tend to be in secondary roles—prestige cameo appearances by a noted theatrical legend rather than roles that contribute to the development of a screen actor. Among these may be counted his appearance in Josefina Molina's* historical drama, *Esquilache* (1988), for which he won a Goya for his supporting role.

Maura, Carmen (Carmen García Maura) (Madrid, 1945). A descendent of the famed nineteenth-century Spanish politician, Antonio Maura, Carmen abandoned her university studies to open an art gallery and to pursue a career in the theater. By the late 1960s she was appearing in minor roles in commercial films as well as in the experimental shorts made by her friends. In 1977 she came to popular attention in her first important role, in Fernando Colomo's* *Tigres de papel* [*Paper Tigers*].* The film not only helped forge the genre of the Madrid Comedies of the 1980s, but also provided Maura with an emblematic screen persona as a member of the generation of disillusioned, young, and progressive Spaniards disoriented by the political transition of the late 1970s. This persona would become a distinctive feature of the many roles Maura played in the 1980s, especially the ones she developed in Pedro Almodóvar's* films.

Principally through her association with Almodóvar, Maura became popularly perceived as the embodiment of a defiant, liberal, and passionate Spanish woman, a role that clearly shaped the diverse range of her performances whether as a working-class housewife, a movie dubber, a transsexual actress, or a former nun. Her leading roles in three Almodóvar films, in particular, *¿Qué he hecho Yo para merecer esto?* [*What Have I Done to Deserve This?*] (1985), *La ley del deseo* [*Law of Desire*]* (1987), and *Mujeres al borde de un ataque de nervios* [*Women on the Verge of a Nervous Breakdown*]* (1988), brought Maura international attention as a brilliant comedy actress capable of a wide range of roles. Though most widely known for her comedic roles, she has a steady list of credits in dramatic works as well, beginning with secondary appearances in Pilar Miró's*

Gary Cooper que estás en los cielos [*Gary Cooper, Who Art in Heaven*] (1980) and Miguel Picazo's* *Extramuros* [*Outside the Walls*] (1985).

Three of her dramatic roles are especially noteworthy: an ex-nun trying to adjust to the cultural changes of the years of transition in José Luis Borau's* *Tata mía* [*My Nanny*] (1987); a Republican-sympathizing musical hall singer during the Civil War in Carlos Saura's* *¡Ay, Carmela!* (1990), for which she won the European film acting prize; and a onetime member of the Basque terrorist group, ETA, thrown into an emotional affair with another terrorist fleeing his pursuers in Mario Camus's* *Sombras en una batalla* [*Shadows in a Battle*] (1993). Each of these roles connects with the dominant features of the strong female identity Maura established as her screen persona.

Mayo, Alfredo (Alfredo Fernández Martínez) (Barcelona, 1911; Palma de Mallorca, 1985). Mayo abandoned his studies in medicine in 1929 for a theatrical career, appearing on stage throughout the 1930s. During the Civil War he was an airplane pilot on the Nationalist side. At the war's end he became more seriously interested in a career in motion pictures. But his first role, that of a frail tuberculosis patient in Eusebio Fernández Ardavín's* production of *La florista de la reina* [*The Queen's Florist*] (1940), was an inauspicious start since Mayo clearly had a robust physique, which belied his role. His lack of ease in the role added to a weak performance. Within a year, however, Carlos Arévalo* would transform Mayo into the virile and swashbuckling Captain Sidi Absalán Balcazár in *¡Harka!* (1941), thereby providing Spanish postwar society with its first heroic, mythic image of the warrior-patriot.

Mayo was cast in a dizzying succession of films that offered audiences a concrete romantic ideal to match the Nationalist rhetoric of the regime. *¡Harka!* was followed that same year by Antonio Román's* *Escuadrilla* [*Squadron*] and the key film of the bellicose genre, José Luis Sáenz de Heredia's* *Raza* [*Race*].* The following year he appeared in Juan de Orduña's* *El frente de los suspiros* [*The Battle Front of Sighs*] and *¡A mí la legión!* [*The Legion's for Me!**]. Through most of these films Mayo's acting talents remained oddly unconvincing; his performances were marred by his tendency to merely recite appropriate dialogue and assume a series of histrionic poses.

Following on the heels of the popular success of his war films, he soon began to appear in romantic melodramas and comedies, frequently paired—as in Luis Marquina's* *Malvaloca* (1942)—with Amparo Rivelles,* with whom Mayo formed the ideal screen couple of the period. Given his limited acting talents and changing cultural values of the period, in the early fifties Mayo's career began to decline steadily. His status changed to that of a supporting actor; he appeared in films such as Juan de Orduña's *El último cuplé* [*The Last Ballad*]* (1956) and *Teresa de Jesús* (1962).

In 1965, however, Mayo's acting fortunes changed radically when he appeared in one of the major roles in Carlos Saura's* *La caza* [*The Hunt*].* Ironically, his character, Paco, is a self-conscious critique of the decaying heroic images that

Mayo himself had authored two decades earlier. The film was followed two years later with *Peppermint Frappé* (1967), another commercial success for Saura and an artistic achievement for Mayo, who, for the first time in his long career, seemed to be developing a talent for character acting. Other directors, however, showed little interest in Mayo. After his work with Saura, he returned to his standard secondary parts, appearing in more than fifty more films before his death in 1985.

Mistral, Jorge (Valencia, 1920; Mexico City, 1972). Mistral abandoned his law studies to strike his fortune in professional theater during the early post–Civil War period, eventually appearing with prestigious theater companies such as those of José Rivero and Ana Adamuz. He made his film debut in 1944 in José Gaspar's *La llamada del mar* [*The Call of the Sea*]. He continued to appear in theatrical productions as well as in films but his movie career was secured in 1945 when he signed an exclusive contract with CIFESA, then the most prestigious Spanish film company. CIFESA promoted Mistral as a romantic young lead in films such as *Misión blanca* [*The White Mission*] (1946), *Locura de amor* [*The Madness of Love*]* (1948), and *Pequeñeces* [*Trifles*] (1950), all three directed by Juan de Orduña.* Thus he was able to forge a screen persona as a Spanish Errol Flynn, becoming perhaps the principal romantic screen idol of the late 1940s in Spain and rivaling the other principal romantic male lead of the decade, the older Alfredo Mayo.* These early screen successes established Mistral's strength as a competent actor in costumed epics, with little indication of a particularly unique acting talent.

In 1950, on an extended theatrical tour of Cuba and Mexico, Mistral broke his exclusive contract with CIFESA and began a period lasting more than a decade in which he appeared in a prodigious number of Mexican, Argentine, Italian, and even Hollywood films. These included the role of Alejandro, the Heathcliff figure from Luis Buñuel's* problematic version of *Wuthering Heights*, shot in Mexico under the title *Abismos de pasión* (1953).

While maintaining his residence in Mexico, Mistral still appeared in Spanish films, such as the Luis Lucia* remake of Armando Palacio Valdés's *La hermana San Sulpicio* [*Sister Saint Sulpicio*] (1952) and *Un caballero andaluz* [*An Andalusian Gentleman*] (1954) both directed by Lucia, and Juan Antonio Bardem's* Spanish-Mexican coproduction, *La venganza* [*The Vengeance*] (1957). By the early 1960s, however, his career had essentially waned and he was appearing only in films he had produced and directed himself. *La fiebre del deseo* [*The Fever of Desire*] and *La piel desnuda* [*Naked Skin*], both completed in 1964, failed critically and commercially.

Molina, Angela (Madrid, 1955). The daughter of famed dancer and film actor, Antonio Molina, Angela studied classical ballet, Spanish dance, and acting at Madrid's Escuela Superior, beginning her film career at the age of nineteen. Her earliest films, *No matarás* [*Thou Shalt Not Kill*] (César F. Ardavín,* 1974), *No* *quiero perder la honra* [*I Don't Want to Lose My Honor*] (Eugenio Martín, 1974), and *Las protegidas* [*The Protected Ones*] (Francisco Lara Polop, 1975), in which she played leading roles, were of mediocre artistic quality at best. Her recognition of this fact moved her to make a crucial decision to consider her options more scrupulously and to accept secondary parts in more serious films. This led to appearances in a number of interesting and important film roles in the next two years, including Antoni Ribas's* *La ciutat cremada* [*Burnt City*]* (1975), Miguel Picazo's* *El hombre que supo amar* [*The Man Who Learned How to Love*] (1976), and Jaime Camino's* *Las largas vacaciones del '36* [*The Long Summer Vacation of '36*] (1976).

Her career received a major boost the next year when she shared the leading female role in Luis Buñuel's* final film, *Ese oscuro objeto del deseo* [*That Obscure Object of Desire*] (1977), which received international acclaim and brought Molina into contact with an immense audience both in Spain and abroad.

During the late 1970s and early 1980s, Molina appeared in a series of major roles in key films, three of which were directed by Manuel Gutiérrez Aragón*: *Corazón del bosque* [*Heart of the Forest*] (1978); *Demonios en el jardín* [*Demons in the Garden*] (1982), and *La mitad del cielo* [*Half Of Heaven*]* (1986). Gutiérrez Aragón, with whom she had earlier worked in one of the principal political films of the early transition, *Camada negra* [*Black Brood*]* (1977), was a major influence in developing Molina's acting talents. He led her away from the narrow repertory of characters she had protrayed thus far and into progressively more demanding and varied roles. By the mid-1980s, when she appeared as the allegorical embodiment of the passionate Spanish female in Bigas Luna's* *Lola* (1985), she had already achieved a certain mythic status as the prototypal Spanish woman in the eyes of international audiences.

While some of her best performances were delivered under the careful direction of Gutiérrez Aragón, Molina made significant dramatic contributions to works by a variety of directors, including José Luis Borau* (*La Sabina* [1979]), Jaime de Armiñán* (*Nunca es tarde* [*Never Too Late*] [1978]), and Jaime Chávarri* (*A un dios desconocido* [*To an Unknown God*] [1977], *Bearn o la sala de la muñecas* [*Bearn or The Doll's Room*] [1983], *Las cosas del querer* [*The Things of Love*] [1989]). As well as contributing important performances in Spanish films, Molina also has achieved a solid international career, frequently appearing in French, German, and Italian films.

Montes, Conchita (María Concepción Carro Alcaraz) (Madrid, 1914). After obtaining her law degree Montes met Edgar Neville,* the noted playwright and film director. At the end of the Civil War, he cast her in her first film, *Frente de Madrid* [*Madrid Front*] (1939), which he codirected with the Italian, Carlo Borguesio. Over the next twenty years, Montes appeared in twelve more Neville films, as well as numerous stage productions scripted by him. Of the Neville works with which she was most closely identified, the most noteworthy were *La vida en un hilo* [*Life on a String*] (1945); *Nada* [*Nothing*] (1947), based on the

Carmen Laforet novel; and *El baile* [*The Dance*] (1959), adapted from Neville's stage success in which Montes also starred.

Montes also translated a number of English stage comedies that she then staged with her own theatrical company. Among the films she starred in by directors other than Neville, special mention should be made of Jerónimo Mihura's *Mi adorado Juan* [*My Beloved Juan*] (1949). Though she generally played a range of light or comic characters, she excelled in roles in which she played a sophisticated or aristocratic woman. Conchita Montes's film career continued with sporadic appearances in films into the early 1990s. She appeared, for instance, in Nicholas Ray's *55 Days at Peking* (1963), Luis García Berlanga's* *La escopeta nacional* [*National Rifle*]* (1977), and Gerardo Vera's *Una mujer bajo la lluvia* [*A Woman in the Rain*] (1992).

Montesinos, Guillermo (Castellón de la Plana, 1948). Interested in theater since his early youth, Montesinos came to Madrid determined to become a professional theatrical actor. During the 1970s he appeared in minor roles in an uneven mix of films, ranging from Juan Antonio Bardem's* political thriller, *Siete días de enero* [*Seven Days in January*] (1978), to Vicente Escrivá's* comic *Gata caliente* [*Hot Cat*] (1978). During this same period he appeared regularly on the Madrid stage in both serious and comic roles.

It was not until the 1980s, however, that Montesinos's film career gained momentum. With dramatic appearances in Pilar Miró's* *El crimen de Cuenca* [*The Crime at Cuenca*]* (1979), Imanol Uribe's* *La fuga de Segovia* [*Flight from Segovia*] (1981), and Miró's *Gary Cooper, que estás en los cielos* [*Gary Cooper, Who Art in Heaven*] (1981), he revealed his ability for serious characterizations in secondary roles. At about the same time, he began to attract critical attention and a popular following for his appearances in impressive minor roles in comic films. These inlcuded Luis García Berlanga's* *La vaquilla* [*The Heifer*] (1985), José Luis García Sánchez's* *La corte de Faraón* [*The Pharoah's Court*] (1985), Fernando Trueba's* *Sé infiel y mires con quién* [*Be Unfaithful and Don't Worry with Whom*] (1985). These were followed by his most acclaimed performances of the decade, Fernando Colomo's* *La vida alegre* [*The Happy Life*] (1987), and Pedro Almodóvar's* *Mujeres al borde de un ataque de nervios* [*Women on the Verge of a Nervous Breakdown*]* (1988), in which he played the role of the taxi driver for all seasons.

During the 1980s, Montesinos appeared in more than thirty films directed by some of the most important filmmakers of the period: Pilar Miró,* Imanol Uribe,* Carlos Saura,* Luis Garcia Berlanga,* Fernando Colomo,* Vicente Aranda,* and Pedro Almodóvar.*

Montiel, Sara (María Antonia Abad Fernández) (Ciudad Real, 1928). After completing schooling in her native Orihuela, Montiel entered a contest for aspiring young actresses through which she came to the attention of film producer Vicente Casanova. Casanova arranged for her screen debut in 1944 in

Ladislao Vajda's* *Te quiero para mí* [*I Want You for Myself*] under the name of María Alejandra. The following year she began to appear under a new stage name, Sara Montiel, in a series of CIFESA films directed by José Luis Sáenz de Heredia.* Of her early roles, the most important, unquestionably, was that of the dance hall singer, Lulú, in Sáenz de Heredia's *Mariona Rebull* (1947), a role that ironically prefigured her greatest film success in *El último cuplé* [*The Last Song*] in 1957.

In 1948 she was cast in an important supporting role in Juan de Orduña's* grandiose historical epic, *Locura de amor* [*The Madness of Love*], the most artistically significant and commercially successful Spanish film of the period. Paired with the romantic idol of the day, Jorge Mistral,* Montiel had the opportunity to extend her acting range in the role of a beautiful though ruthless woman. Over time, her identification with similarly strong-willed female characters became one of the hallmarks of Montiel's screen persona.

During the first half of the 1950s, she appeared in fourteen films shot in Mexico, including three for Hollywood productions. One of these was *Serenade* (1955), directed by Anthony Mann, whom she later married. Although Montiel never had the lead in any of these films, her appearance in mainstream Hollywood films served to establish her as the one Spanish film actress of the decade with an important international presence. This aura only enhanced her triumphant return to Spanish cinema in 1957 in Juan de Orduña's *El último cuplé* [*The Last Song*],* the most commercially successful Spanish film of the 1950s. Part of that success clearly derived from the erotic dimension of Montiel's character. In the midst of the prudish Franco dictatorship, her eroticism seemed to defy the usual constraints of the Spanish film censors.

The astounding success of *The Last Song* not only established Montiel as a Spanish superstar, but also forged a short-lived genre of melodramatic musicals as a spin-off of the film, including Montiel's own subsequent appearance in *La violetera* [*The Flower Seller*] (1958) and *Mi último tango* [*My Last Tango*] (1960), both directed by Luis César Amadori. Her subsequent screen career seemed a transparent effort by Montiel both to regain the broad popularity of that critical success and to capitalize on her erotic screen persona. To this end she was paired anew with Jorge Mistral in the Spanish-Italian coproduction of *Carmen, la de Ronda* [*Carmen, the Girl from Ronda*] (Tulio Demecheli, 1959), but the film was the beginning of Montiel's decline. The 1960s were marked by a variety of film projects with major directors, including Rafael Gil* (*Samba*, 1964), Mario Camus* (*Esa mujer* [*That Woman*], 1969), and Juan Antonio Bardem* (*Varietés*, 1971). But by the 1970s, the commercial appeal of Montiel had clearly diminished.

Montllor, Ovidi (Alcoy, Alicante, 1942). Trained as a mechanic, Montllor became interested in theater in the early 1960s. He performed in a local theater group and eventually ended up in Barcelona pursuing a professional acting career first in the Andrià Gual Company, later in Nuria Espert's theater company. By the mid-1960s, Montllor had begun singing professionally and composing his own songs. By the end of the decade he was one of the popular singers identified with the Catalan *Nova cançó* (New Song) movement, a reaffirmation of Catalan identity through popular music.

He made his first screen appearance in Francesc Betriu's* *Furia española* [*Spanish Fury*] (1975), achieving popular success as a film actor with his second film, the leading male role in José Luis Borau's* *Furtivos* [*Poachers*]* (1975). His performance as the seemingly dim-witted son of Lola Gaos* not only brought him critical acclaim but also established his screen persona as an antisocial, often sexually obsessed, socially marginal character; Montllor was identified with this persona throughout much of the next decade and a half. He later appeared as a similarly dysfunctional character in Borau's *La Sabina* (1979). Subsequent films included Carles Mira's* *Con el culo en el aire* [*Caught with Your Pants Down*] (1980), Imanol Uribe's* *La fuga de Segovia* [*Flight from Segovia*] (1982), and Eloy de la Iglesia's* *El pico* [*The Shoot*]* (1983), all serious films in which Montllor performed adequately but without the kind of special distinction of his performance in *Poachers*. By the end of the decade his roles as moody, often inexpressive characters had led him into a self-parody of his own screen persona. A striking example of this self-parodic mode is foreshadowed in his portrayal of the taciturn Juan Soldes in Mira's *Caught with Your Pants Down* (1980). Having been traumatized by making love for the first time with a prostitute, his character is sent off to a religious convent to be "cured" of his sexual urges, but spends much of the film wandering through the asylum transfixed by his own sexual desire.

Morán, Manuel (Madrid, 1905; Alicante, 1967). After a variety of trades and professions, including working in an insurance company, editing a sports magazine, and managing flamenco dance acts, Morán became involved in professional theater during the Civil War. His earliest stage appearances were in the Falange Theater Group. At the war's end he moved to film acting, playing minor roles in important films of the period. Morán's typical role was that of a popular, earthy type, often a roguish character with comic underpinnings. This ambivalent characterization enabled him to make an easy move back and forth from comic to serious roles. After supporting comic roles in such films as Juan de Orduña's* *Yo no me caso* [*I'm Not Getting Married*] (1944) and José Luis Sáenz de Heredia's* *El destino se disculpa* [*Destiny Apologizes*] (1944), he appeared in Antonio Román's* *Los últimos de Filipinas* [*Martyrs of the Philippines*] (1945), still in a secondary role, but one with more dramatic substance.

By the early 1950s, after having made fifty screen appearances, Morán appeared as one of the lead characters in a film by a virtually unknown filmmaker. The character of the flamenco impressario, Manolo, in Luis García Berlanga's* *Bienvenido, Mister Marshall!* [*Welcome, Mister Marshall!*]* was largely an autobiographical construction that would, in time, become his best-known role. As Manolo, Morán cleverly exploited his hulking physique, a certain humorous, paternalistic tone, and a nearly constant smile that ingratiated him to the characters around him as well as to the audience. Along with José Isbert,* with whom he shared billing in *Mister Marshall*, Morán came to embody the Spanish light comedy of the 1940s and 1950s.

Most of his appearances over his twenty-eight year film career were as supporting characters. Yet in several films, such as *Welcome, Mister Marshall!*, Ladislao Vajda's *Ronda española* [*Spanish Round*] (1951), and Rafael Gil's* *¡Viva lo imposible!* [*Long Live the Impossible!*], he did play leading roles. In 1958 he won the Sindicato Nacional de Espectáculo award for his acting in *Long Live the Impossible!*.

Nieto, José (José García Nieto) (Murcia, 1902; Matalascanas, Huelva, 1982). Educated in Valencia and Madrid, Nieto worked in an insurance company from the ages of fourteen to sixteen, then debuted as a bullfighter under the professional name of Josele. He was an accomplished horseman and because of this skill was noticed by Florián Rey* who enlisted him to show off his talents in his production of *Lazarillo de Tormes* (1925). Nieto appeared in some eight other silent films before going to Hollywood in 1931 to act in the Spanish-language versions of American films. He later worked as a Spanish-language dubber of American films in France, returning to Spain shortly before the outbreak of the Civil War.

In 1939 he appeared in Pedro Puche's *Manolenka*, one of the very few Spanish films premiered at the war's end. This screen success led to an immediate demand for Nieto in a number of films. In 1941 he appeared in Antonio Román's* debut feature, *Escuadrilla* [*Squadron*], and José Luis Sáenz de Heredia's* *Raza* [*Race*],* both of which were major commercial hits. These films established Nieto in the hero mold of Alfredo Mayo,* the principal romantic male lead actor of the period.

Nieto's dark features as well as an urbane acting style, however, enabled him to play more sinister roles than Mayo, as evidenced in *Race* in which he portrays Pedro Churruca, the morally deformed Republican brother, against Mayo's José Churruca, the Nationalist hero. Nieto later appeared in two of Román's other patriotic hits, *Boda en el infierno* [*Wedding in Hell*] (1942), and *Los últimos de Filipinas* [*Martyrs of the Philippines*]* (1945). Besides these heroic, military roles, he revealed his acting range in a number of dramatic and comic films in this period, including Ladislao Vajda's* *Se vende un palacio* [*A Palace for Sale*] (1943) and Rafael Gil's* *Calle sin sol* [*A Street without Sunlight*] (1948).

Despite these successes, Nieto never fully achieved the status of a leading actor and by the early 1950s he dropped to the level of supporting actor. He appeared in a number of important Spanish films of the early 1950s, including Rafael Gil's* *La señora de Fátima* [*The Lady of Fatima*] (1951) and Vajda's *Carne de horca* [*Flesh for the Gallows*] (1954), but much of his professional career during this decade was devoted to appearing in American epic films shot in Spain. His credits include Terence Young's *That Lady* (1955), Robert Rosen's *Alexander the Great* (1956), Stanley Kramer's *Pride and the Passion* (1957), Charles Vidor's *A Farewell to Arms* (1957), King Vidor's *Solomon and Sheba* (1959), and Nicholas Ray's *55 Days at Peking* (1963). Though Nieto continued to work in Spanish and foreign films shot in Spain until 1978—appearing in a total of nearly 140—his roles were usually minor and in no way reflective of his period of prominence during the 1940s.

Pajares, Andrés (Madrid, 1940). In 1957 Pajares abandoned his academic studies for a career as a comic in traveling musical reviews. His success led to appearances in Madrid in a number of the most prominent musical spectacle shows with prestigious singing stars such as Tony Leblanc, Rocío Jurado, and Sara Montiel.* By the mid-1970s, Pajares was appearing regularly on Spanish television variety shows with his own repertory of established comic characters, mostly of an antic, burlesque type.

He started to appear in minor comic roles in films in 1968, developing a parallel career that he continued throughout his rise to popularity in the 1970s. In the early 1980s he assumed leading roles in over a dozen low-budget comic films directed by Mariano Ozores in which he played off his well-established burlesque-comedy persona. With his appearance in Luis García Berlanga's* *Moros y cristianos* [*Moors and Christians*] (1987), his comic style began to evolve from the broad burlesque of his earlier work into a more sustained and controlled dramatic comic style. His evolution reached a new high with his much acclaimed performance in Carlos Saura's* *¡Ay, Carmela!* (1990) for which he won a Goya for Best Dramatic Actor as well as an analogous prize at the Montreal Film Festival.

Paredes, Marisa (Madrid, 1946). Attracted to the world of acting from an early age, Paredes made her theatrical debut in a series of minor roles on the Madrid stage, eventually turning her interest to motion pictures. Her application for entrance into the National Film School (EOC) was turned down because she lacked a basic education degree. Undaunted, she pursued small acting roles in Spanish television as well as theater as she began to study acting seriously. She remained active in theater, films, and television throughout the 1970s, principally in minor roles. The versatility and experience she gained during this period enabled her to take on a series of offbeat parts in the early works of a new generation of Spanish filmmakers in the 1980s. These included roles in Fernando Trueba's* debut film, *Opera prima* [*First Work*]* (1980), Emilio Martínez-Lázaro's* *Sus años dorados* [*Golden Years*] (1980), Pedro Almodóvar's* *Entre tinieblas* [*Dark Habits*] (1984), Agustín Villaronga's *Tras el cristal* [*Beyond The Window*] (1985), and Felipe Vega's *Mientras haya luz* [*While There's Still Light*] (1987). In such performances, Paredes was distinguished by her striking physical appearance—a strong, bony face, flowing hair, and powerful dark eyes, features that made more than one critic remark on her likeness to Joan Crawford.

It was not until the 1990s, however, with her reconnection with Pedro Almodóvar in his international success, *Tacones lejanos* [*High Heels*], in which Paredes played the aging torch singer, Becky del Páramo, that her talents were widely recognized. The success of the film and critical praise for her striking portrayal brought her to the attention of a wider European audience and led to appearances in French and Swiss films for the first time. She also garnered an important leading role in Almodóvar's *La flor de mi secreto* [*The Flower of My Secret*] (1995), in which she played the role of an aging author of sentimental novels caught in her own melodramatic mid-life crisis.

Peña, Luis (Santander, 1918; Madrid, 1977). Son of actors Luis Peña and Eugenia Illescas and brother of the actress Pastora Peña, Luis made his stage debut at the age of six performing in his parents' theatrical company. He began his film career in 1930 but did not achieve prominence until 1940 with his appearance in Antonio Calvache's *Boy*; he eventually became one of the most popular romantic leading male actors of the post–Civil War decade. *Boy* was followed by a succession of popular films that includes Carlos Arévalo's* *¡Harka!* (1941), Juan de Orduña's* *Porque te vi llorar* [*Because I Saw You Cry*] (1942), Luis Marquina's* *Vidas cruzadas* [*Crossed Lives*] (1942), and José Luis Sáenz de Heredia's* *Bambú* [*Bamboo*] (1945).

During the 1940s, as he pursued his film career, Peña continued to appear in theatrical works as well. Critics consider his most impressive acting performances to be in a number of supporting roles in the 1950s, especially José Antonio Nieves Conde's* *Surcos* [*Furrows*]* (1950), Juan Antonio Bardem's* *Calle mayor* [*Main Street*]* (1956), and José María Forqué's* *Amanecer en Puerta Oscura* [*Dawn at Puerta Oscura*] (1957). Though he continued working in motion pictures over the following twenty years, until his death, he mostly played minor roles in often unmemorable films.

Penella, Emma (Manuela Ruiz Penella) (Madrid, 1930). Penella abandoned her secondary education to work as an unpaid trainee at the María Guerrero Theater in Madrid. She made her first uncredited appearance in a Spanish motion picture in 1949 as a stand-in for Amparo Rivelles* in *La duquesa de Benamejí* [*The Duchess of Benamejí*]. In the following five years, she appeared in a variety of secondary film roles, including *Los ojos dejan huellas* [*The Eyes Leave Traces*] (José Luis Sáenz de Heredia,* 1952) and *Carne de horca* [*Flesh for the Gallows*] (Ladislao Vajda,* 1953), but always with her voice dubbed because it was generally felt that she lacked an adequate film voice.

Her status clearly changed in 1954 when Juan Antonio Bardem* cast Penella in *Cómicos* [*Comedians*],* one of his critical successes of the 1950s. Though her performances in this period were strong and striking, she usually was relegated to secondary roles. In 1963 she appeared in Luis García Berlanga's* *El verdugo* [*The Executioner*]* as Carmen, the daughter of Amadeo, the executioner (José Isbert*), a woman whose unplanned pregnancy with a funeral parlor worker sets the stage for one of the most biting Spanish films of the 1960s. Though still a secondary player, Penella's performance was singled out by critics as a serious and penetrating characterization.

With her marriage to film producer Emiliano Piedra,* Penella's career over the next twenty years was shaped by her husband's productions, very often with the scripts and directors tailored to her particular dramatic needs. These included costume dramas directed by Angelino Fons* (*La busca* [*The Search*] [1966]), *Fortunata y Jacinta* [1969], and *La primera entrega* [*The First Delivery* [1974]]), and a screen adaptation of Leopoldo Alas's *La regenta* (1974) directed by Gonzalo Suárez.* Despite acting awards she received for these roles, negative criticism of her performances led her to abandon films for a number of years. She returned to make a striking cameo performance in Carlos Saura's* *El amor brujo* [*Love, the Magician*] (1985). The following year, she played the title role in Eloy de la Iglesia's* immensely successful *La estanquera de Vallecas* [*The Kiosk Vendor from Vallecas*], in which she was able to combine both her strong dramatic and comic talents.

Poncela, Eusebio (Madrid, 1947). After completing dramatic training at the Escuela de Arte Dramático in Madrid, Poncela began a highly successful stage career in the late 1970s, appearing in mainstream as well as experimental productions. However, he was unable to transfer his stage success to a screen career for a number of years. Of his early film appearances, perhaps his most strikingly original role was that of the filmmaker, José Sirgado, in Iván Zulueta's* *Arrebato* [*Rapture*]* (1979). In 1979 he also appeared in a more conventional political thriller, Gillo Pontecorvo's *Operación ogro* [*Operation Ogre*], dealing with the Basque Separatist group ETA's assassination of Prime Minister Carrero-Blanco.

By the mid-1980s, Poncela's presence as a promising film actor was well established. In 1986 he appeared in prominent supporting roles in two important films: Pilar Miró's* *Werther*, in which he played the sensitive suicidal character in a contemporary update of the German Romantic classic, and in Pedro Almodóvar's* *Matador*, in which he played the sexually ambivalent police inspector investigating a chain of serial killings. This latter role was followed by his characterization of the gay filmmaker, Pablo, in Almodóvar's major hit, *La ley del deseo* [*Law of Desire*] (1987). Despite the film's success, Poncela fell back into secondary roles in which he provided often strong, memorable performances. These include Carlos Saura's *El Dorado* (1988), Francisco Regueiro's *Diario de invierno* [*Winter Diary*] (1988), and Imanol Uribe's *El rey pasmado* [*The Flustered King*] (1991).

Puigcorbé, Juanjo (Juan José Puigcorbé Benaiges) (Barcelona, 1955). Abandoning studies in physics and philosophy and letters to pursue studies at the Instituto de Teatro de Barcelona, Puigcorbé made his stage debut in 1976. Over the next four years, he worked with some of the most important Catalonian stage directors, including Lluis Pasqual, Nuria Espert, and Pere Planella. He made his screen debut in Francesc Bellmunt's* comedy of sexual mores, *La orgía* [*The Orgy*] (1978); he also participated in the writing of the film's script. Puigcorbé appeared in the following years in two other Bellmunt hit comedies, *Salut y força al canut* [*Health, Lust, and Fun*] (1979), and *La quinta del porro* [*The Stoned Conscripts*] (1980). After these ensemble comic roles, he gave a more substantive dramatic performance in Gonzalo Herralde's* *Ultimas tardes con Teresa* [*Last Afternoons with Theresa*] (1983).

Throughout the 1980s, Puigcorbé appeared in a variety of supporting roles in increasingly more popular and important films. These included performances in Manuel Gutiérrez Aragón's* *La noche más hermosa* [*The Most Beautiful Night*] (1984), Luis García Berlanga's* *La vaquilla* [*The Heifer*] (1985) amd Gonzalo Suárez's* *La reina anónima* [*The Anonymous Queen*] (1992). Toward the end of the 1980s, he began to appear more regularly on Spanish television, particularly in José María Forqué's* series, *Miguel Servet* (1988). Eventually, Puigcorbé was able to garner more leading roles in films. These include Manuel Gómez Pereira's *Salsa rosa* [*Pink Sauce*] (1991), Carlos Balagué *Mal de amores* [*Amorous Problems*] (1993), and Mariano Barroso's *Hermano del alma* [*Soul Brother*] (1993).

Rabal, Francisco (Aguilas, Murcia, 1926). Rabal began his professional relationship with Spanish film quite modestly, working as an electrician at the newly opened Chamartín Studios in Madrid. He eventually obtained roles as an extra, then secondary roles, until finally in 1950 he was given his first leading role in Luis Escobar's *La honradez de la cerradura* [*The Probity of the Keyhole*]. But it was not until 1953, when he starred in Francisco Rovira Beleta's* *Hay un camino a la derecha* [*There's a Road to the Right*] that Rabal began to establish his star status as one of the most popular male romantic leads in Spanish cinema. From then on he played in a variety of genre films of the 1950s under the supervision of Spain's most commercially successful and critically praised directors: Rafael Gil,* Vicente Escrivá,* José María Forqué,* José Luis Sáenz de Heredia,* and Juan Antonio Bardem.* In 1957 he began to develop an equally impressive presence in international films, first in Gillo Pontecorvo's *La grande strada azzurra* [*The Big Blue Road*], followed the next year by the leading role in Luis Buñuel's* polemical *Nazarín* and two years later by the even more controversial Buñuel film, *Viridiana.** It was largely through the prominence he achieved through the professional association with Buñuel that Rabal was able to solidify his international career in films by Michelangelo Antonioni (*L'eclisse* [*Eclipse*] [1962]), Glauber Rocha (*Cabezas cortadas* [*Severed Heads*] [1970]), and William Friedkin (*The Sorcerer* [1977]).

Despite the obvious lure of international productions, he remained a perennial figure in Spanish film, evolving as the medium evolved, and showing, if anything, greater dramatic force over time. In the decade of the 1980s, for instance, he appeared in films as diverse as Mario Camus's* *La colmena* [*The*

Beehive] (1982), Miguel Hermoso's *Truhanes* [*Ruffians*] (1983), Francisco Regueiro's* *Padre nuestro* (1985), and Pedro Almodóvar's* *¡Atame!* [*Tie Me Up! Tie Me Down!*] (1989). He is one of the few major Spanish actors, along with Fernando Rey,* José Luis López Vázquez,* and Alfredo Landa,* to successfully maintain a career as a lead actor over more than four decades, winning national and international acclaim.

Rellán, Miguel (Miguel Angel Rellán García) (Tetuán Morroco, 1943). Rellán moved from his native Morroco to the Spanish mainland, first to Seville to begin medical studies, then to Madrid where he appeared in independent theater productions in the late 1960s. He made his film debut in a secondary role in Antonio Isasi's *El perro* [*The Dog*] (1976). Thereafter followed a varied range of secondary character roles in a variety of genre films. It was not until a striking performance in José Luis Garci's* *El crack* [*The Crack*] (1981) that he came to the attention of critics.

Over the next decade he appeared in more than fifty films, always in character roles with a decided emphasis on certain comic exaggerated characterizations, such as the right-wing brother of Carmen Maura in José Luis Borau's* *Tata mía* [*My Nanny*] (1987), for which he won a Goya as best supporting actor, or as a stalwart Nationalist officer in Carlos Saura's* *¡Ay, Carmela!* (1991). He also appeared in countless television dramas, making him one of the most ubiquitous of Spanish actors during the decade of the 1980s.

Resines, Antonio (Antonio Fernández Resines) (Torrelavega, Santander, 1954). As a student at the University of Madrid, Resines became friends with a group of film buffs, including Oscar Ladoire,* Fernando Trueba,* and Julio Sánchez Valdéz, all of whom, by the early 1980s, would become professionally active in the Spanish film industry. Through these friendships, Resines was able to establish himself as a skilled comic actor in a long list of Madrid comedies of the 1980s. He also became involved in the establishment of the film production company, Brezal Films.

To the broad Spanish audience, Resines is perhaps the actor most closely identified with the development of the New Madrid Comedy genre that initially took shape around the film work of Fernando Trueba* and Fernando Colomo.* He appeared in several shorts directed by Trueba and later made secondary appearances in Trueba's first two Madrid comedies, *Opera prima* [*First Work*] (1980), and *Sal gorda* [*Coarse Salt* or *Get Lost, Fatty!*] (1983), Resines also appeared in a variety of other films, some in the dramatic genre category, such as Javier Rebolledo's *Siete calles* [*Seven Streets*] (1981) and Mario Camus's* *La colmena* [*The Beehive*]* (1982). Comedy, however, was his chief calling, and he appeared in a number of the biggest comedy hits of the 1980s. After minor appearances in Colomo's *La mano negra* [*The Black Hand*] (1980), and *Estoy en crisis* [*I'm In Crisis*] (1982), he went on to play comic leads in two of Colomo's most commercially successful films of the 1980s: *La línea del cielo*

[*Skyline*] (1983), and *La vida alegre* [*The Happy Life*] (1986). In 1985 he appeared as one of the leads in Trueba's comic ensemble film, *Sé infiel y no mires con quién* [*Be Unfaithful And Don't Worry with Whom*], along with Carmen Maura,* Ana Belén,* Chus Lampreave,* and Verónica Forque.*

Resines's comic range has often appeared limited to critics, yet his portrayal of an ambitious, career-oriented, fast-talking Madrileño type has held him in remarkably good stead with audiences over a decade and a half.

Rey, Fernando (Fernando Casado Arambillet) (La Coruña, Galicia, 1917; Madrid, 1994). An extraordinarily prolific film actor with more than two hundred film appearances to his credit, Fernando Rey was also for the last thirty years of his life Spain's most successful international actor, playing in American, French, and Italian films while actively maintaining an extraordinary career in Spanish cinema as well. Though he made a very brief appearance in Benito Perojo's* film adaptation of Alejandro Casona's *Nuestra Natacha* [*Our Natacha*] (1936), it was not until the end of the Civil War that Rey's career in Spanish cinema truly began. During the early 1940s he played supporting roles in important films such as Antonio Román's* *Los últimos de Filipinas* [*Martyrs of the Philippines*]* (1945), Rafael Gil's* *La pródiga* [*The Prodigal Daughter*] (1946), Juan de Orduña's* *Misión blanca* [*The White Mission*] (1946), and Gil's adaptation of *Don Quijote de la Mancha* (1947). Such costume productions established the earliest of Rey's various screen images, that of the romantic, courtly hero.

His popularity in these roles led to his being cast in one of the leading parts in the major commercial and artistic success of the decade, Juan de Orduña's* *Locura de amor* [*The Madness of Love*]* (1948). With his appearance in Orduña's second major epic two years later, *Agustina de Aragón*, Rey's career was established as a highly marketable romantic actor, well-suited for performances in costume epics. Despite his successes, he was not yet considered of the status of a lead actor such as Alfredo Mayo* in the first post–Civil War decade.

One of the unique features of Rey's career during the 1940s and 1950s was his success as a recognized cinematic "voice." He had worked as a professional film dubber in the 1940s, and by the 1950s, directors were using his voice-over for a varied collection of films. Two of the most successful films that contained his voice-over narration were García Berlanga's* *Bienvenido, Mister Marshall!* [*Welcome, Mister Marshall!*]* (1953) and Ladislao Vajda's* *Marcelino pan y vino* [*Marcelino, Bread and Wine*]* (1954).

In the 1950s Rey appeared in a series of important supporting roles, including Juan Antonio Bardem's* *Cómicos* [*Comedians*]* (1954), *La venganza* [*The Vengeance*] (1957), and the ill-fated adaptation of Valle-Inclán's *Sonatas* (1959). During the location filming in Mexico for this last film, Rey made the acquaintance of Luis Buñuel,* who was later to invite him to play the role of Don Jaime in his controversial *Viridiana** (1961). The international exposure provided by that film enabled Rey to make the leap into international cinema. He appeared in two Orson Welles films in the 1960s, *Chimes at Midnight* (1967) and *Immortal Story* (1968). In 1970 he worked with Buñuel again in *Tristana*,* in the role of the decadent Don Lope, and received national and international acclaim. He would round out the 1970s alternating between appearances in two more Buñuel films, *Discreet Charm of the Bourgeoisie* (1972) and *Ese oscuro objeto del deseo* [*That Obscure Object of Desire*] (1977), while making other Spanish and international films. Perhaps the most important of these was his appearance as an elegant drug dealer in William Friedkin's *The French Connection* (1972). Between the Buñuel and Friedkin films, Rey managed to stabilize a unique film persona as a sophisticated and yet largely unscrupulous gentleman.

During the 1980s and until his death in 1994, Rey maintained an active double focus on his career, playing in American, Italian, and French films, while appearing with regularity on Spanish screens. Arguably the best work of his long career was done during this period. The Spanish films most frequently cited as Rey's most outstanding performances are two directed by Francisco Regueiro:* *Padre nuestro* (1985) and *Diario de invierno* [*Winter Diary*] (1987). Over his long career, Rey received numerous awards for his acting, among the most prestigious and significant being the following: Best Actor for Rafael Gil's* *La duda* [*The Doubt*] (1972) at the San Sebastián Festival; Best Actor for Carlos Saura's* *Elisa vida mía* [*Elisa, My Life*]* (1977) at the Cannes Film Festival; Best Actor at San Sebastián in 1988 for two films, *El aire de un crimen* [*The Scent of a Crime*] (Antonio Isasi) and *Diario de invierno* [*Winter Diary*] (Francisco Regueiro); and a Gold Medal awarded for lifetime contribution by the Spanish Academy of Cinematographic Arts and Sciences in 1991.

Rivelles, Amparo (Madrid, 1925). Like a number of other Spanish film actresses of the 1930s and 1940s, Amparito Rivelles, as she was known for many years, was born into a theatrical family (Rafael Rivelles and María Fernanda Ladrón de Guevara). She made her stage debut at the age of thirteen and appeared in her first motion picture, Armando Vidal's *Mari Juana* (1940), at the age of fifteen. A short time later she signed an exclusive contract with CIFESA, which was to catapult her into star status throughout the 1940s and well into the 1950s. It was during this period that she appeared in some of the most prestigious Spanish films, including the Rafael Gil's* box office success, *El clavo* [*The Nail*] (1944) and two of Juan de Orduña's* historical epics, *La leona de Castilla* [*The Lioness of Castile*] and *Alba de América* [*Dawn in America*], both in 1951.

During the 1940s, she was largely unrivaled as Spain's most popular film actress. She was often romantically paired with Alfredo Mayo,* the quintessential male screen star of the period, in such films as Eduardo Marquina's* *Malvaloca* (1942), José Buch's* *Un caballero famoso* [*A Famous Gentleman*] (1942), and Juan de Orduña's *Deliciosamente tontos* [*Deliciously Daffy*] (1943), and *The Lioness of Castile* (1951).

Rivelles maintained a theatrical as well as a film career and it was the former that brought her to Mexico in 1957 for what was proposed as a brief theatrical tour, but which ended up as a twenty-year residence. During this time, she starred in a number of highly successful melodramatic series for Mexican television. She returned to Spain in 1977 with a near mythic star status, and shortly thereafter appeared in the highly successful television series, *Los gozos y las sombras* [*Joys and Shadows*], directed by Rafael Moreno Alba and based on a novel by Gonzalo Torrente Ballester. Rivelles's career, spanning some four decades in Spain and Mexico, is rumored to have been, in part, the inspiration for the character of Becky del Páramo in Pedro Almodóvar's* 1992 *Tacones lejanos* [*High Heels*].

Sacristán, José (Chinchón, Madrid, 1937). Working as a mechanic until his early twenties, Sacristán developed an interest in theater and performed in nonprofessional local groups from his adolescence on. In 1960 he made the decision to pursue a professional career in acting and joined the company of the Teatro Infanta Isabel as an unpaid trainee. In 1962 he joined the Teatro Popular Español and embarked on a two-year theatrical tour of Latin America. Returning to Madrid, he joined the Teatro Lope de Vega. He finally made his film debut in 1965 in a minor role in Fernando Palacio's *La familia . . . y uno más* [*The Family . . . and One More*], followed that same year by appearances in two comedies directed by Pedro Lazaga. Over the following years he divided his energies between minor comic roles in popular Spanish comedies and similarly small parts in theatrical works.

Sacristán's film career is usually divided into two major periods. The first, running through 1973, includes some four dozen light comedies, including films directed by some of the most successful popular directors of the period (José Luis Sáenz de Heredia,* Mariano Ozores, Pedro Lazaga, Vicente Escrivá,* Roberto Bodegas*). In these films, he played secondary comic roles, usually a clumsy and timid young man who has difficulties with women.

Sacristán's second period began in 1973 with his first leading role in Roberto Bodegas's* *Vida conyugal sana* [*Healthy Married Life*]. With this new status, his cinematic persona gradually moved into more serious and eventually completely surprising dramatic characterizations. Of these, the most noteworthy are roles in three films that reflected the general political transition of the late 1970s. The first is José Luis Garci's* *Asignatura pendiente* [*Pending Examination*]* (1977), in which he plays a labor lawyer who, during the final months of the Franco dictatorship, has an affair with the woman who was his adolescent sweetheart. The character of José, who sees himself as the exemplar of a generation who put off living and were nurtured on false illusions, is a deft balance of Woody Allen style self–deprecating humor and serious acting. Sacristán followed this with his performance as a homosexual politician in Eloy de la Iglesia's* controversial *El diputado* [*The Deputy*] (1978), and as a transvestite in Pedro Olea's* *Un hombre llamado Flor de Otoño* [*A Man Named Spring Flower*] (1978), for which he won the Best Acting Award at the San Sebastián Film Festival.

Other serious roles that earned Sacristán critical praise were those in two ensemble films, *La colmena* [*The Beehive*] (Mario Camus,*1982) and *El viaje a ninguna parte* [*Journey to Nowhere*] (Fernando Fernán-Gómez,* 1986). Throughout the 1980s, he remained popular with Spanish audiences and well esteemed by critics in a diverse range of films. These included comedies such as Manuel Gutiérrez Aragón's* *La noche más hermosa* [*The Most Beautiful Night* (1984) and Luis García Berlanga's* *La vaquilla* [*The Heifer*] (1985), and more serious dramatic roles in Gonzalo Suárez's* *Epílogo* [*Epilogue*] (1983) in addition to two films that he directed himself, *Soldados de plomo* [*Lead Soldiers*] (1983) and *Cara de Acelga* [*Stick-Face*] (1986).

Sampietro, Mercedes (Barcelona, 1947). Showing a keen interest in theater from adolescence on, Sampietro participated in amateur theater groups while involved in a variety of jobs. Eventually she enrolled in a theater school, making her professional debut in a production of José Triana's *La noche de los asesinos* [*Night of the Assassins*] in 1970. During the 1970s, she alternated dramatic roles on Spanish television with work as a dubber for the voices of Jill Clayburgh and Diane Keaton in the Spanish versions of American films. Sampietro made her film debut in 1977 when she appeared in Jaime Chávarri's* *A un dios desconocido* [*To an Unknown God*].

She has made some two dozen films since then, receiving many of her best dramatic roles in films directed by Pilar Miró.* These included *Gary Cooper que estás en los cielos* [*Gary Cooper Who Art in Heaven*] (1980), for which she won the Best Actress award at the San Sebastián Film Festival, *Hablamos esta noche* [*Let's Talk Tonight*] (1982), *Werther* (1986), and *El pájaro de la felicidad* [*The Bird of Happiness*] (1993). Her peformance as a sexually obsessed nun in Miguel Picazo's *Extramuros* [*Outside the Walls*] (1985) won her a Best Actress award at the San Sebastián Film Festival for a second time.

Characteristically, Sampietro's roles have been those of strong, independent women of a taciturn nature experiencing periods of depression. Her expressive eyes give her performances a particular melancholic edge, which contributes to an understated appearance of deeper emotions.

Sánchez-Gijón, Aitana (Rome, Italy, 1969). After professional dramatic studies, Sánchez-Gijón debuted as an actress in Pedro Masó's television series, *Segunda enseñanza* [*Secondary School*] (1982). In the mid-1980s, she made the crossover to film work, appearing first in minor roles in José María Forqué's* *Romanza final* [*Final Romance*] (1986) and Gonzalo Suárez's* *Remando al viento* [*Rowing with the Wind*] (1988). While achieving critical success for her theater work, she played her first leading role in a motion picture in Fernando Colomo's* *Bajarse al moro* [*Going Down to Morroco*] (1988), followed the next year by a strong performance in Fernando Fernán-Gómez's* *El mar y el tiempo* [*The Sea and Time*] (1989). Therein came a succession of noteworthy performances in Manuel

Gutiérrez Aragón's* television version of *Don Quijote* (1991), Pilar Miró's* *El pájaro de la felicidad* [*The Bird of Happiness*] (1993), and a leading role in Adolfo Aristaraín's Spanish-Portuguese-Argentine coproduction, *La ley de la frontera* [*The Law of the Frontier*] (1995). In 1994, Sánchez-Gijón made her debut in an American film, Alfonso Arau's *A Walk in the Clouds*, opposite Keanu Reeves.

Sanz, Jorge (Madrid, 1969). Sanz was discovered at the age of nine when he auditioned for a role in Pedro Masó's film, *La miel* [*The Honey*] (1979). Spanish audiences have literally seen him grow up on movie and television screens. His popularity as a child actor was so great, in fact, that he was cast in the childhood sequences of *Conan the Barbarian* (1982). By 1983 he already had received critical attention as a young actor when he won the award for Best New Actor (*Premio Revelación*) at the San Sebastián Film Festival for his performance in Antonio José Betancor's *Valentina*. By 1986 Sanz's talents and popularity were strong enough for him to carry the lead in Fernando Trueba's* nostalgic comedy of life in the immediate post–Civil War era, *El año de las luces* [*The Year of Light*]. In that film he was romantically paired with Maribel Verdú,* with whom he would be cast with increasing frequency over the coming years. He began developing a series of more powerful and dramatically demanding roles under the mentorship of Vicente Aranda,* who first directed him in *El Lute II: Mañana seré libre* [*Tomorrow I Will Be Free*] (1988); then *Si te dicen que caí* [*If They Tell You I Have Died*] in 1989, for which he won a Goya; then in the international commercial hit, *Amantes* [*Lovers*] in 1990; as well as in the television drama, *Los jinetes del alba* [*Horsemen of the Dawn*] (1991).

From the early 1990s onward, Sanz avoided simple typecasting by playing in both dramatic and light roles, although his performance in Trueba's Oscar-winning *Belle Epoque** and Manuel Gómez Pereira's *¿Por qué lo llaman amor cuando quieren decir sexo?* [*Why Do They Call It Love When They Mean Sex?*] (1993), reinforced both his talent and popularity as a gifted comedy actor.

Serna, Assumpta (Barcelona, 1957). Serna abandoned law studies to devote herself to theatrical training. She made her film debut in 1978 in Francesc Bellmunt's* comedy of youth in the time of political and cultural transition, *La orgía* [*The Orgy*]. Serna's nude appearance in the film helped bring her to the attention of Madrid filmmakers, who were obviously impressed with her sophisticated erotic appearance. She won the lead in Carlos Saura's* *Dulces horas* [*Sweet Hours*] (1982), again appearing nude. Her next major role was in Pedro Almodóvar's* erotic comedy, *Matador* (1986), in which she assumed a Garboesque coolness as a new dimension of her sensuous screen persona.

Despite the assumption by critics that Serna's talents were only "skin deep," she gave a number of striking film performances during the 1980s, including the role of a lesbian nun in Miguel Picazo's* *Extramuros* [*Outside the Walls*] (1985) and the lead role of Sor Juana Inés de la Cruz in María Luisa Bemberg's international coproduction, *Yo, la peor de todas* [*I, the Worst of All*] (1989). Her obvious acting talents, physical beauty, and a notable skill in foreign languages has enabled her to develop her career in a number of international markets, including American prime-time soap operas such as *Falcon Crest*.

Serrano, Julieta (Barcelona, 1933). Born into a theatrical family, the daughter of Vicente Serrano Andrés and Dolores Girall Portell, Julieta Serrano began acting in amateur productions as an adolescent and eventually began a professional career as a member of the José Tamayo theater company. She made her screen debut in Manuel Summers' *El juego de la oca* [*Snakes and Ladders*] (1965), following that with a fairly constant series of suporting roles over the next three decades. Throughout this period, she continued to divide her time between theatrical and film performances, scrupulously selecting those roles that offered her dramatic challenges. In 1971, she appeared as the confused maid, Isabelita, sexually attracted to her female employer, Adela, played by José Luis López Vázquez,* in Jaime de Armiñán's* film, *Mi querida señorita* [*My Dearest Señorita*].

Such offbeat roles became a characteristic feature of Serrano's screen career over the next decades as she appeared in films by Luis García Berlanga* (*Tamaño natural* [*Life-Size*] [1973]), Pedro Almodóvar* (*Pepi, Luci, Bom, y otras chicas del montón* [*Pepi, Luci, Bom, and Other Girls like That*] [1980]) and Eloy de la Iglesia* (*La mujer del ministro* [*The Minister's Wife*] [1981]).

In 1984, Serrano achieved a new prominence in her film career as the drug-addicted lesbian mother superior in Almodóvar's *Entre tinieblas* [*Dark Habits*]. The performance not only reminded critics of her dramatic range but brought her to international note as Almodóvar's career skyrocketed over the next years. Though she often played her parts in Almodóvar's films with an almost deadpan seriousness, her film persona came to be identified with a unique comedic style unrivaled in Spanish cinema. Of the later performances under Almodóvar's direction, the two most critically acclaimed were the comic interpretations of the conservative Catholic mother of Antonio Banderas* in *Matador* (1986) and the psychotic lover scorned by Fernando Guillén* in *Mujeres al borde de un ataque de nervios* [*Women on the Verge of a Nervous Breakdown*] (1988).

Sevilla, Carmen (María del Carmen Galisteo) (Sevilla, 1930). Daughter of the popular songwriter, José García Padilla, better known as Kola, Carmen Sevilla debuted at the age of thirteen in Estrella Castro's dance company. After appearing in other dance troupes, she made her screen debut in 1947 in Juan de Orduña's* *Serenata española* [*Spanish Serenade*], but it was her second film, *Jalisco canta en Sevilla* [*Jalisco Sings in Seville*], a Spanish-Mexican coproduction directed by Fernando de Fuentes, that brought her fame. Along with Luis Mariano, a French actor-singer of Spanish origin, she was cast in a number of films in the early 1950s such as *Violetas imperiales* [*Imperial Violets*] (Richard Pottier, 1952) that allowed her to develop the screen persona of a wholesome

Spanish Catholic girl, which would be featured in a variety of folkloric genre films throughout the 1950s. Sevilla's screen persona, in fact, became something of a popular mythic stereotype for young Spanish women of her generation.

Among her most memorable roles were those in Luis Lucia's* remake of the Florián Rey* hit, *La hermana San Sulpicio* [*Sister Saint Sulpicio*] (1952), followed by *La bella de Cádiz* [*The Beauty from Cadiz*] (1953) and *Un caballero andaluz* [*An Andalusian Gentleman*] (1954). Although she later appeared in Juan Antonio Bardem's* *La vengana* [*The Vengeance*] (1958), an important auteur work of the period, her principal works remained in popular genre films.

In 1962, Sevilla appeared with two other legendary folkloric singer/dancers, Paquita Rico and Lola Flores,* in Luis Saslavsky's *El balcón de la luna* [*The Balcony of the Moon*]. Such an appearance, however, contrasts with the general demise of her artistic career throughout the 1960s. In the mid-1970s, she attempted a comeback with a highly eroticized version of her earlier screen image in films such as Eloy de la Iglesia's* *El techo de cristal* [*The Glass Ceiling*] (1970) and José María Forqué's* *La cera virgen* [*The Wax Virgin*] (1972), as well as Pedro Olea's* *No es bueno que el hombre esté solo* [*A Man Shouldn't Be Alone*] (1973). By the middle of the decade, however, Sevilla had definitively retired from screen acting.

Sol, Laura del (Barcelona, 1961). Born into a family of dancers, Laura del Sol made her professional debut at the age of fifteen in her parents' Spanish classical ballet company. She was later discovered by Emiliano Piedra,* who was preparing Carlos Saura's* second dance film, *Carmen.** Though of limited acting ability, Sol was able to capitalize on her striking physical beauty and talent as a trained dancer to garner critical kudos at home and abroad. The international acclaim the film received helped solidify a double career for Sol, in both Spanish and international film productions. In Spain she appeared in Saura's *Los zancos* [*Stilts*] (1984) in which she costarred with Fernando Fernán-Gómez,* as well as in the third part of Saura's dance trilogy, *El amor brujo* [*Love, the Magician*] (1986). She also played minor roles in both Fernán-Gómez's *El viaje a ninguna parte* [*The Trip to Nowhere*] (1986) and Imanol Uribe's* *El rey pasmado* [*The Flustered King*]* (1991). Abroad, she appeared in Stephen Frear's *The Hit* (1984), Mariano Monicelli's Italian film, *Il fu Matias Pascal* [*The Late Matías Pascal*] (1985); and *Amelia López O'Neil* (1990) by the Chilean director, Valeriana Sarmiento.

Soler Leal, Amparo (Madrid, 1933). Trained first in the theater, Soler Leal made her stage debut at the age of thirteen in the Teatro Nacional María Guerrero. She began film work in her early twenties, receiving critical praise for her role in José María Forqué's* *Usted puede ser un asesino* [*You Could Be a Murderer*] (1961), which she originated on stage. Therein followed an almost uninterrupted career over the next three decades with more than fifty film appearances, many of them rooted in her portrayal of tormented but slightly zany characters. Her comic skills were enlisted over the years by some of Spain's most important comic filmmakers, including Luis Buñuel*(*Le Charme discrète de la bourgeoisie [The Discreet Charm of the Bourgeoisie]* [1972]), Luis García Berlanga* (*Escopeta nacional [National Rifle]** [1977], *Tamaño natural [Life-Size* [1973], *La vaquilla [The Heifer]* [1984]), and Pedro Almodóvar* (¿*Qué he hecho Yo para merecer esto? [What Have I Done to Deserve This?]* [1985]).

These roles were balanced by an equally rich repertory of dramatic performances, such as in the role of the wife of one of the two wrongly accused farmers tortured by the Civil Guard in Pilar Miró's* *El crimen de Cuenca [The Crime at Cuenca]** (1979) or in Miró's later, *Gary Cooper que estás el los cielos [Gary Cooper Who Art in Heaven]* (1980). Despite these very powerful performances, which clearly reflect Soler Leal's range, it is her comic roles in key films by Berlanga, Pedro Masó, and Almodóvar that have solidified her reputation as one of Spain's most versatile comic actresses.

Soto, Luchy (Madrid, 1919; Madrid, 1970). The daughter of actors Manuel Soto and Guadalupe Muñoz Sampedro, Luchy Soto abandoned formal education in her adolescence in order to devote herself completely to the theater. In 1933, at the age of fourteen, she made her film debut in Eusebio Fernández Ardavín's* *La bien pagada [The Well-Paid Woman]*. During the latter years of the Second Republic she appeared in a number of films by important directors such as Benito Perojo* and Rafael J. Sevilla, but her most important appearance was in a secondary role in Florián Rey's* *Morena clara [The Light-Skinned Gypsy]** (1936). At the war's end, Soto established herself as a consummate film actress in works directed by some of the most prominent directors of the day. She played leading roles in two of the most popular war films of the period, Carlos Arévalo's* *¡Harka!* and Antonio Román's* *Escuadrilla [Squadron]*, both made in 1941. She followed this with roles in films directed by José Luis Sáenz de Heredia,* Rafael Gil,* Ramón Torrado, and Juan de Orduña;* she appeared in Orduña's comic hit, *Ella, él y sus millones [She, He, and Her Millions]* (1944).

In 1946 she married film actor Luis Peña,* and retired from film work until the late 1950s, when she began to appear in secondary roles in light comic fare. These included popular comedies directed by Mariano Ozores, Pedro Lazaga, and José María Forqué,* the three most prolific masters of popular Spanish comedies of the period. In 1970, she made her last film, *El jardín de las delicias [Garden of Delights]*, directed by Carlos Saura,* playing opposite another popular comic star turned serious actor, José Luis López Vázquez.* She died shortly afterwards, just as it appeared that she was beginning to redefine her acting range.

Suárez, Emma (Madrid, 1964). Suárez began her theatrical career at the age of fifteen when she apeared in Miguel Angel Rivas's film, *Memorias de Leticia Valle [Memoirs of Leticia Valle]* (1979). During the 1980s Suárez alternated between secondary roles in television, stage, and films, and striking success principally in the theater. Although she appeared in films by important directors in the decade of the 1980s, including José Luis Garci's* *Sesión continua* [*Double Feature*] (1984) and José Luis Borau's* *Tata mía* [*My Nanny*] (1986), these were mostly minor roles that gave her little opportunity to show her dramatic range.

Her breakthrough as a film actress of note came with more extensive performances in Isabel Coixet's *Demasiado viejo para morir joven* [*Too Old to Die Young*] (1988) and in Juan Miñón's *La blanca paloma* [*White Dove*] (1989). Her performances in the 1990s in Julio Medem's* award-winning debut film, *Vacas* [*Cows*] (1992) and *La ardilla roja* [*The Red Squirrel*] (1993), brought Suárez to the critical attention of larger audiences and made it possible for her to obtain more important leading roles, as in Rosa Vergès's *Souvenir* (1993). In 1996 she gave a powerful performance in Medem's third feature, *Tierra* [*Land*].

Torrent, Ana (Madrid, 1966). Torrent was chosen by Víctor Erice* at the age of seven for the role of the precocious heroine of *El espíritu de la colmena* [*Spirit of the Beehive*]* (1973) who identified emotionally with the monster in the James Wale version of *Frankenstein*. Critically acclaimed for her performance, she next appeared in Carlos Saura's* *Cría cuervos* [*Raise Ravens*] (1975), another child role in which her striking black eyes and her penetrating stare into the camera suggested a maturity and grasp beyond her years.

Though she appeared briefly in Saura's next film, *Elisa vida mía* [*Elisa, My Life*]* (1977), it was difficult for her to maintain the impressively high caliber of her career as suggested by her first films. Of her subsequent work, only one film seems to capture the striking facial and gestural qualities that had made Torrent's earliest work so memorable. That film was Jaime de Armiñán's* *El nido* [*The Nest*]* (1980) in which she played a thirteen-year-old girl who makes herself the sexual object of an aging widower, Héctor Alterio.* Armiñán stunningly develops the double-edged intensity of the young actress as she combines elements of eroticism and cruelty in a character who is an adolescent version of Lady Macbeth. Indeed, her performance as the manipultive temptress in *The Nest* won her the Best Actress award at the Montreal Film Festival in 1980.

After the period of her adolescence, Torrent found it increasingly more difficult to find scripts that could match her compelling earlier performances. Appearances as a young woman in   Basilio Martín Patino's* *Los paraísos perdidos* [*Lost Paradises*] (1985) and Julio Medem's* *Vacas* [*Cows*]* (1991), did little to return her to the special status she had enjoyed as a child actress.

Valero, Antonio (Valencia, 1955). After a major success as an actor in Catalan theater productions, Valero made an auspicious film debut in Manuel Gutiérrez Aragón's* *La mitad del cielo* [*Half of Heaven*]* (1986) in the role of Juan, the struggling economics student who becomes emotionally involved with Rosa (Angela Molina*), the aspiring restauranteur. He followed this with a series of other, much praised performances in secondary roles films by Mario Camus.* These include *Después del sueño* [*After the Dream*] (1992) and *Amor propio*

[*Self-esteem*] (1994). In these films, Valero defined himself as a superb supporting actor delivering often powerful performances. This secondary status owes less to any limitations in his acting skills than to his somewhat taciturn appearance and the lack of a defining sexual edge to his film persona, which might move him to the status of lead actor. Camus was able to channel these same features to good effect in the script of *Adosados* [*Row Houses*] (1996) in which Valero assumes the leading role of a repressed and frustrated suburban husband whose dedication to domestic stability leads him into a Kafkaesque personal crisis of his own making.

Velasco, Concha (Concepción Velasco Verona) (Valladolid, 1939). Though trained in classical dance and flamenco, Concha Velasco made her film debut as an adolescent in a secondary role in Raúl Alfonso's *La reina mora* [*The Moorish Queen*] (1954). She returned to the screen some four years later in a series of musicals and comedies that rocketed her to popular stardom. The most popular and characteristic of these were *Muchachas en vacaciones* [*Girls on Vacation*] (José María Elorrieta, 1957) and the even more commercially successful *Las chicas de la Cruz Roja* [*The Girls from the Red Cross*] (Rafael Salvia, 1958). Over the next fifteen years she appeared in more than three dozen light comedies and musicals by the principal comic directors of mainstream commercial cinema: Mariano Ozores, Pedro Lazaga, José María Forqué,* and José Luis Sáenz de Heredia,* including a leading role in Heredia's highly successful remake of *La verbena de la paloma* [*Paloma Fair*] (1963).

Though some of her performances included more serious roles (Sáenz de Heredia's *El indulto* [*The Pardon*] [1960], it was not until she appeared in two films by Pedro Olea* in the mid-1970s, *Tormento* [*Torment*] (1974), and *Pim, pam, pum . . . ¡fuego!* [*Bang, Bang . . . You're Dead!*]* (1975), that she began to be regarded as a serious actress. Over the next decade she continued to appear in a variety of popular films, both serious and comic, while maintaining a parallel career in Spanish musical comedy.

The characteristic persona of Concha Velasco's early career is that of a beguiling, spunky young woman. Her more serious roles, especially for Olea and later in films by Mario Camus* and Jaime de Armiñán,* expanded that image of a strong-willed women. In 1985 she won the Best Actress award at the Valladolid Film Festival for her performance in Armiñán's *La hora bruja* [*The Witching Hour*].

Verdú, Maribel (María Isabel Verdú Rollán) (Madrid, 1970). Chosen by Vicente Aranda* for *El crimen del Capitán Sánchez* [*The Crime of Captain Sánchez*], an episode for the television series, *La huella del crimen* [*The Trace of a Crime*] in 1985, Verdú quickly found herself launched into an extraordinarily active career in films by some of the most important directors of the decade. These included supporting roles in a variety of critical and commercial successes, such as Fernando Trueba's* *El año de las luces* [*The Year of Light*] and Montxo

Armendáriz's* *27 horas* [*Twenty-Seven Hours*], both in 1986; Eloy de la Iglesia's* *La estanquera de Vallecas* [*The Kiosk Vendor from Vallecas*] (1987); Vicente Aranda's *Amantes* [*Lovers*] (1990); and Trueba's Academy Award–winning film, *Belle Epoque* (1992). In such roles Verdú was generally typecast as a young and vulnerable woman who finds herself set upon by young men. Her early pairing with Jorge Sanz* in *The Year of Light* led to the two of them being television film, *Los jinetes del alba* [*Horsemen of the Dawn*] (1991). Though largely cast in secondary roles, her growing dramatic range may be noted in Bigas Luna's* 1993 film, *Huevos de oro* [*Golden Balls*] in which she plays an attractive hustler in the Benidorm beach resort.

Vivó, José, (Barcelona, 1916–1989). Vivó's studies in Engineering were interrupted by the outbreak of the Civil War. He participated on the Republican side and, at the war's end, abandoned his studies for work in the theater, first in a number of Catalonian companies and then in Madrid. He was a member of the prestigious Compañía Nacional María Guerrero and subsequently performed in some of the outstanding theatrical works of the 1960s and 1970s.

Vivó began appearing in films in the mid-1940s, usually in minor roles. It was not until the 1970s when he became a recognizable character actor in roles that ranged from comic stereotypes of simple-minded servants to compassionate renderings of troubled individuals, to the personification of social mediocrities. In Saura's* 1972 film, *Ana y y los lobos* [*Ana and the Wolves*], he achieved a certain status as one of the three obsessive brothers of the doting matriarch played by Rafaela Aparicio.* He later returned to that role in Saura's quasi-sequel, *Mamá cumple cien años* [*Mama Turns 100*] (1979).

Though always a supporting actor, Vivó's status as a character actor grew. Among his credits are a number of films directed by prominent directors of the 1970s and 1980s. Besides Saura, Vivó worked with Jaime Camino* (*Las largas vacaciones del '36* [*The Long Summer Vacation of '36*] [1975]), Juan Antonio Bardem* (*El puente* [*The Long Weekend*] [1976]), Pilar Miró* (*El crimen de Cuenca* [*The Crime at Cuenca*] [1979), Víctor Erice* (*El sur* [*The South*]* [1983]), and Francisco Regueiro* (*Padre nuestro* [1985]). Along with his impressive list of film credits, he has maintained a fairly constant presence on Spanish television, primarily in made-for-television movies.

Appendix: International Awards Won by Spanish Films, 1941–1994

Although international film festivals began with the Venice Bienale in 1932, Spanish films were not officially presented at festivals until after the Spanish Civil War. The following is a list of major international festival awards received by Spanish films since 1941, the first year in which Spanish films won awards.

1941
Venice Film Festival: *Marianela* (1940, Benito Perojo).

1942
Venice Film Festival: *Goyescas* (1942, Benito Perojo). *La aldea maldita* [*Cursed Village*] (1942, Florián Rey) Special Mention.

1953
Cannes Film Festval: *Bienvenido, Mister Marshall!* [*Welcome, Mister Marshall!*] (1953, Luis García Berlanga) Humorous Film Award. *Duende y misterio del flamenco* [*Magic and Mystery of Flamenco*] (1953, Edgar Neville) Honorable Mention.

Venice Film Festival: *La guerra de Dios* [*God's War*] (1953, Rafael Gil) Bronze Lion; OCIC Prize by Screenwriters Circle. *Carne de horca* [*Flesh for the Gallows*] (1953, Ladislao Vajda) Pugnolo Prize.

1954
Venice Film Festival: *El beso de Judas* [*The Kiss of Judas*] (1954, Rafael Gil) Honorable Mention.

1955
Berlin Film Festival: *Marcelino, pan y vino* [*Marcelino, Bread and Wine*] (1953, Ladislao Vajda) Special Jury Award.

Cannes Film Festival: *Muerte de un ciclista* [*Death of a Cyclist*] (1955, Juan Antonio Bardem) FIPRESCI Catholic Film Critics Award for Best Film.

1956

San Sebastián Film Festival: *Todos somos necesarios* [*We're All Necessary*] (1956, José María Nieves Conde) Concha de Oro for Best Film; José Antonio Nieves Conde, Best Director; Alberto Closas, Best Actor.

Venice Film Festival: Betsy Blair, Honorable Mention as leading actress for *Calle Mayor* [*Main Street*] (1956, Juan Antonio Bardem). *Calabuch* (1956, Luis García Berlanga) OICI prize by Screenwriters Circle.

1957

Berlin Film Festival: *Amanecer en Puerta Oscura* [*Dawn in Puerta Oscura*] (1957, José María Forqué) Silver Bear for Best Director.

Venice Film Festvial: *Un traje blanco* [*A White Suit*] (1957, Rafael Gil). Honorable Mention.

1958

Cannes Film Festival: *La venganza* [*The Revenge*] (1957, Juan Antonio Bardem) FIPRESCI Catholic Film Critics Award for Best Film.

1959

San Sebastián Film Festival: Adolfo Marsillach for Best Actor in *Salto a la gloria* [*Jump to Glory*] (1959, León Klimovsky).

1960

Berlin Film Festival: *Lazarillo de Tormes* (1959, Cesar F. Ardavín) Gold Bear for Best Film.

Venice Film Festval: *El cochecito* [*The Little Car*] (1960, Marco Ferreri) FIPRESCI Catholic Film Critics Award for Best Film.

1961

Cannes Film Festvial: *Viridiana* (1961, Luis Buñuel) Gold Palm.

1963

San Sebastián Film Festival: *Del rosa al amarillo* [*From Rose to Yellow*] (1963, Manuel Summers) Concha de Plata for Best Film.

Venice Film Festival: *El verdugo* [*The Executioner*] (1962, Luis García Berlanga) FIPRESCI Catholic Film Critics Award for Best Film.

1964

Cannes Film Festival: *La niña del luto* [*The Girl in Mourning*] (1964, Manuel Summers) Special Jury Prize.

San Sebastián Film Festival: *La tía Tula* [*Aunt Tula*] (1964, Miguel Picazo) Concha de Oro for Best Director.

1966

Berlin Film Festival: *La caza* [*The Hunt*] (1965, Carlos Saura) Silver Bear for Best Director.

San Sebastián Film Festival: *Nueve carta a Berta* [*Nine Letters to Berta*] (1965, Basilio Martín Patino) Concha de Plata for Best Director.

Venice Film Festival: Jacques Perin, Honorable Mention for lead acting in *La busca* [*The Search*] (1966, Angelino Fons).

1967

San Sebastián Film Festival: Serena Vergana, Concha de Plata for Best Actress in *Una historia de amor* [*A Love Story*] (1966, Jorge Grau).

1968

Berlin Film Festival: *Peppermint Frappé* (1967, Carlos Saura) Gold Bear for Best Director.

1969

San Sebastián Film Festival: Concha de Plata for Best Director shared by Claudio Guerín, José Luis Egea, and Víctor Erice for *Los desafíos* [*The Challenges*] (1969).

1972

San Sebastián Film Festival: Best Actor Award to Fernando Rey for *La duda* [*The Doubt*] (1972, Rafael Gil).

1977

Berlin Film Festival: *Camada negra* [*Black Brood*] (1977, Manuel Gutiérrez Aragón) Silver Bear for Best Director. Fernando Fernán-Gómez for Best Actor *El anacoreta* [*The Anchorite*] (1977, Juan Estelrich).

Cannes Film Festival: Fernando Rey for Best Actor in *Elisa vida mía* [*Elisa, My Life*] (1977, Carlos Saura).

San Sebastián Film Festival: Héctor Alterio for Best Actor in *A un dios desconocido* [*To an Unknown God*] (1977, Jaime Chávarri)

1978

Berlin Film Festival: Gold Bear for Best Film shared by *Las palabras de Max* [*Max's Words*] (1978, Emilio Martínez Lázaro) and *Las truchas* [*Trout*] (1977, José Luis García Sánchez).

Karlovy Vary (Czecoslovalkia) Film Festival: Marisol (Pepa Flores) Award for Best Actress in *Los días del pasado* [*Days of the Past*] (1977, Mario Camus).

1979

Moscow Film Festival: Gold Medal, Best Film for *Siete días de enero* [*Seven Days in January*] (1978, Juan Antonio Bardem).

San Sebastián Film Festival: Special Jury Prize to *Mamá cumple 100 años* [*Mama Turns 100*] (1979, Carlos Saura). Perla del Cantábrico Prize to *El proceso de Burgos* [*The Trial at Burgos*] (1979, Imanol Uribe).

1980

Montreal Film Festival: Ana Torrent as Best Actress in *El nido* [*The Nest*] (1980, Jaime de Armiñán).

1981

Berlin Film Festival: Golden Bear for Best Picture, *Deprisa, deprisa* [*Hurry, Hurry!*] (1980, Carlos Saura).

Moscow Film Festival: First Prize for Best Actress, Mercedes Sampietro in *Gary Cooper que estás en los cielos* [*Gary Cooper Who Art in Heaven*] (1980, Pilar Miró).

1982

San Sebastián Film Festival: International Critics' Grand Prize, *Demonios en el jardín* [*Demons in the Garden*] (1982, Manuel Gutiérrez Aragón).

1983

Academy of Motion Picture Arts and Sciences Oscar for Best Foreign Film, *Volver a empezar* [*To Begin Again*] (1982, José Luis Garci).

Berlin Film Festival: Golden Bear for Best Film, shared by *La colmena* [*The Beehive*] (1983, Mario Camus) and *Belfast 1920* (Great Britain, Edward Bennet).

Cannes Film Festival: Best Artistic Contribution, *Carmen* (1983, Carlos Saura).

1984

Cannes Film Festival: Best Actor award shared by Alfredo Landa and Francisco Rabal in *Los santos inocentes* [*Holy Innocents*] (1983, Mario Camus).

San Sebastián Film Festival: Best New Filmmaker prize, *Tú, solo* [*You Alone*] (1984, Teo Escamilla). FIPRESCI Catholic Film Critics Award, *Tasio* (1984, Montxo Armendáriz).

1985

Berlin Film Festival: Silver Bear for Best Actor, Fernando Fernán-Gómez for *Stico* (1984, Jaime de Armiñán).

Montreal Film Festival: Grand Prize of the Americas, *Padre nuestro* (1985, Francisco Regueiro).

San Sebastián Film Festival: Concha de Plata for Best Film, *La corte de Faraón* [*The Pharoah's Court*] (1985, José Luis García Sánchez).

1986

Montreal Film Festival: Special Prize to the "Spanish Trilogy" (*Bodas de sangre* [*Blood Wedding*] [1980]; *Carmen* [1983]; *El amor brujo* [*Love, The Magician*] [1985], Carlos Saura).

San Sebastián Film Festival: Concha de Oro, *La mitad del cielo* [*Half of Heaven*] (1986, Manuel Gutiérrez Aragón). Concha de Plata for Best Film, *27 horas* [*Twenty-seven Hours*] (1986, Montxo Armendáriz). Concha de Plata for Best Actress, Angela Molina, *La mitad del cielo* [*Half of Heaven*] (1986, Manuel Gutiérrez Aragón).

1987

San Sebastián Film Festival: Concha de Plata for Best Actress, Victoria Abril, *El Lute, camina o revienta* [*El Lute: Run or Die*] (1987, Vicente Aranda). Concha de Plata for Best Actor, Imanol Arias, *El Lute, camina o revienta* [*El Lute: Run or Die*] (1987, Vicente Aranda).

1988

Montreal Film Festival: Special Mention for Best Actress, Julia Migenes, *Berlin Blues* (1988, Ricardo Franco).

San Sebastián Film Festival: Concha de Plata for Best Film, *Remando al viento* [*Rowing with the Wind*] (1988, Gonzalo Suárez). Concha de Plata for Best Actor, Fernando Rey for *Diario de invierno* [*Winter Diary*] (1988, Francisco Regueiro) and *El aire de un crimen* [*The Scent of a Crime*] (1988, Antonio

Isasi).

Venice Film Festival: Best Film Script, Pedro Almodóvar, *Mujeres al borde de un ataque de nervios* [*Women on the Verge of a Nervous Breakdown*] (1988, Pedro Almodóvar).

1989

San Sebastián Film Festival: Special Jury Prize for *El mar y el tiempo* [*The Sea and Time*] (1989, Fernando Fernán-Gómez).

1990

European Community Prize, "Felix" Award for Best Actress, Carmen Maura, *¡Ay, Carmela!* (1990, Carlos Saura).

Montreal Film Festival: Best Actor, Antonio Pajares, *¡Ay, Carmela!* (1990, Carlos Saura).

San Sebastián Film Festival: Concha de Oro for Best Film, *Las cartas de Alou* [*Letters from Alou*] (1990, Montxo Armendáriz).

1991

Berlin Film Festival: Best Actress, Victoria Abril, *Amantes* [*Lovers*] (1990, Vicente Aranda).

San Sebastián Film Festival: Concha de Oro for Best Film, *Alas de mariposa* [*Butterfly Wings*] (1991, Juama Bajo Ulloa).

1992

Berlin Film Festival: Silver Bear for Cinematic Qualities, *Beltenebros* (1992, Pilar Miró).

Cannes Film Festival: Special Jury Prize, *El sol del membrillo* [*The Quince Tree Sun*] (1992, Víctor Erice). FIPRESCI Catholic Film Critics Award, *El sol de membrillo* [*The Quince Tree Sun*] (1992, Víctor Erice).

Venice Film Festival: Silver Lion, *Jamón, Jamón* (1992, José Juan Bigas Luna).

1993

Cannes Film Festival: Young Filmmakers Award, *La ardilla roja* [*The Red Squirrel*] (1993, Julio Medem).

Montreal Film Festival: Best Direction, Juanma Bajo Ulloa, *La madre muerta* [*The Dead Mother*] (1993).

San Sebastián Film Festival: Special Jury Prize, *Huevos de oro* [*Golden Balls*] (1993, José Juan Bigas Luna). Best Actor, Juan Echanove, *Madregilda* (1993, Francisco Regueiro).

1994

Academy of Motion Picture Arts and Sciences Oscar for Best Foreign Film, *Belle Epoque* (1992, Fernando Trueba).

Karlovy Vary Film Festival: Grand Prize, *Hermano de mi alma* [*Soul Brother*] (1994, Mariano Barroso).

Montreal Film Festival: Special Jury Prize, *Canción de cuna* [*Cradle Song*] (1994, José Luis Garci). Best Director, José Luis Garci, *Canción de cuna* [*Cradle Song*] (1994).

San Sebastián Film Festival: Concha de Oro for Best Film, *Días contados* [*Running out of Time*] (1994, Imanol Uribe). Best Actor, Javier Bardem for

Días contados [*Running out of Time*] (1994, Imanol Uribe) and *El detective y la muerte* [*The Detective and Death*] (1994, Gonzalo Suárez).

Venice Film Festival: Golden Osella for Best Script, José Juan Bigas Luna and Cuca Canals, *La teta y la luna* [*The Tit and the Moon*] (1994, José Juan Bigas Luna).

Selected Bibliography

Alegre, Luis. "Entrevista: Fernando Trueba." *Dirigido Por*, no. 208 (December 1992): 38–41.

Alvares, Rosa, and Belén Frías. *Vicente Aranda: el cine como pasión.* Valladolid: 36 Semana Internacional de Cine, 1991.

Alberich, Ferrán. *Bajo el signo de la sombra.* Madrid: Filmoteca Española, 1984.

Angulo, Jesús, Carlos F. Heredero, and José Luis Rebordinos (eds.). *Un cineasta llamado Pedro Olea.* San Sebastián: Filmoteca Vasca, 1993.

———. *El cine de Imanol Uribe: entre el documental y la ficción.* San Sebastián: Filmoteca Vasca, 1994.

Angulo, Jesús, and Francisco Llinás (eds.). *Fernando Fernán-Gómez: el hombre que quiso ser Jackie Cooper.* San Sebastián: Ayuntamiento de San Sebastián, 1993.

Aranda, J. Francisco. *Luis Buñuel: biografía crítica.* Barcelona: Editorial Lumen, 1969.

Armiñán, Jaime de. *Diario en blanco y negro.* Madrid: Nickel Odeón, 1994.

Arocena, Carmen. *Víctor Erice.* Madrid: Cátedra, 1996.

Baena, Juan Julio. "*El cochecito.*" *Temas de cine*, no. 6 (1960): 13–14. "Número especial dedicado a la película *El cochecito* invitado al Festival de Venecia."

Balló, Jordi, Ramón Espelt, and Joan Lorente (eds.) *Cinema català 1975-1986.* Barcelona: Columna, 1990.

Barbáchano, Carlos. *Francisco Regueiro.* Madrid: Filmoteca Española, 1989.

Barroso, Jaime. "Homenaje a Luis Cuadrado," *Contracampo*, nos. 10–11, Año 2 (March-April 1980): 14–30.

Batlle, Joan, and Ramón Sala. "Entrevista con Josep Maria Forn," *Contracampo* no. 7, Año 1 (December 1979), 13–19.

Bayón, Miguel. *La cosecha de los 80: el "boom" de los nuevos realizadores españoles.* Murcia: Filmoteca Regional de Murcia, 1990.

Besas, Peter. *Behind the Spanish Lens: Spanish Cinema Under Fascism and Democracy.* Denver: Arden Press, 1985.

Caparrós-Lera, José María. *Arte y política en el cine de la República (1931-*

1939). Barcelona: Ediciones 7 1/2, 1981.

————. *El cine español de la democracia: de la muerte de Franco al "cambio" socialista (1975-1989)*. Barcelona: Anthropos, 1992.

————. *El cine político visto después del franquismo*. Barcelona: Dopesa, 1978.

Castro, Antonio. *El cine español en el banquillo*. Valencia: Fernando Torres, 1974.

César, Samuel R. "*Vacas* de Julio Medem." *Dirigido Por*, no. 201 (April 1992): 81-82.

Colina, José de la, and Tomás Pérez Turrent. *Luis Buñuel: prohibido asomarse al interior*. México City: Joaquín Mortiz, 1986.

Company, Juan M., and Pau Esteve. "Habla Patino." *Dirigido Por*, no. 38 (November 1976): 27–29.

Contracampo. No. 35 (Spring 1984): 6–82. Special issue devoted to Fernando Fernán-Gómez.

Crespo, Pedro. *Jaime de Armiñán: los amores marginales*. Huelva: Festival de Cine Iberoamericano, 1987.

Deveney, Thomas G. *Cain on Screen: Contemporary Spanish Cinema*. Metuchen, NJ: Scarecrow Press, 1993.

D'Lugo, Marvin. *The Films of Carlos Saura: The Practice of Seeing*. Princeton, NJ: Princeton University Press, 1991.

————. "Bigas Luna's *Jamón, Jamón*: Remaking the National in Spanish Cinema." *In Spain Today: Essays on Literature, Culture, Society*, edited by José Colmeiro et al., 67–81. Hanover, NH: Dartmouth College Department of Spanish and Portuguese, 1995.

————. "Catalan Cinema: Historical Experience and Cinematic Practice." *Quarterly Review of Film and Video* 13, nos. 1–3 (1991): 131–147.

Domínguez, Ramón María. *Miguel Delibes: la imagen escrita*. Valladolid: 38 Semana Internacional de Cine, 1993.

Egido, Luis G. *J. A. Bardem*. Huelva: Festival de Cine Iberoamericana, 1983.

Emiliano Piedra. Alcalá de Henares: 13 Festival de Cine de Alcalá de Henares, 1983.

Erlich, Linda. "Interior Gardens: Victor Erice's *Dream of Light* and the Bodegón Tradition." *Cinema Journal* 34, no. 2 (winter 1995): 22–36.

Espelt, Ramón. *Mirada al Món de Bigas Luna*. Barcelona: Editorial Laertes, 1989.

Fernández Cuenca, Carlos. *Fructuoso Gelabert: fundador de la cinematografía española*. Madrid: Filmoteca Española, 1957.

————. *La obra de Fernando Delgado*. Madrid: Circe, 1949.

————. *Recuerdo y presencia de Florián Rey*. San Sebastián: Festival Internacional de Cine, 1962.

Fernández Valenti, Tomás. "*Belle Epoque*: La España soñada." *Dirigido Por*, no. 208 (December 1992): 34–37.

Fiddian, Robin W., and Peter W. Evans. *Challenges to Authority: Fiction and Film in Contemporary Spain*. London: Támesis, 1988.

Font, Domenèc. *Del azul al verde: el cine español durante el franquismo.* Barcelona: Editorial Avance, 1976.

Font, Domenèc, Joan Batlle, and Jesús Garay. "Entrevista con Pepón Coromina," *La mirada: textos sobre cine,* no. 4, Año 1 (October 1978): 28–29.

Francesc, Joan. *El món de Fructuós Gelabert.* Barcelona: Generalitat de Catalunya, Departamento de Cultura, 1988.

Frugone, Juan Carlos. *Rafael Azcona: atrapados por la vida.* Valladolid: 32 Semana de Cine de Valladolid, 1987.

———. *Oficio de gente humilde . . . Mario Camus.* Valladolid: Semana de Cine de Valladolid, 1984.

Fuentes, Víctor. *Buñuel: cine y literatura.* Barcelona: Salvat, 1989.

Galán, Diego. "Aquel cine de los 50." In *Cine español años 50:* 14–21. Vol. 2 of *Tiempos de Cine Español.* San Sebastián: Ayuntamiento de San Sebastián, N.D.

———. "El largo viaje de Carmen en el cine." In *Carmen: el sueño del amor absoluto,* edited by Carlos Saura and Antonio Gades, 34–45. Madrid: Círculo de Lectores, 1984.

———. *Venturas y desventuras de La prima Angélica.* Valencia: Fernando Torres, 1974.

García Domínguez, Ramón. *Miguel Delibes: la imagen escrita.* Valladolid: 38 Semana Internacional de Cine, 1993.

García Fernández, Emilio C. *Historia ilustrada del cine español.* Barcelona: Planeta, 1985.

Gómez Rufo, Antonio. *Berlanga, contra el poder y la gloria.* Madrid: Temas de Hoy, 1990.

Graham, Helen, and Jo Labanyi. *Spanish Cultural Studies: An Introduction.* Oxford: Oxford University Press, 1995.

Guarner, José Luis, and Peter Besas. *El inquietante cine de Vicente Aranda.* Madrid: Imagfic, 1985.

Gubern, Román. *Benito Perojo: pionerismo y supervivencia.* Madrid: Filmoteca Española, 1994.

———. *El cine español en el exilio: 1936-1939.* Barcelona: Editorial Lumen, 1976.

———. *El cine sonoro de la II República (1929–1936).* Barcelona: Editorial Lumen, 1977.

———. *Raza: un ensueño del General Franco.* Madrid: Ediciones 99, 1977.

———. *1936–1939: La guerra de España en la pantalla.* Madrid: Filmoteca Española, 1986.

Gubern, Román, ed. *El paso del mudo al sonoro en el cine español.* Madrid: Universidad Complutense, 1993.

Gutiérrez, Begoña, and José Manuel Porquet. *Imanol Uribe.* Huesca: Festival de Cine de Huesca, 1994.

Gutiérrez-Solana, Ignacio. "Teo Escamilla: contra el estilo." *Casablanca,* no. 9 (September 1981): 31–38.

Harguinday, Angel S. "La saga picaresca de la aristocracia española." *El País Semanal*, no. 180 (21 September 1980): 14–16.

Heredero, Carlos F. *Las huellas del tiempo: cine español 1951–1961*. Valencia: Filmoteca de la Generalitat Valenciana, 1993.

———. *Iván Zulueta: la vanguardia frente al espejo*. Alcalá de Henares: Festival de Cine, 1989.

———. *José Luis Borau: teoría y práctica de un cineasta*. Madrid: Filmoteca Española, 1990.

———. "Iván Zulueta: la visión poliédrica." *Cine español años 50*: 22–31. Vol. 2 of *Tiempos de Cine Español*. San Sebastián: Ayuntamiento de San Sebastián, N. D.

———. *El lenguaje de la luz: entrevistas con directores de fotografía del cine español*. Alcalá de Henares: 24 Festival de Cine de Alcalá de Henares, 1994.

Hernández-Les, Juan. *El cine de Elías Querejeta: un productor singular*. Bilbao: Ediciones Mensajero, 1986.

Hernández-Les, Juan, and Miguel Gato. *El cine de autor en España*. Madrid: Castellote, 1978.

Hernández-Les, Juan, and Manuel Hidalgo. *El último austro-húngaro: conversaciones con Berlanga*. Barcelona: Editorial Anagrama, 1981.

Hernández Ruiz, Javier. *Gonzalo Suárez: un combate ganado con la ficción*. Alcalá de Henares: Festival de Cine, 1991.

Higginbotham, Virginia. *Spanish Film under Franco*. Austin: University of Texas Press, 1988.

Hopewell, John. *Out of the Past: Spanish Cinema after Franco*. London: BFI Books, 1986.

Irazábal Martín, Concha. *Alice, sí está: directoras de cine europeas y norteamericanas 1896–1996*. Madrid: horas y HORAS, 1996.

Kinder, Marsha. "*El nido*." *Film Quarterly* 35. no. 1 (Fall 1981): 34-41.

———. "The Children of Franco in the New Spanish Cinema." *Quarterly Review of Film Studies* 8, no. 2 (Spring 1983): 57–76.

———. "Pleasure and the New Spanish Mentality: A Conversation With Pedro Almodóvar." *Film Quarterly* (Fall 1987): 33–44.

———. *Spanish Cinema: The Politics of Family and Gender*. Los Angeles: Spanish Ministry of Culture and USC School of Cinema and Television, 1989.

———. *Blood Cinema: The Reconstruction of National Identity in Spain*. Berkeley: University of California Press, 1993.

Kovacs, Katherine S. "Half of Heaven." *Film Quarterly* 41, no. 3 (Spring 1988): 33–37.

Lara, Fernando. "*Canciones para después de una guerra*." *Revista de Occidente* (October 1985): 92–101.

Lasa, Joan Francesc. *Els germans Baños: aquell primer cinema català*. Barcelona: Generalitat de Catalunya, Departament de Cultura, 1996.

Llinás, Fracisco. *Directores de fotografía del cine español*. Madrid: Filmoteca Española, 1989.

López Echevarrieta, Alberto. *Cine vasco: ¿realidad o ficción?* Bilbao: Editorial Mensajero, 1982.

————. *Cine vasco: de ayer a hoy.* Bilbao: Editorial Mensajero, 1984.

Marías, Miguel, and Felipe Vega. "Una conversación con Víctor Erice." *Casablanca*, nos. 31–32 (July–August 1983): 59–70.

Martí-Olivella, Jaume. "Toward a New Transcultural Dialogue in Spanish Film." In *Spain Today: Essays on Literature, Culture, Society*, edited by José Colmeiro et al. 47–66. Hanover, NH: Dartmouth College Department of Spanish and Portuguese, 1995.

Méndez-Leite von Haffe, Fernando. *Historia del cine español.* 2 vols. Madrid: Ediciones Rialp, 1965.

Méndez-Leite, Fernando. *Historia del cine español en 100 películas.* Madrid: Jupey, 1975.

Molina-Foix, Vicente. *New Cinema in Spain.* London: BFI, 1977.

Monterde, José Enrique. *Veinte años de cine español (1973–1992): un cine bajo la paradoja.* Barcelona: Paidós, 1993.

Mortimore, Roger, "Buñuel, Sáenz de Heredia, and Filmófono." *Sight & Sound* (Summer 1975): 180–182.

Payán, Miguel Juan. *El cine español de los 90.* Madrid: Ediciones JC, 1993.

Payán, Miguel Juan, and José Luis López. *Manuel Gutiérrez Aragón.* Madrid: Ediciones JC, 1985.

Pérez Gómez, Angel, and José L. Martínez Montalbán. *Cine español 1951–1978: diccionario de directores.* Bilbao: Editorial Mensajero, 1978.

Pérez Manrique, José María. *Montxo Armendáriz: imagen y narración de libertad.* Burgos: Encuentro Internacional de Cine de Burgos, 1993.

Pérez Millán, Juan Antonio. *Pilar Miró: directora de cine.* Valladolid: Semana Internacional de Cine de Valladolid, 1992.

Pérez Perucha, Julio. *El cinema de Edgar Neville.* Valladolid: 27 Semana Internacional de Cine de Valladolid, 1982.

————. *Carlos Serrano de Osma.* Valladolid: 28 Semana Internacional de Cine, 1983.

Porter i Moix, Miquel. *Historia del cinema català (1895–1968).* Barcelona: Editorial Taber, 1969.

Pozo, Santiago. *La industria del cine en España.* Barcelona: Publicaciones i Ediciones de la Universitat de Barcelona, 1984.

Riambau, Esteve (ed.). *Antes del apocalípsis: el cine de Marco Ferreri.* Madrid: Cátedra, 1990.

Rigol, Antoni. "La historia de Cataluña en la pantalla: *La ciutat cremada* (1976) de Antoni Ribas." In *El cine en Cataluña: una aproximación histórica.* Edited by Sergi Alegre, et al. 83–100. Barcelona: Centro de Investigaciones Film-Historia, 1993.

Rodero, José Angel. *Aquel "nuevo cine español" de los '60.* Valladolid: 26 Semana Internacional de Cine de Valladolid, 1981.

Rodríguez Lafuente, Fernando. "Cine español: 1939–1990." In *Cultura*, edited by

Antonio Ramos Gascón, 241–79. Vol 2 of *España Hoy*. Madrid: Cátedra, 1991.

Rotellar, Manuel. *Cine español de la República*. San Sebastián: 25 Festival Internacional del Cine, 1977.

Sánchez Vidal, Agustín. *Borau*. Zaragoza: Caja de Ahorros de la Inmaculada, 1990.

———. *Luis Buñuel: obra cinematográfica*. Madrid: Ediciones JC, 1984.

———. *El cine de Carlos Saura*. Zaragoza: Caja de Ahorros de la Inmaculada, 1988.

———. *El cine de Florián Rey*. Zaragoza: Caja de Ahorros de la Inmaculada, 1991.

———. *El cine de Segundo de Chomón*. Zaragoza: Caja de Ahorros de la Inmaculada, 1992.

Sanz de Soto, Emilio. "1940–1950." In *Cine español 1896–1983*, 102–41, edited by Augusto M. Torres. Madrid: Filmoteca Española, 1983.

Saura, Carlos, and Antonio Gades. *Carmen: el sueño del amor absoluto*. Madrid: Círculos de Lectores, 1985.

Smith, Paul Julian. *Laws of Desire: Questions of Homosexuality in Spanish Writing and Film 1960–1990*. Oxford: Clarendon Press, 1992.

———. *Desire Unlimited: The Cinema of Pedro Almodóvar*. London: Verso, 1994.

———. *Vision Machines: Cinema, Literature and Sexuality in Spain and Cuba, 1983–1993*. London: Verso, 1996.

Torres, Augusto M. (ed.). *Cine español 1896–1983*. Madrid: Filmoteca Española, 1983.

———. *Conversaciones con Manuel Gutiérrez Aragón*. Madrid: Editorial Fundamentos, 1985.

———. *Diccionario del cine español*. Madrid: Espasa Calpe, 1994.

Vera, Pascual. *Vicente Aranda*. Madrid: Ediciones JC, 1989.

Vernon, Kathleen M. "Re-viewing the Spanish Civil War: Franco's Film *Raza*." *Film and History* 16, no. 2 (1986): 26–34.

———. "La politique des auteurs: Narrative Point of View in *Pascual Duarte*, Novel and Film." *Hispania* 72, no. 1 (March 1989): 87–96.

Vernon, Kathleen, and Barbara Morris (eds.). *Post-Franco, Postmodern: The Films of Pedro Almodóvar*. Westport, CT: Greenwood Press, 1995.

Vidal, Nuria. *El cine de Pedro Almodóvar*. Barcelona: Ediciones Destino, 1988.

Vincendeau, Ginette (ed.). *Encyclopedia of European Cinema*. New York: Facts on File, 1995.

Vizcaíno Casas, Fernando. *Historia y anécdota del cine español*. Madrid: Ediciones ADRA, 1976.

———. *De la checa a la meca: una vida del cine*. Barcelona: Planeta, 1988.

Weinrichter, Antonio. *La línea del vientre: el cine de Bigas Luna*. Gijón: Festival de Cine de Gijón, 1992.

Index

Page numbers for main entries appear in **boldface** type.

About the Author

MARVIN D'LUGO is Professor of Spanish and Adjunct Professor of Screen Studies at Clark University. He is the author of *The Films of Carlos Saura: The Practice of Seeing* (1991) and is currently completing a book on theories of national cinema.